TERENCE DAVIES
SCREENPLAYS

Terence Davies, Festival Écrants Mixtes, Lyon, March 2023. (photo: Marie Claire Véricel)

TERENCE DAVIES SCREENPLAYS

VOLUME II: ADAPTATIONS

Edited by James Dowling

THE BRITISH FILM INSTITUTE
Bloomsbury Publishing Plc
50 Bedford Square, London, WC1B 3DP, UK
1359 Broadway, New York, NY 10018, USA
29 Earlsfort Terrace, Dublin 2, Ireland

BLOOMSBURY is a trademark of Bloomsbury Publishing plc

First published in Great Britain 2025 by Bloomsbury
on behalf of the
British Film Institute
21 Stephen Street, London W1T 1LN
www.bfi.org.uk

The BFI is a cultural charity, a National Lottery distributor, and the UK's lead organisation for film and the moving image. We believe society needs stories. Film, television and the moving image bring them to life, helping us to connect and understand each other better. We share the stories of yesterday, search for the stories of today, and shape the stories of tomorrow.

Copyright © Preface James Dowling 2025; © Introduction Lillian Crawford 2025; © Interview, pp. 19–43, Edinburgh International Film Festival (EIFF)
Copyright © Individual screenplays The Terence Davies Estate 1995, 2000, 2011, 2015

The authors have asserted their right under the Copyright, Designs and Patents Act, 1988, to be identified as author of this work.

Cover design by Louise Dugdale
Cover image: *Sunset Song* (2015) Courtesy Mary Evans/All Film Archive/Magnolia Pictures

All rights reserved. No part of this publication may be: i) reproduced or transmitted in any form, electronic or mechanical, including photocopying, recording or by means of any information storage or retrieval system without prior permission in writing from the publishers; or ii) used or reproduced in any way for the training, development or operation of artificial intelligence (AI) technologies, including generative AI technologies. The rights holders expressly reserve this publication from the text and data mining exception as per Article 4(3) of the Digital Single Market Directive (EU) 2019/790

Bloomsbury Publishing Plc does not have any control over, or responsibility for, any third-party websites referred to or in this book. All internet addresses given in this book were correct at the time of going to press. The author and publisher regret any inconvenience caused if addresses have changed or sites have ceased to exist, but can accept no responsibility for any such changes.

For product safety related questions contact productsafety@bloomsbury.com.

A catalogue record for this book is available from the British Library.

ISBN: HB: 9781839029769
      PB: 9781839029752
      ePDF: 9781839029783
      eBook: 9781839029776

Designed and typeset by Tom Cabot/Ketchup

Printed and bound in Great Britain by Bell and Bain Ltd, Glasgow

To find out more about our authors and books visit www.bloomsbury.com and sign up for our newsletters.

ACKNOWLEDGEMENTS

Heartfelt thanks to Jason Wood, Ben Roberts and the British Film Institute for their generous support of this publication.

Interview with Terence Davies by Mark Cousins from *Projections 6: Film-makers on Film-making*, edited by John Boorman and Walter Donohue (London: Faber and Faber, 1996). Reproduced by kind permission of Faber & Faber Ltd and the Estate of Terence Davies.

CONTENTS

Editor's Preface by James Dowling 7
Introduction by Lillian Crawford 9
Interview with Terence Davies by Mark Cousins 29

THE SCREENPLAYS

The Neon Bible (1995) 47
   (From the novel by John Kennedy Toole)

The House of Mirth (2000) 135
   (From the novel by Edith Wharton)

The Deep Blue Sea (2011) 285
   (From the play by Terence Rattigan)

Sunset Song (2015) 355
   (From the novel by Lewis Grassic Gibbon)

The Contributors 496

PREFACE

James Dowling

The first volume of the Terence Davies Screenplays presented Terence's autobiographical works – *The Terence Davies Trilogy* (1983), *Distant Voices, Still Lives* (1988), *The Long Day Closes* (1992) and *Of Time and the City* (2008), along with his interpretations of the lives of poets Emily Dickinson and Siegfried Sassoon – *A Quiet Passion* (2016) and *Benediction* (2021). In this second volume we turn to the middle period of Terence's film output to present his adaptations based on works by John Kennedy Toole, Edith Wharton, Terence Rattigan and Lewis Grassic Gibbon – *The Neon Bible* (1995), *The House of Mirth* (2000), *The Deep Blue Sea* (2011) and *Sunset Song* (2015).

Having spent the period of 1966 to 1992 exploring his autobiography directly through short stories, novels (*Hallelujah Now* was first published in 1984) and films, Terence said that to return to the haunting memories of his early life again after *The Long Day Closes* 'would have killed me'. Instead, literary adaptations provided emotional mirrors in which he could continue to explore his inner life but at a remove. These films are less departures from his autobiographical mode than an extension of it. The characters of David, Lily Bart, Hester Collyer and Chris Guthrie offered psychological terrains of loneliness, longing, repression and hope, in which Terence found his own hidden narrative, expressed not through fact, but through feeling. On his role in *Benediction* (2021), Jack Lowden has spoken of realising early in the film shoot that he wasn't playing Siegfried Sassoon: 'I was actually playing Terence.'

Opposite: Terence Davies on the set of *House of Mirth* (2000). (BFI National Archive)

The House of Mirth (2000): Terence Davies with cinematographer Remi Adefarasin.

It is interesting to note that in Terence's archive there are screenplays for five further adaptations that have not (yet) made it to the screen. These include *Lady into Ice* (2003), based on *He Who Hesitates* by Ed McBain [published 1965]; *Ramblin Man* (2004), based on short stories by Annie Proulx; *Mother of Sorrows* (2012) by Richard McCann [published 2005]; *The Post Office Girl* (2022) by Stefan Zweig [published in Germany, 1982]; and *Firefly* (2023) – from a novel by Janette Jenkins based around Noël Coward's final years, lived out at his home, the Firefly Estate, in Jamaica [published 2013].

In presenting the screenplays in this volume we have drawn on original typed scripts which were found in Terence's archive or shared by the producers of the films. These range from second drafts to final shooting scripts. The scripts have not been depicted here as facsimiles as this would have run to over 600 pages. They are presented in modified formats that are as close to Terence's original layouts as possible.

My deepest thanks to all the producers of Terence's films for allowing the reproduction of the texts in this volume.

A STORY WHICH DESERVES TO BE TOLD

Lillian Crawford

Come, read to me some poem,
Some simple and heartfelt lay,
That shall soothe this restless feeling,
And banish the thoughts of day.

Not from the grand old masters,
Not from the bards sublime,
Whose distant footsteps echo
Through the corridors of Time.[1]

'The Day is Done' (1845),
Henry Longfellow

There were chills up my spine
And some thrills I can't define
Listen, sweet, I repeat
How long has this been goin' on

Oh, I feel that I could melt
Into Heaven I'm hurled
I know how Columbus felt
Finding another world[2]

'How Long Has This Been Going On?'
(1928), George & Ira Gershwin

Cue the bells and fanfare of the Selznick International Trademark. A white bed sheet hangs on a washing line in rural Mississippi. The camera tracks forward towards it. The music swells into the main title from *Gone With the Wind*. The sheet fills the frame like a cinema screen, dissolving not into the orange-coloured sky above Tara, but an inverted American flag with the stars on the right. We move along the impossibly long flag from right to left into a schoolhouse, with a teacher leading her class in the Pledge of Allegiance. A further dissolve into a wooden church, where we move in front of Reverend Watkins as he talks of the distinction between God's love and human love. The camera tracks down to an image of a Bible superimposed with a white Cross bearing the letters 'INRI'. Then we pull back over the congregation, as David says in voiceover: 'If you were different from anybody in town you had to get out. That's why everybody was so much alike.'[3]

The Neon Bible (1995).

The movies, school, church. The Holy Trinity of Terence Davies's childhood memories – this sequence in *The Neon Bible*, released in 1995, mirrors a similar scene in his autobiographical film *The Long Day Closes*, released in 1992. Debbie Reynolds is heard singing 'Tammy' over a shot which moves in bird's-eye-view through a smoke-filled cinema, his own classroom, and the Liverpudlian church of his youth. Davies later described his adaptation of John Kennedy Toole's 1989 novel as a 'transitional work', moving away from his project of artistic self-reflection towards the literary adaptations of his later films.[4] David's story resonated with Davies, not least in the tripartite world of the adolescent boy. As Longfellow demands in 'The Day is Done': 'Read from some humbler poet'. The film is no great epic, no *Gone With the Wind*, but Davies imports cinematic levity on this small American *bildungsroman*.

A familiar tale for Davies, in a displaced setting. It is with this approach that Davies's adaptations must be read – each with their unique resonances to his personal experience and view of the world. There are moments of ellipsis in each of his films, much like the earlier works, in which dialogue and character give way to pure expression through music and image. The sustained image of the white bedsheet recalls the lengthy shot of the rug on the floor of Davies's childhood home in *The Long Day Closes*, and the recurring image throughout the autobiographical films of his mother hanging out the washing. Sheets appear again at the midpoint of his 2000 adaptation of Edith Wharton's *The House of Mirth*, this time

The House of Mirth (2000).

covering the furniture of the palatial home of Bellomont as 'Soave sia il vento' from Mozart's *Così fan tutte* plays on the soundtrack. The camera pans across the houses of the first act of the film, out into the rain, down the lawn, through deserted tennis courts, across the sea as the water changes from grey to blue, dappled with the Mediterranean sunlight of the French Riviera. An elegant oneiric flourish which moves us seamlessly from one time and place to another. The opening montage of Davies's 2011 take on Terence Rattigan's *The Deep Blue Sea* concludes with the spiralling bedsheets of Hester's nest of infidelity, and after Chris resolves to leave her father to die in the 2015 adaptation of *Sunset Song* by Lewis Grassic Gibbon, she hangs a white sheet out of the window. Sheets cover up the past, our darkest secrets, but can be washed and hung out to dry until they are clean and crisp once more.

Do I see it?

On the first page of each book Davies adapted, he wrote the date on which he acquired it, his name, and sometimes 'Working Copy'. His manner of annotation appears to have changed over time – his copy of *Sunset Song*, dated 18/7/84, has simple pencil annotations. Lines mark out passages he could envision on screen in his mind, with passages of dialogue highlighted as speech or voiceover. Davies's copies of *The Neon Bible* (August 1992) and *The House of Mirth* (21/8/96) are covered with bright neon pink and blue highlighter markings. In the former these highlights appear to focus on selecting images which captured Davies's imagination, while in the latter the emphasis is on whittling down Wharton's sumptuous swathes of dialogue into a feature-length screenplay. His commitment to speech and dialogue is evident when reading the three novels alongside their film adaptations, with most of the characters' lines lifted directly from the source material. This avoided Davies's hatred for the penchant of British cinema to adapt the works of authors like Jane Austen into a form of modern dialect: 'I'm sorry, if it's set in 1815, they didn't speak like that in 1815.'[5]

When Davies read *The House of Mirth*, he immediately saw the opening in his mind and knew he could make the film. By contrast, with his adaptation of *Mother of Sorrows* by Richard McCann which remained undeveloped, it was not until the end of the novel that he believed that it would make an excellent film: 'You read and you think can I make it? Do I see it?'[6] Davies read with his director's hat on, sensing the images and their translation to the screen – the novels Davies adapted are all founded in reality, in people's lives. Davies's decision to adapt *The House of Mirth* is surprising in its upper-class setting, yet he told David Dukin at Channel 4 ten years after reading the novel that he wanted to turn it into film due its resonance on an emotional level, one which transcends class: 'We can all respond to loss of some kind because we've all suffered it.'[7] Like *The Neon Bible*, Wharton's novel is set in America, far removed from Davies' British experience.

Sunset Song also exists in a different time and place, in early 20th-century Scotland, but it is captured so evocatively in Grassic Gibbon's poetic prose that the landscape easily takes shape in the mind's eye. After the novel's prologue, the scene is set:

> Below and around where Chris Guthrie lay the June moors whispered and rustled and shook their cloaks, yellow with broom and powdered faintly with purple, that was the heather but not the full passion of its colour yet. And in the east against the cobalt blue of the sky lay the shimmer of the North Sea, that was by Bervie, and maybe the wind would veer there in an hour or so and you'd feel the change in the life and strum of the thing, bringing a streaming coolness out of the sea.[8]

The film begins with this image created quite literally, with the camera sweeping over those moors to find Chris swallowed up by the overgrown field. Dialogue in the novel is embedded within this rich tapestry of text, written in italics, coming and going with the narrative's warp and weft. Davies distils the dialogue from the images in the screenplay, while always connecting what is being said to the changing nature of the land across the seasons and years into the First World War. *Sunset Song* was a long-term passion project for Davies, beginning when he watched the BBC adaptation in black-and-white on the television on Sunday nights in 1971 – at the beginning of the script he writes that, 'It is a story which deserves to be told. It is a film which has to be made.'[9] Eventually Davies was able to bring Chris and the fictional parish of Kinraddie to life in glorious colour.

By contrast to the largely faithful realisations of the three novels, *The Deep Blue Sea* is more a film inspired by Rattigan's play from 1952 than a

The Deep Blue Sea (2011): Rachel Weisz as Hester Collyer. (BFI National Archive)

direct adaptation. The film was developed with funding from the Sir Terence Rattigan Charitable Trust for the playwright's centenary. Unlike the novels, this was not a project which Davies came to with pre-existing love for the material – rather, Davies found the play implausible, uncinematic, and frequently frustrating. The first act consists largely of characters delivering exposition about the affair between Freddie and Hester, something Davies could not abide. After having difficulty creating a first draft which he hoped would satisfy Rattigan's estate, he recalled being told to 'Be radical!' with his adaptation, and it is this radical approach which transforms the staid play into an emotive work of cinema.[10]

Rather than learning about Hester's experience from the characters who find her after her suicide attempt, Davies takes us inside her memories. 'With theatre you have to explain everything. With film you can just show it.'[11] Davies felt that there was a lack of authenticity to the play's setting, largely due to Rattigan's own social background: 'He never lived in a bedsit in Ladbroke after the war. He was living in The Albany, which was very posh.'[12] It was his working-class perspective which afforded Davies the ability to craft a film which feels truer to British post-war experience, highlighting the difference in social mores of which a modern audience may lack understanding. In his version, the landlady Mrs Elton reveals these contextual attitudes, for example when she discovers that Freddie and Hester are living together, she says, 'I run a respectable house here and I don't want any kind of trouble.'[13] By which she means the police, something she is deeply concerned about, especially in the wake of Hester's suicide attempt at a time when it was a criminal offence. Davies transforms Mrs Elton into a grounded foil to Hester's privileged fantasy version of reality.

For a shorter work like *The Neon Bible*, very little needed to be excised. Whereas *The House of Mirth* presented a greater challenge, and it is clear that Davies was strict with stripping back Wharton's prose to find the kernel without losing its sense. The most significant difference between the book and the film is the amalgamation of two female characters: Lily Bart's cousin Grace Stepney subsumes Lawrence Selden's cousin Gerty Farish. The former is Lily's rival to her aunt affections and, crucially, her inheritance, while the latter has a crush on Selden which she overcomes upon realising that Selden loves Lily. In the novel, Lily is snobbish and dismissive towards Gerty, for which her social exclusion is expressed as disproportionate retribution. By removing Gerty and Lily's attitude towards her, Davies makes Lily more empathetic, and by transferring Gerty's crush on Selden to Grace he gives her more complex motivations in the gossip she spreads to her aunt. A small change, perhaps, but an ingenious one.

But there was no snow

> This is the first time I've been on a train. I've sat in this seat here for about two or three hours now. I can't see what's passing by. It's dark now, but when the train left, the sun was just beginning to set, and I could see the red and brown leaves and the tanning grass all along the hillside.[14]

The Neon Bible is narrated by David as a series of memories as he travels away from his hometown by train. He does not know what his destination is; all he knows is where he came from. The film follows this structure – an appealing image for Davies, whose tracking sequences typically move from right to left to denote the passing of time, here with the camera following David's eyeline as he looks up at the bright full moon framed in the darkness of night. 'Perfidia' performed by Glenn Miller and His Orchestra echoes in the distance. David, now a child, sits playing with a toy train and staring out of the window of his house watching the rain. It is Christmas, 'But there was no snow', David says in voiceover. But, as in the script, 'Outside heavy drifts and falling snow'.[15] A childhood fantasy image, similar to the tableau Bud imagines in *The Long Day Closes* as his front door moves away to reveal his family eating Christmas dinner in a snowy street, soundtracked by Mahler's tenth symphony – the one he never finished, the rest left to another's imagination.

In *The House of Mirth*, Lily boards a train and begins to cut the pages of a novel with a knife. She glances Mr Gryce further down the carriage, whom she invites to sit with her. They are interrupted by Bertha, a disappointment to Lily, and she quickly wishes that she was elsewhere, the camera panning up out of the window as they pass through a tunnel. It is a rare non-linear moment in the film, a film which Davies saw as an opportunity to prove that he 'could write a linear narrative in which you seed things that pay off'.[16] Yet memory is still essential to the film, even if we do not explicitly see the events of Lily's life prior to her arrival in New York in 1905. Lily cutting the pages of her novel is a period detail through which Davies evokes specific time and place. In the novel *The Neon Bible*, David experiences a Proustian rush as he conjures the image of his Aunt Mae: 'She smelled so strong of perfume that sometimes you couldn't get near her without your nose stinging and having a hard time getting air.'[17] The passage recalls Davies describing Friday nights helping his sisters to get ready to go out in his 2008 video essay film *Of Time and the City*: 'a dab of scent, maybe only 'Evening in Paris', but making it seem as if the whole world was drenched in Chanel.'[18]

Sunset Song follows a chronological structure much like *The House of Mirth*. Unlike David, Chris is determined to leave the past behind. After the funeral of her mother, in third-person voiceover she says, 'The child in her heart had died then and Chris of the books and dreams died with it and the dark quiet corpse that was her childhood was folded in the tissue paper and was laid away forever.'[19] It is a similar resolution to the one Davies made after finishing his final autobiographical narrative film, *The Long Day Closes*. Yet *The Deep Blue Sea* returned to the ebb and flow of those early films, especially the photograph-album series of snapshots which made up 1988's *Distant Voices, Still Lives*. In the introduction to the script, Davies describes his adaptation as a 'patchwork of memory and real-time', following Hester's train of thought as she contends with the fallout of her attempted suicide and the breakdown of her relationship with Freddie.[20] The opening shots of the street on which Freddie's flat is situated, scarred by the Blitz, is reminiscent of the opening sequence of *The Long Day Closes*. It leads us down a path of introspection carried through the air by the smoke of Hester's cigarette.

There is more voiceover in Davies's scripts than in the finished films, realising that he could allow the images to tell the story without spoken description. Allowing *The House of Mirth* to be told solely through Wharton's dialogue is the film's greatest asset, and its greatest difference to Martin Scorsese's frenetic 1993 adaptation of *The Age of Innocence*. Davies highlighted Joanne Woodward's narration of that film as one of three great voiceovers, along with *Kind Hearts and Coronets* and *Sunset Boulevard*, explaining that he felt such narration in his adaptation would fail to live up to their success.[21] Since the novel is written in the third person, there is no need: show, do not tell, is Davies's guiding principle. This is taken to an extreme in *The Deep Blue Sea*, which condenses the first act of the play into a nine-minute fantasia of wordless stream of consciousness, narrated in the script but purely visual in the film. Hester's life quite literally flashes before our eyes.

Let's have something with a bit of life in it

'You've been a long way away.' 'Yes.' 'Thank you for coming back to me.' Rachmaninov's second piano concerto swells, Laura bursts into tears, and the audience with her. Just as David Lean carries us away with the music playing on Laura's wireless in 1945's *Brief Encounter* into the memory of her affair, so too does Davies in *The Deep Blue Sea* with Samuel Barber's violin concerto. Like Rachmaninov, this is luscious, grandiose music of heightened emotionality which, despite its composer's American nationality, has much in common with Russian Romanticism. Hester is described during the opening sequence as sitting in an armchair in the house of her husband, Sir William Collyer, staring at the fire as the music swells around them. At its conclusion, Hester is listening to the

The Neon Bible (1995): Gena Rowlands as Aunt Mae.

concerto in Freddie's flat on the radio, as Freddie comes in and says, 'Oh Christ! Let's have something with a bit of life in it', before switching over to 'Educating Archie' on the BBC Light programme.[22] Class difference, a collision of tastes, is planted in that moment.

The tension between high and low brow runs throughout Davies's filmography, something which he appears to make little distinction between himself, treating popular and light music with equal reverence to concerti and opera. It is a theme which recurs throughout *The Deep Blue Sea*, much like the concerto itself which flows in and out to signal a return to Hester's interiority. A memory of Hester and Freddie at the National Gallery, standing in front of a Braque painting. Freddie makes a joke, and Hester calls him childish – he has a chip on his shoulder, for it was childish men like him who saved Britain from Nazi invasion. Freddie goes off to find the Impressionists, and later Hester asks him why. 'I only did it for the Monet', he replies, and Hester's snobbish exterior melts away.[23]

Aunt Mae in *The Neon Bible* listens to Glenn Miller with the same sensibility as Hester does listening to Barber: 'Oh, David… it's… so… wonderful…You feel…You feel the light go through you… through your whole body… it's so… oh!'[24] Davies uses unique phrasing here, with underlined words and extended ellipsis to articulate that which Aunt Mae finds so inexpressible about the music. These scenes of sitting by the radio with the family recall similar moments in Davies's autobiographical films, which similarly move between the vocals of Doris Day or Ella Fitzgerald and orchestral swells of Mahler and Vaughan Williams. There is pain in the memory of those songs for Aunt Mae as well as happiness, capturing heart-wrenching melancholy. In an early sequence, the camera tracks over to her performing the Gershwins' 'How Long Has This Been Going On?' to an audience, before jeers and a bottle smashing are heard on the soundtrack. In the script the image of the violence is shown, whereas in the finished film it is only heard. Too painful for Aunt Mae to visualise.

The soundtrack for *The House of Mirth* is Davies's most classical, although unlike his approach to dialogue, he did not limit himself to music of the period or that the characters would be familiar with. He selected the opening and closing theme as the adagio from Alessandro Marcello's oboe concerto after hearing it at the gym. Unlike the grand Romantic music of Davies's other films, the Baroque sensibility suited the film as he did not wish to overtly manipulate the audience's emotions with the film. He described it as 'very formal but with a wonderful kind of life within that formality', believing that, 'Music should be counterpoint, just enough so that you may not even be sure what you feel, but you feel something'.[25] The rest of the film moves from Haydn to Borodin to Mozart, and even to Morton Feldman's music written for the Rothko Chapel which was composed in 1971. It is as if Davies is stripping back the layers of the orchestra in parallel with the undoing of Lily Bart, until the bare minimalist bones of instrumentation remain, before bringing back the Marcello at the close. A more subdued use of recurrence than the Barber in *The Deep Blue Sea*, but equally effective.

Communal singing is an essential part of Davies's films – *Still Lives* is effectively staged as an operetta of memories flowing in and out of a trip to the pub where Davies's family and their friends sang an array of popular tunes. Similar scenes are staged in *The Deep Blue Sea*, even performing 'How You Gonna Keep 'Em Down on the Farm' which is also heard in the death-bed reminiscences of the elderly Tucker in *Death and Transfiguration* from 1983. These melodies were mirrored in *Sunset Song* through the use of Scottish folk tunes which Davies loved dearly. In his introduction to the script, he describes them as:

songs to pull the heartstrings, to make you remember the long-dead,
making you wish for the longed for happiness which we all need
– content and secure in the knowledge that we will never die... for we
are young and in our prime.[26]

'The Flowers of the Forest', with lyrics written by Scottish poet Jean Elliot in 1756 to commemorate the Battle of Flodden of 1513, is a lament against the slaughter of James IV and his men. In the film, as in the book, it is performed by Chris following a cèilidh at her wedding to Ewan. Much of the scene is cut from the finished film, condensing the dancing and exchange of songs which Davies writes out in full. The song also appears in the film's most moving and cinematic sequence, in which a recording by Ronnie Browne plays over a montage of Ewan's execution by firing squad. The camera moves out over No Man's Land, as the sun starts to shine on the waterlogged mud.[27] The recurrence of war, death, pain, suffering, and the women who mourn their dead.

We'll hear nae mair lilting at our ewe-milking;
Women and bairns are heartless and wae;
Sighing and moaning on ilka green loaning-
The Flowers of the Forest are a' wede away.[28]

The undefinable nature of love

The four adaptations written by Davies, like his 2016 biographical film *A Quiet Passion* about Emily Dickinson, revolve around female characters. Aunt Mae holds the same place in David's world as his sisters did – in the novel she is described as covering David with lipstick marks, telling him stories of her days on the stage, her boyfriends, her gifts: 'We'd go out walking, with her so funny with her buttocks all sucked in and her stomach stuck out like a pregnant Jean Harlow'.[29] Camp faux-Hollywood glamour, rejecting the drab domestic life under the thumb of an abusive man which destroys her sister, David's mother. That abuse terrorises David's household much like Father does in *Distant Voices, Still Lives*, with his own father forcing David to play with other boys who beat him and call him a 'sissy'.[30] There is a similar relief to

INTRODUCTION: A STORY WHICH DESERVES TO BE TOLD

David and Aunt Mae in the father's death at the midpoint of *The Neon Bible*, although his presence lingers like the seeds he planted the day he punched David's mother.

No father is present in *The House of Mirth* – in the novel Wharton simply writes, 'It was a relief to Lily when her father died'.[31] Davies makes Hester's father a vicar in *The Deep Blue Sea*, rendering him quite literally the difficult voice of God attempting to turn her away from the sins of the flesh. She tells Collyer that she cannot stand it when he sounds like her father: 'That tone of voice. That same mixture of irritation and sanctimoniousness. It's hard enough to take it when it comes from a vicar, when it comes from you it's insufferable.'[32] Davies observes in women a tendency to marry men like their father, with an echo of history repeating itself in *Distant Voices, Still Lives*, and most explicitly in *Sunset Song*. Like *Distant Voices*, Davies does not show much of the violence of Chris's father, although it is heard and it is felt. Chris and her brother Will lie in bed listening to their father rape their mother, forcing her to have more children when he is drunk, causing her to scream in agony. That same sexual violence occurs in Chris's own life, first with a stranger who comes to work for her father, and later her husband after he returns home on leave from the Western Front.

This violence does not go unpunished. Unlike Davies's own family in *Distant Voices*, Chris stands up to Ewan the morning after he rapes her, picking up a bread knife and telling him, 'I'm not frightened of you!'[33] At the end of *The Neon Bible*, after his mother's death, David grabs a shotgun and kills Reverend Watkins when he attempts to take his mother away. The impact is not shown, but we see the vicar slide down the stairs with the bullet wound in the side of his head. In the novel David describes the moment: 'He didn't scream or anything like I had expected from the movies. He just fell there at the top of the steps and laid quiet.'[34] This captures Davies's own belief in not showing violence explicitly, for it can never do justice to the real thing, and by not showing those images they become more haunting in the viewer's imagination. Due to Davies's loathing of violence and unwillingness to show it in his films, when it does come, the effect is terrifying.

The most violent moment in *The House of Mirth* occurs when Gus Trenor launches a chair against a door to stop Lily from escaping as he attempts to force her to 'thank' him for helping her financially with sex. It is the final moment in Lily's undoing from which she never recovers.

She yearns for a return to her past, as do her friends. Davies frequently uses a device of characters getting older through tableaux or photographs, sometimes quite literally morphing in front of our eyes into their older selves. But when Lily appears in a *tableau vivant* at a party, she briefly appears to have gotten younger. In the novel and in the script, Lily elects to recreate Reynolds's rather drab portrait of Mrs Lloyd, yet in the final film, she appears as Watteau's resplendent personification of Summer. Assuming Gerty's lines from the novel Grace says, 'She has never looked so radiant. I think I like her best in that simple dress. It makes her look like the real Lily [...] The Lily I know.' Selden continues to gaze at Lily even though Grace's eyes are upon him, and says, 'The Lily we know'. He reflects that Lily is only herself with a few people, and since she can become whatever she is believed to be, 'We must think the best of her…'[35] At the end of the film, when Lily is packing and accepting her impoverished status, the dress she wore for the *tableau vivant* is seen on the bed. And when she drinks the accidentally fatal overdose of chloral, the liquid slips from her fingers and 'stains the dress like blood'. Davies describes the final image of Lily's body thus: 'Now no longer beautiful – just a grey corpse in a shabby room.'[36] A bookend title card reads 'New York 1907' – just two years have passed between Lily's Summer and her final Winter.

In her defiance, Lily dies a spinster and a virgin. But forbidden sensuality sparks between Lily and Selden in two key sequences in which Lily allows him to light her cigarettes – an act totally unbecoming in a *jeune fille à marier*. The erotic intimacy of smoking together dances with the flirtatious repartee of Wharton's electrifying dialogue, which Davies holds in tight mid-shot between the two characters. It is dangerous, and more sensual than any explicit sexual act could be. Davies is careful not to go too far – when Selden kisses Lily, he describes it as 'light enough to be loving but not passionate enough to be compromising'.[37] It is a technique borrowed from Hays Code-era Hollywood and British melodrama, films like *Now, Voyager* from 1942 and *It Always Rains on Sunday* from 1947.

Laura and Alec share illicit cigarettes in *Brief Encounter*, as do Hester and Freddie in *The Deep Blue Sea*. Just as smoking creates an oral fixation in the viewer, the cigarette as a fetish object standing in for something one dare not name, the heterosexual infidelity of both films can be read as a stand-in for homosexuality. Rattigan wrote *The Deep Blue Sea* after his lover Kenneth Morgan died by suicide over another man, while Noël Coward similarly used his short play *Still Life*, developed as *Brief Encounter*, as an analogy for gay desire. The fear of discovery, the everyday transformed into something intoxicating, and the settlement for respectability in an era when queerness was ruinous. Davies's most obvious allusion to *Brief Encounter* occurs when Barber's concerto plays as Hester runs into an Underground station as if to throw herself under the train, with the lights and wind flashing on her face just as Laura does at the end of *Brief Encounter* before returning home to her husband. A memory appears – Collyer holding her during the Blitz as fellow Londoners sing 'Molly Malone'. A similar, but altogether different, scene to Davies's sister singing 'Roll Out the Barrel' in the Anderson shelter in *Distant Voices* – a memory which pre-exists Davies's birth.

It is not sex, queer or otherwise, which runs through all four of Davies's adaptations, but love and its endless unknowability. When Lily sees Selden for the last time, she reflects:

> You told me once that you could help me only by loving me. Well... you did love me for a moment and it helped me... But the moment is gone... and I let it go. [...] And one must go on living...[38]

Lily does not go on living, but she intends to – while ambiguous in the film, her death is accidental, not suicide. Davies describes the theme of *The Deep Blue Sea* in his introduction as 'the undefinable nature of love', a subject each of the character's has a different impression of.[39] Mrs Elton, Davies's mouthpiece of reason, holds the key to it from a decades-long marriage: 'It's wiping someone's arse or changing the sheets after they've wet themselves but never letting them lose their dignity so that you can both go on'.[40] Changing the sheets and starting over. Davies's words, not Rattigan's. And so that is what Hester gives to Freddie – the love to acknowledge that he will be better off without her, and so she lets him go.

> Love comforteth like sunshine after rain,
> But Lust's effect is tempest after sun.
> Love's gentle spring doth always fresh remain;
> Lust's winter comes ere summer half be done.
> Love surfeits not, Lust like a glutton dies.
> Love is all truth, Lust full of forgèd lies.[41]

We can only endure

The clean sheet spread out like the cinema screen, awaiting the whirr of the projector to bring its blank canvas to life. 'These licentious books, these dirty books… all the dirtier because they're going to make movies out of them and anyone who doesn't know it is defying God and is an agent of the Devil!', cries Watkins at a Klan book-burning.[42] In the novel *The Neon Bible*, David describes the tension between the Church and the movies, with Watkins trying to close down the moviehouse to stop people seeing pictures rather than attending his Sunday evening meetings.[43] The camera cranes down from the stars at night to the Revivalist congregation moving through the town towards a tent to hear travelling Evangelical preacher Bobbie Lee Taylor as they sing 'The Old Rugged Cross'. The sequence is dynamic, horrifying and moving, with Taylor set up as a charlatan hiding behind the curtain like the Wizard of Oz himself, praying on naïve God-fearing people. The move to the Church is mirrored in *Sunset Song*, as the villagers of Kinraddie congregate to the parish Church soundtrack by the hymn 'All in the April Evening'. The sequences are beautiful, but disturbing in the mob-like movements and apparent lack of individual freedom.

David sits between his mother and Aunt Mae at the revival meeting. 'The shot is from slightly below them so that the audience in the raked setting seem to go up behind them vertiginously'.[44] It is almost identical to the shot in *The Long Day Closes* of Bud sitting between Mother and Helen at the front of the balcony at the cinema, the projector light creating a shaft behind their heads as the waltz from *Carousel* plays. In *The House of Mirth*, the overture from *Così fan tutte* soundtracks the elite of American Golden Age society flocking to the opera house, with Lily and Gus shown in their box. The same occurs in *A Quiet Passion* as the Dickinsons listen to Bellini, and at the end of 2021's *Benediction*, when George and Siegfried Sassoon go to the theatre to see *Stop the World – I Want to Get Off*. Communion is essential to Davies's cinema, of coming together to share in one art. The theatre, the opera, the cinema – these are the sites of adoration, not the Church.

'[B]ut you keep on going, keep on thinking 'one day they'll say 'that's Mae Morgan!' … It's like a drug, it is baby, but when it doesn't happen, you hurt – here…'[45] Each of Davies's characters has a dream, something they are yearning and reaching towards, which they never manage to reach. At the close of *The Neon Bible*, David is travelling away by train to the end of the line: 'The sun's up full now, over the short trees, and I can see the sky's the same clear blue that it was yesterday in the valley', he says in the novel.[46] Without voiceover in *The House of Mirth*, we do not hear Wharton's narrator revealing Lily's tragically misplaced optimism:

> Tomorrow would not be so difficult after all: she felt sure that she would have the strength to meet it. She did not quite remember what it was that she had been afraid to meet, but the uncertainty no longer troubled her. She had been unhappy, and now she was happy – she had felt herself alone, and now the sense of loneliness had vanished.[47]

In the script for *Sunset Song*, Chris goes out to the Stones where she sees Ewan's ghost as a piper plays out over the countryside. He does not appear in film, nor does the final congregation which gathers in the script, a funeral cortége coming to hear the Minister speak on the deaths of the men who gave their lives in the War:

> They died for a world that is past, these men, but they did not die for this that we seem to inherit. Beyond it and us there shines a greater hope and a newer world, undreamt when these men died. But need we doubt which side the battle they would range themselves did they live today, need we doubt the answer they cry to us even now, from the places of the sunset?[48]

All of Davies's films seem to cry out against the sunset, of the closing of a Summer that has long faded from view. In his introduction to the *Sunset Song* script, he writes, 'How can we bear time or subdue nature? We cannot. We can only endure.'[49] It is a conclusion that, for all these reminiscences and journeys into the past, one must carry on. In Davies's script of *The Deep Blue Sea*, after Freddie has left, Hester notices that he has left his driving gloves behind, and a book of Shakespeare's sonnets given to her as a birthday present by Collyer. He then recites Sonnet 143, which concludes:

> So runneth thou after that which flies from thee,
> Whilst I thy babe chase thee afar behind;

But if thou catch thy hope, turn back to me,
And play the mother's part, kiss me, be kind;
So I will pray that thou mayest have thy will,
If thou turn back, and my loud crying still.[50]

The sonnet does not appear in the final film, but it is a moving expression of the love Hester endures. She does not turn back, but lights the fire she had earlier that day attempted to use to gas herself, and throws open the curtains. The Barber returns, and the camera cranes down from the window to the street, drawing parallel between her resolve to continue and that of Blitz-torn London.

After all, tomorrow is another day.

S/TRAX TARA'S THEME SWELLS THEN FINISHES.

FADE TO BLACK

NOTES

1. Henry Wadsworth Longfellow, 'The Day is Done', from *The Belfry of Bruges and Other Poems* (Cambridge, MA: John Owen, 1845).
2. 'How Long Has This Been Going On?' (1928), music by George Gershwin with lyrics by Ira Gershwin, performed by Gena Rowlands in *The Neon Bible*, see pp. 56–7, this volume.
3. *The Neon Bible*, see p. 70, this volume.
4. Davies interviewed by Graham Fuller, 'Summer's End', *Film Comment*, Vol. 27, No. 1 (Jan.–Feb. 2001), p. 55.
5. BFI Online (2018). 'Terence Davies on *Distant Voices, Still Lives*, 30 years later', interview with Sam Wigley. <www.bfi.org.uk/interviews/terence-davies-distant-voices-still-lives-30-years>.
6. Davies interviewed by Roger Shannon for the Institute for Creative Enterprise at Edge Hill University (2016). <www.youtube.com/watch?v=IxokAZFw3i4&ab_channel=EdgeHillUniversityResearch>
7. Davies interview by Philip Horne, 'Beauty's Slow Fade', *Sight & Sound* (Oct. 2000), p. 17.
8. Lewis Grassic Gibbon, *Sunset Song* (Edinburgh: Canongate Books, 2020), p. 29.
9. 'The Song of the Earth' (introduction), Terence Davies, *Sunset Song*, pp. 358–9, this volume.
10. Davies interviewed by Geoff Andrew, 'Reckless Moment', *Sight & Sound*, Vol. 21, No. 12 (Dec. 2011), p. 24.
11. Davies interviewed by Virginie Selavy, '*The Deep Blue Sea*: Interview with Terence Davies', *Electric Sheep* (2011). <www.electricsheepmagazine.co.uk/2011/11/24/the-deep-blue-sea-interview-with-terence-davies/>
12. Davies interviewed by Craig Hubert, 'Terence Davies Dives In', *Interview Magazine* (2012). <www.interviewmagazine.com/film/terence-davies-the-deep-blue-sea/>
13. *The Deep Blue Sea*, see p. 307, this volume.
14. John Kennedy Toole, *The Neon Bible* (London: Grove Press, 2019), p. 3.
15. *The Neon Bible*, see p. 52, this volume.

INTRODUCTION: A STORY WHICH DESERVES TO BE TOLD

16. *Film Comment* (2001), p. 55. See Note 4.
17. Toole, *The Neon Bible* (2019), p. 5.
18. *Of Time and the City*, in *Terence Davies Screenplays: Volume I* (London: BFI/Bloomsbury, 2025), p. 253.
19. *Sunset Song*, see p. 392, this volume.
20. Author's introduction to *The Deep Blue Sea*, see p. 288, this volume.
21. *Sight & Sound* (2000), p.17. See Note 7.
22. *The Deep Blue Sea*, see p. 314, this volume.
23. *The Deep Blue Sea*, see p. 308, this volume.
24. *The Neon Bible*, see p. 102, this volume.
25. *Sight & Sound* (2000), p.17. See Note 7.
26. Author's introduction to *Sunset Song*, p. 358.
27. *Sunset Song*, see p. 492, this volume.
28. 'The Flowers of the Forest', Scottish folk tune, lyrics by Jean Elliot (1756 or 1758), performed by Ronnie Browne.
29. Toole, *The Neon Bible* (2019), p. 9.
30. Ibid., p. 11.
31. Edith Wharton, *The House of Mirth* (London: Penguin, 2012), p. 38.
32. *The Deep Blue Sea*, see p. 332, this volume.
33. *Sunset Song*, see p. 482, this volume.
34. Toole, *The Neon Bible* (2019), p. 158.
35. *The House of Mirth*, see p. 189, this volume.
36. *The House of Mirth*, see p. 282, this volume.
37. *The House of Mirth*, see p. 171, this volume.
38. *The House of Mirth*, see pp. 278–9, this volume.
39. Author's introduction to *The Deep Blue Sea*, see p. 288, this volume.
40. *The Deep Blue Sea*, see p. 343, this volume.
41. William Shakespeare, *Venus and Adonis* (1593), quoted in *The Deep Blue Sea*, see p. 338, this volume.
42. *The Neon Bible*, see p. 62, this volume.
43. Toole, *The Neon Bible* (2019), p. 57.
44. *The Neon Bible*, see p. 85, this volume.
45. *The Neon Bible*, see p. 77, this volume.
46. Toole, *The Neon Bible* (2019), p. 162.
47. Wharton, *The House of Mirth* (2012), p. 376.
48. *Sunset Song*, see p. 494, this volume.
49. Author's introduction to *Sunset Song*, p. 359.
50. William Shakespeare, 'Sonnet 143', quoted in *The Deep Blue Sea*, see p. 351, this volume.

The Neon Bible (1995): Gena Rowlands as Aunt Mae. (BFI National Archive)

INTERVIEW WITH TERENCE DAVIES: DIRECTING *THE NEON BIBLE*

Mark Cousins

[Originally published in *Projections 6: Film-makers on Film-making*, John Boorman & Walter Donohue (eds), Faber and Faber, 1996]

Terence Davies: The film is based on a book called *The Neon Bible* by John Kennedy Toole who is famous for *The Confederacy of Dunces*. This book was actually found by Elizabeth Karlsen who produced the film and, very roughly, it's about a poor white family growing up in the Southern part of the United States. Into the family comes Aunt Mae who represents everything that is glamorous, and this young boy just basically falls in love with her. She is wonderful and full of life. It's about his relationship with her and how the relationship with his mother and father gradually decays as she becomes the dominant person in his life. The Second World War breaks out and the father goes off to fight and gets killed in Italy and the mother slowly declines into a kind of madness. Then at the end he is deserted. That's what it's about; sounds fun doesn't it? It's not nearly as dreary, honestly.

There are some great underwater routines in there. They are out-takes from *Waterworld*, how do you think we got finance? So that's roughly the story. I've chosen some clips that have a lot of camera movement, some with just conventional cutting, and some which are conventional cutting and camera movement and song as well. You know me and song!

```
CLIP: 'WE GOTTA EAT, WE NEED MONEY'.
LONG CLIP THAT ENDS IN SINGING SCENE.
```

Mark Cousins: What was your idea behind the scene where the boy grows up?

TD: Because in the book the fight we've just seen and his father going out and not coming back for hours and hours is the moment where he actually grows up emotionally, I wanted to see him physically grow up in front of us. I didn't know how it was done and when they said 'morphing' I said, 'It's going to cost a fortune.' Why didn't I think in terms of Polaroid, but you don't. What I wanted was for the scene to carry on even though he has grown up and six years have elapsed. Many people don't get that and say, 'This beating must have gone on for a long time,' which was not the intention. Because I know the material well, I've read the novel forty-seven times, you get to the point where you can't read it again, this is the only way you can think of doing that particular bit, and eliding two or three chapters together at a time. You can't film a novel, you just can't; you have to capture the essence of the book as well as its literal narrative. That's what I was trying to say.

MC: Was there any idea behind your making of the film having seen *Night of the Hunter* with Charles Laughton? He did a cross shot that goes out of the window and up to the stars which seems to suggest mind over matter.

TD: Yes, I adore that film and think it's such a masterpiece. I'm afraid I haven't done it as well as Laughton did. *Night of the Hunter* is one of those films I absolutely adore. People who say they don't like it, I want them killed, but that's awful and you can't do that can you? But I'm the same with *Carry on Sergeant*, so what can you do? What's wonderful about *Night of the Hunter* is it is a fairy tale for adults shot through a German Expressionism. There is that wonderful way children have: there is black, there is white, there is evil, there is good. That sequence on the river, it's just one of the greatest sequences ever filmed. A well-known writer, who shall not be named, said to me recently that it is a flawed masterpiece. I said, 'Well could you do as good, even half as good?' The answer is no, none of us could, it's such a great, great masterpiece.

MC: Were you attempting to reach for that effect?

TD: No, this is not in the same class as *Night of the Hunter* and also it is not about the same thing. It would be like making a musical. The touchstone is *Singin' in the Rain* which I saw when I was seven. Nothing is

Young at Heart (1954): Doris Day and Frank Sinatra.

as good. No matter how hard you try, you can't do it. It is very much one of my big touchstones, one of the most important films in my life, but so is the American musical which is what influenced me most of all. *Singin' in the Rain* was my first film at seven; at eleven I discovered Doris Day in *Young at Heart*. That was it, I was lost to her forever. When I grow up I want to be Doris Day, what I lack in freckles and blond hair I more than make up for in willpower, I assure you.

MC: You were going to say something about memory there.

TD: Sorry, I forgot. The way the nature of memory works is you feel and remember the intensity of the moment, the quintessence of the moment and you don't remember what went before or after. You remember it in a sequence of intense moments, and children feel intensely. In the book he goes out onto the veranda and looks at the stars. How do you make that magical? You make him go out and see nothing but stars, because that's what a child would do. We know that's not true, you would see the landscape, you would see the blackness of the shrubbery, then the sky and then the line of the horizon but that's not what you see in memory. You only remember its intensity and how it burned into you. I was trying to get that because I do think that memory has such a hold on us in the way that Eliot describes it at the beginning of *The Four Quartets*. It is ever present, it is not time gone by, it is now; we can oscillate between what happened twenty years ago, what is happening now and what we will be doing next week. In a film, you have to set it up in a way where it's not going to be conventional narrative; it's not going to cut from this to this, because that implies that events follow each other. If you dissolve, it always indicates time passing. No one has ever told us that, but we all read it as that. It can be time passing forward or backward, but it's time passing. What interested me in this was actually to have a scene that was happening now, dissolve, cut within that sequence, and dissolve back. Now what does that mean? Is that parallel time, is it real time within the memory, or what is it? It is Eliot: 'Time present and time past / Are both perhaps present in time future, / And time future contained in time past. / If all time is eternally present / All time is unredeemable.' It is what memory also does; it fixes on the tiny, never the big. 'Then a cloud passed, and the pool was empty' – that's what you remember, and that's what I wanted to try to capture, that essence of the book. John Kennedy Toole wrote it when he was sixteen and there is a lot of weak writing in it: him being bullied by Mrs Watkins at school is not interesting, the fact that Aunt Mae can't cook is not interesting. What *is* interesting is how you feel when you are with someone you intensely love. I drew a little bit on autobiography. I used to mind my sister's children when I was growing up, and very often I would be allowed to stay and very often I went to bed with them and we'd look out of the window if it was a hot night and talk, then go to sleep. That brought back a whole lot of memories for me and I knew it was right to have him in the bed and to have her say, 'We'll pray tonight,' and he just says, 'Amen.' He does that in the book, and then we go into the sequence in the revival tent; I'm interested in the poetry of the ordinary which is why I love Chekhov because he is too. At big moments, people say the banal thing, they don't say the dramatic thing – unless it is *All About Eve,* when you forgive it!

MC: Would you talk about casting Gena Rowlands and also about working with an actor who is so much a part of the collaboration.

TD: When I read the book and Elizabeth said to me, 'Who do you want to play Aunt Mae?' I said, 'Gena Rowlands,' thinking we'd never get her.

She said, 'I'll ring her agent.' She did, and a month later we were in Los Angeles in the Le Tore restaurant on Sunset Boulevard sitting opposite Gena Rowlands. I thought, 'God, it's Gena Rowlands and I'm sitting here. I better say something or she'll think I'm an idiot.' We then sent her a VHS of *Distant Voices, Still Lives* and the *South Bank Show* and she loved them and she liked me and we got on. I told her how I wanted to do the story, but the script wasn't written and she agreed to do it. Her agent said that in twenty-two years she had never ever done that, which was a great compliment. The old ego went sky high and she was a joy to work with. The only slight disagreement we had was that long speech she has at the window. She wanted to play it in a certain way and I said, 'No, I find that a little bit sentimental, but could you just think about it.' It required her to cry and she said, 'I can't cry, I've never cried in a film.' I said, 'Can you imply tears in the voice?' and she said, 'Yes.' Give an idea like that to an American actor and they do wonders with it. That was the first take and I could feel the tears rising up in my throat. This is absurd, I'm supposed to be their fearless leader.

Before we did the scene in the bed, I told her it was summed up by a poem by Philip Larkin – I read her quite a lot of poetry actually – *An Arundel Tomb*, 'What will survive of us is love.' I thought that she would think I was an idiot. She did think I was a bit strange at first because I don't do a lot of coverage, but after two days they saw the rushes and liked them and were absolutely dedicated.

The way she uses her eyes in that long sequence: 'When I was young I could wear clothes and I could always carry a tune. But you get older honey. You get old' – it was so moving.

CLIP: SEQUENCE INCLUDING 'THE OLD RUGGED CROSS' SONG. TIME PASSES, FATHER KILLED IN WAR, AUNT MAE GOES TO WORK IN A FACTORY

MC: Did you write your scenes with certain camera movements in mind? It reminded me of some scenes in *Distant Voices, Still Lives*.

TD: I write the way I feel, and I see it in that way. I see what's in the mise en scène. I see if the camera is tracking or panning down, that's how I see it, so it's very difficult to extrapolate and say, 'Well, I did it because of that.' I was trying to conflate a number of things that happened in the book. Dad had hit her, he's gone out, he's not come back, the war breaks out, he goes away, nothing is resolved and then he is killed. By this time Aunt Mae has gone into a factory and has made friends there. How do you do that interestingly? You deny geography, that's what you do. You can, as you move in and out of blackness, go somewhere else. If any of you know Bruckner's music, there are rolling crescendi and then you end on a cadence and start again. If that doesn't sound horribly pretentious, that was the feeling behind it, that these sequences are conceived over a long stretch like a long tune in a symphony.

MC: Why did you choose that particular hymn for that sequence?

TD: The hymn that is quoted in the book is not terribly interesting and I didn't know the tune. I needed to get across immediately the idea that you know it's a hymn. 'The Old Rugged Cross' I just happened to like and I thought it was that kind of fundamentalist hymn that they would sing. With a piece of music you're trying to say something more than just its function in the narrative. It's got to be a hymn, but it should be one that has a true ambiguity like in the next sequence where she sings in the factory. In the book she sings a blues song and it was not right. I wanted something that summed up her emotions. She wants to get a man, and she never succeeds. The man she goes away with is not right, but that's never resolved. Also, she's got to sing for herself and for those women. Their menfolk have gone away to war and a lot of them will not be coming back. So, because I love Rodgers and Hart, I

The Neon Bible (1995): While the menfolk are away at war.

chose 'My Romance' because that sums up everything; all that romance about wanting someone – 'My romance doesn't need a thing but you' – and how you want those people that you love that have gone away. Even the people that you don't love that have gone away; you still want them. It was a way of trying to get all of those things within a single song. It has all those resonances for me.

When we finished the film someone said, 'How about a score?' I said, 'No, the music that's in it, that's all there needs to be. We don't need someone putting in "Aunt Mae's Theme" or something like that.' This I *didn't* want, and they just looked at me as if I'd just landed from the planet Thorg, and I had. I got terribly kind of 'poker-up-the-arse' about it: if I had wanted a score, I would have asked for one. At the end of the day, you can only really follow your instinct. This is going to sound terribly arrogant, but you can only make it for yourself because you can't go out to please other people. A film is either liked or it's not; there is no way of knowing which. So, if you pass me on Princes Street, please be generous.

CLIP: SINGING SEQUENCE

MC: You were saying that people don't make musicals anymore, but you do, don't you?

TD: Sort of, but it's not *Pajama Game*, it's not *I'll Never be Jealous Again*, it's not even Betty Grable in *Mother Wore Tights*. I wish it were. There is too much angst in my films. Musicals have got to be jolly, ending on a bright note so that you go out on to the street thinking 'Isn't life wonderful.' You don't go out of my films thinking life is wonderful.

MC: Maybe not the mood of the musicals, but if you compare the camera moves in the title number *of Singin' in the Rain* with some of your camera moves, there is still a sense of epic sweep.

TD: That's a huge compliment, thank you. That film is so seminal to me. It's one of the films which literally did change my life and I weep almost all the way through it if I watch it now, because I can remember the happiness it gave me when I sat in the Odeon Cinema in 1953 with my elder sister. I'll never forget it as long as I live, never. When you love something as much as that you can't have any kind of distance on it. When I look at my own films I think that they are very poor compared to that, because those were the great days of Hollywood. You went to the cinema, queued, and saw these films, and it created the land of magic. I can remember shortly after *Singin' in the Rain* was released and my sister took me to see it. In those days, if a girl had an American for a boyfriend it was just so swish. She had an American boyfriend and he came down the street in the middle of this Liverpool slum in a white suit. Everybody came out to look at him and they knocked on the door just to hear his voice, the accent. He brought us six pairs of nylons, a big thing of Wrigley's Spearmint chewing-gum, some peanut butter and a percolator. We didn't know what a percolator was, so we used it for paint.

There's sophistication for you. When I see those films, it's not just the films that come back. I can remember being taken to see *Young at Heart* and we got the last two seats in the Liverpool Forum. I went with my older sister Helen. We slightly missed the opening credits. It was a very hot Sunday afternoon and we went to the early performance and we came out and walked up the road because we couldn't get a tram. She went faint, and she was wearing a little black costume suit with a little blouse with a frilly collar. I can still see it now. It's so vivid, so when I see those films I know where I saw them, which route I took and who I saw them with. But when I see my own, I don't think they will ever have that effect on anybody.

MC: There are a number of things connecting there. You are talking about the precise memory of things, yet it seems to me, say, the last shot in *Young at Heart* where the camera goes through the window to see Frank Sinatra on the piano: you've done the camera through the window so many times in your films it seems that in some way you are borrowing the perfect form of these films, using them to express something much darker and more serious.

TD: I think there must be, because once you are exposed to something you can't then 'un-know' it. No matter how much you think you haven't borrowed, you do, and that can be a good thing or a bad thing. The film begins by going into the window and it comes out at the end. It's like a perfect arc. But that wonderful track of Judy Garland's when she sings 'The Boy Next Door' at the window, just sublime. I'd have done anything to do that, anything. Even in *Mother Wore Tights* with Betty Grable – and it's not a good musical – there is one wonderful moment when she sings 'Cocomo Indiana' with Dan Dailey. These are wonderful tracks and it is as smooth as silk – 'Gee I'd like to be back home again, in Cocomo In-di-ana' – it's just gorgeous! But, alas, we don't make musicals in England. What have we got? Musicals by 'Andrew Rice-Pudding', 'Don't Queue for me, I'm the Cleaner'. Wonderful!

MC: You are speaking of your influences and they are all pre-Cinemascope. In this film were you trying to evoke the Cinemascope feelings of the 1950s, and were you trying to comment on the shape of the screen by having frame within frame, and sometimes screen within screen? Later in the film you have washing hanging up which acts as a Cinemascope screen – or am I reading into this too much?

TD: The first Cinemascope film I actually saw was *The Robe*, again in 1953, and it was the first Cinemascope film ever made. I can remember going to see it at a packed cinema, the curtains went back and the audience gasped. You just saw this huge, epic thing. There was a wonderful performance by a man called Jay Robinson who played Caligula which made me want to be an actor because he had all the best lines. He was terribly camp, but just wonderful.

There is a wonderful bit with Jean Simmons in it where he says, 'Ahh, the Lady Diana. As beautiful as ever ... and as cold.' I thought, 'Isn't this dramatic?' When I went out to see Gena, the casting director

The Robe (1953): Jay Robinson as Caligula.

said, 'Is there anyone you would like to see?' and I said, 'Yes, I want to see Jay Robinson. Is he still alive, because he had such an important impact on my life?' He was alive and living in Los Angeles and we had tea together. I said, 'I can repeat all your dialogue now,' and I did. He was so lovely. He didn't make many films – *The Robe*, *Demetrius and the Gladiators*, the remake of *My Man Godfrey* and *The Virgin Queen* – but he's still got this wonderfully rich, bump-it-with-a-trumpet voice, like those wonderful strippers in *Gypsy* who sing 'If you wanna make it, twinkle while you shake it. If you wanna grind it, wait till you've refined it. If you wanna bump it, bump it with a trumpet!'

So the influence was actually that film. When you want people in the middle of the frame, how do you make it alive? What you do is make the texture behind them alive. But I used much more asymmetry than I ever used before because the beginning of that second sequence with the people walking down the street was originally supposed to be them walking this way and we are tracking that way. Dull, so dull. So we just moved the camera round – not a lot – and the scene came alive because you have got interest all down the frame for the length of time it takes for that track. It was interesting how you can create that epic quality. It's very easy to make it epic, you have just got to put a lot of extras in. To make it intimate, and feel intimate rather than big – that's different. In this film I had three hundred extras, more than I've ever had in my entire life. When they said you have got three hundred I wondered what I would do with them. My crew were wonderful. I said that I really needed help with the extras because I'd only ever had half a dozen up to now – coming from the Third World! – and they were fantastic.

The frames within frames, I think that's an unconscious thing. I just do it. In *The Long Day Closes* it's the carpet; in *The Neon Bible* it's the sheet, and in the next one it's going to be cutlery.

MC: How do you get shadows in colour? I always thought that once you get colour in film, you negate all shadow.

TD: What I did was I looked at a lot of photographs that were taken at the beginning of the war by Eudora Welty, Dorothea Lange and Walker Evans. Now, they are all in black and white, but with the sunlight being very strong, you get very deep shadow, but you also get detail in the shadow. I said to my cinematographer, Mick Coulter, 'I want a reproduction of this, but in colour, like three-strip Technicolor, where you can get very deep but very detailed shadows.' Look at Douglas Sirk, for instance: you can always see detail in the shadows. I don't know technically how he did it; I just said this is what I want and he gave it to me. It's a question that only he could really answer. They were based on black and white photographs, not colour ones.

MC: I know with *Distant Voices, Still Lives* you said you didn't rehearse very much. Did you have to rehearse more for this one?

TD: It was almost exactly the same. The only thing that we did differently was that we read through the script to begin with, just for the accent, rather than for the performance, because I needed to attune my ear to that accent. We based it actually on Diana Scarwid's accent because she is actually from Savanna which is very gentle. We finished reading it and I then read them the opening of *The Four Quartets* by Eliot which is really foot-tapping. Then I told them to go away and read the script; don't read it too often, but read the scenes the night before. Then we rehearsed them. Sometimes I read them poetry, sometimes I didn't. With Diana I usually quoted music rather than poetry. They give the performance so quickly. I remember the first day we were working with Diana and all she had was one line – it was a sequence of pans and it ends on her saying 'Who do you think the murderer is, David?' By this point she has started to slide into madness. While we were going through it, with Gena first and then Jacob, then her, she just sat in the chair and you could see her literally becoming this woman. It was breathtaking. We came to do it and it was just fabulous. She had to say hardly anything, just this one line, and even I felt moved … and I wrote the thing!

There was another moment when we had been doing pick-up shots all day which are very boring – people going in and out of doors, very dull – and you just can't make them come alive. We had two shots with her at the end of the day and it was a very hot day and everyone was very tired and these shots were last. She came on and she electrified that crew. In the first take you could feel this electricity go through you; it was so moving. When people do things like that I want to adopt them legally, I get so excited. But by the same token when it doesn't go well I get really depressed. Unfortunately, when you are the director that communicates itself to other people. In America the director is God, literally, but I don't believe in all that and think it's a lot of nonsense and I become terribly like Thora Hird.

MC: You were talking about music and said that there were certain songs in the book that didn't appeal to you. Do the alternatives suggest themselves while you are reading the book?

TD: It depends. Sometimes you know the sort of song you want, but you're not sure which one. I have quite a lot of knowledge about American popular songwriting up until the rise of Elvis Presley because I don't really like rock 'n' roll and that's when my interest in pop music really did cease. I know that great tradition which is now, alas, no more. Songwriters now aren't writing anything that's got any wit in it. Can you imagine a Cole Porter now? You can't because nobody is writing like that. The sheer wit of the man. One song begins 'Ravel is chasing Debussy, The aphid is chasing the pea. The gander is chasing the goosey, but nobody is chasing me,' which has become my theme song because it is alas all too true. When I was writing the whole of the ending sequence, I was listening to Radio Three and one night they had a programme of Stephen Foster songs and the only ones that I knew were 'Camptown Races' and 'The Old Folks at Home'. I thought I would listen to it anyway, sung by Thomas Hamson who has now become a very big opera star and lead singer, and he sang the song 'Hard Times Come Again No More', and I thought that's it, that's what I need. Those things have always been serendipity. I've always managed to hear them just when I needed them, and I dashed out to the music discount store on The Strand and I got the last copy, and I thought I'm destined to have this. So it depends, sometimes you know what you want, sometimes it occurs to you, sometimes someone suggests something to you and you say 'It's not that but it's this.' The film opens and closes with a hymn called 'Oh Lord How Long'. A friend of Elizabeth Karlsen got me this old Baptist manual from America, a hymnal, and he played the song and sang it. The words were not that interesting, but the tune was wonderful. I thought, it's got to be a solo instrument, so I said, 'Can we record it on a cor anglais and an oboe?' When I heard it played back it had that wonderful, open American sound like Copland, and you could see how he had got his influence from American folk song and American hymnals. You have to be open to things like that, they come to you and find you. I love music and when it's right it gives me such pleasure. Can you imagine *Psycho* without that wonderful score? You can't. As soon as you hear that *moto perpetuo* you are frightened, and on edge, and when she goes into the house, and it's all played with strings with the mutes on, it's just Fabbo! I get terribly worked up about that, which shows you how boring my private life is.

MC: How do you explain the contrast between the sobriety there is on screen and the jollity of you in person?

TD: I'm actually very miserable. No, I don't say that as a joke, I really am. I get very depressed, very easily. I've poured my life into making films at the expense of a private life and if there are any film-makers amongst you, it is not worth it. There's nothing more depressing than going back to a hotel room after people have said they like what you do, or were very responsive, and you end up going into a hotel room alone. There is no one to put their arms round you and say well done or never mind. That's depressing. You get sick of getting on and off planes on your own. There are times when you cannot bring yourself to go to another festival, but you go because you don't want to let anyone down. I want to be entertaining, I don't want to be miserable, and I don't want to let anybody down who is connected with the film. But at home I get very low indeed. In the last year two members of my family have died, and that's very hard to cope with because I loved them very much. I wish I was intrinsically happy but I'm intrinsically miserable. You try to compensate for it by trying to be funny but there is something unseemly about that, because what you are actually doing is saying 'Love me, love me, love me', and at forty-nine that's really rather unseemly. I've stopped biting the furniture though, so that's one thing I've achieved over the last few years. Actually, I'm really terribly miserable.

MC: Why not give up film-making then?

TD: Well, I don't know what else I'd do. I need to make films, but I don't like all the crap that surrounds it. Cannes was very damaging. I came back feeling completely worthless and completely talentless and that will take a long time to get over.

People were unbelievably nasty: there was someone who, after a screening of *The Long Day Closes,* sent me a letter which was two pages of complete viciousness, I mean, unbelievably vicious. So I wrote back and said 'Please take your bile out on somebody else.' This was a friend, which was very hurtful. There was some booing at the press-showing, but not at the evening showing where we got a standing ovation. I got back and there was a letter from the same gentleman saying 'I'm sorry it went badly.' I mean, it's gloating, and you think, 'Aahh, why do people do it?' Life is too short, and so am I.

MC: They booed the Antonioni film *L'Eclisse* at Cannes.

TD: But when you're on the receiving end of it it's very hard. Especially when you've poured everything into it. The work means more than it should. I think the best thing is to be married, or if you are gay have a partner, and what should be of secondary importance is your work. It's the other way round with me, and it's a mug's game. I'm sick of doing things alone, really so fed up with it. You think, 'Oh well, I want to help the film' and all that, and then you come to something like this – and you all laughed at the first joke and I can't tell you what balm it is, truly, truly, I really am grateful – but you don't want to let the film down, so I try to be jolly.

MC: You recite poetry so much I just want to ask you, do you think there are similarities between film-editing and the way poetry gets written – the condensation, the elliptical things – because you seem to like it a lot, and also music?

TD: Yes I do. I think music is the closest of all the art forms to film because notes on their own don't mean anything. They only mean something when they are juxtaposed with other chords and notes.

A great composer latches on to our inner harmonic so that when something is resolved, either in the minor or the major, we recognize it and therefore are moved. Poetry is the same but not quite as powerful, it's still the same. You know the way Eliot constantly elides but repeats; he will always repeat something: 'Do I dare?' and, 'Do I dare?' So it is like hearing a trill at the end of a cadence in a Mozart symphony, and you can hear that trill in Mahler but played on double basses: it's still a trill but the difference is huge, it's huge. You read a sonnet by Shakespeare and it can have the bleakness of 'Prufrock' but its form is utterly perfect. I can read something like 'Like as the waves make towards the pebbled shore' and have exactly the same kind of terror that I do when I read 'Prufrock' – 'I grow old … I grow old … I shall wear the bottoms of my trousers rolled. Shall I part my hair behind, do I dare eat a peach?' All that terror of being alive. Film can create that same terror of being alive, but over small things.

MC: What are your opinions about the essence of being a director?

TD: Arrogance is the wrong word, but I think you have to be driven by something you need, a need to make films. Although I try to make the films as cooperative as possible, because it is a co-operative effort, there has to be a central vision, and that vision has to be the director's. It couldn't be anybody else's. You cannot make a film by committee. So you have got to have that, and you've got to have the willpower to carry on doing it when people have said horrible things about what you've done. When you begin a new film all those terrors come back and you've got to try to control them because they are terrors. You walk out on to a set and there are seventy people, and they are looking to you and you've got to do it, you've got to pull it out of the bag every time; that's your job. There is something terribly exciting about that. You think, I want to pull this big sequence off, I hope I can, and then somehow you do. I think the essence is that you've got to have a vision, and that vision can be great or small, but it has got to be there, and more than anything else you've got to be true to it, you can't compromise it. If you compromise it, there's no point in doing it. I would rather not work than compromise something I believed in, that's why I would never survive in Hollywood, never. An actor would only have to say, 'I want an extra close-up,' and I'd say, 'You'll get the close-up you deserve, and no more.' And I would say that but, of course, I would be sacked. If it's Tom Cruise or Keanu Reeves or Christian Slater they've got the power because everyone wants to go and see them, they don't go and see it for the director. So I wouldn't survive there, and anyway it's so grim out there I don't know how people do. Those that go out and survive and make a success of it deserve knighthoods because it's awful. I had a tiny taste of it – very, very unpleasant. I didn't like it at all, I couldn't wait to get back. But I think you've got to have a great deal of tenacity. It's no good if you are thin-skinned, and I am very thin-skinned. So it's a question of tenacity, vision, needing to do it. More than wanting it, you've got to need it.

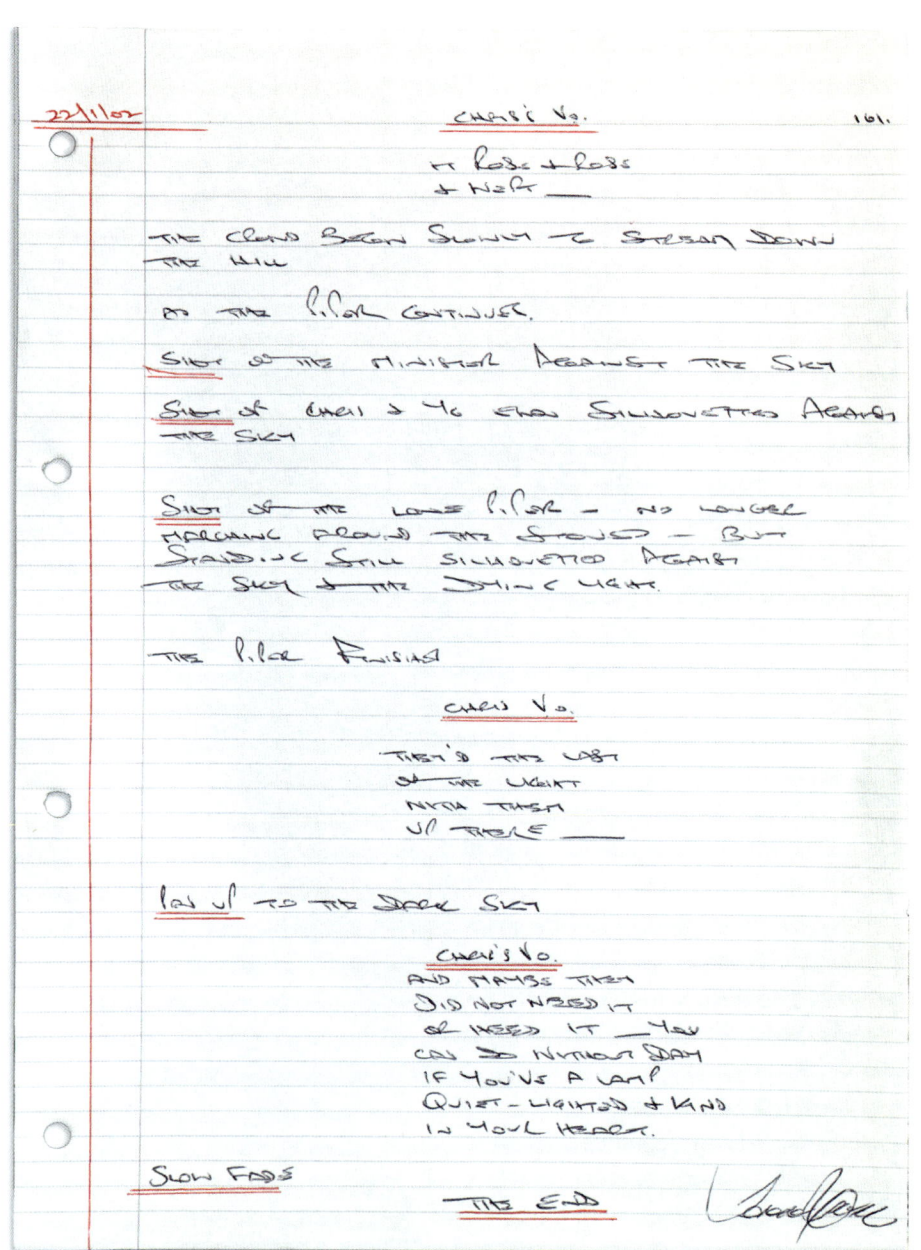

Sunset Song (2015): first draft, closing scene. (© The Terence Davies Estate, held by the Terence Davies Archive at Edge Hill University)

THE SCREENPLAYS

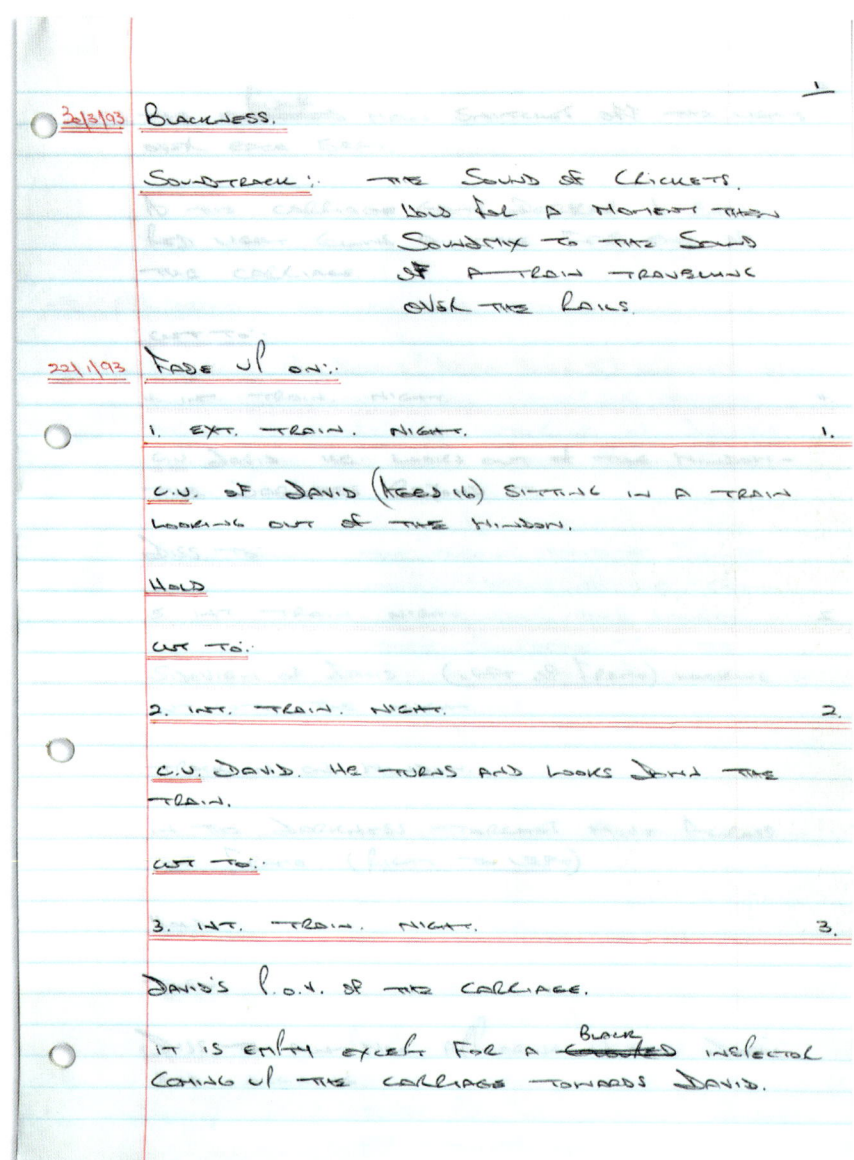

The Neon Bible (1995): first draft, opening scene. (© The Terence Davies Estate, held by the Terence Davies Archive at Edge Hill University)

THE NEON BIBLE (1995)

The Neon Bible (1995): Aunt Mae (Gena Rowlands) and young David (Drake Bell).

The Neon Bible
11 March 1994 (Second Draft)

The cast and crew of *The Neon Bible* include:

DAVID (aged 15)	Jacob Tierney
DAVID (aged 10)	Drake Bell
AUNT MAE	Gena Rowlands
DAVID'S MOTHER	Diana Scarwid
DAVID'S FATHER	Denis Leary
BOBBIE LEE TAYLOR	Leo Burmester
MISS SCOVER	Frances Conroy
REVEREND WATKINS	Peter McRobbie
FLORA	Joan Glover
Written and Directed by	Terence Davies
From the novel by	John Kennedy Toole
Producers	Elizabeth Karlsen
	Olivia Stewart
Director of Photography	Michael Coulter
Production Designer	Christopher Hobbs
Editor	Charles Rees
Costume Designer	Monica Howe
Art Director	Philip Messina
Music Director	Robert Lockhart
Casting Director	Laura Rosenthal

A Three Rivers Ltd production (1995) with:
Film4 Productions / Screen Partners Ltd / Scala Productions / European Script Fund / Academy Pictures / Channel Four Films / Iberoamericana Films Producción S.A.

"THE NEON BIBLE"
A SCREENPLAY BY
TERENCE DAVIES
(AFTER A NOVEL BY JOHN KENNEDY TOOLE)

Developed with the assistance of the European Script
Fund initiative of the media programme European
Community

SECOND DRAFT 11TH MARCH 1994

BLACKNESS

SOUNDTRACK: THE SOUND OF CRICKETS. HOLD FOR A MOMENT THEN SOUND MIX TO THE SOUND OF A TRAIN TRAVELLING OVER THE RAILS. FADE UP ON:

1. EXT. TRAIN NIGHT.

CLOSE UP OF DAVID (AGED 16) SITTING IN A TRAIN LOOKING OUT OF THE WINDOW.

HOLD

                                                                                                              CUT TO:

2. INT. TRAIN. NIGHT.

CLOSE UP DAVID. HE TURNS AND LOOKS DOWN THE TRAIN.

                                                                                                              CUT TO:

3. INT. TRAIN. NIGHT.

DAVID'S POV OF THE CARRIAGE. IT IS EMPTY EXCEPT FOR A BLACK INSPECTOR COMING UP THE CARRIAGE TOWARDS DAVID.
THE BLACK MAN SWITCHES OFF THE LIGHTS OVER EACH SEAT.
AS THE CARRIAGE GETS DARKER A SMALL RED LIGHT GLOWS AT THE FAR END OF THE CARRIAGE.

                                                                                                               CUT TO:

4. INT. TRAIN. NIGHT.

CLOSE UP DAVID. HE LOOKS OUT OF THE WINDOW – THE DARKNESS BEYOND IT.

                                                                                               DISSOLVE TO:

5. INT. TRAIN. NIGHT.

SIDEVIEW OF DAVID (LEFT OF FRAME) LOOKING OUT INTO THE NIGHT.
TRACK IN ON WINDOW
IN THE DARKNESS TORCHES MOVE ACROSS THE FRAME (RIGHT TO LEFT) THEN
DISSOLVE TO: AUNT MAE APPEARING IN THE DARK AND LAUGHING.
SOUNDTRACK: GLENN MILLER BRIEFLY PLAYING "PERFIDIA".
 ECHOING AND FAR AWAY.

                                                                                               DISSOLVE TO:

THE NEON BIBLE

6. EXT. TRAIN WINDOW. NIGHT.

MID CLOSE UP OF DAVID (AGED 4 OR 5) LOOKING OUT INTO THE NIGHT. THE INTERIOR OF THE TRAIN IS NOW THE INTERIOR OF DAVID'S HOUSE (THE SECOND ONE). THE ROOM FILLED WITH PEOPLE.
SOUNDTRACK: THE TRAIN'S WHISTLE SOUNDS. THE WHEELS OF THE TRAIN GET LOUDER AND LOUDER THEN SOUND MIX TO THE SOUND OF RAIN FALLING ON A TIN ROOF.
IT BEGINS TO RAIN.
DAVID KEEPS LOOKING OUT OF THE TRAIN WINDOW.
SLOWLY TRACK IN ON HIM.

SOUNDTRACK:
                    DAVID (VOICE OVER)
                        (AGED 16)
People came to see us that Christmas ... they were nice, those people ... they brought me things ...

                                              DISSOLVE TO:

7. INT. DAVID'S HOUSE. NIGHT.

YOUNG DAVID ON THE WINDOW SEAT. HE TURNS AROUND TO FACE THE ROOM.
TRACK BACK FROM HIM TO MID SHOT
PEOPLE BEGIN TO DROP PRESENTS ONTO THE WINDOW SEAT FOR HIM

                    DAVID (VOICE OVER)
                      A wooden train ...

IT IS PUT DOWN FOR HIM.

                    DAVID'S VOICE OVER
                      Some candy ...

IT IS PUT DOWN FOR HIM.

                    DAVID'S VOICE OVER
       ... a book of Bible stories from the Preacher ...

                                                        CUT TO:

8. INT. DAVID'S HOUSE. NIGHT 8..

CLOSE UP REVEREND WATKINS IN THE MIDST OF A GROUP WHICH CONSISTS ALSO OF SARAH AND FRANK - DAVID'S PARENTS

                    REVEREND WATKINS
                       For Jesus
                                                        CUT TO:

8A. INT. DAVID'S HOUSE. NIGHT 8A.

<u>CLOSE UP</u> DAVID. HE BEGINS TO PLAY WITH THE TRAIN.

                    DAVID'S VOICE OVER
   ... and a cake by mail order from the Olde English Baking
                   Company in Wisconsin.
                                                        CUT TO:

9. INT. DAVID'S HOUSE. NIGHT.

THE ROOM THRONGS WITH PEOPLE COMING IN FROM THE HALL TO THE
LIVING ROOM BLOWING AND RUBBING THEIR HANDS TOGETHER AND
SHAKING THEIR COATS.

                    DAVID'S VOICE OVER
   I don't remember any children of my own age corning round that
   Christmas ... as a matter of fact I don't remember seeing any
                   other children at all ...

                                                        CUT TO:

10. INT. DAVID'S HOUSE. NIGHT 10.

DAVID AT THE WINDOW PLAYING WITH HIS TRAIN.

                    DAVID'S VOICE OVER
                    But there was no snow ...

OUTSIDE HEAVY DRIFTS AND FALLING SNOW.

                    DAVID'S VOICE OVER
                    No ... not that year ...

SOMETHING HITS THE WINDOW AND HE TURNS AROUND

                                                    DISSOLVE TO:

11. EXT/INT. DAVID'S HOUSE. NIGHT.

<u>WIDE SHOT</u>. THE EXTERIOR OF THE SHOT IS OF THE PORCH – HEAVY
SNOW AND DRIFTS. THE WALL OF THE HOUSE DIVIDES THE SHOT.
THE INTERIOR OF THE SHOT IS THE LIVING ROOM. DAVID ON THE WINDOW
SEAT. HE IS NOW KNEELING ON IT AND LOOKING OUT OF THE WINDOW.

THE NEON BIBLE

> DAVID'S VOICE OVER
> Then that spring Aunt Mae came to live with us.

DISSOLVE TO:

12. EXT/INT. DAVID'S HOUSE. NIGHT.

EXACTLY AS THE PRECEDING SHOT ONLY NOW THE SNOW IS MELTING AND SLEET IS FALLING.
AUNT MAE STANDING ON THE PORCH IN FRONT OF THE WINDOW AND IS LIT FROM IT.
DAVID ON THE WINDOW SEAT IS LOOKING OUT AT HER.
SHE STRIKES A POSE AS IF FINISHING A NUMBER ON STAGE.

CUT TO:

13. EXT. PORCH. DAVID'S HOUSE. NIGHT.

<u>CLOSE UP</u> AUNT MAE

> AUNT MAE (TO DAVID)
> David! Honey!

CUT TO:

14. EXT. PORCH. DAVID'S HOUSE. NIGHT.

<u>CLOSE UP</u> DAVID LOOKING THROUGH THE WINDOW. HE BEAMS.

> DAVID'S VOICE OVER
> Next to the train I remember Aunt Mae most.

CUT TO:

15. EXT. PORCH. DAVID'S HOUSE. NIGHT.

DAVID COMES RUNNING OUT OF THE HOUSE TO AUNT MAE.
<u>PAN RIGHT TO LEFT</u> WITH HIM.
AUNT MAE LIFTING UP DAVID

DISSOLVE TO:

16. EXT. PORCH. DAVID'S HOUSE. NIGHT.

EXACTLY THE SAME SHOT AS ABOVE ONLY THIS TIME SARAH (DAVID'S MOTHER) IS STANDING IN THE SAME POSITION AS AUNT MAE.
DAVID COMES RUNNING OUT OF THE HOUSE INTO SARAH'S ARMS.
<u>PAN RIGHT TO LEFT</u> WITH HIM.

SARAH CARRYING HIM TO THE SEAT ON THE PORCH (IN FRONT OF THE LIVING ROOM WINDOW). A WARM SPRING NIGHT.
THEY SIT DOWN.

                SARAH
             Night! Night!

                                      CUT TO:

17. EXT. PATH IN FRONT OF DAVID'S HOUSE. NIGHT.

SEVERAL WOMEN LEAVE THE HOUSE.

                WOMEN
       Goodnight, Sarah. Goodnight.

AUNT MAE AT THE FRONT DOOR OF THE HOUSE. SHE WEARS A LOW CUT GOWN AND CARRIES A SCRAPBOOK.

                AUNT MAE
             Goodnight!

THE LADIES DON'T REPLY.

                                      CUT TO:

18. EXT. PORCH. DAVID'S HOUSE. NIGHT.

<u>MID-SHOT</u> SARAH AND DAVID ON THE SEAT IN FRONT OF THE WINDOW.

               SARAH (TO MAE)
You had no right to dress that way. You deliberately hurt me and all Frank's friends. If I knew you were going to act this way, I would never have let you come to live with us.

                                      CUT TO:

19. EXT PORCH. DAVID'S HOUSE. NIGHT.

<u>CLOSE UP</u> AUNT MAE

                AUNT MAE
    (PULLING HER CLEAVAGE SLIGHTLY TOGETHER)
But Sarah I didn't know they'd take on that way – why I've worn this gown before audiences from Charleston to New Orleans ... I forgot to show you my clippings didn't I?

SHE MOVES TOWARDS SARAH AND DAVID.

                                      CUT TO:

THE NEON BIBLE

20. EXT. PORCH. DAVID'S HOUSE. NIGHT.

AUNT MAE SITS DOWN ON THE SEAT IN FRONT OF THE WINDOW SO THAT DAVID IS NOW BETWEEN HER AND SARAH.

          AUNT MAE (LEAFING THROUGH THE SCRAPBOOK)
    The notices! The notices! They were superb – particularly about this gown –

SARAH GETS UP AND MOVES TO THE FRONT DOOR WITH DAVID.

                    SARAH
    Look, Aunt Mae, on stage that gown may have been quite successful but you don't know what it's like to live in a small town like this. If Frank heard about things like this, he won't let you stay here. Now don't ever do that to me again.

SHE AND DAVID GO INTO THE HOUSE.

                                      CUT TO:

21. EXT. PORCH. DAVID'S HOUSE. NIGHT.

<u>CLOSE UP</u> AUNT MAE (<u>HEAD ON</u>) SITTING ON THE SEAT IN FRONT OF THE WINDOW.
SHE BEGINS TO LEAF THROUGH THE SCRAPBOOK.
DAVID APPEARS AT THE HALF OPEN WINDOW BEHIND AUNT MAE (SLIGHTLY TO HER RIGHT)

                    AUNT MAE (BEAMING)
    "Mae Morgan – Popular Singer at the Rivoli"
                    (SEES DAVID)
    D'you know, David, once a Duke kissed my hand, asked me to marry him and live with him in Europe then drank wine out of my slipper.

                                        CUT TO:

22. EXT. PORCH. DAVID'S HOUSE. NIGHT.

<u>SHOT OF</u> FRANK (DAVID'S FATHER) COMING UP THE PORCH STEPS AND INTO THE HOUSE.

                      FRANK
    He must've been drunk, huh!

                                        CUT TO:

23. EXT. PORCH. DAVID'S HOUSE. NIGHT.

<u>2 SHOT</u> - DAVID AND AUNT MAE (<u>HEAD ON</u>)
SHE TURNS BACK TO DAVID AND MAKES A FACE.
DAVID GIGGLES.

>   AUNT MAE
>   Well, what would he know about any old Duke anyway.

SHE LIFTS THE BOOK UP FOR DAVID TO SEE.

>   AUNT MAE
>   Memphis - Biloxi - Oh I've played 'em all!

>   FRANK'S VOICE OVER
>   I don't want her here!

>   SARAH'S VOICE OVER
>   Frank she's got no place else to go.

AUNT MAE CLOSES THE SCRAPBOOK.

>   AUNT MAE (VISIBLY HURT)
>   You'd better run along, honey, before Poppa blows my brains
>   out.

>   DAVID
>   Goodnight, Aunt Mae.

HE DISAPPEARS.

>   AUNT MAE
>   Night, honey.

<u>TRACK AROUND</u> (<u>LEFT TO RIGHT</u>) TO <u>SIDEVIEW</u> OF AUNT MAE ON THE SEAT.

<u>SOUNDTRACK</u>: A SOLO TRUMPET PLAYING THE INTRO TO GERSHWIN'S "HOW LONG HAS THIS BEEN GOING ON" IS HEARD.

WHEN AUNT MAE IS IN PROFILE.

                                                    DISSOLVE TO:

24. INT. NIGHTCLUB. NIGHT.

<u>MID CLOSE UP</u> (<u>SIDEVIEW</u>) OF AUNT MAE. SHE STANDS IN THE SPOTLIGHT - A TRIANGLE OF SMOKY WHITE LIGHT - AND BEGINS TO SING INTO THE MICROPHONE.

THE NEON BIBLE

                    AUNT MAE (SINGING)
                 "I could cry salty tears,
               Where have I been all these years"

TRACK BACK TO MID-LONG SHOT
SHE IS ON THE SMALL STAGE (EXTREME FRAME RIGHT) IN THE
FOREGROUND EMPTY TABLES AND CHAIRS. EXTREME LEFT OF FRAME A
GROUP OF SAILORS AT THE BAR SHOUT AND WHISTLE AT HER.

                    AUNT MAE (SINGING)
                       "Little wow,
                    Please tell me now,
              How long has this been going on ..."

SUDDENLY ONE OF THE SAILORS THROWS A BOTTLE AT HER.

                                                    CUT TO:

25. INT. NIGHTCLUB. NIGHT.

CLOSE UP AUNT MAE. THE BOTTLE HITS HER ON THE SIDE OF THE
HEAD AND SHE FALLS BACKWARDS (THE CAMERA GOING WITH HER) INTO
A SEA OF GIRLS' ARMS.

                                                DISSOLVE TO:

26. EXT. PORCH. DAVID'S HOUSE. NIGHT.

CLOSE UP AUNT MAE (FRONTVIEW). FRANK AND SARAH'S VOICES
SUBSIDING INTO ANGRY SILENCE.
AUNT MAE JUST SITS THERE.

                    AUNT MAE (SINGING)
             "Kiss me twice and then once more,
             That makes thrice, let's make it four,
                What a break for heaven's sake,
                How long has this been going on."

                                                    CUT TO:

27. EXT. PORCH. DAVID'S HOUSE. DAY.

CLOSE UP (TWO SHOT) FROM BEHIND OF DAVID BEING CARRIED FROM
THE HOUSE BY HIS FATHER.
DAVID IS CRYING AND STRETCHING BACK OVER HIS FATHER'S
SHOULDER TO HIS UNSEEN MOTHER.

                                                    CUT TO:

28. EXT. NEIGHBOUR'S FRONT YARD. DAY.

CLOSE UP DAVID. HE JUST STANDS THERE.

                    BRUCE (VOICE OVER)
              You've been crying!

                        DAVID
                      (STILL TEARFUL)
                No, I haven't.

                                                    CUT TO:

29. EXT. NEIGHBOUR'S FRONT YARD. DAY.

CLOSE UP BRUCE WHO IS SLIGHTLY OLDER THAN DAVID.

                        BRUCE
                Can you fight?

                                                    CUT TO:

30. EXT. NEIGHBOUR'S FRONT YARD. DAY.

CLOSE UP DAVID

                        DAVID
                    (SHAKES HEAD)

BRUCE SLAPS HIM.

                                                    CUT TO:

31. NEIGHBOUR'S FRONT YARD. DAY.

CLOSE UP BRUCE.

                        BRUCE
                Can you jump?

                                                    CUT TO:

32. NEIGHBOUR'S FRONT YARD. DAY.

CLOSE UP DAVID

                        DAVID
                      No.

BRUCE SLAPS HIM AGAIN.

                                                    CUT TO:

33. EXT. NEIGHBOUR'S FRONT YARD. DAY.

<u>CLOSE UP</u> BRUCE.

>   BRUCE
>   Can't you do <u>anything</u>?

CUT TO:

34. EXT. NEIGHBOUR'S FRONT YARD. DAY.

<u>CLOSE UP</u> DAVID

>   DAVID (TIMIDLY)
>   No.

BRUCE REALLY HITS HIM THIS TIME AND DAVID FALLS, CRYING, ON THE SEAT OF HIS PANTS.

>   BRUCE'S VOICE OVER
>   Arh, you're just a cissy!

DAVID WAILS AS HE SITS THERE - HIS NOSE BLEEDING.

CUT TO:

35. EXT. PORCH. DAVID'S HOUSE. EARLY EVENING.

<u>CLOSE UP</u> (2 SHOT) FROM BEHIND OF DAVID BEING CARRIED INTO THE HOUSE BY HIS FATHER. DAVID'S NOSE STILL BLEEDING. DROPS OF BLOOD FALLING ON TO THE BACK OF FATHER'S WHITE SHIRT. DAVID STILL CRYING AND BLOOD-SMEARED.

CUT TO:

36. INT. KITCHEN. DAVID'S HOUSE. EARLY EVE.

<u>3 SHOT</u> SARAH AND AUNT MAE FACING CAMERA. DAVID FACING THEM - BACK TO CAMERA.

>   SARAH (ANGRY)
>   You shouldn't have taken him, Frank!

CUT TO:

37. INT. KITCHEN. DAVID'S HOUSE. EARLY EVENING.

<u>CLOSE UP</u> FRANK (AT DOOR)

>   FRANK (ANGRY)
>   He's gotta play with other kids -

                    (INDICATING AUNT MAE)
         Bein' here with her ain't healthy - it ain't healthy!

WALKS OUT.

                                                          CUT TO:

38. INT. KITCHEN. DAVID'S HOUSE. EARLY EVENING.

<u>CLOSE UP</u> <u>2 SHOT</u> AUNT MAE AND SARAH

                         AUNT MAE (SHOUTING)
                         You louse!
                                                          CUT TO:

39. INT. KITCHEN. DAVID'S HOUSE. EARLY EVENING.

<u>3 SHOT</u> DAVID IN THE MIDDLE. AUNT MAE <u>LEFT OF FRAME</u>, SARAH <u>FRAME RIGHT</u>.

                         DAVID (WAILING)
         Bruce's mom made me stay on the porch till Poppa came -

                         SARAH (SOOTHING)
                    Alright, David, alright.

                         AUNT MAE (SOOTHING TOO)
                      Never you mind, honey.

THEY FINISH WIPING HIS FACE AND HE STOPS CRYING.

                              SARAH
                 I'll sleep with you tonight David.
                      Would you like that?

DAVID NODS AND SMILES.

                              SARAH
                          (TO AUNT MAE)
              I couldn't sleep with Frank, not tonight.

                            AUNT MAE
                (RUNNING HER WET HANDS THROUGH DAVID'S
                 HAIR AND LOOKING AT HIM ASKANCE)
                    There! Just like Franchot Tone!

DAVID SMILES.
                                                          CUT TO:

THE NEON BIBLE

40. EXT. BARBER'S SHOP. DAY.

3 SHOT (BACKVIEW) AUNT MAE (FRAME LEFT) AND DAVID (EXTREME FRAME RIGHT) LOOKING INTO THE WINDOW OF THE SHOP.
THEY ARE ALSO REFLECTED IN IT. IN BETWEEN THEM (INSIDE THE BARBERS) AN ELDERLY BARBER IS CUTTING SOMEONE'S HAIR. THE INTERIOR OF THE SHOP IS DARK. ABOVE DAVID'S HEAD (STUCK INSIDE THE WINDOW) IS A YOUNG MAN IN AN UNDERSHIRT SMILING IN AN ADVERT FOR RAZOR BLADES.
THE BARBER LOOKS UP AT AUNT MAE AND DAVID.

CUT TO:

41. INT. BARBER'S SHOP. DAY.

CLOSE UP AUNT MAE SEEN THROUGH THE WINDOW. SHE WINKS VERY SLOWLY WITH ONE EYE AT THE BARBER.

CUT TO:

42. EXT. BARBER'S SHOP. DAY.

3 SHOT AUNT MAE, BARBER, DAVID THE BARBER SMILES

                    AUNT MAE
             (LOOKING DOWN AT DAVID)
               Come one, Franchot!

DAVID GIGGLES.

                    DAVID
                Okay, Aunt Mae

CUT TO:

43. (SCENE CUT).

44. EXT. SIDEWALK/BARBERS SHOP. DAY.

2 SHOT (BACKVIEW) AUNT MAE AND DAVID. THEY WALK AWAY FROM THE SHOP DOWN THE SIDEWALK (PAN RIGHT TO LEFT).
DAVID RUNNING SLIGHTLY BEHIND AUNT MAE AND GIGGLING.

                    AUNT MAE
           (WALKING LIKE A FILM STAR)
        Miss Jean Harlow, if you please!

               DAVID'S VOICE OVER
She was my only playmate and mother was glad we were such good
                   friends.

CUT TO:

44A. EXT. STREET. DAY.

SIDEVIEW OF AUNT MAE AND DAVID WALKING DOWN SIDEWALK.
TRACK WITH THEM (RIGHT TO LEFT)
SPFX.
AFTER A SHORT TIME WITHOUT A DISSOLVE DAY TURNS INTO NIGHT.
CONTINUE TRACKING WITH THEM (RIGHT TO LEFT) TO SODA FOUNTAIN.
WHEN THEY REACH IT THE TRACK STOPS.
THEY GO IN AND SIT DOWN AT ONE OF THE WINDOW BOOTHS.

                                                    CUT TO:

44B. INT. SODA FOUNTAIN. NIGHT.

DAVID STANDING ON THE SEAT (FRAME RIGHT) LOOKING OUT OF
WINDOW. AUNT MAE OPPOSITE HIM (FRAME LEFT)
GEORGE THE BARBER CARRYING SODAS JOINS THEM AND SITS DOWN
NEXT TO AUNT MAE.
REFLECTED IN THE GLASS OF THE WINDOW THE NEON BIBLE SIGN.
DAVID POINTS TO THE NEON BIBLE SIGN.

                        DAVID
                  Look, Aunt Mae ...

SHE LOOKS DIRECTLY OUT AT CAMERA.

                                                DISSOLVE TO:

44C. EXT. SODA FOUNTAIN. NIGHT.

THE WINDOW OF THE SODA FOUNTAIN NOW BLACK.
THE SODA FOUNTAIN CLOSED.
THE NEON BIBLE SIGN REFLECTED IN THE WINDOW
THEN
FLAMES APPEAR AT THE BOTTOM OF THE FRAME LICKING UP THE
WINDOW.
PAN (LEFT TO RIGHT) AWAY FROM WINDOW TO A FIRE IN MAIN STREET.
BOOKS ARE BEING THROWN ONTO A BONFIRE BY THE REV. WATKINS,
HIS WIFE AND BY WHITE HOODED MEMBERS OF THE KKK.

                     REVEREND WATKINS
       (HIS FACE CONTORTED WITH HATRED) (A SMILING RANTING BIGOT)
             ... the sly and the tricky in this community
      want you to read these licentious books, these dirty books ...
        all the dirtier because they're going to make movies out of
        them and anyone who doesn't know it is defying God and is an
                         agent of the Devil! ...

CONTINUE PANNING AWAY (LEFT TO RIGHT) INTO BLACKNESS
                                                DISSOLVE TO:

THE NEON BIBLE

44D. EXT. FIELD. NIGHT.

CONTINUE PANNING (RIGHT TO LEFT) FROM BLACKNESS TO YOUNG
DAVID BEING CARRIED ON HIS FATHER'S SHOULDERS.
TORCH LIGHT ONLY.
A CROWD WHOOPS AND CHEERS.
SO DOES DAVID'S FATHER. DAVID BEMUSED
THEN
DAVID JUMPS AS HE IS FRIGHTENED BY A FLASH OF FLAMES
REFLECTED ON HIM AND HIS FATHER.
ECSTATIC CHEERS.
THEN
PAN AWAY (LEFT TO RIGHT) TO

44E. EXT. FIELD. NIGHT.

A CROWD OF MEN WITH THEIR SONS CARRYING TORCHES. AT THE FRONT
OF THE CROWD KKK MEMBERS BELOW A TREE
TWO BLACK MEN HAVE BEEN HUNG AND ONE IS SET ON FIRE.
CONTINUE PANNING (RIGHT TO LEFT) TO TREE AND AWAY FROM THE
CROWD.

            DAVID'S VOICE OVER (AS A CHILD)
            What are they doing Aunt Mae?

THE SECOND BLACK MAN IS SET ALIGHT.
CHEERS AND WHOOPS.

            AUNT MAE'S VOICE OVER
            They're burning books David ...
            They're burning Gone With The Wind.

PAN (LEFT TO RIGHT) TO BLACKNESS

                                                                          DISSOLVE TO:

44F. EXT. BARBERS SHOP WINDOW. NIGHT.

REFLECTED IN IT - A FIRE.
ABOVE THE FLAMES THE FACE OF A YOUNG BLACK BOY (AGED 16)
LOOKS TOWARDS THE CAMERA IN TERROR.

                                                                           DISSOLVE TO:

                            44G. EXT. TRAIN WINDOW. NIGHT.

HOLD ON WINDOW. DAVID LOOKING OUT. UPPER FRAME LEFT A LARGE
MOON IS REFLECTED IN THE GLASS.
HOLD

THEN DAVID REACHES UP AND TOUCHES THE MOON.

DISSOLVE TO:

45. INT. DAVID'S HOUSE. NIGHT.

AUNT MAE'S BEDROOM
EXACT REVERSE OF 44B.
SHOT OF DAVID AT THE WINDOW (BACKVIEW). THROUGH THE WINDOW A HUGE MOON UPPER FRAME RIGHT. HE REACHES UP AND TOUCHES THE MOON.
HOLD

AUNT MAE'S VOICE OVER
David, honey! Will you get me that little bottle from the closet?
(PAUSE)
The one with the white label.

CUT TO:

46. INT. AUNT MAE'S BEDROOM. NIGHT.

CLOSE UP (SIDEVIEW) OF DAVID AT THE CLOSET DOORS. HE OPENS THEM. HE TAKES OUT THE BOTTLE AND EXITS. ON THE INSIDE OF THE CLOSET DOOR FACING THE CAMERA IS PASTED THE ADVERT FROM THE BARBER'S SHOP OF THE YOUNG MAN IN THE UNDERSHIRT ADVERTISING RAZOR BLADES. THERE ARE LIPSTICK KISSES ALL OVER HIS FACE.
HOLD

CUT TO:

47/48. INT. AUNT MAE'S BEDROOM. NIGHT..

2 SHOT AUNT MAE (SIDEVIEW - FRAME LEFT) DAVID (CENTRE FRAME) FACES CAMERA.
AUNT MAE'S HAIR IS STREAMING OUT OVER A BOWL.
DAVID HANDS HER THE PEROXIDE AND SHE BEGINS TO POUR THE PEROXIDE OVER HER HAIR.
HE WATCHES AS HER HAIR GOES BLONDER AND BLONDER.

CUT TO:

49. INT. PORCH. DAY.

SHOT OF GEORGE THE BARBER (FROM INSIDE THE HOUSE - THROUGH THE SCREEN DOOR).

GEORGE
Mae -

CUT TO:

50. EXT. PORCH. DAY.

SHOT OF AUNT MAE SEEN FROM GEORGE'S POV THROUGH THE SCREEN DOOR.

THE NEON BIBLE

> AUNT MAE (GIRLISH)
> Why - George - This is little David.

CUT TO:

51. INT. PORCH. DAY.

CLOSE UP GEORGE

> GEORGE
> Hello little David

CUT TO:

52. INT. PORCH. DAY.

SHOT OF DAVID (NEXT TO HIM AUNT MAE).
DAVID JUST BACKS AWAY INTO THE HOUSE WITHOUT SPEAKING AND RUNS UPSTAIRS.

CUT TO:

53. INT. AUNT MAE'S BEDROOM. DAY.

CLOSE UP DAVID (BACKVIEW) AT THE WINDOW. HE LEANS OUT OVER THE PORCH TO TRY TO SEE AND HEAR WHAT IS GOING ON.

> AUNT MAE'S VOICE OVER
> (HER LAUGHTER A MIXTURE OF THE
> GIRLISH AND THE IMPROPER)
> Oh George - Georgy!

CUT TO:

56. INT. KITCHEN. DAY.

2 SHOT SARAH AND FRANK AT THE TABLE. SHE DRINKS COFFEE. HE IDLY GLANCES THROUGH THE PAPER. IN BACKGROUND, FRANK'S GUN BEHIND THE STOVE.

> SARAH
> D'you think they'll get serious?

> FRANK (LAUGHING)
> Not if he has to drink wine out of her slipper -
> he'll never live long enough to marry her!

> SARAH
> Frank!

> FRANK
> Nah - I think he'll be good for her.

CUT TO:

55. INT. KITCHEN. DAY.

SHOT OF DAVID STANDING AT THE DOOR. THEY DON'T NOTICE HIM SO HE WALKS SLOWLY AWAY DRAGGING THE WOODEN TRAIN BEHIND HIM.

                                                                       CUT TO:

56. EXT. PORCH. DAY.

SHOT OF DAVID COMING ON TO IT. PAN WITH HIM (RIGHT TO LEFT). HE IS LOOKING FOR AUNT MAE.

                                                                       CUT TO:

57. EXT. PORCH. DAY.

2 SHOT (DAVID'S POV) OF AUNT MAE AND GEORGE WALKING AWAY FROM THE HOUSE.
PAN WITH THEM (LEFT TO RIGHT)
THEY ARE TALKING AND LAUGHING.

                                                                       CUT TO:

58. EXT. PORCH. DAY/EARLY EVENING.

SHOT OF DAVID WAITING.
THEN WITHOUT A DISSOLVE IT GRADUALLY GETS DARK AND THE HOUSE LIGHTS GO ON. DAVID IS LIT FROM THE WINDOW.
THE SOUND OF AUNT MAE AND GEORGE TALKING IS HEARD.
DAVID LOOKS TOWARDS THEM.

                                                                       CUT TO:

59. EXT. PORCH. NIGHT.

DAVID'S POV SHOT OF AUNT MAE AND GEORGE COMING UP ONTO THE PORCH AND STOPPING AT THE FRONT DOOR.
PAN WITH THEM (RIGHT TO LEFT)
THEY STOP AT THE FRONT DOOR. SHE HAS LEAVES STUCK TO THE BACK OF HER DRESS AND HER HAIR. GEORGE STARTS TO BRUSH THE LEAVES OFF HER DRESS AND HIS HAND COMES TO REST ON HER BUTTOCKS. SHE ADJUSTS HER DRESS AND THEY GO INSIDE.

                                                                       CUT TO:

60. EXT. PORCH. NIGHT.

WIDE SHOT OF DAVID STANDING ON THE PORCH. THE WHOLE HOUSE LIT UP BEHIND HIM. HE LOOKS UP AT THE HOUSE.
SLOWLY HE GOES INTO THE HOUSE DRAGGING HIS WOODEN TRAIN BEHIND HIM.
HOLD

THE NEON BIBLE

> DAVID'S VOICE OVER
> He carried on with Aunt Mae all through that
> summer and into part of the Fall.
> Then one day George didn't come around anymore.

DISSOLVE TO:

61. EXT. BACK YARD. AFTERNOON.

<u>2 SHOT</u> DAVID STANDS, AUNT MAE SITTING IN THE DIRT. A FINE DAY. DAVID PLAYS WITH SOME CARS. HE RUNS AROUND HER. AUNT MAE READING HER LETTER. HER FACE CRUMBLING AT THE CONTENTS.

> DAVID
> (STOPPING AT HER SHOULDER)
> It's your turn, Aunt Mae.

PAUSE

> AUNT MAE (DISTRACTED)
> Oh, I'm sorry David.
>
> (TO HERSELF)
> You bastard, George!

SHE LEAVES.
DAVID JUST STANDS THERE AS HE WATCHES HER GO.

DISSOLVE TO:

61B. <u>SPFX</u>. EXT. BACK YARD. AFTERNOON.

YOUNG DAVID CHANGES (<u>WITHOUT A DISSOLVE</u>) TO A SLIGHTLY OLDER DAVID AGED APPROXIMATELY 8-10. HE STANDS THERE FACING CAMERA.

DISSOLVE TO:

62. EXT. BACK YARD. AFTERNOON.

<u>SLIGHTLY OLDER DAVID'S POV</u>
LINES OF WASHING FILL THE FRAME. WHITE SHEETS BILLOWING SOFTLY IN THE WIND OF THE WARM AFTERNOON.
ONLY SARAH'S HEAD AND HANDS ARE SEEN AS SHE CONTINUES TO HANG THE WASHING. SHE EXITS <u>FRAME LEFT</u>.
<u>TRACK IN</u> ON THE WASHING.

> DAVID'S VOICE OVER
> The movies and school ...

WHEN THE SHEETS ENTIRELY FILL THE SCREEN.

DISSOLVE TO:

63. "GONE WITH THE WIND" POSTER.

TRACK IN ON IT.
SOUNDTRACK: TARA'S THEME HEARD.

                                                             DISSOLVE TO:

64. "JEZEBEL" OR "DARK VICTORY" POSTER.

TRACK IN ON IT.
SOUNDTRACK: TARA'S THEME HEARD.

                                                             DISSOLVE TO:

65. "THE GARDEN OF ALLAH" POSTER.

TRACK IN ON IT.

SOUNDTRACK: TARA'S THEME FADES.

                      DAVID'S VOICE OVER
                    School and the movies ...
                          DISSOLVE TO:

66. EXT. TRAIN. NIGHT.

MEDIUM LONG SHOT OF THE TRAIN.
DAVID (AGES 16) IS FRAMED AT THE WINDOW WHICH IS EXTREME RIGHT OF FRAME WITH THE TRAIN RUNNING (RIGHT TO LEFT) DOWN THE ENTIRE SCREEN.
HOLD

                                                            DISSOLVE TO:

67. THE STARS AND STRIPES.

THE FLAG FILLS THE ENTIRE FRAME. FRAME, THE STRIPES RUNNING DOWN FRAME.
THE STARS EXTREME RIGHT OF (RIGHT TO LEFT) THE ENTIRE

                            MRS. WATKINS' VOICE OVER
      "I pledge allegiance to the flag of the United States of
                                    America ..."

HOLD SHOT
SOUND DISSOLVE

                     MRS. WATKINS AND HER CLASS VOICE OVER
        "... and the Republic for which it stands ..."

                                                          DISSOLVE TO:

THE NEON BIBLE

68. INT. MRS. WATKINS' CLASSROOM. DAY..

<u>WIDE SHOT</u> OF CLASSROOM (<u>SIDEVIEW</u>)
MRS. WATKINS STANDS AT THE HEAD OF THE CLASS (EXTREME <u>FRAME RIGHT</u>). THE REST OF THE CLASS (AT THEIR DESKS) RUNS DOWN THE ENTIRE LENGTH OF THE FRAME (<u>RIGHT TO LEFT</u>).

     ALL RECITING
     (HANDS OVER HEARTS)
 ... one nation, indivisible,
with liberty and justice for all. ...

    DAVID'S VOICE OVER (AGED 16)
   School, the movies.. . and God.

            <u>DISSOLVE TO:</u>

68A. INT. CHURCH. NIGHT.

REVEREND WATKINS IN THE PULPIT. THE NEON BIBLE LIT UP AND HUGE ABOVE AND BEHIND HIM.
HE STRETCHES OUT HIS ARMS WIDE - LIKE CHRIST CRUCIFIED.

     REVEREND WATKINS
 ... I thank the Lord that I had to struggle coming up,
   I wouldn't want it any other way ...
 I think I can appreciate the other man's position but I
think I can do more for my fellow man having experienced the
     Christian power of God's love ...

<u>CRANE DOWN FROM HIM</u>.
            <u>DISSOLVE TO:</u>

68B. INT. CHURCH. NIGHT.

<u>SHOT OF</u> HIS CONGREGATION LISTENING AND FANNING THEMSELVES.

BEGIN TO <u>CRANE DOWN</u> OVER THEM.

    REVEREND WATKINS' VOICE OVER
 ... his love isn't like human love, His love is straight and
true ... for all God-fearing people know His way, and live by
      His will ...

FADE HIS VOICE
<u>CONTINUE CRANE DOWN</u>

                    DAVID'S VOICE OVER
    If you were different from anybody in town you had to
       get out. That's why everybody was so much alike. They
       used to tell us in school to think for yourselves but you
                     couldn't do that in town ...

                                                    DISSOLVE TO:

68C. EXT. PORCH. DAVID'S HOUSE. LATE AFTERNOON.

CONTINUE CRANING DOWN TO HOUSE BATHED IN A RED LIGHT FROM THE
LATE AFTERNOON SUN.

                    DAVID'S VOICE OVER
        You had to think what your father thought all
     his life, and that was the way everybody thought ...

                 RADIO ANNOUNCER'S VOICE OVER
    Earl K. Long calls himself The Last of the Red-Hot Poppas, a
             political wizard, a poor man's Philosopher.
                 Ladies and gentlemen – Earl K. Long

CRANE STOPS ON <u>MID LONG SHOT OF</u> HOUSE

            EARL K. LONG VOICE OVER (ADDRESSING A RALLY)
             ... they called in last night at Antoines ...
    I don't know how to get into Antoines ... I was lead in there
      once in my life and lead out ... they didn't have a single
     thing on the bill of fare that I could read ... if you've ever
      been there you know that's true ... and it cost about eighteen
        dollars ... I can go to a cafeteria and eat for six bits ...
       the only reason I say that is just to let you know that I'm
       just an old ordinary gezebo, I don't belong to the bosses and
      the club – you could tell that by looking at me couldn't you?
           Couldn't you? There's two reasons: – they don't want me, I
                          don't want them ...
LAUGHTER.
APPLAUSE.
FRANK WHOOPS WITH APPROVAL AND APPLAUDS TOO.
                                                    DISSOLVE TO:

69. EXT. PORCH. LATE AFTERNOON.

<u>FRAME RIGHT</u> THE SUN LOW AND RED (SEEN THROUGH THE UPRIGHTS
OF THE PORCH). SLIGHTLY LEFT OF THE SUN IS THE RENNING SMOKE
STACK (THE NAME "RENNINGS" RUNS ALL THE WAY DOWN IT) MAKING
THE SMOKE STACK LOOK LIKE "A BLACK MATCHSTICK IN FRONT OF AN
ORANGE LIGHT BULB".

THE NEON BIBLE

> SARAH'S VOICE OVER
> Don't go to the union meeting, Frank,
> You can't lose this job too.

> FRANK'S VOICE OVER
> Sarah we're fighting for our lives.
> Sarah I'm fighting for you ...

> FRANK'S VOICE OVER (A GATHERING FURY)
> They're the people that are keepin' us poor
> - those damn rich bastards!

> DAVID'S VOICE OVER (CALLING SOFTLY)
> Poppa, Poppa ...

> SARAH'S VOICE OVER lWEARY OF THE ARGUMENT)
> Frank ... come on in, Frank ...

>> CUT TO:

70. INT. LIVING ROOM. LATE AFTERNOON.

BATHED IN RED FROM THE LOW RED SUN COMING THROUGH THE CURTAINS AND WINDOW.
<u>SHOT OF</u> FATHER THROUGH THE LIVING ROOM WINDOW.
(<u>BACKVIEW</u> FROM INSIDE LIVING ROOM)
HE SITS ON THE PORCH - ON THE SEAT UNDER THE WINDOW - ROCKING HIMSELF FASTER AND FASTER, HIS LEGS ON THE PORCH RAIL.

> FRANK
> (SLIGHTLY TURNING AROUND)
> I ain't goin' in there - it's hotter 'n' hell ...

>> CUT TO:

71. INT. LIVING ROOM. LATE AFTERNOON.

<u>CLOSE UP</u> DAVID (<u>FATHER'S POV</u>)

> DAVID
> (LOOKING THROUGH THE PORCH, SOFTLY TO HIMSELF - PUZZLED)
> Poppa?

>> CUT TO:

72. INT. LIVING ROOM. LATE AFTERNOON.

<u>WIDE SHOT OF</u> OPEN FRONT DOOR (<u>FRAME LEFT</u>) AND OPEN WINDOW (<u>FRAME RIGHT</u>).
(<u>DAVID'S POV</u> OF FATHER)

                        FRANK
        (NOW ROCKING FASTER AND FASTER IN A PAROXYSM OF FURY)
                    They're the ones!
                Them and those damned politicians!

HE JUMPS UP FROM THE PORCH SEAT AND RUNS AWAY FROM THE HOUSE.
THEN

72A. SAME SHOT.

<u>WITHOUT A DISSOLVE</u> AFTERNOON FADES TO EARLY EVENING.

FATHER RETURNS UP THE STEPS AND INTO THE HOUSE. HE CARRIES A BAG.

                                                        CUT TO:

73. INT. LIVING ROOM/STAIRS. EARLY EVENING.

DAVID COMES RUNNING INTO SHOT FROM THE LIVING ROOM. FATHER
PASSES HIM (<u>LEFT TO RIGHT</u>)

                    DAVID (CALLING)
                  Mother! Poppa's here!

                    SARAH'S VOICE OVER
                         Good!
                                                        CUT TO:

74. INT. HALLWAY. EARLY EVENING.

<u>SHOT OF</u> STAIRS AND HALLWAY.
FATHER WALKING DOWN HALLWAY AWAY FROM CAMERA TOWARDS KITCHEN.
SARAH COMES OUT OF THE KITCHEN AND SEES FRANK.

                        SARAH
                   Has he the mon ...?

                    (SEES THE BAG)

                  Frank, what's that?

                        FRANK
                  Seeds, Sarah – seeds!

                        SARAH
                Seeds? What are they for?

                    FRANK (VERY EXCITED)
            I'm gonna grow things – on the hill ...

THE NEON BIBLE

> SARAH
> That's crazy – nothing'll grow there
> – anyway what did you buy them with?

> FRANK
> The money from the gas station.

> SARAH (INCREDULOUS)
> All of it?

> fRANK (EXCITED)
> All of it.

> SARAH (DECISIVE)
> Take the seeds back – tonight Frank
> – get the money back tonight.
> There's no food. We've gotta eat.

                                                                CUT TO:

75. INT. HALLWAY. EARLY EVENING.

DAVID – FRIGHTENED – COMES TO THE FOOT OF THE STAIRS.
(DAVID IN <u>CLOSE UP</u>)

> SARAH'S VOICE OVER
> You have a son to feed.

                                                                 CUT TO:

76. INT. HALLWAY. EARLY EVENING.

<u>2 SHOT</u> (<u>SIDEVIEW</u>) SARAH AND FRANK

> FRANK
> There's money to be made on the hills back there –
> plenty of money ...

SARAH GRABS AT HIM.
FRANK WALKS BACK TOWARDS THE FRONT DOOR FOLLOWED BY SARAH.
<u>TRACK</u> WITH THEM (<u>RIGHT TO LEFT</u>)

> FRANK
> Dammit let me go!

> SARAH (FRANTIC)
> We've got no money!

                    FRANK
Dammit I can spend my own money like I want – you want money?
Go sell some of Mae's jewellery down at the bar room. There's
some women upstairs there that like that cheap kinda stuff.

                    SARAH
             (BOTH FRANTIC AND FURIOUS)
Call Aunt Mae what you want to! I know what you think of her.
              You've got a son to feed!
            We have to eat! We need money!

THEY HAVE NOW REACHED THE FRONT DOOR. SARAH STILL HANGING
ONTO FRANK.

                    FRANK
         Get off me! Dammit to hell get off me!

HE PULLS HIS ARM FREE OF SARAH THEN DELIBERATELY PUNCHES HER
FULL IN THE FACE. THE FORCE OF THE BLOW KNOCKS HER BACKWARDS.

                                                   CUT TO:

77. INT. FOOT OF THE STAIRS. EARLY EVENING.

SARAH COMES CRASHING INTO SHOT HITTING HER HEAD ON THE
BANNISTER. BLOOD STARTS POURING FROM HER MOUTH.
DAVID ENTERS SHOT AND CRADLES HER HEAD.

                FRANK'S VOICE OVER
         I'm gonna plant these seeds! You hear me!

                DAVID (FRIGHTENED)
              Aunt Mae! Aunt Mae!

                                                   CUT TO:

78. INT. MOTHER'S BEDROOM. NIGHT.

SHOT OF DAVID STANDING IN DOORWAY.

                    DAVID (SOFTLY)
              Is she gonna die, Aunt Mae?
                                                   CUT TO:

79. INT. MOTHER'S BEDROOM. NIGHT.

2 SHOT AUNT MAE BY SARAH'S BEDSIDE. SARAH IN BED MOANING
SLIGHTLY. AUNT MAE BATHING SARAH'S MOUTH (IN DARKNESS).

                        AUNT MAE
        No, honey ... she's just lost a tooth and her dignity ...
                        that's all ...

SHE CONTINUES TO BATH SARAH.
SILENCE IN THE DARK.

                        AUNT MAE
                    Where's Poppa?
                                                    CUT TO:

80. INT. MOTHER'S BEDROOM. NIGHT.

SHOT OF DAVID.

                        DAVID
                    I'll go find him.

HE EXITS.
                                                    CUT TO:

81. EXT. PORCH. NIGHT.

SHOT OF DAVID COMING OUT OF THE HOUSE TOWARDS CAMERA. HE
STOPS NEAR THE PORCH STEPS.
SILENCE.
HE JUST STANDS THERE.
                                            CUT/DISSOLVE TO:

82. EXT. PORCH. NIGHT.

EXACT REVERSE OF PREVIOUS SHOT
DAVID STANDS ON THE EDGE OF THE PORCH WITH THE HUGE SKY IN
FRONT OF HIM FILLED WITH STARS AND A MOON. IN THE DISTANCE
THE NEON BIBLE COMES ON.
HOLD ON SHOT
SPFX THEN WITHOUT A DISSOLVE DAVID LITERALLY GETS BIGGER, HE
LITERALLY GROWS UP IN FRONT OF OUR EYES.
                                                    CUT TO:

83. INT. MOTHER'S BEDROOM. NIGHT.

OLDER DAVID (14-16) COMES TO DOORWAY AND STANDS IN THE DARK.

                        DAVID
                    How is she?
                                                    CUT TO:

84. INT. MOTHER'S BEDROOM. NIGHT.

<u>SHOT OF</u> AUNT MAE COVERING SARAH UP THEN SITTING BACK IN THE CHAIR. THE MOONLIGHT MAKES HER HAIR LOOK HALOED IN THE DARK AND SEEM SERENE.

> AUNT MAE
> She'll be alright, David.

<u>DAVID COMES INTO SHOT</u> AND SITS AT THE FOOT OF THE BED (<u>FRAME LEFT</u>). SILENCE.

> DAVID
> What about Poppa, Aunt Mae?

> AUNT MAE
> Don't worry about him. There's no place else for him to go. He'll show up.

SILENCE.
AUNT MAE FINISHES BATHING THE SLEEPING SARAH. AUNT MAE LOOKS OUT OF THE WINDOW.
PAUSE.

> CUT TO:

85. INT. MOTHER'S BEDROOM. NIGHT.

<u>CLOSE UP</u> DAVID (<u>AUNT MAE'S POV</u>)

> DAVID
> Tell me about the stage, Aunt Mae ...
> tell me about Biloxi ...

> CUT TO:

86. INT. MOTHER'S BEDROOM. NIGHT.

<u>CLOSE UP</u> AUNT MAE (<u>DAVID'S POV</u>)

> AUNT MAE
> (MORE TO HERSELF THAN DAVID)
> Oh I felt lucky if I got a job at some little dance hall in Mobile or Baton Rouge ... but I <u>loved</u> the stage, David, I loved the spotlights and the bright costumes and feeling the beat of the band under me ...

LOOKS AT DAVID.

                          AUNT MAE
         I never sang good, honey ... I knew that but when I was
         younger I looked good in clothes and could carry a tune ...

                                                              CUT TO:

87. INT. MOTHER'S BEDROOM. NIGHT.

<u>CLOSE UP</u> DAVID. HE JUST LOOKS AT HER.

                       AUNT MAE'S VOICE OVER
                   But you get old, David, honey ...
                          you get older ...

                                                              CUT TO:

88. INT. MOTHER'S BEDROOM. NIGHT.

<u>SLIGHTLY WIDE SHOT</u> AUNT MAE GETS UP AND GOES TO THE WINDOW
(POSSIBLY <u>PAN WITH HER</u>).

                            AUNT MAE
          ... but you keep on going, keep on thinking "one day they'll
         see me and I'll cut a record", one day they'll say "that's Mae
         Morgan!" ... It's like a drug, it is baby, but when it doesn't
                          happen, you hurt – here ...

SHE INDICATES HER HEART AND SOFTLY BEGINS TO WEEP.
DAVID COMES INTO SHOT AND HUGS HER - STANDING CLOSE TO HER
BELLY, SHE PUTS HER ARMS AROUND HIM AND STROKES HIS HEAD AND
BACK.

                            AUNT MAE
             ... and then some guy thinks your "awful nice" and so
             does the next guy and the next and the next, til you
            get to be a used up piece of goods so to speak then no
                          honest man wants ...

<u>TRACK IN</u> ON DAVID TILL HE IS IN <u>CLOSE UP</u>.
AUNT MAE CONTINUES TO WEEP SOFTLY, TEARS FALLING ON HER
FOREARM
- DAVID HUGGING HER TIGHTER.

                       AUNT MAE'S VOICE OVER
                   ... the last job was the crummiest
             someone threw a bottle at me – "Watch out Mae!" Then wham!

BEGIN SLOWLY TO <u>CRANE UP</u> TO AUNT MAE.
<u>CRANE UP STOPS</u> WHEN SHE IS IN <u>CLOSE UP</u>.

                              AUNT MAE
            ... the girls got together and bought me my ticket here
            ... but here I'm just a sore thumb, you know that, David
              I went on the stage to show off 'cos no-one ever paid
                       any attention to me otherwise ...
                          It hurts, David, it hurts
               I just wanted to be happy with you all, here ...
           we all have our hurts, David - big and small - and old Aunt
                      Mae ain't feeling too good tonight ...

(OVER THE DISSOLVE)

     Sleep with me tonight, honey ... I feel lonesome ...

                                                         DISSOLVE TO:

89. INT. AUNT MAE'S BEDROOM. NIGHT.

2 SHOT (SIDEVIEW) OF AUNT MAE AND DAVID LYING ON HER SHALLOW
BED. AUNT MAE NEAREST CAMERA, DAVID (ON HER RIGHT) FURTHEST
FROM CAMERA. BEYOND THEM (FACING CAMERA) THE BEDROOM WINDOW
WHICH IS OPEN.
IN THE DARKNESS THEY ARE SILENT IN BED LOOKING OUT OF THE
WINDOW TO A CLEAR, STAR FILLED NIGHT SKY.

                              AUNT MAE
                Do you ever pray before you go to sleep, honey?

                               DAVID
                             Sometimes.

                              AUNT MAE
                     (DRAWING HIM CLOSER TO HER)
         Well, we'll pray tonight ... we'll pray that your mother
                        feels well tomorrow ...

BEGIN TO CRANE UP AND TRACK OVER THEM INTO THE WINDOW.

                         AUNT MAE'S VOICE OVER
               ... and that nothing happens to your Pappa ...

TRACK THROUGH THE WINDOW - STARS FILLING THE NIGHT SKY.

                         AUNT MAE'S VOICE OVER
                   ... and that you and I won't hurt
                     too bad tomorrow or ever again ...

THE NEON BIBLE

                    DAVID'S VOICE OVER
                        Amen.

HOLD ON THE STAR FILLED NIGHT SKY THEN CRANE DOWN TO THE NEON BIBLE LIT UP AND FILLING FRAME.
HOLD ON THE NEON BIBLE.

SOUNDTRACK: REVIVALIST CONGREGATION
                        VOICE OVER (SINGING)
                    (ACCOMPANIED ON A HARMONIUM)
        "On a hill far away stood an old rugged cross,
            the emblem of suffering and shame;
                And I love that old cross
              where the dearest and best,
        for a world of lost sinners was slain ..."

CRANE DOWN FROM THE NEON BIBLE TO BLACKNESS

SOUNDTRACK: REVIVALIST CONGREGATION
                        VOICE OVER (SINGING)
         "So I'll Cherish the old rugged cross,
          till my trophies at last I lay down,
         I will cling to the old rugged cross,
        And exchange it some day for a crown ..."

DISSOLVE OUT OF DARKNESS.
THEN:
                                          CRANE DOWN TO:

90. EXT. MAIN STREET. NIGHT.

SHOT OF A CANVAS STRETCHED ACROSS MAIN STREET ON A ROPE - IT FILLS THE FRAME.
HOLD ON CANVAS. IT READS:

                  "SALVATION! SALVATION!
                    BOBBIE LEE TAYLOR
                        OF MEMPHIS
                    2 WEEKS! 2 WEEKS!"

SOUNDTRACK: REVIVALIST CONGREGATION
                        VOICE OVER (SINGING)
     "Oh that old rugged cross, so despised by the world,
          has a wonderous attraction for me,
       For the dear Lamb of God left his glory above,
             to bear it to dark Calvary ..."

                        CRANE DOWN AND PAN (RIGHT TO LEFT) TO:

91. EXT. MAIN STREET. NIGHT..

WIDE SHOT TORCHES BEING CARRIED. THE STREET IS FILLED WITH TOWNSPEOPLE GOING TO THE REVIVALIST MEETING.
PEOPLE ON FOOT, IN CARS. THE SIDEWALKS JAMMED WITH PEOPLE - LIKE A MARDI GRAS.
IN THE MIDST OF THE THRONG SARAH, DAVID AND AUNT MAE ARE SEEN.

SOUNDTRACK: REVIVALIST CONGREGATION
VOICE OVER (SINGING)
"In the old rugged cross, Stain'd with blood so divine,
A wondrous beauty I see, For t'was on that old cross,
Jesus suffered and died
To pardon and sanctify me ..."

CONTINUE CRANE DOWN THEN PAN (RIGHT TO LEFT) AND TRACK WITH CROWD TO:

92. EXT. MAIN STREET. NIGHT.

HIGH SHOT OVER THE HEADS OF THE CROWD TO A WIDE SHOT OF BOBBY LEE'S TENT IN THE DISTANCE. IT EXUDES A YELLOW/RED GLOW FROM INSIDE - A MIXTURE OF TORCHES AND KEROSENE LAMPS.
TRACK WITH CROWD TOWARDS IT.

SOUNDTRACK: REVIVALIST CONGREGATION
VOICE OVER (SINGING)
"To that old rugged cross I will ever be true,
Its shame and reproach gladly bear,
Then he'll call me some day
To my home far away,
Where his glory for ever i'll share ..."

DISSOLVE TO:

93. EXT. TENT. NIGHT.

A DARK HOLE AT THE TENT'S ENTRANCE. TRACK IN ON IT WITH THE CROWD THEN PRECEDE THE CROWD INTO DARKNESS.

SOUNDTRACK: REVIVALIST CONGREGATION
VOICE OVER (SINGING)
"So I'll cherish the old rugged cross,
Till my trophies at last I lay down"

DISSOLVE TO:

THE NEON BIBLE

94. INT. TENT. NIGHT.

EXACT REVERSE OF PREVIOUS SHOT
TRACK BACK OUT OF THE DARKNESS TO WIDE SHOT. THE TENT (WITH RAKED SEATING) FILLED WITH SINGING PEOPLE.

SOUNDTRACK: REVIVALIST CONGREGATION
                VOICE OVER (SINGING)
       "I will cling to the old rugged cross,
         And exchange it some day for a crown"

IT IS NOW SILENT EXCEPT FOR THE PEOPLE FANNING THEMSELVES AND CHAIRS CREAKING.
AN AIR OF EXPECTANCY AS THEY WAIT.
HOLD

SOUNDTRACK:
                MAN'S VOICE OVER (TANNOY)
  "It has been wonderful to be in this town with Bobbie Lee, my
     friends. God bless all of you - may the heavens shine
   down upon you, Christian and sinner alike - you are all our
              brothers and sisters in Christ ..."
                                                    CUT TO:

95. INT. TENT. NIGHT.

CLOSE UP (SIDEVIEW) OF BOBBIE LEE TAYLOR LOOKING AT THE AUDIENCE THROUGH A SMALL FLAP IN THE TENT.
BLACKNESS ALL AROUND HIM. HE IS LIT ONLY FROM THE LIGHT COMING THROUGH THE APERTURE.
BOBBIE LEE LOOKS AT THE CROWD AND MIMES TO THE TANNOY VOICE - A PRACTISED RITUAL.

                MAN'S VOICE OVER (TANNOY)
   "... by now there is no need for me to introduce Bobbie Lee to
         you all - you have come to love him ..."

                BOBBIE LEE
           (ALOUD BUT SOFTLY TO HIMSELF)
                Good crowd ...
                good money

AND CONTINUES TO MIME TO THE VOICE OVER.

                MAN'S VOICE OVER (TANNOY)
   "... everybody loves a dedicated Christian, sinners fear one -
         you have shown you love this chosen boy"

BOBBIE PREPARES HIMSELF TO GO TO MEET HIS PUBLIC.

>   MAN'S VOICE OVER (TANNOY)
>   "... here is your Bobbie Lee!"

BOBBIE OPENS THE TENT FLAP AND WALKS OUT. THE AUDIENCE APPLAUDS.
                                                       CUT TO:

96. INT. TENT. NIGHT.

WIDE SHOT (HEAD ON) OF BOBBIE LEE COMING TO THE FRONT OF THE
STAGE, TO WHERE THE LECTERN IS. ON IT A BIBLE. HE WALKS TO IT.
HE DOESN'T SPEAK. HE FINDS A PLACE IN THE BIBLE.
SILENCE AS HE LOOKS AT IT AND THEN AT THE AUDIENCE.
                                                       CUT TO:

97. INT. TENT. NIGHT.

WIDE SHOT OF AUDIENCE. PEOPLE MOVE UNEASILY IN THEIR CHAIRS
WHICH CREAK. SOME PEOPLE COUGH.
                                                       CUT TO:

98. INT. TENT. NIGHT.

CLOSE UP BOBBIE LEE. HE RUNS HIS EYES OVER THE AUDIENCE,
CLEARS HIS THROAT THEN SOFTLY BEGINS TO SPEAK.

>   BOBBIE LEE
> Here we are gathered together again for another glorious night
> of conversion and salvation. I was praying right before I came
> up here that the testimonies would be many. I was praying that
>   more lost souls would give themselves up to
>   the glory of Jee-Sus Christ ...
>   CUT TO:

99. INT. TENT. NIGHT.

3 SHOT DAVID IN THE MIDDLE OF SARAH AND AUNT MAE. THE SHOT IS
FROM SLIGHTLY BELOW THEM SO THAT THE AUDIENCE IN THE RAKED
SEATING SEEM TO GO UP BEHIND THEM VERTIGINOUSLY.

>   BOBBIE LEE'S VOICE OVER
>   (SOFT AND FAR AWAY)
>   ... I feel in my soul tha t these prayers will be answered,
>   that sinners will surrender to Him by the hundredfold ...

DAVID LEANS FORWARD AND LOOKS DOWN.
                                                       CUT TO:

THE NEON BIBLE

100. INT. TENT. NIGHT.

THE REVERSE OF PREVIOUS SHOT - THE AUDIENCE SEEMING EVEN MORE VERTIGINOUS AS THEY SLOPE DOWN TOWARDS BOBBIE LEE WHO SEEMS SMALL AND FAR AWAY.

                  BOBBIE LEE'S VOICE OVER
                    (SOFT AND FAR AWAY)
... He don't care who you are. He don't care if you're rich or poor. He don't care if you're babe or grandfather. He just cares if you've got a soul to give him.
                        (LOUDER)
        That's all Jee-Sus cares about! ...

PAUSE.

                                        CUT TO:

101. INT. TENT. NIGHT.

<u>WIDE SHOT OF</u> AUDIENCE WITH BOBBIE LEE IN FOREGROUND (BACK TO CAMERA).

                          BOBBIE LEE
Take it fr0m me, my friends, that is all. What more could he want? He don't want worldly riches. They lead to lust, they lead to sin. He owns a universe. He wants for nothing - except your souls ...

                                        CUT TO:

102. INT. NIGHT. TENT.

<u>CLOSE UP</u> (<u>SIDEVIEW</u>) BOBBIE LEE.

                          BOBBIE LEE
Today our nation is having a mortal struggle with the Devil. In our cities girls are giving themselves up to the oldest profession - they go where they want, to dances and honky-tonk at army bases without a restraining hand ...

                                        CUT TO:

103. INT. TENT. NIGHT.

<u>3 SHOT</u> SARAH, DAVID AND AUNT MAE. DAVID LISTENS. SARAH'S EYES ARE SHINING. AUNT MAE LOOKS DOWN - A MIXTURE OF GUILT AND UNEASE.

                  BOBBIE LEE'S VOICE OVER
                    (SOFT AND FAR AWAY)
The Devil is tempting these women, drawing them into his web ...

                                        CUT TO:

104. INT. TENT. NIGHT.

CLOSE UP (FRONTVIEW) BOBBIE LEE.

> BOBBIE LEE
> (REALLY GETTING INTO HIS STRIDE NOW)
> When they're dancing d'you think they're thinking of Jee-Sus? You can bet your life they aren't! Jee-Sus has no place on the dancefloor. No, sir, that is the playground of the Devil.

PAUSE

> BOBBIE LEE
> Now, may I ask you a question? Are you fighting the Devil, are you falling under his influence?

CUT TO:

105. INT. TENT. NIGHT.

2 SHOT (SIDEVIEW) (DAVID STANDING IN FRONT OF HIS SEAT). AUNT MAE STILL VERY UNEASY. A WOMAN SOBS. AUNT MAE AND DAVID LOOK BACK INTO THE CROWD (THEIR LEFT AND RIGHT) AND CATCH SIGHT OF SARAH.

> BOBBIE LEE'S VOICE OVER
> There's a voice, a voice from the wilderness! She don't fear Jee-Sus, she wants his compassion ...

MORE SOBS AND SHOUTS OF 'OH, LORD! OH, LORD JESUS!" DAVID LOOKS TOWARDS CAMERA.

CUT TO:

106. INT. TENT. NIGHT.

2 SHOT (SIDEVIEW) DAVID AND HIS MOTHER, SARAH, HER EYES SHINING AND TEARS RUNNING DOWN HER CHEEKS.

> SARAH (SOFTLY)
> Oh Lord, Oh sweet Lord Jesus!

MEN AND WOMAN ALONG THE ROW BOTH WEEPING AND EYES LOOKING ECSTATIC.

> BOBBIE LEE'S VOICE OVER
> (MORE AND MORE EXCITED)
> How many other of you women are stifling tears of repentance? Don't be afraid, let Jee-Sus know you're sorry. Cry to him for mercy!

CUT TO:

THE NEON BIBLE

107. INT. TENT. NIGHT.

WIDE SHOT (HEAD ON) OF AUDIENCE. BOBBIE LEE'S POV NOW, ONE BY ONE, PEOPLE ARE STANDING UP OR FALLING TO THEIR KNEES AS THEY TESTIFY - BOBBIE LEE'S VOICE OVER POUNDING OUT OVER AND OVER.

                      FIRST WOMAN
     I'm Mrs. Ollie Wingate ... for a long time now

                     (BEGINS TO WEEP)
... for a long time now I've been feeling that I needed
               the help of Jesus ...

                     SECOND WOMAN
Most of you know me, I own the grocery on Main -
I am resigned to the Lord ... I want to repent and
          be converted to his way ...

                                                 CUT TO:

108. INT. TENT. NIGHT.

CLOSE UP (HEAD ON) BOBBIE LEE NOW MORE AND MORE ECSTATIC.

                      BOBBIE LEE
Here they are. They want to dedicate themselves to Jee-Sus.
  What a glorious turn their lives have taken tonight ...
               we'll let them speak ...

BEGIN TO SLOWLY TRACK AROUND AND BACK TO LONG SHOT SO THAT BOBBIE LEE IS EXTREME FRAME RIGHT THE AUDIENCE IS IN FRONT OF HIM (CENTRE FRAME) ON THE GROUND AND THE RAKED SEATING IS EXTREME FRAME LEFT (WITH A BLACK HOLE UNDERNEATH IT EXTREME FRAME LEFT.) THE HARMONIUM HAS STARTED SOFTLY TO PLAY "GOING HOME". ONE BY ONE THE AUDIENCE JOINS IT UNTIL EVENTUALLY THE WHOLE AUDIENCE IS SINGING.

                    CONGREGATION
                       (SINGING)
   "Goin' home, goin' home, I'm a-goin' home
        Quiet night, some still day
         I'm just goin' home ..."

PEOPLE STANDING, KNEELING, THEIR ARMS OUTSTRETCHED TOWARDS BOBBIE LEE.

                    BOBBIE LEE
    Weren't those words of inspiration?
      Let's hear from this boy ...

A YOUNG BOY STANDS UP, RAISING HIS ARMS

     BILLY SUNDAY THOMPSON
   I'm Billy Sunday Thompson. I want to
    dedicate myself to Jesus ...

     CONGREGATION (SINGING)
    "It's not far, just close by,
    Through an open door;
    Work all done, care laid by,
    goin' to fear no more ..."

     BOBBIE LEE (ECSTATIC)
  Those were the words of a babe - testify, testify,
    the Lord will take you any time ...

<u>HOLD ON LONG SHOT</u>

      BOBBIE LEE
     Come to Jee-Sus!
     Finally come to Jee-Sus!

     CONGREGATION (SINGING)
    "Mother's there, expecting me,
     Others leading too
    Lots of friends gathered there,
    All the friends I knew ..."

<u>BEGIN TO PAN</u> (<u>RIGHT TO LEFT</u>) TOWARDS THE DARK TUNNEL ENTRANCE TO THE TENT.

     CONGREGATION (SINGING)
    "Home, home, I'm a-goin' home
    Nothin' lost, all is gained
    No more threat nor pain,
    No more stumbling on the way,
    No more longin' for the day,
    Goin' to run no more ..."

     BOBBIE LEE'S VOICE OVER
 ... Open your hearts, feel that light beaming in - walk into
the Garden of Eden with him and feel the strength of Jee-Sus
    coming into your soul ...

<u>SOUND DISSOLVE</u>: BOBBIE LEE'S VOICE OVER WITH F.D. ROOSEVELT'S DECLARATION OF WAR TO CONGRESS.

THE NEON BIBLE

                    F.D. ROOSEVELT'S VOICE OVER
     "Yesterday - December 7th 1941 - a date which will live in infamy
        - the United States of America was suddenly and deliberately
           attacked by naval and air forces of the Empire of Japan ..."

BLACK ENTRANCE TO THE TENT IS FRAMED.
TRACK IN ON IT AND INTO BLACKNESS

                    CONGREGATION VOICE OVER (SINGING)
                       "Morning Star lights the way;
                          Restless dreams of dawn
                         Shadows gone, break of day
                          Real life's just begun ..."

                       F.D. ROOSEVELT'S VOICE OVER
                    "Yesterday the Japanese government
                  Also launched an attack against Malaya ..."

                                                        DISSOLVE TO:

109. EXT. MAIN STREET. DAY.

WIDE SHOT (HIGH) SOLDIERS MARCHING TOWARDS THE RAILROAD
STATION FOLLOWED BY FAMILY AND FRIENDS.

                       F.D. ROOSEVELT'S VOICE OVER
                 "Last night Japanese forces attacked Hong Kong.
                  Last night Japanese forces attacked Guam ..."

                    CONGREGATION VOICE OVER (SINGING)
                            "There's no break,
                             there's no end
                           Just a leading on;
                              Wide awake,
                              with a smile
                           Goin on and on ..."

                                                        DISSOLVE TO:

110. EXT. RAILROAD STATION. DAY.

CRANE DOWN FROM HIGH SHOT TO 4 SHOT OF DAVID, SARAH, AUNT MAE
AND FRANK, WHO IS IN UNIFORM. THEY STAND ON THE PLATFORM.

                       F.D. ROOSEVELT'S VOICE OVER
         "Last night Japanese forces attacked the Phillipine Islands.
          Last night Japanese forces attacked Wako Island. Last night
                    Japanese forces attacked Midway Island ..."

THE GROUP DON'T SPEAK. FRANK OPENLY CRYING. SARAH TOO. AUNT MAE TRYING TO CONTROL HERSELF. DAVID JUST LOOKS. FRANK AND SARAH KISS THEN PART AND HE GETS ONTO THE TRAIN.
<u>HOLD ON</u> <u>3 SHOT</u> THEY WAVE SADLY.

      F.D. ROOSEVELT'S VOICE OVER
 "... Our interests are in grave danger. With confidence in our
        Armed Forces ..."

<u>PAN</u> (<u>RIGHT TO LEFT</u>) TO TRAIN FILLING AND FILLED WITH SOLDIERS. FRANK DISAPPEARS FROM VIEW. TRAIN MOVES OFF.
<u>TRACK WITH IT</u> (HIGH SHOT + CRANE?)

      F.D. ROOSEVELT'S VOICE OVER
 "... with the unbounded determination of our people - we will
     gain the inevitable triumph.
       So help us, God ..."

    CONGREGATION VOICE OVER (SINGING)
  "Goin' home, goin' home, I'm just goin' home,
     Quiet night, some still day
     I'm Just Goin' Home."

<u>SOUND DISSOLVE</u> TO: FACTORY GIRLS AND CROWD SINGING "<u>CHATTANOOGA CHOO CHOO</u>" ACCOMPANIED BY A SMALL BAND CONSISTING OF A PIANO, A BASS FIDDLE, A BANJO AND A TRUMPET.

      FACTORY GIRLS AND CROWD
      VOICE OVER (SINGING)
 "Pardon me boy, is this the Chattanooga Choo Choo?
 Track 29,
 Well you can give me a shine, I can afford,
 To board the Chattanooga Choo Choo I got my fare,
 And just a trifle to spare,
 You leave the Pennsylvania Station 'bout a quarter to four,
 Read a magazine and then you're in Baltimore,
 Dinner in the diner,
 Nothin' could be finer,
 Than to have your ham and eggs in Carolina ..."

            DISSOLVE TO:

111. INT. FACTORY. NIGHT.

<u>CONTINUE TRACK</u> (IN HIGH SHOT) DOWN THE LONG LINE OF MACHINES IN SEMI-DARKNESS - THE SPILL FROM THE COLOURED LIGHTS PLAYING ON THEM AS WE <u>TRACK</u> OVER THEM.

THE NEON BIBLE

                    FACTORY GIRLS AND CROWD
                        VOICE OVER (SINGING)
"When you hear that whistle blowin' eight to the bar, then you
            know that Tennessee is not very far,
        Shove all the coal in, gotta keep them rollin'
          Whoo! Whoo! Chattanooga there you are ..."

CONTINUE TRACK (IN HIGH SHOT)
WHEN THE END OF THE MACHINE LINE IS REACHED WE SEE THAT A
SMALL DANCE FLOOR AND BANDSTAND HAVE BEEN CREATED. THE DANCE
FLOOR PACKED WITH JITTERBUGGING WOMEN AND SOME OLDER MEN.
COLOURED DISKS TURN IN FRONT OF THE LIGHTS WHICH SEND A
MULTI-COLOURED PATTERN ACROSS THE DANCE FLOOR AND DANCERS.
THOSE NOT DANCING STAND BY OR SIT ON THE MACHINES. EVERYONE
IS SINGING.

CONTINUE TRACK
ON ONE MACHINE (OVERLOOKING THE DANCE FLOOR) SIT SARAH AND
DAVID BOTH SINGING AND MOVING IN TIME TO THE SONG - BOTH
REALLY HAPPY.
AS WE TRACK PAST AND OVER THEM

                                SARAH
                      Look at those two go!

                                DAVID
                              (SHOUTING)
                        Swing her Aunt Mae!

                            ALL (SINGING)
              "There's gonna be a certain party at the station,
                            Satins and lace,
                     I used to call funny face"

CONTINUE TRACKING TO DANCEFLOOR
IN THE MIDST OF THE DANCERS AUNT MAE AND HER PARTNER (FLORA)
ARE JITTERBUGGING REALLY WELL. SO WELL, IN FACT, THAT ALL THE
OTHERS STOP DANCING AND FORM A CIRCLE TO WATCH AND SING AS
THE COUPLE "TAKE THE FLOOR".

                         EVERYONE (SINGING)
                    "She's gonna smile until I
        Tell her that I'll never roam, so Chattanooga Choo Choo
                  Won't you choo choo me home! ..."

TRACK AROUND (LEFT TO RIGHT) AND CRANE DOWN TO AUNT MAE AND
HER PARTNER

                    EVERYONE (SINGING)
    "Chattanooga, Chattanooga, Chattanooga, Chattanooga,
    So Chattanooga choo choo, won't you choo choo me home!"

WILD APPLAUSE. AUNT MAE FANNING HERSELF WITH HER HAND. SHE
TAKES SOMEONE'S GLASS OF BEER AND TAKES A LONG DRINK. THEN
BELCHES AND PEOPLE LAUGH.

                            FLORA
                    (SHUSHING EVERYONE)
    You've seen how Miss Morgan can dance - well she can sing too!

                            AUNT MAE
                (EMBARRASSED YET GLAD IT'S BEEN SAID)
            Oh Flora, I haven't sung in years!

                            FLORA
    So she's gonna sing for us right now! Miss Mae Morgan!

EVERYONE CHEERS AND CLAPS.
AUNT MAE GOES SEMI-RELUCTANTLY TO THE BAND STAND (<u>TRACK</u> AND
<u>PAN LEFT TO RIGHT</u>) WITH HER.
LAUGHTER.

                            AUNT MAE
                        (INTO MICROPHONE)
            Well it's not gonna be "God Bless America".

THE TRUMPETER BEGINS THE FIRST FEW NOTES OF "MY ROMANCE" THE
REST OF THE BAND JOIN SOFTLY IN AND SHE BEGINS TO SING AND
SINGS REALLY WELL.
<u>TRACK IN</u> ON AUNT MAE. <u>TRACK STOPS</u> WHEN SHE IS IN <u>CLOSE UP</u>

                        AUNT MAE (SINGING)
    "My romance doesn't have to have a moon in the sky,
      My romance doesn't need a blue lagoon standing by,
No month of may, no twinkling stars, no hideaway, no soft guitars,
      My romance doesn't need a castle rising in Spain,
        Nor a dance to a constantly, surprising refrain,
                    Wide awake I can make,
                My most fantastic dreams come true,
            My romance doesn't need a thing but you".

SHE FINISHES VERY NEAR TO TEARS. LOUD APPLAUSE.

                    BASS FIDDLE PLAYER (CLYDE)
                You're good. We should talk.
                                                        <u>CUT TO:</u>

THE NEON BIBLE

112. INT. PROPELLER FACTORY. NIGHT.

<u>2 SHOT</u> SARAH AND DAVID. HE LOOKS UP AT HER. SHE IS FIGHTING TO KEEP THE TEARS BACK.

<u>CUT TO:</u>

113. EXT. PROPELLER FACTORY. NIGHT.

SARAH, DAVID , AUNT MAE COMING OUT OF THE FACTORY WITH EVERYONE ELSE (SHOT HEAD-ON).
"GOODNIGHTS" ALL ROUND.

<u>CUT TO:</u>

114. EXT. HOUSE. NIGHT.

EXACT REVERSE OF PREVIOUS SHOT
SARAH, DAVID, AUNT MAE FROM BEHIND WALKING OVER THE CINDER PATH TO THE HOUSE.
THEY REACH THE PORCH STEPS AND TURN AROUND TO LOOK DOWN AT THE TOWN.

AUNT MAE
(EMBRACING DAVID AND SARAH)
You know I never thought I'd be happy here.

THEY LOOK UP AT THE NIGHT SKY.
<u>HOLD</u>
THEN
THE FRAME BLEACHES OUT TO THE GLARING WHITE OF THE SUN.

FRANK'S VOICE OVER
The sun isn't prettier anywhere else than it is here in Italy. It's the brightest and yellow-est I ever saw ... I'm staying in a farmhouse a thousand years old ... they've got olives too ... there's been some pretty heavy fighting...

<u>THE GLARE BLEACHES AWAY TO:</u>

115. EXT. FIELD.

DAVID (<u>SIDEVIEW</u>) WADING THROUGH SHOULDER-HIGH GRASS (<u>LEFT TO RIGHT</u>). A BRILLIANT SUMMER DAY.

FRANK'S VOICE OVER
I marched along the Appian Way, that's a very famous road in history - so tell your teacher ... oh I saw where the Pope lives too ... I miss everyone of you more than I ever thought I would ...

(BEGIN TO FADE HIS VOICE) AND CROSS FADE TO DAVID'S.

> FRANK'S VOICE OVER
> ... but most of the fighting is over now ...

> DAVID'S VOICE OVER (AGED 16)
> The war had been on for quite a while when Poppa got his notice from the draft. He didn't have to go, but he more or less enlisted ...

DAVID CONTINUES WALKING (LEFT TO RIGHT). SLIGHTLY BEHIND HIM SOME GIRLS FROM HIS CLASS. BOYS' LAUGHTER IS HEARD AND DAVID AND THE GIRLS LOOK BACK.

CUT TO:

116. EXT. FIELD. DAY.

BOYS FROM DAVID'S CLASS SNIGGERING IN A HUDDLE THEN MAKING MASTURBATING GESTURES TO THE GIRLS.

CUT TO:

117. EXT. FIELD. DAY.

SHOT OF DAVID AND THE GIRLS (FROM BEHIND). THEIR TEACHER (MISS MOORE) SLIGHTLY IN FRONT OF THEM - ALL IN WHITE.
THE GIRLS ARE 'SHOCKED' BUT DAVID JUST LOOKS BLANKLY AT THE BOYS.
HE CONTINUES WALKING WITH THE GIRLS FOLLOWING MISS MOORE.
A TRAIN WHISTLE IS HEARD AND THEY ALL STOP AND LOOK TOWARDS IT.

CUT TO:

118. EXT. TRAIN. DAY.

IN LONG SHOT A TRAIN TRAVELLING LEFT TO RIGHT ACROSS THE HORIZON.
HOLD

CUT TO:

119. EXT. DAVID'S HOUSE. DAY 119.

SHOT OF THE PINES - RUSTLING SOFTLY IN A SOFT SUMMER BREEZE AND THE HOUSE QUIET, LAZY IN THE SUN.
PAN DOWN TO PORCH THEN:
TRACK IN ON IT.
ALL THE DOORS OF THE HOUSE ARE OPEN AS WE GET TO FRONT DOOR.

CUT TO:

THE NEON BIBLE

120. INT. DAVID'S HOUSE. DAY.

SOMETHING BURNING. THEN HE HEARS HISSING.
SPREAD IN FRONT OF HER ON THE TABLE ARE FRANK'S LETTERS FROM ITALY AND THE TIN BOX THEY WERE KEPT IN, AND A TELEGRAM. SHE IS SOBBING.

                SARAH (HYSTERICAL)
             Frank! Oh, Frank!

                                              CUT TO:

122. INT. KITCHEN. DAY.

SHOT OF DAVID COMING TO THE TABLE. HE SITS DOWN.

                    DAVID
                (TO SARAH)
                    Poppa?

SHE CONTINUES TO CRY AND THEN DAVID TAKES THE CRUMPLED TELEGRAM OUT OF HER HAND.
HE STRAIGHTENS IT AND READS IT. HE GETS UP AND GOES OUT.

                                              CUT TO:

123. EXT. PORCH. DAY.

SHOT OF DAVID (FRONTVIEW) COMING OUT ON THE PORCH AND STOPPING BY THE PORCH STEPS.
SLOWLY HE STARTS TO WEEP HIS WEEPING TURNING TO PAROXYSM.

HOLD

                    DAVID
               Poppa - oh Poppa!

                                              CUT TO:

123A. EXTERIOR PORCH. DAY.

EXACT REVERSE OF PREVIOUS SHOT.

                DAVID (WEEPING)
             Poppa ... Oh, Poppa!
HOLD

                                              CUT TO:

124. EXT. TRAIN STATION. DAY.

A TRAIN PULLS INTO SHOT (LEFT TO RIGHT) PAUSE
THEN THE DOORS ARE OPENED TO REVEAL A LINE OF COFFINS, ALL
DRAPED WITH THE STARS AND STRIPES.

>   DAVID'S VOICE OVER
>   Then the war was over. And all the soldiers came home.

SOUND DISSOLVE
>   SARAH'S VOICE OVER
>   Maybe it's this one?
>   It could be this grave, Mae?
>   CUT TO:

125. INT. KITCHEN. DAVID'S HOUSE. DAY.

CLOSE UP PHOTOGRAPH OF MASS WAR GRAVES AND CROSSES. SARAH'S
WEDDING RING HAND MOVING ACROSS IT.
>   CUT TO:

126. INT. KITCHEN. DAVID'S HOUSE. DAY.

2 SHOT SARAH AND DAVID AT TABLE. SARAH HOLDS UP THE
PHOTOGRAPHS FOR AUNT MAE TO SEE.

>   SARAH
>   (OSCILLATING BETWEEN SMILES AND TEARS)
>   Maybe this one - it could be that one, Mae.

DAVID AND SARAH LOOK TO AUNT MAE.
>   CUT TO:

127. INT. KITCHEN. DAVID'S HOUSE. DAY.

CLOSE UP AUNT MAE AT KITCHEN DOOR. A CAR HORN SOUNDS.

>   CLYDE'S VOICE OVER
>   Mae! Hey, Mae!

>   AUNT MAE
>   Comin' Clyde honey!
>   (AWKWARD)
>   Look, David honey, I gotta go. We're playing at a wedding over
>   at the county seat ...

CAR HORN GOES AGAIN.

THE NEON BIBLE

>   AUNT MAE
>   ... and it's good money

AN AWKWARD SILENCE. SHE EXITS.

CUT TO:

128. EXT. DAVID'S HOUSE. DAY.

SHOT (FROM PORCH) OF AUNT MAE GETTING INTO CLYDE'S TRUCK. HIS BASS FIDDLE PROPPED UP IN THE BACK.
WHEN SHE'S GOT IN AND SETTLED HERSELF WE SEE (THROUGH THE SMALL WINDOW AT THE BACK OF THE CAB) AUNT MAE KISSING CLYDE. THE TRUCK MOVES OFF.

CUT TO:

129. EXT. PORCH. DAVID'S HOUSE. DAY.

<u>CLOSE UP</u> (HEAD ON) OF DAVID. HE WATCHES THE TRUCK DRIVE OFF. PAUSE.

>   SARAH'S VOICE OVER
>   Oh David, just look!

HE LOOKS OVER HIS SHOULDER.

CUT TO:

130. EXT. PORCH. DAVID'S HOUSE. DAY.

<u>CLOSE UP</u> (BACK VIEW) DAVID. HE LOOKS BACK OVER HIS SHOULDER.

>   SARAH'S VOICE OVER
>   ... Big cabbages - big, big cabbages your Poppa grew ...

<u>HOLD</u>

>   AUNT MAE'S VOICE OVER
>   Say it again, David ... It 's so beautiful...

DISSOLVE TO:

130A. EXT/INT. PORCH AND HALL. DAVID'S HOUSE. DAY.

<u>TRACK IN</u> ON FRONT DOOR AND INTO, THEN DOWN THE HALLWAY.

>   DAVID'S VOICE OVER (RECITING)
>   "Then read from the treasured volume
>   The poem of thy choice.
>   And lend to the rhyme of the poet
>   The beauty of thy voice.
>   And the night shall be filled with music ..."

DISSOLVE TO:

130B. INT. CLASSROOM. DAY.

MR. FARNEY AT THE HEAD OF THE CLASS RECITING FROM A BOOK.
TRACK IN ON HIM.
SOUND DISSOLVE

> MR. FARNEY
> "And the night shall be filled with music,
> And the cares, that infest the day,
> Shall fold their tents, like the arabs,
> And as silently steal away"

　　　　　　　　　　　　　　　　　　　　　　DISSOLVE TO:

131. INT. SCHOOL. DAY.

SHOT OF THE CORRIDOR - ON EITHER SIDE OF WHICH THE CLASSROOM DOORS ARE CLOSED - DARK WOOD GLOWING IN THE DARK INTERIOR.
TRACK DOWN CORRIDOR.
THE DOOR AT THE END OF THE CORRIDOR IS OPEN.
THROUGH IT - IN BRILLIANT SUNSHINE - THE GRADUATING CLASS STANDS SINGING "DIXIE" ACCOMPANIED ON THE PIANO BY MR FARNEY.

> CLASS (SINGING)
> "I wish I was in the land of cotton,
> Old times they are not forgotten,
> Look away! Look away! Look Away! Dixieland!"

　　　　　　　　　　　　　　　　　　　　　　DISSOLVE TO:

132. INT. GRADUATION HALL. NIGHT.

GRADUATING CLASS STAND ON STAGE SINGING. PARENTS SEATED IN FRONT (BACKS TO CAMERA). MR FARNEY PLAYING THE PIANO.
TRACK IN ON THE CLASS

> CLASS (SINGING)
> "In Dixie Land I'll take my stand,
> to live and die in Dixie!
> Away! Away! Away down South in Dixie"

TRACK STOPS WHEN THEY'VE FINISHED. (DAVID CENTRE STAGE)

> CLASS (SINGING)
> "Away! Away! Away down South in Dixie."

AUDIENCE APPLAUDS.

　　　　　　　　　　　　　　　　　　　　　　　　CUT TO:

133. INT GRADUATION HALL. NIGHT.

2 SHOT. AUNT MAE AND CLYDE SITTING IN THE AUDIENCE.

                    CLYDE
                 (TO DAVID)
       You goin' to high school, Boy?

                                            CUT TO:

134. INT. GRADUATION HALL. NIGHT.

CLOSE UP DAVID. HIS FELLOW PUPILS COMING OFF THE STAGE BEHIND HIM.

                    DAVID
               (SHAKES HIS HEAD)
     I gotta job in MR Williams' drugstore.

                                            CUT TO:

135. INT. GRADUATION HALL. NIGHT.

2 SHOT AUNT MAE AND CLYDE

            AUNT MAE (ENCOURAGING)
Well, you're the first person in our family to finish grade
                school, anyway.

             (GIVES HIM A PRESENT)
       I'm real proud of you, David.

                                            CUT TO:

136. INT. GRADUATION HALL. NIGHT.

CLOSE UP DAVID.

               DAVID (BEAMING)
Oh, Aunt Mae! It's a watch! It must have cost at
            least thirty dollars!

                                            CUT TO:

137. INT. GRADUATION HALL. NIGHT.

2 SHOT. AUNT MAE AND CLYDE.

                        AUNT MAE
                (IN HER BEST HOLLYWOOD VOICE)
                    Oh much, much more!

SHE LAUGHS.

CUT TO:

138. EXT. GRADUATION HALL. NIGHT.

3 SHOT. DAVID, AUNT MAE AND CLYDE COMING OUT ONTO THE STREET WITH THE REST OF THE PEOPLE.

                        DAVID
                Is any one with mother?

                        AUNT MAE
                Yeah - Flora's sitting with her tonight.

DAVID GOES TO EXIT FRAME LEFT.

                        AUNT MAE
            Over here, David. Clyde's going to drive us home.

CUT TO:

139. EXT. GRADUATION HALL/STREET. NIGHT.

SHOT OF BACK OF CLYDE'S TRUCK.
DAVID SITS ON THE BACK WITH CLYDE'S BASS FIDDLE. AUNT MAE AND CLYDE INSIDE THE CAB.

                        AUNT MAE
                (LEANING OUT OF DOOR WINDOW)
            You can ride up here with us if you want, David.

                        CLYDE
                    (STARTING THE ENGINE)
            No, Mae. There ain't enough room for him up here.

                THE TRUCK MOVES OFF.

                        CLYDE
        I'd bet he'd rather ride in the back than up here with us.

CUT TO:

140. EXT. GRADUATION HALL/STREET. NIGHT.

SHOT OF STREET (DAVID'S POV) FROM THE BACK OF THE TRUCK. THE
STREET ALIVE WITH PEOPLE "LIKE A RIVER FLOWING".
PEOPLE WALKING HOME. HOUSES.
SOME PARTIES GOING ON IN SOME OF THE
HOLD ON SHOT.

>   AUNT MAE'S VOICE OVER (FURIOUS)
>   Clyde! You cut that out!

                                                              CUT TO:

141. INT. TRUCK. NIGHT.

THE TRUCK HAS STOPPED.
2 SHOT AUNT MAE AND CLYDE (HEAD ON)
HIS HEAD COMPLETELY MASKS HER FACE AS HE KISSES HER AND SAYS
SOMETHING SOFTLY TO HER.

>   AUNT MAE
>   Alright Clyde, in a little while.

THEY HEAR A NOISE AND LOOK TOWARDS CAMERA.

                                                              CUT TO:

142. INT. TRUCK. NIGHT.

SHOT OF DAVID AT AUNT MAE'S SIDE OF THE TRUCK.
(HER POV)
HE JUST LOOKS AT THEM.

                                                              CUT TO:

143. EXT. TRUCK. NIGHT.

2 SHOT (DAVID'S POV). AUNT MAE AND CLYDE.

>   AUNT MAE (SLIGHTLY EMBARRASSED)
>   Look, honey, go wait there by the path
>   for me. I'm going to stay here with Clyde for a while ...

                                                              CUT TO:

144. INT. TRUCK. NIGHT.

DAVID (THEIR POV) JUMPS DOWN OFF THE RUNNING BOARD AND WALKS
AWAY FROM THE TRUCK.

                    AUNT MAE'S VOICE OVER
                    Now don't go off you hear!

HE KEEPS WALKING BUT LOOKS BACK.

                                                    CUT TO:

145. EXT. TRUCK. NIGHT.

DAVID'S POV. OF TRUCK. 2 SHOT AUNT MAE AND CLYDE. AUNT MAE
LEANS OUT OF THE WINDOW.

                    AUNT MAE (SHOUTING)
    ... I don't want to walk up the path alone - I won't be too
                            long ...

AND CLYDE PULLS HER TO HIM AND THEY DISAPPEAR BELOW THE
WINDSHIELD - EXCEPT FOR AUNT MAE'S HAT.
HOLD
THE CAB STARTS TO GENTLY SHAKE UP AND DOWN AS THEY BECOME
MORE AND MORE PERCUSSIVE.

                                                    CUT TO:

146. EXT. BOTTOM OF TRUCK. NIGHT.

CLOSE UP DAVID HE JUST LOOKS AT THE TRUCK. SLIGHT GROANS AND
LOW LAUGHTER OF CLYDE AND AUNT MAE.
HE LOOKS UP AT THE SKY AND SNIFFS THE AIR.
HOLD

                                                    CUT TO:

147. EXT. BOTTOM OF HILL. NIGHT.

SHOT OF TRUCK. AUNT MAE GETS OUT AND STRAIGHTENS HER DRESS.

                    AUNT MAE (COUGHS)
                    Good night, Clyde.

HE DRIVES OFF WITHOUT RESPONDING.
AUNT MAE TURNS TOWARDS DAVID, SMILES, AND EXTENDS HER HAND.

                                                    CUT TO:

148. EXT DAVID'S HOUSE. NIGHT.

SHOT OF AUNT MAE AND DAVID COMING TOWARDS PORCH. AS THEY
APPROACH THEY LOOK VERY DISTURBED.

                                                    CUT TO:

149. EXT. PORCH. NIGHT.

SHOT OF HOUSE - DOORS AND WINDOWS OPEN. ALL THE LIGHTS ON - A MIXTURE OF ELECTRIC LIGHT AND KEROSENE LAMPS, CURTAINS BILLOWING.
SARAH'S VOICE CAN BE HEARD. SHE IS TALKING TO HERSELF.
THEN SARAH COMES TO THE FRONT DOOR BUT SHE REMAINS BEHIND THE SCREEN DOOR. SHE LOOKS 'WILD'.

CUT TO:

150. EXT. PORCH. NIGHT.

2 SHOT AUNT MAE AND DAVID VERY UPSET.

AUNT MAE
Where's Flora, Sarah? Sarah, where's Flora?

CUT TO:

151. EXT. PORCH. NIGHT.

SHOT OF SARAH. ON HER FACE, THE LOOK OF SOMEONE UNSTABLE. AN INTIMATION OF THE MADNESS WHICH WILL EVENTUALLY ENFOLD HER.

SARAH
(SMILING THROUGH TEARS)
Flora? Oh yes. She told me I was crazy, Mae. Right to my face. She wasn't here 30 minutes. I've been sitting here waiting for you two to come in. Yes, Flora wasn't here 30 minutes.

CUT TO:

152. EXT. PORCH. NIGHT.

CLOSE UP AUNT MAE. SHE LOOKS VERY WEARY.

CUT TO:

153. EXT. PORCH. NIGHT.

CLOSE UP DAVID. HE IS SILENT.
SPFX SUPERIMPOSE OVER HIS CLOSE UP THE TRAIN ON WHICH HE IS TRAVELLING.

DISSOLVE TO:

153A. INT. TRAIN. NIGHT.

LONG SHOT OF DAVID SITTING ON HIS SEAT LOOKING OUT OF THE WINDOW. TRACK UP ALONG AISLE TOWARDS DAVID. CARRIAGE EMPTY.

SOUNDTRACK: A POLICE WHISTLE IS HEARD

                RADIO ANNOUNCER (VOICE OVER)
    "Now – 'Gangbusters' – presented in co-operation
    with police and federal law enforcement departments
           throughout the United States."
"The only national programme that brings you authentic police
                case histories."

(CAR HORN FOLLOWED BY A POLICE SIREN IS HEARD THEN MACHINE-GUN FIRE)

                RADIO ANNOUNCER (VOICE OVER)
      "Tonight's 'Gangbusters' presents the case of
         "The Appointment with Death ..."'

<u>PAN</u> (<u>RIGHT TO LEFT</u>) TO DAVID IN <u>CLOSE UP</u> AND <u>CONTINUE TRACK</u> TOWARDS THE DARKNESS OUTSIDE THE WINDOW.

                RADIO ANNOUNCER (VOICE OVER)
    "when a courageous policewoman waited for a deadly
      killer whom police didn't even know ..."

{FADE HIS VOICE)
BLACKNESS FRAMED BEYOND THE CARRIAGE WINDOW
                                                              DISSOLVE TO:

153B. INT. LIVING ROOM. NIGHT.

OUT OF BLACKNESS TO ROOM IN SEMI-DARKNESS. <u>CLOSE UP</u> AUNT MAE DANCING AROUND ROOM.

<u>SOUNDTRACK</u>: "PERFIDIA" ON RADIO PLAYED BY GLENN MILLER.

AUNT MAE DANCING IN TIME TO THE MUSIC – IN A DREAMY HALF-WORLD OF HER OWN. HER ARMS AND HANDS WEAVING AN INVISIBLE PATTERN IN THE AIR AS SHE SWAYS TO THE MUSIC

                        AUNT MAE
        Oh, David ... it's ... so ... <u>wonderful</u> ...
  You feel ... You feel the light go <u>through</u> you ... through
           your <u>whole</u> body ... it's so oh!

(SHE CAN'T FIND THE WORDS TO EXPRESS IT)
(SHE CONTINUES DANCING AND HUMMING)

<u>PAN AWAY</u> FROM HER (<u>RIGHT TO LEFT</u>) THEN
                                                               DISSOLVE TO:

THE NEON BIBLE

153C. INT. LIVING ROOM. NIGHT.

PAN (RIGHT TO LEFT) TO DAVID SEATED BY RADIO. HE SMILES.

SOUNDTRACK: "PERFIDIA" FADES. PAN AWAY FROM DAVID (LEFT TO RIGHT)

                                                                                                    DISSOLVE TO:

153D. INT. LIVING ROOM. NIGHT.

PAN (LEFT TO RIGHT) TO CLOSE UP SARAH BY RADIO.

SOUNDTRACK:

                      REVEREND WATKINS' VOICE OVER
                          (ON RADIO)
... The streets are so populated with many pregnant women, it's disgusting, soldiers coming home married to foreign women when we should be looking out and seeing that good American blood in the valley won't lose its purity ... Chinese women, pregnant women, women who sing with bands are corrupting American blood ...

THE RADIO IS SUDDENLY HEARD BEING SWITCHED OFF.

                          AUNT MAE'S VOICE OVER
        How can you listen to that trash, Sarah? How?

                                  SARAH
                          (IN A HALF-WORLD)
       Who do you think the murderer is, David? Who?

                                                             DISSOLVE TO:

153E. EXT. MAIN STREET. DAY.

CLOSE UP OLD, INSANE WOMAN IN A CAR. SHE LOOKS STRAIGHT OUT AT CAMERA.

SOUNDTRACK:
                                  RADIO
                   (FROM "THE SHADOW") (A LOW LAUGH)

                          THE SHADOW VOICE OVER
                            The Shadow knows.
(A LONG LOW LAUGH)
                                                                  CUT TO:

153F. INT. DRUGSTORE. DAY.

<u>CLOSE UP</u> DAVID (BEHIND COUNTER NEAR THE WINDOW).

     REVEREND WATKINS' VOICE OVER
       Bye.

     MR. WILLIAMS' VOICE OVER
      Bye, Reverend.

REVEREND WATKINS IS HEARD WALKING OUT OF THE DRUGSTORE.

     MR. WILLIAMS' VOICE OVER
   Reverend Watkins is a good Christian man.

     DAVID(NOT CONVINCED)
      Yeah.

              CUT TO:

153G. EXT. /INT. DRUGSTORE. DAY.

<u>DAVID'S POV</u>. REVEREND WATKINS GETS INTO THE CAR WITH THE OLD WOMAN IN THE BACK. "STATE ASYLUM" ON THE SIDE OF THE CAR. IT DRIVES OFF.

              CUT TO:

154. EXT. DRUGSTORE. DAY 154.

<u>MID WIDE SHOT</u>. WINDOW OF STORE <u>FRAME LEFT</u>. DAVID BEHIND IT. THE GLASS DOUBLE DOORS OF THE STORE FILL THE REST OF THE FRAME. A "NO-COLOREDS" SIGN HANGS ON THE DOOR ON THE LOWER RIGHT.

     JO LYNNE'S VOICE OVER
   Do you have this month's "Modern Romance"?

DAVID LOOKS TOWARDS CAMERA. SFPX
AS HE DOES SO JO LYNNE IS REFLECTED IN THE GLASS OF THE DOUBLE DOORS

              CUT TO:

155. INT. DRUGSTORE. DAY.

<u>CLOSE UP</u> DAVID.
HE CLEARS HIS THROAT.

              CUT TO:

THE NEON BIBLE

156. INT. DRUGSTORE. DAY.

CLOSE UP JO LYNNE.

                        JO LYNNE
I asked if you had this month's "Modern Romance".

                                                  CUT TO:

157. INT. DRUGSTORE. DAY.

CLOSE UP DAVID

                        DAVID
Yes, I know. I don't know if we have it but I'll look ...

HE TURNS AROUND TO MAGAZINE RACK BEHIND HIM AND STARTS LOOKING FOR THE MAGAZINE SHE'S ASKED FOR.

                   JO LYNNE'S VOICE OVER
                          Thanks.

HOLD ON DAVID.

                                                  CUT TO:

158. INT. DRUGSTORE. DAY.

CLOSE UP JO LYNNE.

                        JO LYNNE
Do you work here all the time?
PAUSE

                   DAVID'S VOICE OVER
Yes I do. All the times the store's open and from thirty minutes before it does.

SHE WATCHES HIM.

                        JO LYNNE
How old are you? About 19?

                                                  CUT TO:

159. INT. DRUGSTORE. DAY.

CLOSE UP DAVID BACK TO CAMERA.
HE HAS FOUND THE MAGAZINE BUT DOESN'T TURN AROUND.

                    DAVID
              ... and a half ...

PAUSE
THEN DAVID TURNS AROUND TO FACE JO LYNNE SILENCE.

                    DAVID
         You're from out of the valley, aren't you?
                                              CUT TO:

160. INT. DRUGSTORE. DAY.

<u>CLOSE UP</u> JO LYNNE

                    JO LYNNE
     Yes, we came here to take care of my grandpa. He got sick.
       If he gets better , we're going home again, Springhill.

                                              CUT TO:

161. INT. DRUGSTORE. DAY.

<u>2 SHOT</u> <u>SIDEVIEW</u> DAVID (<u>FRAME LEFT</u>). JO LYNNE (<u>FRAME RIGHT</u>).
MR WILLIAMS IS IN THE DISPENSARY BEYOND.

                    DAVID
            That's where you're from?

                    JO LYNNE
            Yes. You ever been there?

                    DAVID
         No, I've never been out of the valley.

                    JO LYNNE
         Well, if you do ever get out don't go there.
                 This place is prettier.

MR. WILLIAMS COMES FROM THE DISPENSARY WITH JO LYNNE'S
PRESCRIPTION.
SHE PAYS AND LEAVES. DAVID WATCHES HER GO.
                                              CUT TO:

162. INT. DRUGSTORE, DAY.

JO LYNNE GOING OUT OF THE DOUBLE DOORS (<u>DAVID'S POV</u>). HALF
WAY OUT SHE TURNS AND SMILES AT DAVID.

THE NEON BIBLE

                    JO LYNNE
            I forgot to tell you 'goodbye'.

                                                CUT TO:

163. INT. DRUGSTORE. DAY.

<u>CLOSE UP</u> DAVID (<u>JO LYNNE'S POV</u>)

                    DAVID (BEAMING)
                      Oh, goodbye.

SHE LEAVES.

                                                CUT TO:

164. INT. DRUGSTORE. DAY.

<u>CLOSE UP</u> MR WILLIAMS IN THE DISPENSARY (<u>DAVID'S POV</u>)

                    MR. WILLIAMS
            (SHAKING HIS HEAD AND SMILING)
                      Nineteen!

                                                CUT TO:

165. INT. DRUGSTORE. DAY.

<u>CLOSE UP</u> DAVID (<u>MR. WILLIAMS' POV</u>}

                    DAVID (GIGGLING)
                      And a half!

<u>PAN AND TRACK</u> (<u>RIGHT TO LEFT</u>) AWAY FROM DAVID AT THE COUNTER
TOWARDS WINDOWS AND DOUBLE DOORS OF THE STORE.

                    DAVID'S VOICE OVER
            Aunt Mae, I saw a girl in the store I really liked.

                    AUNT MAE'S VOICE OVER
              Why don't you ask her out, Dave?

                    DAVID'S VOICE OVER
              Suppose she won't go out with me?

                    AUNT MAE'S VOICE OVER
                Don't worry, Dave, You're a
                nice looking boy, she will. Ask her.

PAN AND TRACK STOP WHEN DOORS AND WINDOWS ARE FRAMED.
SPFX
THEN WITHOUT A DISSOLVE
LATE AFTERNOON TURNS TO DUSK.

                                                    CUT TO:

165A. EXT. MISS SCOVER'S HOUSE. DUSK/LATE AFTERNOON.

SHOT OF DAVID FROM MISS SCOVER'S PORCH. HE COMES TO A STOP ON HIS BIKE BY THE PORCH.
ALL OVER THE PORCH - CATS EVERYWHERE. DAVID COMES TOWARDS THE FRONT DOOR.

                    MISS SCOVER'S VOICE OVER
                We're going outside, Baby. Outside.

DAVID STOPS
                              DAVID
                    I've brought your medicine
                    from the drugstore, Miss Scover.

                                                    CUT TO:

165B. EXT. MISS SCOVER'S HOUSE. DUSK/LATE AFTERNOON.

DAVID'S POV OF MISS SCOVER AT HER FRONT DOOR. SHE IS WEARING A DRESSING GOWN. SHE IS ABOUT 40 BUT A THIN, RADDLED 40. SHE CARRIES A CAT WHICH SHE KISSES BEHIND ITS EAR.

                              MISS SCOVER
                         (TO DAVID, QUIETLY)
                    Come in, boy, while I get the money.

SHE TURNS AND GOES INSIDE THE HOUSE.

                                                    CUT TO:

165C. INT. MISS SCOVER'S HOUSE. DUSK/LATE AFTERNOON.

HER POV OF DAVID.
DAVID COMES AND STANDS JUST INSIDE THE DOOR.

                                                    CUT TO:

165D. INT. MISS SCOVER'S HOUSE. DUSK/LATE AFTERNOON.

DAVID'S POV OF HER LIVING ROOM. IT IS DARK. LIGHT SPILLING INTO THE ROOM FROM THE BEDROOM.

THE LIVING ROOM IS VERY DIRTY AND VERY UNTIDY. MISS SCOVER
DISAPPEARS INTO THE BEDROOM. SILENCE.
CURTAINS SHUT.
THEN SHE RE-EMERGES INTO THE LIVING ROOM HOLDING THE MONEY.

                MISS SCOVER
          How old are you?

                                  CUT TO:

165E. INT. MISS SCOVER'S HOUSE. DUSK/LATE AFTERNOON.

<u>HER POV</u> OF DAVID. HE TAKES A HALF STEP FORWARD THEN STOPS.

                    DAVID
                 Fifteen.

AND HOLDS OUT HIS HAND FOR THE MONEY.

                                  CUT TO:

165F. INT. MISS SCOVER'S HOUSE. DUSK/LATE AFTERNOON.

<u>DAVID'S POV</u> OF MISS SCOVER

                MISS SCOVER
        Do you deliver at night?

                                  CUT TO:

165G. INT. MISS SCOVER'S HOUSE. DUSK/LATE AFTERNOON.

<u>HER POV</u> OF DAVID.

                    DAVID
         Tuesdays and Thursdays.

                                  CUT TO:

165H. INT. MISS SCOVER'S HOUSE. DUSK/LATE AFTERNOON.

<u>DAVID'S POV</u> OF HER
MISS SCOVER MAKES NO ATTEMPT TO MOVE BUT OFFERS HIM THE MONEY.
SILENCE.

                MISS SCOVER
     Next time, come back Thursday.

AND SHE FLIPS A COIN AT HIM.

CUT TO:

165I. EXT. PORCH. DAVID'S HOUSE. LATE AFTERNOON/EARLY EVENING.

<u>CLOSE UP</u> DAVID. SILENCE.

                          DAVID
            (TO AUNT MAE BUT LOOKING DOWN AT HIMSELF)
                  Aunt Mae - how do I look?

CUT TO:

165J. EXT. PORCH. DAVID'S HOUSE. LATE AFTERNOON/EARLY EVENING.

HIS <u>POV</u> OF AUNT MAE.

                 AUNT MAE (LOOKING AT HIM)
    You'll be a fine looking boy in about a year or so ...
    your body's getting some lines ... and your face is
           getting to look like a man's too ...

CUT TO:

165K. EXT. PORCH. DAVID'S HOUSE. LATE AFTERNOON/EARLY EVENING.

<u>CLOSE UP</u> DAVID (<u>SIDEVIEW</u>)
HE LOOKS AWAY FROM AUNT MAE AND DIRECTLY AT CAMERA.

CUT TO:

165L. EXT. MISS SCOVER'S PORCH. LATE AFTERNOON/EARLY EVENING.

CATS ALL OVER THE PORCH. A LIGHT ON IN THE FRONT ROOM.
THE CATS SCATTER WHEN DAVID COMES ONTO THE PORCH AND RINGS
THE BELL.

CUT TO:

165M. EXT. MISS SCOVER'S PORCH. LATE AFTERNOON/EARLY EVENING.

<u>CLOSE UP</u> MISS SCOVER OPENING THE FRONT DOOR. SHE WEARS A
SILKY ROBE THIS TIME. HER FACE IN SHADOW BUT HER BOSSOM
OBVIOUS.

                     MISS SCOVER
            (HER VOICE THROATY AND NERVOUS)
         Come in, boy, while I get my purse.

CUT TO:

THE NEON BIBLE

165N INT. MISS SCOVER'S HOUSE. LATE AFTERNOON/EARLY EVENING.

HER POV OF DAVID

              DAVID
        No ... I can't ...

                                  CUT TO:

165O. EXT. MISS SCOVER'S PORCH. LATE AFTERNOON/EARLY EVENING.

DAVID'S POV OF HER

            MISS SCOVER
      Just for a little while ...
        It's damp out here ...

                                  CUT TO:

165 P. INT. MISS SCOVER'S HOUSE. LATE AFTERNOON/EARLY EVENING.

HER POV OF HIM

              DAVID
        (SHAKES HIS HEAD)
              No.

                                  CUT TO:

165Q. EXT. MISS SCOVER'S PORCH. LATE AFTERNOON/EARLY EVENING.

DAVID'S POV OF HER
SHE TAKES THE MONEY FROM HER ROBE AND THROWS IT AT HIM THEN SLAMS THE DOOR SHUT.

                               DISSOLVE TO:

165R. INT. DRUGSTORE. LATE AFTERNOON/EARLY EVENING.

THE INTERIOR OF THE SHOP IS FILLED WITH A RED LIGHT FROM THE LOW, RED, LATE AFTERNOON SUN.
SHOT OF DAVID TIDYING THE COUNTER (BACKVIEW?) THE DOORBELL TINKLES AND HE LOOKS UP/AROUND.

                                    CUT TO:

165S. INT. DRUGSTORE. LATE AFTERNOON/EARLY EVENING.

DAVID'S POV OF 4 OR 5 BOYS (THE ONES FROM THE SCHOOL FIELD TRIP WITH MISS MOORE).

THEY COME TOWARDS HIM IN A PACK.

>   HEAD BOY
>   Where are they?

(PAUSE)

>   Where does the old guy keep them? Under the counter?
>   Are they under the counter?

                                                    CUT TO:

165T. INT. DRUGSTORE. LATE AFTERNOON/EARLY EVENING.

<u>CLOSE UP</u> DAVID

>   DAVID
>   (HALF KNOWING WHAT THEY MEAN)
>   What?

                                                    CUT TO:

165U. INT. DRUGSTORE. LATE AFTERNOON/EARLY EVENING.

<u>DAVID'S POV</u> OF BOYS. THEY ARE A MIXTURE OF SCHOOLBOY BRAVADO AND EMBARRASSMENT. THEY GIGGLE.

>   HEAD BOY
>   You know! Them!

                                                    CUT TO:

165V. INT. DRUGSTORE. LATE AFTERNOON/EARLY EVENING.

<u>CLOSE UP</u> DAVID
HE DOESN'T ANSWER.

                                                    CUT TO:

165W. INT. DRUGSTOBE. LATE AFTERNOON/EARLY EVENING.

<u>DAVID'S POV</u> OF BOYS.

>   HEAD BOY
>   God, you're dumb! Rubbers!

THEY ALL SNIGGER.

                                                    CUT TO:

THE NEON BIBLE

165X. INT. DRUGSTORE. LATE AFTERNOON/EARLY EVENING.

<u>CLOSE UP</u> DAVID

                        DAVID
                 (VERY EMBARRASSED)
                 I don't know.

                                                     CUT TO:

165Y. INT. DRUGSTORE. LATE AFTERNOON/EARLY EVENING.

<u>DAVID'S POV</u> OF BOYS.

                       HEAD BOY
              Geez, he's <u>so dumb</u>!

THEY SWAGGER OUT.

                                                     CUT TO:

166. EXT. CINEMA. DUSK.

<u>MID SHOT</u> (<u>SIDEVIEW</u>) OF DAVID AND JO LYNNE IN THE QUEUE AS IT SHUFFLES FORWARD.

                     JO LYNNE
              How much is it?

                      DAVID
              30 cents apiece.

THE QUEUE SHUFFLES FORWARD REVEALING A POSTER FOR "MILDRED PIERCE" STARRING JOAN CRAWFORD.

                                                    CUT TO:

167. INT. CINEMA. NIGHT.

<u>2 SHOT</u> (FRONT) OF DAVID AND JO LYNNE'S HANDS. (DAVID RIGHT OF FRAME, JO LYNNE LEFT)
GINGERLY DAVID TAKES HER HAND AND SHE THEN CRADLES IT ON HER LAP.

<u>CRANE UP TO</u>:
<u>2 SHOT</u> DAVID AND JO LYNNE.
JO LYNNE IS RAPT AS SHE LOOKS AT THE SCREEN. DAVID CAN'T TAKE HIS EYES FROM JO LYNNE.

EVE ARDEN'S VOICE OVER
(FROM "MILDRED PIERCE")
Leave something on me, I might catch cold.

CONTINUE CRANE UP INTO DARKNESS TOWARDS PROJECTOR LIGHT.

JO LYNNE'S VOICE OVER
Let's go for a walk, let's go up and
see those houses they're building, David.

DAVID'S VOICE OVER
I thought your grandfather wanted you home.

PROJECTOR LIGHT FRAMED THEN CONTINUE CRANE TO DARKNESS.

JO LYNNE'S VOICE OVER
We won't be there long ... I just want to see ...

DISSOLVE TO:

168. EXT. HILL. NIGHT.

CRANE UP OUT OF DARKNESS TO FRAME DAVID AND JO LYNNE SITTING ON THE FRONT STEPS OF A HOUSE NOT YET COMPLETED (BACK VIEW). FRAMES OF HOUSES IN VARIOUS STAGES OF COMPLETION RUN DOWN THE HILL TOWARDS THE TOWN.
WIND IN THE TREES.

CUT TO:

169. EXT. HILL. NIGHT.

2 SHOT FRONTVIEW. DAVID AND JO LYNNE.

JO LYNNE
I liked the movie.

DAVID
So did I.

THEY LOOK AT EACH OTHER.
SILENCE EXCEPT FOR THE WIND IN THE TREES.
SLOWLY THEY GRAVITATE TOWARDS THEIR FIRST CLUMSY KISS.
THEY KISS.
SILENCE.
THEY LOOK AT THE UNFINISHED HOUSES. THEN DAVID PUTS HIS ARM AROUND HER.

CUT TO:

170. EXT. HILL. NIGHT.

<u>2 SHOT</u> (BACKVIEW) SHOULDER.
DAVID AND JO LYNNE, HIS ARM AROUND HER.

        EVE ARDEN'S VOICE OVER (FROM 'MILDRED PIERCE')
  You know I think alligators have the right idea - they eat
                         their young.

                                                              CUT TO:

171. INT. LIVING ROOM. DAVID'S HOUSE. NIGHT.

THE ROOM IS IN SEMI-DARKNESS, LIT ONLY BY THE MOONLIGHT FROM THE WINDOW AND THE ELECTRIC LIGHT FROM DOWN THE HALL IN THE KITCHEN.
<u>CLOSE UP</u> SARAH SHE JUST SITS IN THE HALF DARKNESS, STARING AT DAVID.
<u>HOLD</u> ON SHOT SILENCE

                      AUNT MAE'S VOICE OVER
              Sarah - Come and eat! Sarah!

SHE CONTINUES TO SIT THERE AND STARE. SILENCE

                                                             CUT TO:

172. INT. LIVING ROOM. DAVID'S HOUSE. NIGHT.

<u>CLOSE UP</u> DAVID AT THE WINDOW AND LIT FROM IT. (<u>SARAH'S POV</u>)
HE STARES AT MOTHER FOR A MOMENT THEN LOOKS AWAY - VERY UNEASY AT BEING WITH HER.
SILENCE. <u>HOLD</u> ON SHOT
THEN HE LOOKS OUT OF THE WINDOW.
AUNT MAE'S FOOTSTEPS ARE HEARD COMING UP THE HALL THEN INTO THE ROOM.
DAVID LOOKS TOWARDS THE DOOR.

                                                             CUT TO:

173. INT. LIVING ROOM. DAVID'S HOUSE. NIGHT.

<u>DAVID'S POV</u> <u>2 SHOT</u>. AUNT MAE COMING INTO THE ROOM. SARAH GETS UP FROM THE CHAIR AND EXITS.

                            AUNT MAE
            (USHERING HER TOWARDS THE KITCHEN)
                        Go eat, Sarah.

SARAH SHUFFLES SILENTLY OUT. <u>HOLD</u> ON SHOT
AUNT MAE SITS DOWN IN SARAH'S CHAIR.

                    AUNT MAE (UNEASY)
                Well, how was work today?

                                                            CUT TO:

174. INT. LIVING ROOM. DAVID'S HOUSE. NIGHT.

<u>CLOSE UP</u> DAVID NOT LOOKING AT HER.

                          DAVID
                Things were just slow but OK, I guess.
SILENCE.

                    AUNT MAE'S VOICE OVER
                      What's the matter?

                          DAVID
                   (QUICKLY LOOKING AT HER)
                         Nothing.

                                                            CUT TO:

175. INT. LIVING ROOM. DAVID'S HOUSE. NIGHT.

<u>CLOSE UP</u> AUNT MAE.
SILENCE.
SHE JUST LOOKS DOWN.

                          AUNT MAE
                I've got something to tell you, Dave.

AN UNEASY PAUSE.
SILENCE

                          AUNT MAE
                I got a letter from Clyde today.
                   (SHE OFFERS HIM THE LETTER)
                Here - read it for yourself.

                                                            CUT TO:

176. INT. LIVING ROOM. DAVID'S HOUSE. NIGHT.

<u>CLOSE UP</u> DAVID.
HE DOESN'T RESPOND EXCEPT TO LOOK AWAY.

                                                            CUT TO:

THE NEON BIBLE

177. INT. LIVING ROOM. DAVID'S HOUSE. NIGHT.

CLOSE UP AUNT MAE.

                        AUNT MAE
                  (NOW VERY AWKWARD)
Clyde thinks he can get us a good job, a permanent one in Nashville on the radio or records ...

SILENCE
                        AUNT MAE
   ... well, hon, what d'you think about it?

                                            CUT TO:

178. INT. LIVING ROOM. DAVID'S HOUSE. NIGHT.

CLOSE UP DAVID.

                        DAVID
            (LOOKING OUT OF THE WINDOW)
   I don't know, Aunt Mae, what does it mean?
               (HE LOOKS AT HER)
         What about me and mother?

                                            CUT TO:

179. INT. LIVING ROOM. DAVID'S HOUSE. NIGHT.

CLOSE UP AUNT MAE.

                        AUNT MAE
That's it, hon. If we get a job I can send for you two. Clyde thinks we could make a lot of money.

                                            CUT TO:

180. INT. LIVING ROOM. DAVID'S HOUSE. NIGHT.

CLOSE UP DAVID.

                        DAVID
                   (SCARED)
But what am I going to do with mother? I work all day, I can't leave her here alone -

                                            CUT TO:

181. INT. LIVING ROOM. DAVID'S HOUSE. NIGHT.

CLOSE UP AUNT MAE.

>   AUNT MAE (VERY GINGERLY)
>   She isn't any trouble. Look. Quit your job.

>   CUT TO:

182. INT. LIVING ROOM. DAVID'S HOUSE. NIGHT.

CLOSE UP DAVID

>   DAVID (INDIGNANT)
>   If I quit my job I'll lose about the best I could get
>   anywhere.

>   CUT TO:

183. INT. LIVING ROOM. DAVID'S HOUSE. NIGHT.

CLOSE UP AUNT MAE

>   AUNT MAE (QUIETLY INSISTENT)
>   Quit your job at the store. Then you can stay here all day
>   with mother, d'you hear? In a week, maybe two, you'll get the
>   tickets for Nashville from me ...

>   CUT TO:

184. INT. LIVING ROOM. DAVID'S HOUSE. NIGHT.

CLOSE UP DAVID
HE IS SILENT. COMPLETELY OUTMANOEUVRED BY THE FAIT ACCOMPLI.

>   AUNT MAE'S VOICE OVER
>   There's nothing to worry about, hon, really.

>   CUT TO:

185. INT. LIVING ROOM. DAVID'S HOUSE. NIGHT.

CLOSE UP AUNT MAE

>   AUNT MAE
>   It's a big chance for me, Dave. I can get on the radio and
>   records - and I'll be getting enough money for you to quit
>   work and join me.

LONG PAUSE
>
> AUNT MAE
> Look, hon, I'm taking the bus out of here the day after tomorrow. And don't worry. It won't be long before you and mother get a train ticket from me, you hear?

SILENCE
>
> AUNT MAE
> Now, tell MR Williams tomorrow that you want to quit.

<u>PAN</u> (<u>LEFT TO RIGHT</u>) FROM AUNT MAE TO SARAH IN THE DOORWAY. SHE CARRIES PINECONES IN HER SKIRT. SHE IS SMILING.

> SARAH
> There.
> You see how they're growing? From a little seed your Poppa planted they're growing all over, but I saw them come up in the clearing first.
> I saw them first.

>> CUT TO:

186. INT. LIVING ROOM. DAVID'S HOUSE. NIGHT.

<u>CLOSE UP</u> DAVID AT THE WINDOW.
HE LOOKS OUT.

> DAVID'S VOICE OVER
> Everything was changing ... Mother ... Aunt Mae ... and then Jo Lynne left.

>> CUT TO:

186A. INT. KITCHEN. DAVID'S HOUSE. DAY.

<u>SHOT OF</u> SARAH AT SINK.
BLOOD COMING FROM HER MOUTH. SHE COUGHS. THEN SHE CATCHES SIGHT OF SOMEONE. SHE LOOKS TOWARDS THE CAMERA.

> SARAH (SHOUTING)
> GET OUT!

>> CUT TO:

187. INT. DRUGSTORE. DAY.

<u>CLOSE UP</u> DAVID. HE IS SLAPPED HARD ACROSS THE FACE. HE IS MOMENTARILY STUNNED.

>> CUT TO:

188. INT. DRUGSTORE. DAY.

CLOSE UP JO LYNNE

>   JO LYNNE (FRIGHTENED)
> What's the matter with you? We only went out once ...
>   let me go! ...

                                                    CUT TO:

189. INT. DRUGSTORE. DAY.

2 SHOT (SIDEVIEW) DAVID AND JO LYNNE. HE HAS HOLD OF HER AND SHE STRUGGLES TO GET FREE.

TRACK WITH THEM (LEFT TO RIGHT) TOWARDS THE DOOR.

>   DAVID
> We could get married, Jo Lynne, the State'll marry us ...

SHE IS NOW VERY FRIGHTENED AND SLAPS HIM AGAIN IN THE FACE.

>   JO LYNNE (CRYING)
>   Let me go!
>   You're crazy - like your mother!

SHE BREAKS AWAY FROM HIM.
PAN WITH HER (LEFT TO RIGHT) AS SHE RUNS OUT OF THE DOOR OF THE STORE. SHE IS CRYING.

                                                    CUT TO:

190. INT. DRUGSTORE. DAY.

CLOSE UP DAVID, HIS FACE BLEEDING. HE STANDS THERE FOR A SECOND THEN WIPES THE BLOOD AWAY. SOME OF IT DROPS ON HIS SHIRT.

                                                    CUT TO:

191. INT. DRUGSTORE. EVENING.

SHOT OF DOUBLE DOORS LEADING TO THE STREET.
DAVID WALKS INTO SHOT. HE FINISHES PUTTING HIS COAT ON AND PUTS THE 'CLOSED' SIGN ON THE DOOR.

                                                    CUT TO:

THE NEON BIBLE

192. INT. DRUGSTORE. EVENING.

<u>SHOT OF</u> MR WILLIAMS COMING OUT OF THE DISPENSARY. HE IS PUTTING ON HIS COAT. HE WALKS TO THE TILL. <u>PAN WITH HIM</u> (<u>RIGHT TO LEFT</u>)

          MR. WILLIAMS
      Well, goodnight, David.

                                          CUT TO:

193. INT. DRUGSTORE. EVENING.

<u>CLOSE UP</u> DAVID

              DAVID
     I have to quit, MR Williams.

                                          CUT TO:

194. INT. DRUGSTORE. EVENING.

<u>CLOSE UP</u> MR WILLIAMS

       MR. WILLIAMS (SMILING)
     Are you making fun, David?

                                          CUT TO:

195. INT. DRUGSTORE. EVENING.

<u>CLOSE UP</u> DAVID

              DAVID
No, MR Williams, I really mean it. I have to leave because Aunt Mae is going to Nashville tomorrow and there's no one to look after Mother but me.

                                          CUT TO:

196. INT. DRUGSTORE. EVENING.

<u>CLOSE UP</u> MR WILLIAMS

          MR. WILLIAMS
But you need to earn money, David. You can't do it all alone ... she could get help. Rev. Watkins could help ...

                                          CUT TO:

197. INT. DRUGSTORE. EVENING.

CLOSE UP DAVID

                        DAVID
                       (ANGRY)
  No one's going to take my mother to the crazy house or the
      poor folks asylum! I won't let anyone touch her!

HE CALMS DOWN THEN LOOKS AT MR WILLIAMS.

                                                                   CUT TO:

198. INT. DRUGSTORE. EVENING.

2 SHOT MR WILLIAMS (FRAME LEFT) AND ACROSS THE COUNTER (FRAME RIGHT) DAVID.

                     MR. WILLIAMS
                      (QUIETLY)
              Alright, David, alright.

HE TURNS AROUND TO THE CASH REGISTER AND TAKES SOME MONEY OUT, PUTS IT IN AN ENVELOPE AND GIVES IT TO DAVID, WHO TAKES IT AND PUTS IT IN HIS POCKET.

                        DAVID
            Thank you, MR Williams.

THEY SHAKE HANDS.

                                                                    CUT TO:

199. INT. AUNT MAE'S BEDROOM. DAY.

2 SHOT DAVID (FRAME LEFT) AUNT MAE (FRAME RIGHT). HE WATCHES HER PACK.
SHE FINISHES.
DAVID PICKS UP HER SCRAPBOOK AND HANDS IT TO HER. SHE PUTS IT INSIDE THE CASE AND CLOSES IT.
THEN PUTS HER HAT ON WITH A PIN IN IT.

                                                                   CUT TO:

200. EXT. PORCH. DAY 200.

A WIND GETTING UP.
SHOT (SIDEVIEW) OF AUNT MAE COMING OUT OF THE HOUSE FOLLOWED BY DAVID.

THE NEON BIBLE

SHE STOPS AT THE TOP OF THE PORCH STEPS AND PUTS DOWN HER SUITCASE WHICH HAS LABELS OF "NEW ORLEANS", "BILOXI" AND "MOBILE" ON IT.
DAVID CLOSES THE FRONT DOOR.

> AUNT MAE
> Where's Sarah?

> DAVID
> Out back somewheres - shall I get her?

> AUNT MAE
> No, hon, there isn't time.

CUT TO:

201. EXT. BARBER'S SHOP. DAY.

WIND GETTING STRONGER.
2 SHOT (FRONTVIEW) DAVID AND AUNT MAE SITTING ON A BENCH IN FRONT OF THE BARBER'S SHOP WAITING FOR THE BUS.
SILENCE BETWEEN THEM.

CUT TO:

202. EXT. BARBER'S SHOP. DAY.

CLOSE UP DAVID (SIDEVIEW. AUNT MAE POV) HE JUST LOOKS AT HER. HOLD

CUT TO:

203. EXT. BARBER'S SHOP. DAY.

CLOSE UP AUNT MAE (SIDEVIEW DAVID'S POV)
SHE LOOKS UP AND DOWN THE STREET THEN LOOKS AT DAVID.
HER EYES FULL OF TEARS.

> AUNT MAE
> (A SAD SMILE)
> It's the cold breeze, hon,
> always makes my eyes water.

CUT TO:

204. EXT. MAIN STREET. BUS. DAY.

THE BUS COMES INTO SHOT (RIGHT TO LEFT), THE WINDOWS FILLING THE FRAME.

CUT TO:

205. EXT. MAIN STREET. BUS. DAY.

SHOT (<u>SIDEVIEW</u>) OF AUNT MAE AND DAVID RUNNING TOWARDS THE BUS, DAVID CARRYING HER SUITCASE.

THEY GET TO THE BUS. AUNT MAE KISSES DAVID, HE KISSES HER. SHE TAKES HER CASE AND GETS ON BOARD.

CUT TO:

206. EXT. MAIN STREET. BUS. DAY.

AS IN SCENE 204 (<u>DAVID'S POV</u>)
AUNT MAE MOVES DOWN INSIDE THE DARK INTERIOR OF THE BUS AND WAVES TO DAVID.

THE BUS MOVES OFF.

SOUNDTRACK:
THE INTRODUCTION TO STEPHEN FOSTER'S "HARD TIMES COME AGAIN NO MORE" IS HEARD.

THE BUS MOVES OFF, KICKING UP DUST. (<u>PAN</u> WITH IT LEFT TO RIGHT). <u>HOLD</u> AS IT DRIVES OFF FOR EVER.
THE WIND (WHICH IS GETTING STRONGER ALL THE TIME) MAKES THE DUST SWIRL, COMPLETELY OBSCURING THE BUS.

SPFX DISSOLVE TO:

207. EXT. MAIN STREET. DAY.

THE DUST SWIRLS AWAY TO REVEAL <u>CLOSE UP</u> DAVID.

HE WAVES AND SMILES SADLY AS HE WATCHES AUNT MAE GO AWAY FOREVER.

SOUNDTRACK:

BARITONE BEGINS TO SING THE STEPHEN FOSTER.
 "There are sounds in life's pleasures
  and countless many tears,
 While we all sup sorrow with the fool,
 There's a song that will linger for ever in our ears,
  Oh, hard times come again no more ..."

THE NEON BIBLE

THE WIND PICKS UP A BLOWS DUST AND BUS FUMES AT HIM. HE BLANCHES.
THE WIND GETS STRONGER AND BLOWS THE WHITE DUST AROUND HIM UNTIL IT COMPLETELY OBSCURES HIM.
THEN
SPFX/DISSOLVE
THEN THE DUST CLEARS TO REVEAL

208. EXT. DAVID'S HOUSE. DUSK.

SOUNDTRACK: "HARD TIMES COME AGAIN NO MORE" CONTINUES.

>   "'Tis the sound, the sigh of the weary,
> Hard times, hard times come again no more,
>   Many days you have lingered around
>   My cabin door,
>   Oh, hard times come again no more ..."

A HIGH WIND.
DAVID RUNS UP TOWARDS THE HOUSE.
PAN WITH HIM (LEFT TO RIGHT) TO HOUSE WHICH IS IN DARKNESS EXCEPT FOR A WEAK LIGHT IN THE KITCHEN. FRONT DOOR OPEN AND BANGING IN THE WIND.

DAVID RUNS UP THE PORCH STEPS AND GOES INSIDE THE HOUSE.
TRACK (FROM BEHIND) WITH HIM INTO THE HOUSE.

                                             DISSOLVE TO:

209. INT. DAVID'S HOUSE. HALL. DUSK.

TRACK BACK FROM FRONT DOOR AS DAVID COMES THROUGH IT.
THE FRONT AND SCREEN DOORS BANG IN THE WIND. DAVID CLOSES THEM.

SOUNDTRACK: "HARD TIMES" CONTINUES.

>   "'Tis the sigh that is wafted across the troubled wave,
>   'Tis the wail that is heard about the shore,
>   'Tis a dirge that is murmured around a lowly grave,
>   Oh, hard times come again no more ..."

CONTINUE TRACKING BACK AND TO SIDEVIEW OF DAVID AS HE LOOKS INTO THE DARK LIVING ROOM AND THEN WALKS ALONG THE HALL TOWARDS THE STAIRS.

                    DAVID (SOFTLY)
                      Mother! ...

NO REPLY
CONTINUE TRACKING (LEFT TO RIGHT) AS DAVID GOES UP THE STAIRS.

                         DAVID
                       Mother ...

THEN (CONTINUE TRACKING LEFT TO RIGHT) PRECEDE HIM ALONG THE
HALL, ALONG THE STAIRS THEN CRANE UP TO THE LANDING.
BLOOD DRIPS FROM THE LANDING.

            DAVID'S VOICE OVER (COUNTING THE STAIRS)
                       13 - 14 - 15 ...

TRACK INTO THE BLOOD DRIPPING AND BEYOND THE BANISTERS A BUNDLE
- BARELY VISIBLE IN THE HALF LIGHT COMING FROM THE KITCHEN.

SOUNDTRACK: "HARD TIMES" CONTINUES.

            "'Tis the sound, the sigh of the weary,
           Hard times, hard times, come again no more,
              Many days you have lingered around
                        My cabin door,
             Oh, hard times come again no more ..."

CRANE UP OVER THE LANDING BANNISTERS AND THE BUNDLE AND
PAN (LEFT TO RIGHT) TO DAVID COMING UP THE STAIRS ONTO THE
LANDING AND THEN TOWARDS CAMERA.
DAVID WALKS INTO CLOSE UP A LOOK OF HORROR DAWNING ON HIS
FACE. HE STARTS TO CRY.
                                                    CUT TO:

210. INT. LANDING. DUSK.

CLOSE UP MOTHER. SHE IS WRAPPED IN A BLANKET, BLOOD BUBBLING
FROM HER MOUTH.

                                                    CUT TO:

211. INT. LANDING. DUSK.

CLOSE UP SIDEVIEW MOTHER AND DAVID.
HE KNEELS DOWN AND TAKES HER HEAD IN HIS HANDS.

                        DAVID (CRYING)
                      Mother - Mother ...

THE NEON BIBLE

HE DOESN'T KNOW WHAT TO DO.

                                                                      CUT TO:

212. INT. LANDING. DUSK.

SHOT OF DAVID AND MOTHER (HEAD-ON).
HE PUTS HIS HANDS UNDER HER ARMS AND DRAGS HER TO THE FARTHER BEDROOM AND PUTS HER ON THE BED.

                                                                      CUT TO:

213. INT. MOTHER'S BEDROOM. DUSK..

CLOSE UP (SIDEVIEW) OF MOTHER ON BED, DAVID KNEELING AT HER SIDE, FACING CAMERA.

SOUNDTRACK: "HARD TIMES" CONTINUES.

> "While we seek mirth and beauty
> and music light and gay,
> There are frail forms fainting at the door
> Though their voices are silent,
> their pleading looks will say,
> Oh, hard times come again no more"

DAVID PULLS THE BLANKET AROUND MOTHER AND TRIES TO STAUNCH THE BLOOD COMING FROM HER MOUTH WITH PART OF IT.
BUT IT'S NO USE. SHE DRIFTS INTO AND OUT OF CONSCIOUSNESS.
HE STROKES HER FOREHEAD AS SHE STARTS TO HAVE DIFFICULTY BREATHING.
DAVID CANNOT STOP CRYING.
HOLD

                                                                       CUT TO:

214. INT. MOTHER'S BEDROOM. DUSK.

SHOT OF DAVID AND MOTHHER ON BED (FRONTVIEW).
DAVID (STILL CRYING) IS SITTING ON THE BED NEXT TO MOTHER WHO IS IN HIS ARMS IN A HALF SITTING POSITION.
HE CRADLES HER GENTLY.
HOLD

SOUNDTRACK: "HARD TIMES" CONTINUES.

> "'Tis the sound, the sigh of the weary,
> Hard times, hard times come again no more,
> Many days you have lingered Around my cabin door,
> Oh, hard times come again no more."

HER BREATHING BECOMES "LIKE A SIGH, A SORT OF CHOKING SIGH".
SHE TREMBLES FOR A MOMENT AND HER LIPS MOVE WITH DIFFICULTY
AS SHE TRIES TO SPEAK

                    MOTHER
                 (SOFTLY DYING)
                    Frank ...

HER BREATHING STOPS AND SHE LAYS STILL IN DAVID'S ARMS. HE
CANNOT STOP CRYING AS HE CRADLES HER.
HE PUTS HIS FACE TO HERS AND KISSES HER.
<u>TRACK</u> AND <u>PAN AWAY</u> (<u>RIGHT TO LEFT</u>) TO BEDROOM WINDOW.
OUTSIDE THE PINES ARE LASHED IN THE HEAVY WIND.
<u>SPFX</u> THEN
THE WIND DROPS THEN DUSK TURNS INTO NIGHT.

                                                                       <u>CUT TO:</u>

215. EXT. BACK OF DAVID'S HOUSE. NIGHT.

<u>SHOT OF</u> DAVID FROM BEHIND FINISHING DIGGING A SHALLOW GRAVE.
HE IS KNEELING.
TO HIS RIGHT THE BODY OF HIS MOTHER WRAPPED IN A BLANKET.
HER FEET EXPOSED.
DAVID IS LIT FROM THE LIGHT COMING FROM THE KITCHEN WINDOW.
HE DRAGS HER LITTLE BODY AND PUTS IT IN THE GRAVE AND COVERS
IT WITH EARTH.
HE KNEELS THERE FOR A MOMENT.

                                                                       <u>CUT TO:</u>

216. EXT. BACK OF DAVID'S HOUSE. NIGHT 216.

<u>SHOT OF</u> DAVID GETTING UP FROM THE GRAVE AND WALKING TOWARDS A
WATER BUTT, JUST BELOW THE KITCHEN WINDOW. AS HE APPROACHES
IT HE THROWS THE SHOVEL UNDER THE HOUSE.
<u>TRACK WITH HIM</u> FROM BEHIND.
<u>TRACK STOPS</u> WHEN HE IS AT THE WATER BUTT.
HE WASHES OFF THE DIRT AND BLOOD FROM HIS FACE AND HANDS.
SUDDENLY A NOISE IS HEARD AND HE LOOKS UP QUICKLY.
ANOTHER NOISE AND QUIETLY DAVID MOVES TOWARDS THE BACK DOOR
OF THE HOUSE.

                                                                       <u>CUT TO:</u>

217. INT. HALL. DAVID'S HOUSE. NIGHT.

<u>SHOT OF</u> DAVID BEHIND THE SCREEN DOOR OF THE DOOR AT THE BACK
OF THE HOUSE.

                    MAN'S VOICE OVER
                      Hello, Son.

                           DAVID
                  (COMING INTO THE HALL)
                     My name's David.
               (HE TAKES A STEP OR TWO FORWARD)
                     What do you want?

                                                      CUT TO:

218. INT. HALL. DAVID'S HOUSE. NIGHT.

SHOT OF A MAN BY THE FRONT DOOR. HE IS IN SILHOUETTE IN THE DARKNESS. HIS FACE CANNOT BE SEEN.

                            MAN
    I'm here on behalf of the State, son. Now you know your mother
         needs a better place to stay, you can't take care of
       her by yourself. With your Aunt here it was different ...

                                                      CUT TO:

219. INT. HALL. DAVID'S HOUSE. NIGHT.

CLOSE UP DAVID (HEAD ON BY KITCHEN DOOR)

                           DAVID
              She isn't going with you. She isn't here.

                                                      CUT TO:

220. INT. HALL/STAIRS. DAVID'S HOUSE. NIGHT.

MAN STARTS UP STAIRS.

                            MAN
        Now son, you don't understand - I'll get her myself.

                                                      CUT TO:

221. INT. HALL. DAVID'S HOUSE. NIGHT.

CLOSE UP DAVID

                       DAVID (SCARED)
         She's not up there. You can't come in here like that ...

HE WATCHES THE MAN GO UP THE STAIRS

> MAN'S VOICE OVER
> I want to see that what's done is best for us all ...

DAVID FRANTIC

> DAVID (SHOUTING)
> Get the hell out of this house, you bastard!

> MAN'S VOICE OVER
> I won't listen to any more of your profanity, boy.

CUT TO:

222. INT. KITCHEN. DAVID'S HOUSE. NIGHT.

<u>SHOT OF</u> DAVID IN HALL, FRANTIC. HE TAKES THE SHOTGUN FROM INSIDE THE KITCHEN DOOR.

> DAVID
> Get out!

HE RAISES THE GUN AND FIRES.
THE MAN IS HEARD FALLING THEN HIS BODY SLIDES DOWN THE STAIRS. HIS HEAD AND SHOULDERS IN FRONT OF DAVID.
THE MAN'S FACE IS TURNED TOWARDS THE CAMERA. BLOOD OOZES FROM THE BACK OF HIS HEAD AND DRIPS DOWN. IT IS REVEREND WATKINS.
THE KICK FROM THE GUN HAS SPUN DAVID BACK INTO THE KITCHEN.
HE LOOKS AT THE MAN THEN LOOKS AWAY - HORRIFIED BY WHAT HE HAS DONE.
HE DROPS THE GUN AND SHIVERS. HIS HANDS WRAPPING AROUND HIS BODY.
HE FEELS SOMETHING IN HIS COAT AND TAKES IT OUT.
IT IS THE ENVELOPE CONTAINING THE MONEY FROM MR WILLIAMS.
HE IS STILL FOR A MOMENT.
THEN HE HAS DECIDED.
HE RUNS FROM THE HOUSE.
THE BODY OF REVEREND WATKINS LIES ON THE STAIRS, BLOOD DRIPPING.
<u>TRACK IN</u> ON REVEREND WATKINS' BODY.

> DAVID'S VOICE OVER (AGED 16)
> I didn't ask the conductor where this train went.
> I know I should, but I just gave him Mr Williams' envelope and told him to let me off where it didn't pay for the ride anymore ...

<u>CRANE DOWN</u> TO BLACKNESS.
THEN

DISSOLVE TO:

223. EXT. TRAIN. NIGHT.

<u>HIGH SHOT OF</u> TRAIN AS IT MOVES THROUGH THE NIGHT
(MOVING <u>RIGHT TO LEFT</u> ACROSS THE FRAME).

                    DAVID'S VOICE OVER (AGED 16)
Maybe they're up at the house now too. But I'm not scared now with the train getting this far away ...

<u>CRANE DOWN</u> TO WINDOW

                    DAVID'S VOICE OVER (AGED 16)
Maybe I'll get a job. Maybe I'll save some money and go to Nashville to look for Aunt Mae. I guess they think that's where I am. I guess they think I went to look for her.

DAVID BEHIND THE GLASS LOOKING OUT OF THE WINDOW INTO
THE BLACKNESS. HE TURNS AND LOOKS DOWN THE INSIDE OF THE
CARRIAGE.

                                              DISSOLVE TO:

224. INT. TRAIN. NIGHT.

<u>CLOSE UP</u> (<u>HEAD ON</u>) DAVID AT THE WINDOW. HE IS VERY TIRED AND
YAWNS THEN LOOKS DOWN THE INTERIOR OF THE CARRIAGE.

                                              DISSOLVE TO:

225. INT. TRAIN. NIGHT.

<u>DAVID'S POV</u> THE CARRIAGE CONTAINS A SOLDIER SLEEPING AND AN
OLD LADY TRYING TO KEEP AWAKE. THE BLACK CONDUCTOR WALKS DOWN
THE AISLE (AWAY FROM CAMERA).

                                              DISSOLVE TO:

226. INT. TRAIN. NIGHT.

DAVID <u>CLOSE UP</u> (<u>SIDEVIEW</u>) HE FALLS ASLEEP. THROUGH THE WINDOW
BLACKNESS AND A MOON.

                      MR. FARNEY'S VOICE OVER
          (READING LONGFELLOW'S "LIGHT OF STARS")
     "The night is come, but not too soon;
            And sinking silently,
        All silently, the little moon,
       Drops down behind the sky."

TRACK IN ON THE WINDOW TO THE DARKNESS OUTSIDE.

> MR. FARNEY'S VOICE OVER
> "There is no light in earth or heaven
> But the cold light of stars;
> And the first watch of night is given
> To the red planet Mars."

DISSOLVE TO:

227. EXT. TRAIN. NIGHT.

DAVID ASLEEP BEHIND THE WINDOW. TRACK BACK TO MID LONG SHOT.

> MAN'S VOICE OVER
> "Is it the tender star of love?
> The star of love and dreams?
> O no! from that blue tent above,
> A hero's armor gleams ..."

HOLD ON LONG SHOT

> "And earnest thoughts within me rise,
> When I behold afar,
> Suspended in the evening skies,
> The shield of that red star ..."

THEN SPFX
WHILST THE SHOT OF DAVID SLEEPING BEHIND THE WINDOW OF THE CARRIAGE REMAINS STATIC CENTRE FRAME THE REST OF THE TRAIN FLIES BY THROUGH THE SHOT OF DAVID AND STROBES (RIGHT TO LEFT). THE TRAIN SEEMS TO HAVE NO END.

> MR. FARNEY'S VOICE OVER
> "O star of strength! I see thee stand
> And smile upon my pain;
> Thou beckonest with thy hand,
> And I am strong again ..."

PAN AWAY (RIGHT TO LEFT):

"THE NEON BIBLE" LIT UP AND FILLING THE FRAME AMIDST THE SURROUNDING DARKNESS.

> MR. FARNEY'S VOICE OVER
> "Within my breast there is no light
> But the cold light of stars;

THE NEON BIBLE

> I give the first watch of the night
> To the red planet Mars.
>
> "The star of the unconquered will,
> He rises in my breast,
> Serene, and resolute, and still,
> And calm, and self-possessed."

DISSOLVE TO:

228. EXT. TRAIN. NIGHT.

<u>LONG SHOT OF</u> THE TRAIN MOVING ACROSS THE HORIZON (<u>RIGHT TO LEFT</u>). BEHIND IT IN THE SKY DAWN IS BREAKING.
<u>HOLD</u> ON SHOT

> MR. FARNEY'S VOICE OVER
> "And thou, too, whosoe'er thou art,
> That readest this brief psalm,
> As one by one thy hopes depart,
> Be resolute and calm ..."

THE TRAIN LEAVES FRAME AND DISAPPEARS. <u>HOLD</u> ON THE <u>SHOT OF</u> THE HORIZON.
DAWN GETTING BRIGHTER AND BRIGHTER.

> MR. FARNEY'S VOICE OVER
> "O fear not in a world like this,
> And thou shalt know erelong,
> Know how sublime a thing it is
> To suffer and be strong."

THE SUN IS NOW FULLY UP. A BRILLIANT NEW DAY.
<u>HOLD</u> ON SHOT
CLOSING CREDITS

THE END

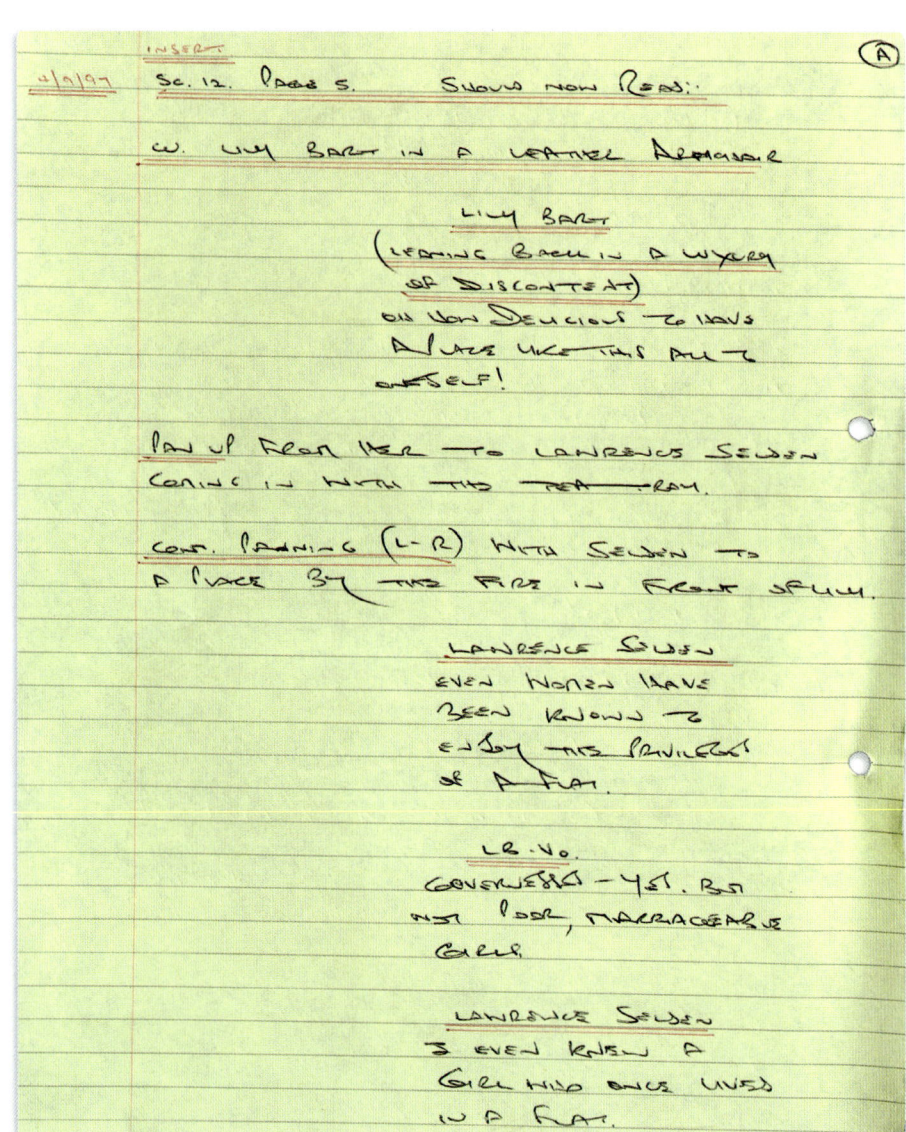

The House of Mirth (2000): first draft, Scene 12 insert. (© The Terence Davies Estate, held by the Terence Davies Archive at Edge Hill University)

THE HOUSE OF MIRTH (2000)

The House of Mirth (2000): Gillian Anderson as Lily Bart.

The House of Mirth
30 September 1997 (2nd Draft)

Cast and crew of *The House of Mirth* include:

LILY BART	Gillian Anderson
LAWRENCE SELDEN	Eric Stoltz
GUS TRENOR	Dan Aykroyd
MRS PENISTON	Eleanor Bron
GEORGE DORSET	Terry Kinney
BERTHA DORSET	Laura Linney
SIMON ROSEDALE	Anthony LaPaglia
GRACE STEPNEY	Jodhi May
MRS CARRY FISHER	Elizabeth McGovern
Written and Directed by	Terence Davies
From the novel by	Edith Wharton
Producer	Olivia Stewart
Director of Photography	Remi Adefarasin
Editor	Michael Parker
Production Designer	Don Taylor
Costume Designer	Monica Howe
Music Director	Adrian Johnston
Casting	Kerry Barden, Billy Hopkins, Suzanne Smith Crowley

A Three Rivers Ltd production (2000) with:
Granada Film Ltd / The Arts Council of England / Film Four / The Scottish Arts Council / Showtime / The Scottish Film Fund.

"THE HOUSE OF MIRTH"

SCREENPLAY BY
TERENCE DAVIES
ADAPTED FROM THE NOVEL BY
EDITH WHARTON

Developed with the support of Channel Four Films
and the MEDIA Programme of the European Union

2nd DRAFT
SEPTEMBER 30th 1997

OPENING CREDITS
A SERIES OF PRINTS OF OLD NEW YORK.

SOUNDTRACK: THE SLOW MOVEMENT OF THE MARCELLO OBOE CONCERTO IS HEARD.
IT RUNS UNDERNEATH THE CREDITS AND OPENING SEQUENCE.
THE FINAL PRINT IS OF THE INTERIOR OF GRAND CENTRAL STATION.
HOLD.
GRADUALLY - IN A LONG DISSOLVE - IT COMES TO LIFE.

TITLE: 'NEW YORK 1905'.

                                              DISSOLVE TO:

1. INT. DAY. PLATFORM, GRAND CENTRAL STATION. A STEAM TRAIN PULLING INTO THE PLATFORM.

SOUNDTRACK: THE MARCELLO OBOE CONCERTO CONTINUES.
THE TRAIN STOPS - STEAM RISING FROM THE ENGINE.
THE STEAM FILLS THE ENTIRE FRAME TO WHITE.

                                   DISSOLVE (OUT OF WHITE) TO:

2. INT. DAY. PLATFORM, GRAND CENTRAL STATION.

SHOT OF STEAM - LILY BART EMERGES FROM IT. SHE WALKS TOWARD CAMERA.
A GROUP OF LADIES WITH UNFURLED PARASOLS WALK PAST HER, OBLITERATING HER.
TRACK WITH THE PARASOLS (R-L). THEY LEAVE FRAME REVEALING:
LAWRENCE SELDEN WALKING ACROSS THE CONCOURSE.

SOUNDTRACK: THE MARCELLO OBOE CONCERTO CONTINUES.
SELDEN STOPS AND LOOKS OVER AT LILY BART.
TRACK STOPS.
                                                    CUT TO:
SELDEN'S POV OF LILY.

SOUNDTRACK: THE MARCELLO OBOE CONCERTO CONTINUES.
PAN WITH LILY BART (L-R) IN MID-LONG SHOT AS SHE WALKS THROUGH THE STATION AMIDST THE CROWD.
TRACK IN ON HER.
WHEN WE GET TO MEDIUM CLOSE UP SHE STOPS.

TRACK STOPS.

SOUNDTRACK: THE MUSIC ENDS. SHE LOOKS DIRECTLY AT CAMERA.

THE HOUSE OF MIRTH

> LILY BART (SMILING)
> Mr. Selden - What luck!

<u>CUT TO:</u>

<u>CLOSE UP</u> LAWRENCE SELDEN.

> LAWRENCE SELDEN (SMILING)
> Good luck?

<u>CUT TO:</u>

<u>CLOSE UP</u> LILY BART.

> LILY BART (SMILING)
> Yes. I'm on my way to the Gus Trenors at Bellomont and I've missed the 3.15 to Rhinebeck and there isn't another train 'til half-past five.
>
> How nice of you to come to my rescue!

<u>CUT TO:</u>

<u>CLOSE UP</u> LAWRENCE SELDEN.

> LAWRENCE SELDEN
> It's my mission in life.
> (SMILING)
> And what form should my rescue take?

<u>CUT TO:</u>

<u>CLOSE UP</u> LILY BART.

> LILY BART
> Oh almost any.

THEY BEGIN TO MOVE OFF.

<u>CUT TO:</u>

<u>2 SHOT</u> (<u>FRONT VIEW</u>) LAWRENCE SELDEN AND LILY BART.
<u>TRACK BACK</u> WITH THEM AS THEY WALK.

> LAWRENCE SELDEN
> Shall we go over to Sherry's for a cup of tea?
>
> LILY BART (GRIMACING SLIGHTLY)
> I'm dying for tea - but isn't there a quieter place?
>
> LAWRENCE SELDEN (TESTING THE WATER)
> I live near here.
>
> LILY BART
> (KNOWING THAT SHE SHOULDN'T)
> At 'The Benedick' still?

                    LAWRENCE SELDEN
                         Yes ...
                    (THROWING THE BAIT)
                   ... on the top floor.

                       LILY BART
                   Is it cool up there?

            LAWRENCE SELDEN (TOUCHING HER ARM)
                     Come up and see.

LILLY BART STOPS. SO DOES SELDEN.

                                                      CUT TO:

CLOSE UP LILY BART.
                       LILY BART
               (AFTER A PAUSE. TAKING HIS ARM)
                    I'll take the risk.

                                                      CUT TO:

CLOSE UP LAWRENCE SELDEN.

                LAWRENCE SELDEN (CHARMING)
                   Oh I'm not dangerous.

                                                      CUT TO:

3. INT. DAY. LAWRENCE SELDEN'S APARTMENT. THE BENEDICK.

CLOSE UP LILY BART IN A LEATHER ARMCHAIR.

                       LILY BART
              (LEANING BACK IN A LUXURY OF DISCONTENT.)
    Oh how delicious to have a place like this all to oneself!

PAN UP FROM HER TO SELDEN COMING IN WITH THE TEA TRAY.
CONTINUE PANNING (L-R) WITH SELDEN TO A PLACE BY THE FIRE IN
FRONT OF LILY.

                    LAWRENCE SELDEN
   Even women have been known to enjoy the privileges of a flat.

                 LILY BART (VOICE OVER)
     Governesses - yes. But not poor, marriageable girls.

                    LAWRENCE SELDEN
        I even knew a girl who once lived in a flat.

                                                      CUT TO:

THE HOUSE OF MIRTH

<u>CLOSE UP</u> LILY BART.

      LILY BART
   Oh you mean Grace Stepney
    (SMILES UNKINDLY)
   I said 'marriageable'.

              <u>CUT TO:</u>

<u>2 SHOT</u>.
THEY BOTH LAUGH.

      LILY BART
It was horrible of me to say that about my own cousin, but I do sometimes feel that Grace is the possessor of an unscrupulous good nature.

THEY BOTH SMILE.
A MOMENTARY PAUSE.

              <u>CUT TO:</u>

<u>CLOSE UP</u> LILY BART.

      LILY BART
But if I were as dutiful a niece as she I would now be at Richfield playing Bezique with Aunt Julia.

Oh! If l could only do over my Aunt's drawing room I know I should be a better woman.

              <u>CUT TO:</u>

<u>CLOSE UP</u> LAWRENCE SELDEN.

     LAWRENCE SELDEN
    (SYMPATHETICALLY)
   Is it so very bad?

              <u>CUT TO:</u>

<u>CLOSE UP</u> LILY BART.

      LILY BART
That shows how seldom you come there. Why don't you come oftener?

              <u>CUT TO:</u>

<u>CLOSE UP</u> LAWRENCE SELDEN.

     LAWRENCE SELDEN
When I do come it's not to look at Mrs Peniston's furniture.

<u>2 SHOT</u> LILY BART AND LAWRENCE SELDEN (LILY <u>FRAME RIGHT</u>. SELDEN <u>FRAME LEFT</u>.)

LILY LEANS FORWARD AND PUTS HER CUP ON THE TRAY IN FRONT OF SELDEN.

      LILY BART
   Nonsense. You don't come at all - and yet
    we get on so well when we meet.

                CUT TO:

SELDEN POURS TEA FOR BOTH OF THEM.

      LAWRENCE SELDEN
     Cream or lemon?

      LILY BART
      Lemon.

SELDEN SLICES THE LEMON, PUTS THE LEMON INTO BOTH CUPS AND HANDS LILY HER TEA.

                CUT TO:

<u>CLOSE UP</u> LILY BART.

      LILY BART
    But that is not the reason.

                CUT TO:

<u>CLOSE UP</u> LAWRENCE SELDEN.

      LAWRENCE SELDEN
     The reason for what?

                CUT TO:

<u>CLOSE UP</u> LILY BART.
      LILY BART
    For your never coming.
   I wish I could make you out.
 Of course there are men who dislike me and others who are
      afraid of me ... (LAUGHS)
 They think I want to marry them. (SHE SMILES UP AT HIM).
    But I don't think you dislike me - and
   you can't possibly think I want to marry you.

<u>CLOSE UP</u> LAWRENCE SELDEN.

     LAWRENCE SELDEN (LAUGHS)
    No - I absolve you from that.

                CUT TO:

<u>CLOSE UP</u> LILY BART. THIS IS NOT THE REPLY SHE WAS LOOKING FOR.

THE HOUSE OF MIRTH

                    LILY BART
              (HURT, BUT RECOVERING)
                   Well then - ?   CUT TO:

<u>CLOSE UP</u> LAWRENCE SELDEN. HE GETS UP AND MOVES.
TO THE MANTELPIECE CARRYING HIS TEA.
<u>CRANE UP</u> WITH HIM AND <u>PAN</u> (<u>L-R</u>).

                  LAWRENCE SELDEN
            Well then perhaps <u>that's</u> the reason.
                                                        CUT TO:

<u>CLOSE UP</u> LILY BART (<u>SELDEN'S POV</u>).

                       LILY
                      What?

                                                        CUT TO:

<u>CLOSE UP</u> LAWRENCE SELDEN (<u>LILY'S POV</u>).

                  LAWRENCE SELDEN
     The fact that you don't want to marry me. Perhaps I don't
      regard it as such a strong inducement to go and see you.

WE HEAR HER LAUGH.
                                                        CUT TO:
<u>CLOSE UP</u> LILY BART (<u>SELDEN'S POV</u>).
SHE IS STILL LAUGHING.

                    LILY BART
            Dear Mr Selden it is stupid of you
    to be disingenuous and it isn't like you to be stupid.

SHE GETS UP AND MOVES TO THE WINDOW BEHIND SELDEN.
<u>CRANE UP</u> WITH HER AND <u>PAN</u> (<u>L-R</u>) TO THE WINDOW.
SHE STARES OUT OF IT, HER BACK TO SELDEN.

                    LILY BART
                  (RATHER GRAVE)
Don't you see that what I need is a friend who won't be afraid
       to say disagreeable things to me when I need them.
   Sometimes I have fancied that you might be that friend - I
  don't know why - but I have always felt that I don't have to
                 pretend with you or be on my guard ...
            (HER VOICE DROPS AND SHE BECOMES GRAVER)
            You don't know how much I need such a friend.

SILENCE.
                                                        CUT TO:

CLOSE UP LAWRENCE SELDEN. HE DOESN'T SPEAK AN AWKWARD SILENCE.

CUT TO:

CLOSE UP LILY BART.

                    LILY BART
      (MORE LIVELY BUT WITHOUT TURNING AROUND)
I've been about too long - people are getting tired of me;
      they are beginning to say I ought to marry.

CUT TO:

CLOSE UP LAWRENCE SELDEN.

              LAWRENCE SELDEN
            Well, why don't you?

CUT TO:

CLOSE UP LILY BART.
SHE TURNS AROUND SMILING.

                    LILY BART
                  (BLUSHING)
Ah I see you are a friend after all and that was one of the
          disagreeable things I was asking for.

CUT TO:

CLOSE UP LAWRENCE SELDEN.

         LAWRENCE SELDEN (AMICABLY)
It wasn't meant to be disagreeable. But isn't marriage your
   vocation? Isn't it what you're all brought up for?

CUT TO:

CLOSE UP LILY BART.

              LILY BART (SIGHS)
              I suppose so.

CUT TO:

CLOSE UP LAWRENCE SELDEN (WIDER SHOT).

              LAWRENCE SELDEN
    And so why not take the plunge and have it over.

SHE JOINS HIM IN A 2 SHOT.

                    LILY BART
You speak as if I ought to marry the first man who came along.

THE HOUSE OF MIRTH

                    LAWRENCE SELDEN
            I didn't mean to imply that you are as
                    hard put to it as that.

                                                    CUT TO:

CLOSE UP LILY BART (SELDEN'S POV).
SHE SHAKES HER HEAD.

                    LILY BART (AFTER A PAUSE)
                       You collect do you?
                     First Editions and things?

SELDEN NODS AND SMILES.

                         LILY BART
            And Americana - do you collect Americana?

                      LAWRENCE SELDEN
                 No. That's rather out of my line.

                         LILY BART
            And Americana are horribly dull I suppose?

                      LAWRENCE SELDEN
              Should fancy so - except to the historian.

                    LILY BART (TO HERSELF)
           And yet they fetch fabulous prices, don't they?

                      LAWRENCE SELDEN
                Only the very rich can afford to buy them.

PAUSE.
                         LILY BART
 And, you know that I am not rich. But life is very expensive.

LONG PAUSE.
HE OFFERS HER A CIGARETTE. SHE TAKES ONE AND THEN SOME OTHERS
WHICH SHE PUTS IN HER RETICULE. SHE LIGHTS HER CIGARETTE.
SHE FINISHES LIGHTING HER CIGARETTE, INHALES, THEN BLOWS THE
SMOKE OUT, HER FACE SHROUDED FOR A MOMENT.
SHE LOOKS AT HIM INTENTLY.

                         LILY BART
     Do you ever mind not being rich enough? And having to work -
                       do you mind that?

                                                    CUT TO:

<u>CLOSE UP</u> LAWRENCE SELDEN.

                LAWRENCE SELDEN
Oh the work itself is not so bad - I'm rather fond of the law.

                                <u>CUT TO:</u>
<u>CLOSE UP</u> LILY BART.

                LILY BART (INTENTLY)
But do you mind enough to marry to get out of it?

                                <u>CUT TO:</u>
<u>CLOSE UP</u> LAWRENCE SELDEN.

               LAWRENCE SELDEN (LAUGHING)
                    God forbid!

HER REFLECTION APPEARS IN THE MIRROR OVER THE MANTELPIECE BEHIND SELDEN.

                    LILY BART
Ah there's the difference - a girl must - a man if he chooses.

                LAWRENCE SELDEN
    Perhaps you'll meet your fate tonight at the Trenors.

                    LILY BART
        (STILL LOOKING AT HIM VIA THE MIRROR)
           I thought you might be going there.

                LAWRENCE SELDEN
           Those big parties bore me.

                    LILY BART
              As they do me.

                LAWRENCE SELDEN
              Then why go?

                    LILY BART
       You forget - it's part of the business.
           (SHE GLANCES AT THE CLOCK)
     Dear me! I must be off. It's after five!

SHE DOESN'T MOVE, BUT CHECKS HERSELF IN THE MIRROR, THEN LOWERS HER VEIL. SHE MOVES TO THE DOOR. SELDEN FOLLOWS HER. <u>PAN WITH HIM</u> (<u>L-R</u>) TO THE DOOR.

THE HOUSE OF MIRTH

>   LAWRENCE SELDEN
>   (AS HE FOLLOWS HER - WANTING HER TO STAY)
>   Let me see you to the station.

>   LILY BART (NOT WANTING TO GO)
>   No. Goodbye here please. It's been delightful.

THEY SHAKE HANDS.

                                                    CUT TO:

4. INT. DAY. LANDING. THE BENEDICK.

2 SHOT AT DOOR.

>   LAWRENCE SELDEN (HOLDING HER HAND)
>   Goodbye then.

SHE EXITS.

                                                    CUT TO:

5. INT. DAY. LANDING AND STAIRS. THE BENEDICK.

SHOT OF LILY BART RAPIDLY DESCENDING THE STAIRS.

>   LAWRENCE SELDEN (VOICE OVER)
>   Good luck at Bellomont!

                                                    CUT TO:

6. INT. DAY. LANDING. THE BENEDICK.

MID-SHOT OF A CHARWOMAN SCRUBBING THE FLOOR. THE SOUND OF
LILY'S SKIRTS RUSTLING AS SHE GETS CLOSER.
THE CHARWOMAN LOOKS UP AT LILY.

>   LILY BART (VOICE OVER)
>   I beg your pardon.

THE CHARWOMAN PUSHES HER PAIL ASIDE AND LILY DESCENDS THE STAIRS.
THE CHARWOMAN TURNS AND WATCHES HER DESCEND THE STAIRS.
AT THE TURN IN THE LANDING LILY GLANCES BACK UP AT THE
CHARWOMAN, THEN CONTINUES HER DESCENT.

                                                    CUT TO:

7. INT. DAY. LOBBY THE BENEDICK.

SHOT OF LILY COMING TOWARDS CAMERA.

>   SIM ROSEDALE (VOICE OVER)
>   Miss Bart? Well - of all people.

LILY STOPS IN HER TRACKS. SHE IS CLEARLY FLUSTERED AT SEEING HIM AND AFRAID OF THE PERCEIVED COMPROMISE.

                  LILY BART
          (DISTURBED YET TRYING TO BE POLITE)
          Oh Mr Rosedale - how are you?

SIM ROSEDALE ENTERS SHOT.

                SIM ROSEDALE
    Been up to town for a little shopping?

SHE IS FLUSTERED AND DOESN'T ANSWER STRAIGHT AWAY.

                  LILY BART
            (NOT LOOKING AT HIM)
    Yes - I came up to see my dressmaker.

            SIM ROSEDALE (GRINNING)
I didn't know there were any dressmakers in 'The Benedick'.

                  LILY BART
          (TRYING TO LOOK PUZZLED)
    Oh is that the name of this building?

          SIM ROSEDALE (STILL GRINNING)
        Yes. I happen to own it.
    The name means 'a confirmed bachelor'.

AWKWARD SILENCE.

       LILY BART (CHANGING THE SUBJECT)
      I'm just on my way to the Trenors.

                SIM ROSEDALE
    You must let me take you to the station.

           LILY BART (BARELY CIVIL)
                No. Thanks.
You're very kind but I couldn't think of troubling you.

SHE LEAVES SHOT.
<u>HOLD ON</u> SIM ROSEDALE. HE LOOKS AT HER.
                                                      <u>CUT TO:</u>

<u>SIM ROSEDALE'S POV</u> OF LOBBY AND STREET BEYOND, LILY MOVING TOWARDS THE STREET.

THE HOUSE OF MIRTH

TRACK IN ON STREET WITH HER (BACKVIEW).
DISSOLVE TO:

8. INT. DAY. TRAIN.

TRACK BACK DOWN TRAIN CORRIDOR (FRONT VIEW).
LILY BART, FINDING A SEAT, CAREFULLY ARRANGES HERSELF IN IT.
PAN (L-R) TO SEAT.
SHE LOOKS UP AT SOMEONE FURTHER DOWN THE CARRIAGE. SHE TAKES A BOOK AND KNIFE FROM HER TRAVELLING BAG AND BEGINS TO CUT THE PAGES OF A NOVEL - ALL THE WHILE STEALING GLANCES AT SOMEONE SLIGHTLY FURTHER DOWN THE CARRIAGE.
CUT TO:

LILY BART'S POV OF PERCY GRYCE WHO IS SITTING A COUPLE OF SEATS AWAY FROM HER.
HE IS READING A NEWSPAPER - BUT A BIT TOO INTENTLY.
HE FINISHES READING AND LOOKS OUT OF THE WINDOW THEN UP THE CARRIAGE. HE CATCHES SIGHT OF LILY BART.
HE NERVOUSLY NODS TO HER.
CUT TO:

LILY BART (GRYCE'S POV).
HER EYES HAVE DROPPED AND SHE CONTINUES TO CUT THE PAGES. THEN SHE LOOKS UP, FIRST UNDER HER LASHES, THEN FULLY AT PERCY GRYCE.
SHE GIVES HIM A RADIANT SMILE.

> LILY BART
> (SMILING)
> Ah MR Gryce - it's you! The seat next to
> me is empty - do take it.

CUT TO:

PERCY GRYCE (LILY'S POV).
PERCY GRYCE - IMMENSELY EMBARRASSED - COMES TO HER BUT SITS OPPOSITE HER.
AS HE SITS DOWN:

> LILY BART (VOICE OVER)
> I suppose you're going to Bellomont?

> PERCY GRYCE (VERY SHY)
> Yes - for a week.

CUT TO:

CLOSE UP LILY BART.

                       LILY BART
              A whole week - how delicious.
                                                        CUT TO:
CLOSE UP PERCY GRYCE.

                       PERCY GRYCE
                  And will you be there?

CLOSE UP LILY BART.

                    LILY BART (FLIRTING)
                Yes - and I'm as old as the hills.
                           (LAUGHS)
                                                        CUT TO:
CLOSE UP PERCY GRYCE.
HE SMILES BUT IS STILL VERY SHY. A SILENCE BETWEEN THEM.

                       LILY BART
                Is your mother keeping well?
                                                        CUT TO:
CLOSE UP PERCY GRYCE.

                 PERCY GRYCE (SMILING TIMIDLY)
                Yes, she has a very strong constitution

                         SILENCE.
                  LILY BART (VOICE OVER)
              Are you both still living at Albany?

PERCY NODS AND AGAIN IS SILENT.
                                                        CUT TO:

2 SHOT (SIDEVIEW) OF LILY BART AND PERCY GRYCE.
THROUGH THE WINDOW THE LAST FEW PEOPLE RUNNING FOR THE TRAIN
BEFORE IT PULLS OUT.
IT MOVES OFF WITH A JOLT. SILENCE STILL BETWEEN THEM.

                       LILY BART
             And how are you getting on with your Americana?

                 PERCY GRYCE (A LITTLE BOLDER)
                   I've got a few new things.

                       LILY BART
            Your uncle had a very fine collection I believe.

                       PERCY GRYCE
              Yes ... he ... collected for many years but ...

THE HOUSE OF MIRTH

<u>CLOSE UP</u> BERTHA DORSET FLUSTERED AT JUST HAVING CAUGHT THE TRAIN.

>BERTHA DORSET (BREATHLESS)
>I must have this seat next to you Lily!

SHE DROPS INTO THE SEAT.

>BERTHA DORSET
>(STILL BREATHLESS)
>Oh!
>(SEEING PERCY GRYCE)
>Oh how do you do, MR Gryce?

CUT TO:

<u>CLOSE UP</u> PERCY GRYCE (<u>HER POV</u>).
HE BLUSHES AND HALF SMILES.

CUT TO:

<u>2 SHOT</u> BERTHA DORSET AND LILY BART.

>BERTHA DORSET
>I came across from Mount Kisco in the motor-car this morning then kicked my heels at Garrisons for an <u>hour</u> - without even a cigarette.
>I don't suppose you have a single one left, have you, Lily?

>LILY BART
>(LOOKING AT PERCY GRYCE)
>What an absurd question Bertha!

BERTHA QUICKLY LOOKS AT LILY.
.
>BERTHA DORSET
>You don't smoke? Since when have you given it up?

SLIGHT PAUSE.
BERTHA LOOKS AT PERCY BRYCE

>BERTHA DORSET
>And you don't either MR Gryce?

CUT TO:

<u>CLOSE UP</u> PERCY GRYCE. HE SHAKES HIS HEAD.
<u>CLOSE UP</u> BERTHA DORSET.

>BERTHA DORSET
>Ah - of course.
>How stupid of me.

SHE SMILES AS SHE LEANS BACK AGAINST THE CUSHIONS.
PAN (L-R) PAST BERTHA AND LILY TO THE WINDOW.
THE TRAIN ENTERS A TUNNEL
HOLD ON BLACK AND SMOKE FOR A MOMENT.

>   JUDY TRENOR (VOICE OVER)
>   Lily dear - my secretary has been called away
>   if it is not too much of a bore will you help me with
>   some invitations?

THEN DISSOLVE TO:

9. INT. DAY. STUDY BELLOMONT.

PAN (L-R) FROM OPEN WINDOWS OVERLOOKING THE GROUNDS TO JUDY TRENOR AT HER WRITING DESK, WHICH IS COVERED IN A CHAOS OF PAPERS.
PAN ENDS ON A 2 SHOT. JUDY TRENOR CENTRE FRAME, LILY BART FRAME RIGHT.

>   JUDY TRENOR
>   It was simply inhuman of Pragg to go off now. When I was in
>   Tuxedo I asked a lot of people down and I've mislaid the list
>   and can't remember who's coming.
>   And this week is going to be a failure too.

>   LILY BART
>   Oh Judy, as if any one were ever bored at Bellomont!

>   JUDY TRENOR
>   Everything has gone wrong.
>   And now Bertha Dorset is furious with me.

>   LILY BART
>   Furious with you? Why?

>   JUDY TRENOR
>   Because I told her that Lawrence Selden was coming; but he
>   wouldn't, after all, and she's quite unreasonable enough to
>   think it's my fault.

CLOSE UP. LILY BART. NOT LOOKING AT JUDY.

>   LILY BART
>   (QUIETLY - A BIT TOO CASUAL)
>   I thought that was all over ...

CUT TO:

CLOSE UP JUDY TRENOR.

THE HOUSE OF MIRTH

                    JUDY TRENOR
              So it is - on his side.
  I believe I'll call up Lawrence on the telephone and tell
              him he simply <u>must</u> come.

                                                  CUT TO:

CLOSE UP LILY BART.

                  LILY BART (BLUSHES)
                      Oh don't.

               JUDY TRENOR (VOICE OVER)
                   Good gracious Lily!
                Do you dislike him so much?

               LILY BART (STILL FLUSTERED)
                 Not at all. I like him.
                                                  CUT TO:

CLOSE UP JUDY TRENOR.

                    JUDY TRENOR
  Oh, I don't say there's any real harm in Bertha but she
  delights in making people miserable - especially her husband;
  poor George - when he isn't jealous, she pretends to be.
                       (PAUSE)
        But she <u>is</u> dangerous. And you're not nasty. And for
   always getting what she wants in the long run, commend me
                    to a nasty woman.

                                                  CUT TO:

CLOSE UP LILY BART.

                    LILY BART
           I thought you were so fond of Bertha.
                                                  CUT TO:

CLOSE UP JUDY TRENOR.

                    JUDY TRENOR
  Oh I am - it's much safer to be fond of dangerous people.

                                                  CUT TO:

<u>2 SHOT</u> JUDY TRENOR AND LILY BART.
THEY BOTH CONTINUE TO WRITE IN SILENCE.

                    JUDY TRENOR
  Did you know his father made a fortune out of inventing a
           device which excludes fresh air from hotels.

                    LILY BART
                     Who?

                    JUDY TRENOR
               Well to be sure, Lily!
                    Percy Gryce!

LILY STOPS WRITING AND LOOKS UP.

                    JUDY TRENOR
     But he's horribly shy and easily shocked and - and -

                    LILY BART
     Why don't you say it Judy? I have the reputation of being on
                   the hunt for a husband.

                    JUDY TRENOR
     Oh he wouldn't believe it of you - at first. But don't
     wear the scarlet for dinner and don't smoke if you can
                      help it, Lily dear.

                    LILY BART
     You are very kind Judy. I'll lock up my cigarettes and wear
               that last year's dress you gave me.

                    JUDY TRENOR
         Lily? ... I asked him here on purpose for you.

                    LILY BART
     Mr. Gryce and I are getting to be very good friends.

LILY CONTINUES TO WRITE BUT JUDY STOPS.

                    JUDY TRENOR
     Lily what an awful life you'll lead - nothing but Percy's
            eight hundred thousand a year and old books.
                       PAUSE
     You're quite sure that you wouldn't like me to telephone
                      Lawrence Selden?

                    LILY BART
                  (NOT LOOKING UP)
                     Quite sure.

HOLD.

                                                        CUT TO:

THE HOUSE OF MIRTH

10. EXT. DAY. TERRACE BELLOMONT.

<u>SHOT OF</u> GROUP BESIDE THE TEA TABLE. THE GROUP CONSISTS OF BERTHA AND GEORGE DORSET, GUS TRENOR AND JUDY TRENOR, CARRY FISHER AND EVIE VAN OSBURGH
JUDY TRENOR DISPENSES TEA.

BERTHA DORSET
I do enjoy the quiet, don't you, Lily?

CUT TO:

<u>SHOT OF</u> LILY AS SHE LIES ON A DAY BED AGAINST THE HONEYSUCKLE. HER EYES ARE CLOSED - SHE HAS BEEN LISTENING TO THE HALF-HEARD SMALL TALK. SHE OPENS HER EYES, LOOKS AT BERTHA AND HALF SMILES.

CUT TO:

2 <u>SHOT</u> BERTHA AND GEORGE DORSET.

BERTHA DORSET
I wish the men would always stay away - it's really much nicer without them.
Oh you don't count George; one never talks to one's husband.

CUT TO:

2 <u>SHOT</u> JUDY AND GUS TRENOR.

JUDY TRENOR
But wives never like their husbands talking to other women.

CUT TO:

2 <u>SHOT</u> BERTHA AND GEORGE DORSET.

BERTHA DORSET
Only if the women in question are slightly too eligible ... or divorced.

GEORGE DORSET (JOVIAL)
Wives may do as they wish. Husbands are expected to be like money - influential but silent.

CUT TO:

2 <u>SHOT</u> JUDY AND GUS TRENOR.

GUS TRENOR (JOLLY)
If divorcees were more acceptable I might be tempted.

                    JUDY TRENOR (SHOCKED)
                            Gus!
LAUGHTER.
                                                    CUT TO:

2 SHOT BERTHA DORSET AND JUDY TRENOR.

                        BERTHA DORSET
    The problem with divorcees is that their alimony is always
                paid by other women's spouses.

                                                    CUT TO:

2 SHOT CARRY FISHER AND EVIE VAN OSBURGH.

                        CARRY FISHER
      But that doesn't necessarily mean social exclusion.

                                                    CUT TO:

CLOSE UP LILY BART.

                          LILY BART
     Not if the divorcee is penitent enough. And the quickest way
     to be socially forgiven is by being remarried only to the very
            wealthy and having God on one's visiting list.

                                                    CUT TO:

CLOSE UP BERTHA DORSET.

                        BERTHA DORSET
     Don't be sacrilegious Lily, you'll shock MR Gryce. He already
     deplores women who play bridge for money; if he hears that you
     disapprove of God as well nothing will prevent him from going
                       back to Albany and mother.

A SILENCE DESCENDS - ESPECIALLY BETWEEN LILY AND BERTHA -
A SILENCE FULL OF MUTUAL PIQUE AND VAGUE THREAT.

                                                    CUT TO:

2 SHOT CARRY FISHER AND EVIE VAN OSBURGH.
CARRY TAKES HER TEA, LEAVES THE TABLE AND JOINS LILY.

                       EVIE VAN OSBURGH
                          (TIMIDLY)
       Mr. Gryce has enough taste to be the owner of a fine
                       collection of books.

                                                    CUT TO:

CLOSE UP BERTHA DORSET.

THE HOUSE OF MIRTH

          BERTHA DORSET (LAUGHING)
Nonsense - any man of his age still living at home is incapable of evolving a taste of his own.

                                      CUT TO:

<u>CLOSE UP</u> EVIE VAN OSBURGH.

         EVIE VAN OSBURGH (WITH A VAGUE PIQUE)
I'm sure I don't see why you laugh at him. I think he's <u>very</u> nice.

<u>CLOSE UP</u> BERTHA DORSET.

          BERTHA DORSET (LAUGHING ALL THE MORE)
                  Of course you do dear!

                                      CUT TO.

<u>2 SHOT</u> LILY AND CARRY FISHER. CARRY SITS ON THE END OF LILY'S DAY BED. BERTHA'S LAUGHTER IN THE BACKGROUND.

         CARRY FISHER (QUIETLY AND AS A WARNING)
Lily, when a woman has the beauty men admire and women envy, it is wise to tread carefully. If you have a grudge against Bertha pay her back when you are married.

                      LILY BART
After a while, Carry, it becomes wearying always having to win people's good opinion by charm alone.

                                      CUT TO:

<u>CLOSE UP</u> CARRY FISHER.

                   CARRY FISHER
When a girl has no mother to calculate for her she must be on the alert herself.

                                      CUT TO:

<u>CLOSE UP</u> LILY BART.

                      LILY BART
My parents equipped me for a certain sort of life without bequeathing me the means of sustaining it. Without parents to give advice and a good bank balance to confirm that advice ... we are at the mercy of those who choose to help us.

                                      CUT TO:

CLOSE UP CARRY FISHER.

                       CARRY FISHER
But, Lily, you have at least Mrs Peniston's generosity.

CLOSE UP LILY BART.

                          LILY BART
Aunt Julia is very kind. But sometimes that sort of largesse can be as comforting as the Arctic. Dispensing financial assistance out of duty or under a sense of distant family obligation is no substitute for love freely given.

FOOTSTEPS ARE HEARD. SHE LOOKS TOWARDS THEM AND SMILES AUTOMATICALLY.
SEEING WHO IT IS, HER SMILE HALF-FADES.
                                                                   CUT TO:
HER POV OF LAWRENCE SELDEN.

                     LAWRENCE SELDEN
     You see I came after all.
PAUSE.

HE IS JOINED BY BERTHA DORSET, WHO SLIPS HER ARM THROUGH HIS AND SMILES BROADLY AT LILY.
                                                                    CUT TO:
CLOSE UP LILY BART BLUSHING AND FORCING A SMILE.
HOLD.
SOUNDTRACK:
                 JUDY TRENOR (VOICE OVER)
He didn't even write me - he just came of his own accord. Perhaps it's not over with Bertha after all.

                                                                    CUT TO:

11. INT. NIGHT. DINING ROOM BELLOMONT.

WIDE SHOT OF A VERY LARGE DINING TABLE AND A LARGE NUMBER OF GUESTS.
LILLY BART IN CENTRE FRAME. FACING CAMERA. GEORGE DORSET TO HER RIGHT. TRACKING ON HER.
DINNER TALK
SHE LOOKS UP AND DOWN THE TABLE AT THE OTHER GUESTS. SHE IS IN A QUIET REVERIE.
TRACK STOPS WHEN SHE IS IN CLOSE UP.
SHE LOOKS ACROSS AT THE GUESTS IMMEDIATELY OPPOSITE HER.
                                                                    CUT TO:

THE HOUSE OF MIRTH

<u>CLOSE UP</u> LAWRENCE SELDEN (<u>HER POV</u>). HE SEEMS CHARMING AND DESIRABLE.
                                                    <u>CUT TO:</u>

<u>CLOSE UP</u> LILY BART.
SHE LOOKS TO SELDEN'S LEFT.
                                                    <u>CUT TO:</u>

<u>CLOSE UP</u> PERCY GRYCE (<u>HER POV</u>). HE SEEMS VERY DULL.
                                                    <u>CUT TO:</u>

<u>SHOT</u> LILY BART AND GEORGE DORSET.
HE CHUCKLES AND SHE IS ROUSED FROM HER REVERIE.
                                                    <u>CUT TO:</u>

                    GEORGE DORSET (CHUCKLING)
                        I do say look at her

<u>SHOT</u> BERTHA DORSET AND TO HER RIGHT LAWRENCE SELDEN,
TO HER LEFT PERCY GRYCE.
SHE IS BEING VERY CHARMING, FIRST TO PERCY GRYCE AND THEN TO
LAWRENCE SELDEN.

                    GEORGE DORSET (VOICE OVER)
        One would suppose she's really gone on that poor devil and
              it's all the other way round, I assure you.

                                                    <u>CUT TO:</u>

<u>2 SHOT</u> LILY BART AND GEORGE DORSET.

                            LILY BART
                Aren't you horribly jealous of her?

                    GEORGE DORSET (BUFFOONISH)
                Abominably! Keeps me awake at night!
                        (PUSHES HIS PLATE AWAY)
                            (AMIABLY)
            I can't eat a mouthful of this stuff you know.

                                                    <u>DISSOLVE TO:</u>

12. NIGHT. DINING ROOM BELLOMONT.

ALL THE MEN OF THE PARTY SITTING AT ONE END OF THE TABLE.
THERE IS INTIMATE SMALL-TALK THEN SILENCE AS THEY ALL -
EXCEPT PERCY GRYCE - ENJOY THEIR CIGARS AND PORT.

LAWRENCE SELDEN
(TO PERCY GRYCE)
Will you join us at cards, MR Gryce?

PERCY GRYCE
(SHOCKED)
I'm afraid not.
I never gamble.

CUT TO:

13. INT. NIGHT. MAIN ROOM BELLOMONT.

THE MAIN ROOM IS ARCADED WITH A GALLERY SUPPORTED ON YELLOW MARBLE COLUMNS. LOTS OF POTTED PLANTS AROUND THE WALL.
A CRIMSON CARPET. DOGS DOZING BY THE FIRE. HANGING FROM THE CEILING A GREAT CENTRAL LANTERN.
2 SHOT LILY BART AND PERCY GRYCE SITTING TOGETHER.

LILY BART
Perhaps you'll be kind enough to keep me from playing bridge tonight, Mr.Gryce.

PERCY GRYCE
Of course Miss Bart.

LILY BART
I've no head for the game or the rules of betting - I've been 'dragged' into it and have lost an appalling amount of money.

PERCY GRYCE TRIES NOT TO LOOK TOO SHOCKED.

LILY BART
(CHARMING)
Mr. Gryce I've shocked you.

PERCY GRYCE
(WITH GREAT DIFFICULTY)
Whilst I do not approve of cards, Miss Bart, I do approve of you.

LILY BART
(SMILING)
I hope that means I am forgiven for I am penitent.

AN AWKWARD PAUSE THEN LAUGHTER. THEY LOOK TOWARDS IT.

CUT TO:

THE HOUSE OF MIRTH

WIDE SHOT. THE CARD PLAYERS HAVING A GOOD TIME.

                                                CUT TO:

2 SHOT LILY BART AND PERCY GRYCE.

                        PERCY GRYCE
                Will you go to Church tomorrow?

                        LILY BART
        Yes. I try to encourage Judy's daughters to attend ...
                         (SOFTLY)
        ... they are not always as scrupulous in these matters as
                        they might be.

                        PERCY GRYCE
                May I accompany you, Miss Bart?

                        LILY BART
                    Of course, MR Gryce.

                                                CUT TO:

14. INT. DAY. LILY BART'S BEDROOM. BELLOMONT.

SHOT OF LILY, DRESSED FOR CHURCH, MOVING SLOWLY TO THE WINDOW. WOMEN'S VOICES ARE HEARD MOVING PAST HER BEDROOM DOOR.

(PAN R-L).

CHURCH BELLS IN THE DISTANCE.
SHE STOPS AT THE WINDOW.
HOLD.

                                                CUT TO:

HER POV OF PERCY GRYCE - DRESSED FOR CHURCH AND STANDING ON THE GRAVEL PATH BY THE HORSE-DRAWN CARRIAGE.
HE STANDS THERE FOR A MOMENT THEN TURNS TOWARDS THE HOUSE AND LOOKS UP AT LILY'S WINDOW.

                                                CUT TO:

SHOT OF LILY MOVING AWAY FROM THE WINDOW - NOT WANTING PERCY GRYCE TO SEE HER, AND NOW NOT WANTING TO GO TO CHURCH WITH HIM.

HOLD FOR A MOMENT.

                                                CUT TO:

15. EXT. DAY. DRIVE. BELLOMONT.

SHOT OF PERCY GRYCE WAITING BY THE HORSE-DRAWN CARRIAGE.
HE PACES UP AND DOWN ANXIOUSLY LOOKING AT HIS WATCH.

SOUNDTRACK: CHURCH BELLS.
HE STOPS (BACK TO CAMERA) THEN TURNS AS VOICES AND FOOTSTEPS
ARE HEARD COMING FROM THE HOUSE.

                                          CUT TO:

16. EXT. DAY. HOUSE BELLOMONT.

SHOT OF FRONT OF HOUSE (PERCY GRYCE'S POV).
OUT COME THE CHURCH-GOERS - MURIEL AND HILDA TRENOR, MR AND
MRS WEATHERALL AND LADY CRESSIDA RAITH.
PAN WITH THEM (R-L) TO CARRIAGE.
PERCY GRYCE HELPS THE LADIES INTO THE CARRIAGE. HE LOOKS BACK
AT THE HOUSE ONE MORE TIME FOR LILY, THEN GETS IN HIMSELF.
HE HAS WAITED FOR HER AND SHE HAS HUMILIATED HIM.
PAN (R-L) WITH THE CARRIAGE AS IT DRIVES TO CHURCH
SOUNDTRACK: CHURCH BELLS

                                          CUT TO:

SHOT OF LILY'S BEDROOM WINDOW. WE HEAR THE CARRIAGES DRIVING
AWAY, THEN LILY APPEARS AT THE WINDOW AND WATCHES IT GO.

                                          CUT TO:

17. DAY. LILY BART'S BEDROOM. BELLOMONT.

SHOT OF LILY PICKING UP HER PRAYER BOOK AND SUNSHADE. SHE
MOVES SLOWLY TO THE DOOR AND EXITS.
PAN WITH HER (L-R).

                                          CUT TO:

18. DAY. HALL. BELLOMONT.

SHOT OF LILY COMING ONTO THE LANDING THEN DESCENDING THE STAIRS.

SOUNDTRACK: CHURCH BELLS.

PAN WITH HER (L-R) DOWN TO THE BOTTOM OF THE STAIRCASE, THEN
CONTINUE PANNING (L-R) TO GET HER TO THE LIBRARY DOORS.
SHE OPENS THEM AND GOES IN.

                                          CUT TO:

THE HOUSE OF MIRTH

19. INT. DAY. LIBRARY BELLOMONT.

<u>CLOSE UP</u> LILY. SHE COMES TO CAMERA AND STOPS ABRUPTLY.
<u>SOUNDTRACK</u>: CHURCH BELLS.

                    LILY BART
             Dear me, am I late?

                                                            CUT TO:

<u>LILY'S POV</u>.
TWO SLIGHTLY ANGLED WING-CHAIRS. THE ONE ON THE LEFT SEATS A WOMAN. ONLY HER SKIRT AND HAND CAN BE SEEN. ON THE RIGHT THE LEGS OF A MAN SEATED IN THE CHAIR.

<u>SOUNDTRACK</u>: CHURCH BELLS.

                BERTHA DORSET (VOICE OVER)
                      (TARTLY)
                    Late for what?

                    LAWRENCE SELDEN
                    Late for whom?

BERTHA DORSET GETS UP OUT OF THE DEPTHS OF THE ARMCHAIR.
SO DOES LAWRENCE SELDEN, WHO SMILES.

                    BERTHA DORSET
          Perhaps you had an earlier engagement?

                                                            CUT TO:

<u>SHOT OF</u> LILY (<u>BERTHA'S POV</u>).

<u>SOUNDTRACK</u>: CHURCH BELLS.

                    LILY BART
                    Yes, I had.

AS SHE SPEAKS SHE WALKS TOWARDS SELDEN.
<u>PAN WITH HER</u> (<u>R-L</u>) TO A <u>2 SHOT</u> (LILY AND SELDEN).
                                                            CUT TO:

<u>SHOT OF</u> BERTHA DORSET (<u>THEIR POV</u>).
<u>SOUNDTRACK</u>: CHURCH BELLS.

                    BERTHA DORSET
                    (ILL-TEMPERED)
           Perhaps I am in the way then?

                                                            CUT TO:

SHOT OF LILY AND SELDEN SMILING BUT NEITHER SPEAKING.
SOUNDTRACK:: CHURCH BELLS.

                                                    CUT TO:

CLOSE UP BERTHA DORSET.
SOUNDTRACK: CHURCH BELLS.

                    BERTHA DORSET
            Mr Selden is at your disposal.
        I never interfere Mr Selden's engagements.

                                                    CUT TO:

2 SHOT LILY BART AND LAWRENCE SELDEN.
SOUNDTRACK: CHURCH BELLS.

                      LILY BART
                      (SMILING)
    But I have no engagement with Mr Selden! My engagement was to
    go to church and I'm afraid the carriages have left without me.
                (TO LAWRENCE SELDEN)
              Have they left do you know?

                    LAWRENCE SELDEN
          Yes I heard them drive away sometime since.

LILY MOVES TOWARDS THE GLASS DOORS WHICH LEAD OUTSIDE.
PAN WITH HER (R-L).

                      LILY BART
              Then I shall have to walk.

                                                    CUT TO:

2 SHOT LAWRENCE SELDEN AND BERTHA DORSET.
SOUNDTRACK: CHURCH BELLS.

                    BERTHA DORSET
                    (STILL TART)
              It's too late to get there.

                                                    CUT TO:

CLOSE UP LILY BART.
SOUNDTRACK: CHURCH BELLS.

                      LILY BART
                      (SMILING)
      Well, I shall have the credit for trying at any rate.

THE HOUSE OF MIRTH

SHE WALKS OUT INTO THE LONG VISTA TOWARDS THE GARDEN.
HOLD.

                                                                                            CUT TO:

2 SHOT BERTHA DORSET AND LAWRENCE SELDEN
SOUNDTRACK: CHURCH BELLS
BERTHA FLOUNCES OUT OF THE LIBRARY IN A HUFF.
SELDEN WATCHES HER GO THEN LOOKS ROUND AND WATCHES LILY.

                                                                                           CUT TO:

20. EXT. DAY. WOODLAND. BELLOMONT.

SHOT OF LILY WALKING SLOWLY THROUGH THE WOOD.
SOUNDTRACK: THE CHURCH BELLS STOP.
SHE STOPS, LISTENING TO THE SILENCE, THEN CONTINUES TO WALK
SLOWLY.
PAN WITH, THEN FROM, HER (R-L).

                                                                    DISSOLVE TO:

21. EXT. DAY. WOODLAND. BELLOMONT.

PAN (R-L) THROUGH GREENERY TO A PARASOL. LILY SITTING ON A BENCH
HOLD.
THEN FOOTSTEPS OVER LEAVES ARE HEARD.
THE PARASOL IS FURLED REVEALING LILY'S FACE SMILING. SHE
REMAINS SEATED.

                                LILY BART
                 You must be quite breathless.

                                                                                            CUT TO:

SHOT OF LAWRENCE SELDEN

                              LAWRENCE SELDEN
  How fast you walk. I thought I'd never catch up with you.

                                                                    CUT TO:

WIDER SHOT OF LILY BART

                              LILY BART
     But I've been sitting here for nearly an hour.

SELDEN SITS DOWN ON THE BENCH NEXT TO HER.

LAWRENCE SELDEN
Waiting for me I hope.

LILY BART
Waiting to see if you would come.

CUT TO:

CLOSE UP LAWRENCE SELDEN.

LAWRENCE SELDEN
Weren't you sure that I would?

CUT TO:

CLOSE UP LILY BART.

LILY BART
If I waited long enough. But I only had a limited time to give to the experience.

CUT TO:

CLOSE UP LAWRENCE SELDEN.

LAWRENCE SELDEN
Why limited?

CUT TO:

CLOSE UP LILY BART.

LILY BART
By my other engagement.

THE CHURCH-GOERS ARE HEARD WALKING BACK TO THE HOUSE.

CUT TO:

THE CHURCH PARTY PASS BY WITHOUT SEEING THEM, PERCY GRYCE AT THE REAR WITH EVIE VAN OSBURGH.

CUT TO:

2 SHOT LILY BART AND LAWRENCE SELDEN.

LAWRENCE SELDEN
Now I see why you were getting up on your Americana.

LILY BART (STANDING)
That was why I was waiting for you to thank you for having given me so many points!

THE HOUSE OF MIRTH

> LAWRENCE SELDEN (STANDING)
> You can hardly do justice to the subject in so short a time.

THEY BOTH START WALKING BACK TO THE HOUSE
<u>PAN WITH</u> THEM (<u>R-L</u>)

> LAWRENCE SELDEN
> Won't you devote the afternoon to it? We'll take a walk and you can thank me at your leisure.

<u>HOLD ON THEM</u> AS THEY WALK BACK TO THE HOUSE.
THEN <u>TRACK AROUND</u> (<u>R-L</u>) AND BEGIN TO <u>CRANE UP</u> THROUGH HEAVY FOLIAGE AND RISING GROUND.
THEN TRACK FORWARD THROUGH THE PERFECT AFTERNOON.

<u>SOUNDTRACK</u>:
ONLY THE SOUNDS OF FOOTSTEPS THROUGH FOLIAGE AND SLIGHT WIND RUSTLING THROUGH THE TREES.

> LAWRENCE SELDEN (VOICE OVER)
> Let us sit here.

<u>TRACK/CRANE STOPS</u> WHEN HIGH GROUND IS REACHED.
THEN <u>TRACK AROUND</u> (<u>L-R</u>) TO LILY.
SHE IS SEATED ON A ROCK AND SHE IS SLIGHTLY BREATHLESS FROM THE CLIMB.

> LILY BART (FANNING HERSELF)
> I have broken two engagements for you today and both of them with Percy Gryce.

<u>CONTINUE TRACKING</u> (<u>L-R</u>) TO SELDEN.

> LILY BART (VOICE OVER)
> How many have you broken for me?

<u>TRACK STOPS</u> WHEN SELDEN IS IN <u>CLOSE UP</u>/<u>MID SHOT</u>.

> LAWRENCE SELDEN (LEANS BACK)
> None.
> My only engagement at Bellomont was with you.

                                                             CUT TO:

<u>MID SHOT</u> LILY BART.

> LILY BART (FAINTLY SMILING)
> Did you really come to Bellomont to see me?
>
>   CUT TO:

CLOSE UP LAWRENCE SELDEN.

                LAWRENCE SELDEN
                Of course I did.

                                        CUT TO:

CLOSE UP LILY BART.

                LILY BART
            (MURMURING MEDITATIVELY)
                Why?

                                        CUT TO:

CLOSE UP LAWRENCE SELDEN.

                LAWRENCE SELDEN
    Because I always like to see what you're doing.
        You're such a wonderful spectacle.

                                        CUT TO:

CLOSE UP LILY BART.

                LILY BART
  Now that you are here you can see the effect first hand.

                                        CUT TO:

CLOSE UP LAWRENCE SELDEN.

            LAWRENCE SELDEN (SMILING)
  I don't flatter myself that my coming here has deflected your
          course of action by a hair's-breadth.

                                      CUT TO:

2 SHOT.
SILENCE BETWEEN THEM.
HE TAKES OUT HIS CIGARETTE CASE.

                LILY BART
            (LEANING FORWARD)
    Oh do give me one - I haven't smoked for days!

HE OFFERS HER A CIGARETTE. SHE TAKES IT BUT HE DOESN'T LIGHT
EITHER HERS OR HIS OWN.

                LAWRENCE SELDEN
        Why such unnatural abstinence?

THE HOUSE OF MIRTH

LILY BART
Because it is not considered becoming in a <u>jeune fille à marier</u> and at the present moment I am a <u>jeune fille à marier</u>.

SILENCE.

LILY BART
You must suppose me a dull kind of person if you think that I never yield to an impulse.

LAWRENCE SELDEN
But I don't suppose that. Your genius lies in converting impulses into intentions.

LILY BART
My genius?
My genius would appear to be my ability to do the wrong thing at the right time.

LAWRENCE SELDEN
Or vice-versa.

LILY BART (GRAVER)
Is there any final test of genius but success! And I certainly haven't succeeded.

LAWRENCE SELDEN
But you will marry someone very rich.

SLIGHT PAUSE.
LILY BART
What a miserable future you foresee for me.

LAWRENCE SELDEN
Haven't you seen it for yourself?

LILY BART
Of course. But it looks much darker when you show it to me.

CUT TO:

<u>CLOSE UP</u> LILY BART.
LILY BART
(NEAR TO TEARS BUT NOT CRYING)
Why do you do this to me?
Why do you make the things I have chosen seem hateful to me, if you have nothing to give me instead?

CUT TO:

CLOSE UP LAWRENCE SELDEN.

>   LAWRENCE SELDEN (NOW SERIOUS)
>   No - I have nothing to give you.
>   If I had, it should be yours, you know that.

CUT TO:

CLOSE UP LILY BART.

>   LILY BART
>   But you belittle me in being so sure they are the only things
>   I care for.

CUT TO:

CLOSE UP LAWRENCE SELDEN.

>   LAWRENCE SELDEN
>   Isn't it natural that I should try to belittle all the things
>   I can't offer you?

SILENCE.

CUT TO:

2 SHOT.
>   LILY BART
>   Do you want to marry me?
>
>   LAWRENCE SELDEN (LAUGHS)
>   No I don't - but perhaps I should if you did.
>
>   LILY BART
>   It would be a great risk - I have never concealed from you how
>   great.

HE DOESN'T REPLY.
SHE STANDS AND SELDEN GETS UP.

>   LILY BART
>   You are a coward.

SHE PUTS THE CIGARETTE TO HER LIPS AND SELDEN LIGHTS IT.

>   LAWRENCE SELDEN
>   No - it is you who are the coward.

HE LIGHTS HIS OWN.
LONG PAUSE.
>   LILY BART
>   Were you serious?

THE HOUSE OF MIRTH

                    LAWRENCE SELDEN
            Why not? I took no risk in being so.

THEY LOOK AT EACH OTHER FOR A MOMENT IN THE RAPIDLY FALLING DUSK.
HE LEANS FORWARDS AND KISSES HER LIGHTLY. THE KISS IS
LIGHT ENOUGH TO BE LOVING BUT NOT PASSIONATE ENOUGH TO BE
COMPROMISING.
SHE RECEIVES HIS KISS AND IS HALF-DELIGHTED AND HALF AFRAID.

                    LILY BART (SOFTLY)
Why is it that when we meet we always play this elaborate game?

FOR A MOMENT HE DOESN'T ANSWER.
THEN:
                    LAWRENCE SELDEN
            It's getting late. Let us go down.

                                                    CUT TO:

22. EXT. DUSK THE ROAD LEADING FROM BELLOMONT.

<u>SHOT OF</u> SELDEN AND LILY COMING DOWN SOME SLOPING GROUND.
<u>PAN WITH</u> THEM (<u>L-R</u>) AS THEY DESCEND TO THE ROAD.
A MOTOR-CAR IS HEARD COMING TOWARDS THEM. THEY STOP AND LOOK
AT IT. AS IT DRIVES BY IT KICKS UP A LOT OF DUST.

                                                    CUT TO:

23. EXT. DUSK ROAD BELLOMONT.

<u>PAN WITH</u> THE CAR (<u>R-L</u>) <u>THEIR POV</u> IT CONTAINS PERCY GRYCE.

                LAWRENCE SELDEN (VOICE OVER)
    I do believe that Percy Gryce is leaving I wonder what drove
                            him away?

                    LILY BART (VOICE OVER)
            I'm afraid we may have shocked him.

<u>HOLD ON</u> THE DISAPPEARING CAR AND THE DUST FILLING THE SCREEN.
<u>HOLD ON</u> THE DUST.
<u>SOUNDTRACK</u>:
                    JUDY TRENOR (VOICE OVER)
        All I can say is, Lily, that I can't make you out!
        We could none of us imagine your putting up with him for a
                moment unless you meant to marry him.

                                                DISSOLVE TO:

24. INT./EXT. NIGHT. TRAIN.

DISSOLVE OUT OF SMOKE FROM CAR TO SMOKE FROM STEAM ENGINE. TRACK BACK TO A SHOT OF LILY LOOKING OUT OF A WINDOW AT THE SMOKE IN THE TUNNEL OUTSIDE THE WINDOW.

> JUDY TRENOR (VOICE OVER)
> Even Bertha Dorset kept her hands off -
> I will say that - 'til Lawrence Selden came down and you dragged him away from her.

TRACK STOPS WHEN LILY IS IN MID SHOT FRAME RIGHT. SHE CONTINUES TO LOOK OUT OF THE WINDOW.

> LILY BART (VOICE OVER)
> I thought MR Gryce meant to stay all week.

> JUDY TRENOR (VOICE OVER)
> He did mean to stay - that's the worst of it.
> It shows that he's running away from you;
> that Bertha's done her work and poisoned him.

> LILY BART (VOICE OVER)
> Oh he's not completely lost - there are ways

> JUDY TRENOR (VOICE OVER)
> Whatever you do Lily, do nothing.

SILENCE.
LILY CONTINUES TO LOOK OUT OF THE WINDOW.

> LILY BART (VOICE OVER)
> What was it Bertha really told Percy?

> JUDY TRENOR (VOICE OVER)
> Don't ask me - horrors - I told you Bertha was
> dangerous - they're all alike you know; they
> hold their tongues for years and you think you're
> safe; but when the opportunity comes they
> remember everything including your borrowing money.

> LILY BART (VOICE OVER)
> But that was from my father's cousin. I repaid it of course.

> JUDY TRENOR (VOICE OVER)
> Well Bertha wouldn't remember that. Besides, it was the
> idea of the gambling debt that frightened Percy off.
> Oh Bertha knew her man!

> Oh Lily, you'll never do anything if you're not serious.

SILENCE. JUST THE SOUND OF THE TRAIN.
LILY LOOKS OUT OF THE WINDOW INTO THE DARKNESS.
<u>TRACK IN</u> ON THE WINDOW AND THE BLACKNESS BEYOND.
<u>HOLD ON</u> DARKNESS.

> GUS TRENOR (VOICE OVER)
> Out of spirits?
>
> LILY BART (VOICE OVER)
> I'm a little dull.

THE FRAME IS FILLED WITH BLACKNESS.

<u>DISSOLVE TO:</u>

25. EXT./INT. NIGHT. CAB/NEW YORK.

<u>DISSOLVE FROM BLACK</u> TO THE BLACK LEATHER OF THE OUTSIDE OF THE CAB.
<u>TRACK AROUND</u> (R-L) TO <u>2 SHOT</u> OF GUS TRENOR AND LILY SFITING IN THE CAB.
<u>TRACK STOPS</u> IN <u>2 SHOT</u>.

> GUS TRENOR
> Is your last box of Doucet dresses a failure, or did my wife rook you out of everything at bridge?
>
> LILY BART
> I have to give up Doucet dresses and bridge.
> I can't afford either anymore (SLIGHT PAUSE)
> And Judy thinks me a bore.
> (PREGNANT PAUSE)
> The fact is Judy is angry with me.
>
> GUS TRENOR
> Angry with you? Nonsense. My wife's devoted to you.
>
> LILY BART
> She is the best friend I have and that is why I mind vexing her.
> I want to make my peace with her.

SILENCE.

> LILY BART (WITH A HALF LAUGH)
> She has set her heart on my marrying money - a great deal of money.

GUS TRENOR (APPALLED)
You don't mean Percy Gryce! Good Lord! How on earth could Judy think you would do such a thing?

LILY BART
(LOWERING HER EYES THEN WITH A SIGH)
I sometimes think men understand a woman's motives better than their own sex do.

GUS TRENOR
Good Lord. I could have <u>told</u> Judy.

SILENCE.

GUS TRENOR
Oh by the way, Miss Lily, I wish you'd try to persuade Judy to be civil to Rosedale - I did a very neat stroke of business through him last week and if she would only ask him to dine now and then I could get almost anything out of him. He's going to be richer than all of us one of these days ...

<u>CUT TO:</u>

<u>CLOSE UP</u> LILY BART.
SHE SMILES DIPLOMATICALLY THEN PAUSES FOR A
JUDICIOUS MOMENT, THEN SPEAKS.

LILY BART
Would you do me a favour? A very great favour?

<u>CUT TO:</u>

<u>CLOSE UP</u> GUS TRENOR.

GUS TRENOR
Why, of course.

<u>CUT TO:</u>

<u>CLOSE UP</u> LILY BART.

LILY BART
I thought you would understand; that's why I wanted to speak to you.
(PAUSE)
I don't mean to bore you with all this but I am entirely dependent on my Aunt, and though she is very kind she makes me no regular allowance. I have a tiny income of my own but it's been badly invested. It seems to bring in less and less each year. And recently I've lost money at cards. I have paid my debts of course, but I don't dare tell my Aunt.

THE HOUSE OF MIRTH

>   (NEAR TO TEARS)
>   I can no longer go on living my present life.

CUT TO:

CLOSE UP GUS TRENOR.

>   GUS TRENOR
>   And Percy Gryce?

CUT TO:

CLOSE UP LILY BART.

>   LILY BART
>   I can't make that sort of marriage.

CUT TO:

CLOSE UP GUS TRENOR.

>   GUS TRENOR
> And so you gave him the sack, and that's the reason he lit out
>   by the first train this morning?

CUT TO:

CLOSE UP LILY BART.
SHE JUST LOOKS DOWN. SILENCE.

CUT TO:

2 SHOT.

>   GUS TRENOR
> If you will trust me I can make a handsome sum for you without
>   endangering your capital.

>   LILY BART (GRATEFUL)
> I am so ignorant of money matters, but I would be so grateful
>   to have a good advisor.

>   GUS TRENOR (SMILING)
>   Leave it to me. I'll find a solution.

PAN (R-L) TO CLOSE UP LILY.
SHE LEANS BACK RELIEVED AND SMILING AT HIM.
CONTINUE PANNING (R-L).

DISSOLVE TO:

26. EXT. DAY. CARRIAGE. NEW YORK.

CONTINUE PANNING (R-L) TO A 2 SHOT OF MRS PENISTON AND GRACE STEPNEY IN AN OPEN CARRIAGE, DRIVING THROUGH THE PARK.

MRS PENISTON
Really, Lily, you are as careless and frivolous as your poor parents were. I don't see why you go to Bellomont if you don't remember what happened or whom you saw there.

CUT TO:

CLOSE UP LILY BART.

LILY BART (RATHER WEARILY)
But there was no one new - just the usual throng.

CUT TO:

2 SHOT MRS PENISTON AND GRACE STEPNEY.

MRS PENISTON
When I was a girl I used to keep every menu from every dinner and write the names on the back.

GRACE STEPNEY (TIMIDLY)
Was Mr Selden there?

CUT TO:

CLOSE UP LILY BART.

LILY BART
Yes - he came later.

CUT TO:

2 SHOT MRS PENISTON AND GRACE STEPNEY.

GRACE STEPNEY
And Mr Rosedale - was he there?

CUT TO:

CLOSE UP LILY BART.

LILY BART (SLIGHTLY SURPRISED)
No. Of course not.
Why do you ask?

CUT TO:

2 SHOT MRS PENISTON AND GRACE STEPNEY.

GRACE STEPNEY
Oh passing interest, merely.
Mr. Selden tells me that socially Mr Rosedale is very ubiquitous now.

                    MRS PENISTON
    I have always thought that men like Rosedale and their
    methods of gaining fortunes were, at best, questionable, at
    worst, criminal. To grow richer at a time when most people's
    investments are shrinking strikes me as being in very bad taste.

                    GRACE STEPNEY
        But society still uses such men - if only obliquely.

                                                      CUT TO:

<u>CLOSE UP</u> LILY BART.

                        LILY BART
        If obliquity were a vice we should all be tainted.

                                                      CUT TO:

<u>2 SHOT</u> MRS PENISTON AND GRACE STEPNEY.

                    MRS PENISTON
    Only someone without family could make such a vulgar remark.

                                                      CUT TO:

<u>CLOSE UP</u> LILY BART.

                LILY BART (ABSOLUTELY CHARMING)
                    Aunt Julia you are my family.

                                                      CUT TO:

<u>2 SHOT</u> MRS PENISTON AND GRACE STEPNEY.

                MRS PENISTON (COMPLETELY WON OVER)
        There are times, Lily, when you are far too charming for your
                            own good.

THE CARRIAGE STOPS. IT HAS ARRIVED AT MRS PENISTON'S HOUSE.

                                                      CUT TO:

27. EXT. DAY. STREET/CARRIAGE. NEW YORK.

<u>WIDE SHOT</u>. THEY ALL GET OUT OF THE CARRIAGE AND MOUNT THE
STEPS TO THE HOUSE.
<u>PAN UP</u> WITH THEM.

                    MRS PENISTON
        Just as I thought! It's extraordinary that I cannot teach
        the parlour-maid to draw the blinds down evenly! Will you
                        see to it Grace?

                    GRACE STEPNEY
                      Of course.

THEY GO IN.

                                                    CUT TO:

28. INT. DAY. HALL & VESTIBULE, MRS PENISTON'S HOUSE.

<u>GROUP SHOT</u> MRS PENISTON, GRACE, LILY AND JENNINGS THE BUTLER. THE LADIES MOVE TO THE STAIRS.

                    MRS PENISTON
    Jennings we will take tea in the upstairs sitting room. Lily,
            you can read me the obituaries.

                     LILY BART
                (STILL VERY CHARMING)
    Oh Aunt Julia, Grace does it so much better than me - she can
    make the most insignificant death seem interesting. I will see
                      to the blinds.

                    MRS PENISTON
            Very well, you may join us later.

LILY GOES OFF TO THE DRAWING ROOM, MRS PENISTON AND GRACE GO UPSTAIRS.

                    MRS PENISTON
    Grace don't forget to give me my digitalis before tea.

                                                    CUT TO:

29. INT. DAY. HALL & VESTIBULE, MRS PENISTON'S HOUSE.

<u>SHOT</u> (<u>FROM BEHIND</u>) OF LILY GOING TO THE DRAWING ROOM DOORS AND OPENING THEM. SHE STANDS FOR A MOMENT LOOKING INTO THE GLOOMY ROOM THEN GOES IN.

                                                    CUT TO:

30. INT. DAY. DRAWING ROOM. MRS PENISTON'S HOUSE.

<u>SHOT</u> (FROM INSIDE THE DARK ROOM) OF LILY COMING IN AND CLOSING THE DOORS. SHE STANDS FOR A MOMENT IN THE SILENCE, THE ROOM SUFFOCATING HER. SHE MOVES TOWARDS THE PIANO. <u>PAN WITH HER</u> (<u>L-R</u>). SHE OPENS THE PIANO LID AND BEGINS TO PICK OUT A TUNE ON THE KEYS (A PIANO ARRANGEMENT OF THE SLOW MOVEMENT OF THE MARCELLO OBOE CONCERTO).

THE HOUSE OF MIRTH

BUT THE ROOM (INDEED THE HOUSE) SEEMS TO SUFFOCATE EVEN THIS, AND SHE STOPS PLAYING AND PUTS THE LID DOWN.
SHE STANDS STILL FOR A MOMENT THEN LOOKS TOWARDS HER REFLECTION IN THE LARGE MIRROR ABOVE THE FIREPLACE.

CUT TO:

SHOT OF MIRROR - LILY REFLECTED IN IT. ALSO REFLECTED IN IT IS A LARGE CHANDELIER AND A BRONZE STATUE OF THE DYING GLADIATOR.
IN FRONT OF THE MIRROR - ON THE MANTELPIECE - IS A LARGE, HEAVY ORMULU CLOCK SURMOUNTED BY A HELMETED MINERVA. IT STANDS BETWEEN TWO MALACHITE VASES.
THE CLOCK TICKS HEAVILY IN THE TOMB-LIKE SILENCE, THEN CHIMES THE HOUR. WE SEE (IN REFLECTION) LILY MOVE TOWARDS THE WINDOW.

CUT TO:

SHOT OF LILY COMING TO THE WINDOWS.
SHE RAISES ONE BLIND A FRACTION AND THEN THE OTHER, BUT WHAT EXTRA LIGHT DOES COME IN SCARCELY LIFTS THE GLOOM OF THE ROOM, FURNISHED (LIKE THE REST OF THE HOUSE) IN HEAVY MAHOGANY AND BLACK WALNUT.
SHE STANDS LOOKING OUT OF THE WINDOW - LIKE SOMEONE LONGING FOR FREEDOM.
THE FRONT DOORBELL IS HEARD RINGING BUT SHE DOESN'T REACT. THEN WE HEAR ONE OF THE DRAWING ROOM DOORS OPEN AND SHE LOOKS ROUND IN SURPRISE.

CUT TO:

SHOT OF THE CHARWOMAN FROM THE BENEDICK SQUEEZING PAST THE PARLOUR MAID AND COMING INTO THE ROOM.

            PARLOUR MAID
    It's a Mrs Haffen, Miss. She won't say what she wants.

THE PARLOUR MAID EXITS CLOSING THE DOOR.

            LILY BART (VOICE OVER)
        Do you want to see me?

MRS HAFFEN DOESN'T SPEAK FOR A MOMENT.

            MRS HAFFEN
        I have something you might like to see.

CUT TO:

CLOSE UP LILY BART VERY INTRIGUED. AFTER A PAUSE.

                    LILY BART
            You have something belonging to me?
                                                    CUT TO:

CLOSE UP MRS HAFFEN.

                    MRS HAFFEN
            Not exactly. It's mine as much as anybody's.

SHE TAKES FROM HER BAG A PARCEL WRAPPED IN NEWSPAPER.
                                                    CUT TO:

CLOSE UP LILY BART.

                    LILY BART
I don't understand. If the parcel is not mine, why are you here?

                                                    CUT TO:

CLOSE UP MRS HAFFEN.

                    MRS HAFFEN
I'm coming to that. My husband lost his job at The Benedick
        and so did I - we've been sick ... it's been hard ...

                                                    CUT TO:

CLOSE UP LILY. SHE MOVES BACK TO THE MANTELPIECE.
PAN WITH HER (L-R).

                    LILY BART
        I'm sorry you have been in trouble but if you have
            anything to say to me please do so.

                                                    CUT TO:

MID SHOT MRS HAFFEN.

                    MRS HAFFEN
(SHE OPENS THE PARCEL AND LETTERS SPILL OUT OF IT ONTO THE TABLE)
        When I was working at The Benedick I was in charge of
        cleaning the gentlemen's rooms. Most gentlemen are careful
        about the letters they get - burn them in winter, tear
                them into bits in Summer ...

                                                    CUT TO:

CLOSE UP LILY. SHE IS REPELLED.

                    MRS HAFFEN (VOICE OVER)
        - But Mr Selden wasn't so particular - he'd tear them through
            once then put them in the basket for anyone to see ...

THE HOUSE OF MIRTH

SILENCE.

                      LILY BART
I know nothing of these letters. I have no idea why you have brought them here.

                                                CUT TO:
<u>CLOSE UP</u> MRS HAFFEN.

                      MRS HAFFEN
To sell them.

SILENCE.

                    MRS HAFFEN
I saw you coming out of Mr Selden's rooms so I guessed they were worth more to you than me.

                                                CUT TO:
<u>2 SHOT</u>.
NEITHER MOVE. SILENCE. THEN LILY WALKS TO THE TABLE AND PICKS UP THE LETTERS AND BEGINS TO READ. SILENCE.
<u>CLOSE UP</u> LILY READING. FADE UP THE SOUND OF BERTHA DORSET'S VOICE READING THE LETTERS.

                BERTHA DORSET (VOICE OVER)
... My darling Lawrence, you are my consolation, my only joy ... in you I find more freedom and support than I have ever known ... in you I find love ...

FADE HER VOICE. THEN, AS LILY IS READING THE NEXT LETTER, FADE UP BERTHA'S VOICE AGAIN.

                BERTHA DORSET (VOICE OVER)
... I cannot bear George near me, when he touches me I want to scream ... his very presence is unbearable ... Oh Lawrence! The only thing worse than being married to a boor is being married to a rich boor ...

<u>FADE</u> HER VOICE. LILY CONTINUES LEAFING THROUGH THE LETTERS. <u>FADE UP</u> BERTHA'S VOICE.

                BERTHA DORSET (VOICE OVER)
... You promised me that we would meet when George was next away from town ... although you have forbidden me to come to you I will, I must ... you cannot deny me in this, I will not be denied in this ... not seeing you is so painful to me.
                    Your devoted Bertha.

CLOSE UP OF LETTERS WHICH LILY IS HOLDING. BERTHA'S VOICE FADES. WE SEE THAT AT THE BOTTOM OF EACH LETTER IS BERTHA DORSET'S SIGNATURE.
CLOSE UP LILY. SHE IS CALMER.
2 SHOT.

       LILY BART
    What do you want me to pay you for them?

       MRS HAFFEN
     One hundred and fifty.

       LILY BART
      Seventy five.

       MRS HAFFEN
    One hundred and twenty five.

       LILY BART
      One hundred.

       MRS HAFFEN
     I've got to live too.

       LILY BART
I have offered all that I am prepared to give for the letters.

SILENCE.

       LILY BART
   But there may be other ways of getting them.

     MRS HAFFEN (ACQUIESCING)
      One hundred.

LILY PAYS HER AND MRS HAFFEN LEAVES.
                CUT TO:

CLOSE UP LILY SMILING.
SHE TURNS AND LOOKS INTO THE MIRROR.

       LILY BART
"If you would forgive your enemy first, inflict a hurt on them."

LOOKING RADIANT.

       LILY BART
   Bertha - how could you have been so indiscreet.

THE HOUSE OF MIRTH

WE HEAR THE DOOR OPEN.
CUT TO:

SHOT OF GRACE STEPNEY AT THE DOOR.

GRACE STEPNEY
Lily, Aunt Julia would like to see you ... she is unwell.

CUT TO:

CLOSE UP LILY STILL LOOKING INTO THE MIRROR.

LILY BART (CHARMING BUT FIRM)
Not now Grace.

IN REFLECTION WE SEE GRACE LEAVE AND CLOSE THE DOOR.
HOLD.
DISSOLVE TO:

31. INT. DAY. CHURCH.

THE CHURCH IS DECORATED WITH ORCHIDS AND CRAMMED WITH FASHIONABLE GUESTS.
SIDEVIEW SHOT OF LAWRENCE SELDEN SITTING IN ONE OF THE PEWS. HE LOOKS TOWARDS CAMERA, NODS AND SMILES.
CUT TO:

SIDEVIEW SHOT OF LILY BART AND GRACE STEPNEY IN THE PEW OPPOSITE (SELDEN'S POV)
THEY LOOK AT HIM AND NOD AND SMILE. LILY THEN LOOKS AHEAD WHILE GRACE, FOR A MOMENT, LOOKS AT LILY THEN LOWERS HER EYES. IN GRACE'S EYES ONE CAN SEE THE DISAPPOINTMENT AS SHE REALISES THAT SHE CAN NEVER COMPETE WITH LILY FOR SELDEN.
TRACK IN ON LILY (SIDEVIEW) AND PAN (R-L) TO A SHOT IN WHICH WE SEE LILY TWO OR THREE PEWS BEHIND PERCY GRYCE. HE SEEMS PRIM BUT ACCEPTABLE.
LILY STEALS A GLANCE BACK AT SELDEN, THEN LOOKS AHEAD.
CONTINUE TRACKING AND PANNING (R-L) TO THE COUPLE AT THE ALTER.

MINISTER
... I now pronounce you man and wife.

THEY KISS AND TURN.
IT IS JACK STEPNEY AND GWEN VAN OSBURGH.
THEY WALK UP THE AISLE.
TRACK BACK WITH THEM.
DISSOLVE TO:

32. INT. DAY. VAN OSBURGH MANSION.

<u>TRACK BACK</u> (IN A <u>2 SHOT</u>) WITH LILY BART AND GRACE STEPNEY. THEY ARE WALKING DOWN EITHER SIDE OF A HUGE TABLE LADEN WITH WEDDING PRESENTS.

   GRACE STEPNEY (LOOKING AT A LARGE PENDANT IN DISBELIEF)
  It's as big as a dinner plate! Who can it be from?

     LILY BART (READING THE LABEL)
       'Sim Rosedale'.
    That explains the vulgarity.

      GRACE STEPNEY
 Well, Gwen can always exchange it for something else.
     Oh this is exquisite!

     LILY BART (READING THE LABEL)
  One wouldn't expect anything less from MR Gryce.

<u>CONTINUE TRACKING BACK</u>.

      GRACE STEPNEY
 They say Edie Van Osburgh and MR Gryce have become fast
 friends since he left Bellomont. But I forgot. You and he
   became friends at Mrs Trenor's, didn't you?

    LILY BART (SMILING BUT NIGGLED)
 Grace I envy you your power to construe romance from the most
      prosaic circumstances.

THEY REACH THE END OF THE TABLE.
<u>TRACK STOPS</u>.
GRACE EXITS.
LILY LOOKS UP AND STARTS SLIGHTLY.
               <u>CUT TO</u>:

<u>2 SHOT</u> <u>OF</u> EVIE VAN OSBURGH (THE YOUNGER SISTER OF THE BRIDE) AND PERCY GRYCE IN INTIMATE CONVERSATION.
               <u>CUT TO</u>:

<u>SHOT OF</u> LILY. SHE LOOKS UNEASY AT WHAT SHE HAS SEEN.

      GUS TRENOR (VOICE OVER)
    I never saw you look so lovely.

THE HOUSE OF MIRTH

> LILY BART (TURNING AND SMILING)
> Oh - Gus -

HE JOINS HER IN A 2 SHOT.

> GUS TRENOR (A BIT TOO LOUDLY)
> Well, Lily, I've got a cheque for you.

> LILY BART
> (DROPPING HER VOICE IN EMBARRASSMENT LEST ANYONE SHOULD HEAR.)
> Another dividend?

SHE DRAWS HIM TOWARDS THE CONSERVATORY, WHICH LIES JUST BEYOND THEM.

> GUS TRENOR
> You have both Rosedale and I to thank for it.
> I've made you five thousand on his 'tip' and I've re-invested four on your behalf.
> (INTIMATELY)
> And there's a promise of another 'big rise'.

> LILY BART
> (STILL EMBARRASSED AND NOW DISTURBED)
> I can't thank you properly now.

> GUS TRENOR (GETTING ANNOYED)
> I don't want to be thanked - I want you to be nice to Rosedale and me - I'd like to see you now and then - come on over to Bellomont - I'll send the motor -

> LILY BART (LAUGHING BUT DISTURBED)
> Really, you say the most absurd things! Besides it's impossible. My aunt has come back to town and I must stay with her for the rest of the season.

GUS TRENOR IS SILENT AND RATHER GLUM

> LILY BART
> Come to see me and Aunt Peniston the next afternoon you are in town and you can tell me how better to invest my small fortune.

THE CROWD HAS THICKENED AND THEY ARE SEPARATED.

33. INT. DAY. TERRACE. VAN OSBURGH MANSION.

LILY GOES INTO THE CONSERVATORY PROPER THEN OUT ONTO THE TERRACE. SHE STANDS FOR A MOMENT FANNING HERSELF.

                    LAWRENCE SELDEN (VOICE OVER)
                          This is luck!

SHE SPINS AROUND, COMPLETELY TAKEN OFF-GUARD.

                                                    CUT TO:

CLOSE UP LAWRENCE SELDEN.

                         LAWRENCE SELDEN
   I was wondering if I should be able to have a word with you.

                                                    CUT TO:

CLOSE UP LILY BART.

                            LILY BART
   I have not recovered my self-respect since you showed me how
                       poor my ambitions were.

                                                    CUT TO:

CLOSE UP LAWRENCE SELDEN.

                         LAWRENCE SELDEN
     On the contrary, I thought that I had been the means of
     proving they were more important to you than anything else.

                                                    CUT TO:

WIDE SHOT LOOKING BACK INTO THE CONSERVATORY FROM THE TERRACE.
GUS TRENOR AND SIM ROSEDALE COMING TOWARDS LILY AND SELDEN.

                           GUS TRENOR
                 I thought you'd given us the slip Lily.

                          SIM ROSEDALE
                 We've been hunting all over for you.

GUS TRENOR SMILES AND LEAVES SIM ROSEDALE, LILY AND SELDEN
STANDING UNEASILY TOGETHER.
SILENCE.

                          SIM ROSEDALE
                            {TO LILY}
   My object in hunting for you was to invite you to my box at
   the opera on opening night. Gus has promised to come to town
         on purpose - he's a tremendous admirer of yours.
   I fancy he'd go much farther for the pleasure of seeing you.

THE HOUSE OF MIRTH

                    LILY BART
                  (BARELY CIVIL)
      The Trenors are my best friends - I think
      we should all go a long way to see each other.

SILENCE.

                    SIM ROSEDALE
                    (SMILING)
    How's your luck been going on Wall Street lately? I hear Gus
       pulled off a nice little pile for you last month.

                    LILY BART
               (LIGHTLY BUT ANGERED)
       I had a little money to invest and MR Trenor helps
                    me in such matters.
      I had a lucky 'turn' - is that what you call it? You make a
               great many yourself I believe.

A VERY UNEASY SILENCE.

              SIM ROSEDALE (TO BREAK THE SILENCE)
                       (TO LILY)
    Is that the latest creation of the dressmaker you go to see at
    The Benedick? If so, it is a great success. Isn't it Mr Selden?

SELDEN DOES NOT REPLY.

                 LILY BART (VERY UNEASY)
      That's nice of you. But it would be nicer still if you got me
                    a glass of lemonade.

SIM ROSEDALE SMILES AND GOES FOR THE LEMONADE.
IN THE BACKGROUND (BUT VISIBLY) PERCY GRYCE AND EVIE VAN
OSBURGH WALK BACK INTO THE CONSERVATORY.
LILY IS VERY UNEASY AT THE SIGHT. SELDEN WATCHES THEM AND
THEN HER

                    LAWRENCE SELDEN
       They met six weeks ago at Bertha Dorset's and have been
                    devoted ever since ...

LILY TRIES TO LOOK UNCONCERNED.

                    LAWRENCE SELDEN
      ... The engagement is to be announced next week. They say it
    will be just the nicest marriage possible - one dull fortune
                    marrying another ....
                                                       CUT TO:

CLOSE UP LILY BART

          LILY BART
   (SMILING AND TRYING TO BE BRAVE IN THE FACE OF DEFEAT)
    Evie Van Osburgh and Percy Gryce? Well, Well.

SHE STANDS GAZING AFTER THEM.
                   DISSOLVE TO:

34. INT. EVENING. VAN OSBURGH MANSION.

SHOT OF CURTAINS IN FRONT OF AN IMPROVISED STAGE SET UP AT ONE END OF THE BALLROOM.
HOLD FOR A MOMENT THEN THE CURTAINS GO BACK TO REVEAL A YOUNG SOCIALITE REPRESENTING A FIGURE IN A TITIAN PAINTING - A TABLEAU VIVANT.
AUDIENCE POLITELY APPLAUDS.
                   CUT TO:

SHOT OF AUDIENCE APPLAUDING - THEY ARE THE WEDDING GUESTS.
A PAUSE.
THEN THEY APPLAUD AGAIN.
                   CUT TO:

THE SECOND TABLEAU VIVANT.
THE CURTAINS GO BACK TO REVEAL A SECOND SOCIALITE THIS TIME REPRESENTING A GIRL IN A VAN DYKE (OR VERMEER?) PAINTING.

HOLD.

THE CURTAIN IS LOWERED.
SILENCE.

THEN THE CURTAIN GOES UP TO REVEAL THE THIRD TABLEAU VIVANT.
IT IS LILY BART AS REYNOLDS' 'MRS LLOYD'.
THE AUDIENCE AUDIBLY SAY 'OH!' AND APPLAUD VIGOROUSLY.
HOLD ON LILY WHO HOLDS THE POSE, CONFIDENT SHE HAS MADE A GREAT IMPACT.
THE AUDIENCE CONTINUE TO APPLAUD AS THE CURTAIN DROPS.

PAN AWAY FROM HER (L-R) TO AUDIENCE STILL APPLAUDING AND PICK UP LAWRENCE SELDEN AND GRACE STEPNEY STANDING NEXT TO ONE ANOTHER.
IN A 2 SHOT.
THE APPLAUSE CONTINUES FOR A MOMENT THEN LITTLE GROUPS FORM INTO INTIMATE CIRCLES AS EVERYONE STARTS TOWARDS THE DINING ROOM WHICH IS BEYOND THE BALLROOM.

GRACE STEPNEY
She has never looked so radiant. I think I like her best in that simple dress. It makes her look like the real Lily ...
(SHE LOOKS LOVINGLY AT SELDEN)
... The Lily I know.

LAWRENCE SELDEN
(NOT LOOKING AT GRACE OR AWARE OF HER FEELINGS)
The Lily we know ...

GRACE LOOKS AWAY FROM HIM TRYING TO HIDE HER DEJECTION.

LAWRENCE SELDEN
She is herself with a few people only ... (PENSIVE)
She has it in her to become whatever she is believed to be ...

HE LOOKS AT GRACE EARNESTLY.
SHE LOOKS AT HIM TRYING TO CONCEAL HOW SHE FEELS.

LAWRENCE SELDEN
... We must think the best of her ...

GRACE STEPNEY (PUTTING A BRAVE FACE ON AND SMILING)
I'll tell her that!
(SHE LOOKS AT LILY)
She always says you dislike her.

PEOPLE HAVE STARTED WALKING TOWARDS THE DINING ROOM.

LAWRENCE SELDEN
Well, Grace, how was life at Richfield?

GRACE STEPNEY
Quiet. Aunt Peniston sees very little company.

LAWRENCE SELDEN
I'm sure your being there gave her much pleasure.

GRACE STEPNEY (TRYING TO BE JOVIAL)
Yes, I'm as reliable as roast mutton. But Aunt Julia is not alone in preferring Lily's erratic brilliance.

LAWRENCE OFFERS HER HIS ARM AND SHE TAKES IT.
THEY TURN AWAY FROM CAMERA AND WALK TOWARDS THE DINING ROOM.

LAWRENCE SELDEN
You should marry Grace.

TERENCE DAVIES SCREENPLAYS: VOL. II

                    GRACE STEPNEY
        (WITH AN EDGE TO HER VOICE BUT WITH A SMILE)
               We should all marry, Mr Selden.

PAN AWAY FROM THEM (R-L).

                                              DISSOLVE TO:

35. EXT. NIGHT. GARDEN. VAN OSBURGH MANSION.

CONTINUE PANNING (R-L) TO PICK UP IN A 2 SHOT SELDEN AND LILY
ARM IN ARM GOING DOWN THE TERRACE STEPS AND INTO THE GARDEN.
LILY AND SELDEN WALK DOWN INTO THE GARDEN AND SIT ON A BENCH
NEAR THE FOUNTAIN.
MUSIC FROM THE HOUSE IS HEARD. THEY DON'T SPEAK.
HOLD ON A 2 SHOT.
THEN TRACK IN ON THEM.
TRACK ENDS ON A CLOSER 2 SHOT.
AFTER A LONG PAUSE LILY SPEAKS.

                        LILY BART
                  You never speak to me.

                     LAWRENCE SELDEN
              I'm never near you long enough.
PAUSE.
                        LILY BART
                You think hard things of me.

                     LAWRENCE SELDEN
                I think of you at any rate.

                        LILY BART
             Then why do we never see each other?

                     LAWRENCE SELDEN
      I have my law practice and you are always surrounded by
                          admirers.

                        LILY BART
            There are no admirers at my aunt's house.

                     LAWRENCE SELDEN
        Then perhaps I might take tea with you at Mrs Peniston's
                         next week.

                    LILY BART (EAGERLY)
  Yes, come at four on Friday. Then we can talk. I have so much to
  say to you - I need your help. You promised once to help me ...

THE HOUSE OF MIRTH

                    LAWRENCE SELDEN
        The one way I can help you is by loving you.

SHE LOOKS AT HIM AND HE AT HER.
THEY DON'T MOVE FOR A MOMENT. THEN THEY KISS.

                        LILY BART
            (VERY QUIETLY AS SHE CONTINUES TO HOLD HIM)
                Love me ... but don't tell me so ...

HOLD ON THEM IN THE SILENCE.
THEN SHE GETS UP AND RUNS INTO THE HOUSE, LEAVING SELDEN
ALONE. HE JUST STANDS THERE.
PAN (L-R) AWAY FROM HIM. AS WE PAN WE SEE GUS TRENOR ANGRILY
LOOKING AT THEM.
                                            DISSOLVE TO:

36. INT. NIGHT. VAN OSBURGH MANSION.

SHOT OF THE VESTIBULE AND HALL. PEOPLE PUTTING ON THEIR
OUTDOOR COATS IN ORDER TO LEAVE.
IN A GROUP NEAREST CAMERA ARE GUS TRENOR, SIM ROSEDALE AND
LAWRENCE SELDEN.

                        GUS TRENOR
                   Selden - going too?

SELDEN JUST SMILES, PUTS ON HIS COAT AND GOES OUT THROUGH THE
DOOR, FOLLOWED BY SIM ROSEDALE, GUS TRENOR AND OTHERS.

                    LAWRENCE SELDEN
                (OVER HIS SHOULDER TO GUS TRENOR)
                Aren't you staying for supper?

                        GUS TRENOR
            (TETCHILY, TO HIMSELF, BUT MEANING TO BE OVERHEARD)
                            No.
     When people crowd their rooms so that you can't get near
     anyone you want to speak to I'd sooner do without. My wife was
     right to stay away; she says life's too short to spend it in
                    breaking new people in.

TRACK OUT WITH HIM AND THE PEOPLE LEAVING.
SOUNDTRACK: COSÌ FAN TUTTE OVERTURE

                                        DISSOLVE IN DARKNESS TO:

37. EXT. NIGHT. OPERA HOUSE. NEW YORK.

CARRIAGES DISGORGING THE WEALTHY AUDIENCE FROM PRIVATE CARRIAGES AND CABS. THEY CRISS-CROSS IN FRONT OF THE CAMERA. <u>TRACK IN</u> ON THEM.

DISSOLVE TO:

38. EXT./INT NIGHT. OPERA HOUSE. NEW YORK.

<u>CONTINUE TRACKING</u> FROM BEHIND WITH THE CROWD, BUT WITH A GROUP NEAREST CAMERA CONSISTING OF LILY BART (WHO WALKS SLIGHTLY AHEAD) FOLLOWED BY GUS TRENOR, SIM ROSEDALE, MR AND MRS JACK STEPNEY AND BERTHA AND GEORGE DORSET.

> SIM ROSEDALE
> I never knew 'til tonight what a figure Lily has.

> GUS TRENOR
> Everybody knows. Bad taste I call it.

TRENOR AND ROSEDALE GO A LITTLE AHEAD.

<u>SOUNDTRACK</u>: <u>COSÌ FAN TUTTE</u> OVERTURE
<u>CONTINUE TRACKING</u> INTO THE OPERA HOUSE AND UP THE STAIRS.

> JACK STEPNEY
> When a girl's as good looking as that she'd better marry, then no questions are asked. She cannot go on claiming the privileges of marriage without assuming its obligations!

> GEORGE DORSET
> Perhaps Lily is about to assume them in the shape of Mr Rosedale.

> JACK STEPNEY
> Good Lord! One doesn't marry someone like Rosedale!

> BERTHA DORSET (LAUGHING)
> In Lily's case it's a mistake to have too high a standard.

> GWEN STEPNEY
> She looks as though she were up for auction.

<u>SOUNDTRACK</u>: <u>COSÌ FAN TUTTE</u> OVERTURE CONTINUES.

DISSOLVE TO:

39. NIGHT. DORSET'S BOX. OPERA HOUSE.

BERTHA DORSET AND GWEN STEPNEY COME INTO THE BOX AND SIT DOWN FOLLOWED BY JACK STEPNEY AND GEORGE DORSET.

> GEORGE DORSET
> Thank God it's in Italian, then we can eat late - when it's Wagner we have to eat <u>days</u> before!

DISSOLVE TO:

40. NIGHT. MRS PENISTON'S BOX. OPERA HOUSE.

<u>2 SHOT</u> MRS PENISTON AND GRACE STEPNEY IN A BOX. MRS PENISTON IS IN THE CENTRE OF THE BOX, GRACE TO HER RIGHT, CONCEALED SLIGHTLY BEHIND THE CURTAINS WHICH HANG OUTSIDE THE BOX. MRS PENISTON IS SURVEYING THE AUDIENCE THROUGH HER OPERA GLASSES.

<u>SOUNDTRACK</u>: <u>COSÌ FAN TUTTE</u> OVERTURE CONTINUES.

> MRS PENISTON
> (DISQUIETED)
> Lily and Gus Trenor you say?

> GRACE STEPNEY
> Aunt Peniston, of course I don't mean ...

> MRS PENISTON
> (GROWING ANGRY)
> Then what do you mean Grace? Do people say he's in love with her?

> GRACE STEPNEY (WITH A SMILE)
> People always say unpleasant things. It is a pity, though, that Lily makes herself so conspi<u>cu</u>ous.

> MRS PENISTON
> <u>Conspicuous</u>! Does he mean to divorce then marry her?

> GRACE STEPNEY
> No - it's - it's a flirtation - nothing more.

> MRS PENISTON
> A flirtation? With a married man? Such things were never heard of in my day. And my own niece!

CUT TO:

41. INT. NIGHT. ROSEDALE'S BOX. OPERA HOUSE.

<u>SHOT OF</u> SIM ROSEDALE'S BOX.
<u>SOUNDTRACK</u>: <u>COSÌ FAN TUTTE</u> OVERTURE CONTINUES.
LILY ENTERS FIRST, FOLLOWED BY GUS TRENOR AND SIM ROSEDALE.
SHE HOLDS THE STAGE FOR A MOMENT BEFORE SITTING DOWN.
SHE THEN SITS.
SHE SEES MRS PENISTON AND NODS IN HER DIRECTION.

                                        DISSOLVE TO:

42. NIGHT MRS PENISTON'S BOX. OPERA HOUSE.

<u>SOUNDTRACK</u>: <u>COSÌ FAN TUTTE</u> OVERTURE CONTINUES.
GRACE (PARTIALLY CONCEALED BY THE BOX CURTAIN) HAS NOT SEEN
LILY. MRS PENISTON GIVES A SHORT NOD IN LILY'S DIRECTION.

                    MRS PENISTON
                What else is being said?

                    GRACE STEPNEY
                That Gus Trenor pays her bills.

                MRS PENISTON (OUTRAGED)
        Rubbish! Lily has her own income and I provide for her
                    very handsomely.
PAUSE.
                    GRACE STEPNEY
                There are her gambling debts.

                    MRS PENISTON
                    What do you mean?
        Who told you that my niece plays cards for money?

                    GRACE STEPNEY
    Mrs Gryce. She told me herself that it was Lily's gambling
                debts that frightened Percy.
    In fact people are inclined to excuse her on that account.

                    MRS PENISTON
                 To excuse her for what?

                    GRACE STEPNEY
        For accepting the attentions of men like Gus Trenor.

MRS PENISTON SITS THERE FURIOUS.
SILENCE.

THE HOUSE OF MIRTH

                    MRS PENISTON
Thank you for telling me Grace. But I must say this unwelcome information has completely ruined the Mozart for me.

SHE PUTS THE OPERA GLASSES TO HER EYES AGAIN.
                                           DISSOLVE TO:

43. NIGHT OPERA. HOUSE.

SOUNDTRACK: COSÌ FAN TUTTE OVERTURE CONTINUES.
SHOT OF LAWRENCE SELDEN COMING DOWN THE AISLE TOWARDS HIS SEAT.
TRACK BACK WITH HIM.
AND TRACK STOPS WHEN HE SITS DOWN.
HE LOOKS UP TO SIM ROSEDALE'S BOX.
                                           DISSOLVE TO:

44. INT. NIGHT. SIM ROSEDALE'S BOX, OPERA HOUSE.

SHOT OF BOX. LILY AND GUS TRENOR TOGETHER SLIGHTLY AWAY FROM SIM ROSEDALE.
SOUNDTRACK: COSÌ FAN TUTTE OVERTURE CONTINUES.
                                               CUT TO:

2 SHOT (LILY BART AND GUS TRENOR).

                    GUS TRENOR
                  (CONSPIRATORIAL)
Look here Lily - Judy and I have been in town for weeks - when am I going to see you?

        LILY BART (LIGHTLY BUT CLEARLY EMBARRASSED)
You can find me any afternoon at my aunt's. Come there some afternoon and we can have a quiet talk.

                    GUS TRENOR
You put me off with that at the Van Osburgh wedding, but the plain truth is now that you've got what you wanted out of me you'd rather not see me.

                LILY BART (SHOCKED)
Don't be foolish Gus. If you want to see me come to my aunt's.

                    GUS TRENOR
Lily - let's leave before the first act starts - Judy's as cross as two sticks when she's away from Bellomont - come to the house now?

                    LILY BART
              Is Judy unwell?

                    GUS TRENOR
         Well a visit from you might be just what's needed.

                    LILY BART
              Very well Gus - I'll come with you.

THEY LEAVE, GIVING BRIEF APOLOGIES TO SIM ROSEDALE.
SOUNDTRACK: COSÌ FAN TUTTE OVERTURE CONTINUES.
                                                    DISSOLVE TO:

45. NIGHT. OPERA HOUSE.

SHOT OF LAWRENCE SELDEN.
THE OVERTURE FINISHES. THE HOUSE LIGHTS GOES DOWN.
APPLAUSE.
THE CURTAIN RISES.
SELDEN HAS BEEN WATCHING THE BOX AND SEES, TO HIS DISMAY,
LILY LEAVE WITH GUS TRENOR.
HE HURRIEDLY GETS UP FROM HIS SEAT AND LEAVES.
                                                         CUT TO:

46. EXT. NIGHT. OPERA HOUSE NEW YORK.

SHOT OF LILY AND GUS TRENOR GETTING INTO A CARRIAGE. IT
DRIVES OFF.
PAN (L-R) AWAY FROM IT TO A CLOSE UP OF SELDEN WATCHING IT
RECEDE. HE LOOKS BOTH CRESTFALLEN AND ANGRY.
HE WALKS AWAY FROM THE OPERA HOUSE INTO THE NIGHT.
                                                         CUT TO:

47. INT. NIGHT. TRENOR HOUSE.

WIDE SHOT OF THE FRONT DOOR FROM THE VESTIBULE.
THE HOUSE IS DARK AND SILENT, AND LOOKS UNINHABITED.
THE FRONT DOOR OPENS AND GUS TRENOR AND LILY ENTER.
LILY SLIGHTLY UNEASY, GUS GENIAL.

                    GUS TRENOR
         Doesn't it look as if it were waiting
              for the body to be brought down?

HE LAUGHS A LITTLE. SHE DOESN'T RESPOND.
                                                         CUT TO:

THE HOUSE OF MIRTH

SHOT (SIDEVIEW) OF THEM BOTH WALKING THROUGH THE SILENT. DARK HOUSE.

                    GUS TRENOR
    Come into the den. It's the only comfortable room
                    in the house.

                                      CUT TO:

48. INT. NIGHT. DEN TRENOR HOUSE.

SHOT OF THE ROOM. IT IS LARGE AND COMFORTABLE. IT LOOKS AS THOUGH IT IS OCCUPIED. A FIRE BURNS.
LILY ENTERS SHOT.

                    LILY BART
                Where's Judy?

WE HEAR THE DOORS CLOSE BEHIND HER. GUS TRENOR GOES TO THE FIREPLACE.

                    GUS TRENOR
     The fact is she's not up to seeing anybody.

                    LILY BART
   Do you mean Judy is not well enough to see me?

             GUS TRENOR (TURNING AND SMILING)
    Devil of a headache - quite knocked out by it.

       LILY BART (AFRAID BUT MASKING IT WITH A SMILE)
  In that case will you have the goodness to call me a cab?

                    GUS TRENOR
              Why must you go?

                    LILY BART
    It's late and we are alone. I must insist.

             GUS TRENOR (ANGRY AND SMILING)
 It's always the same old story! You can't give me five minutes
           but are charming to others.

HE TAKES A STEP TOWARDS HER.

                  GUS TRENOR
  I only went to that damned stupid opera to be with you.

>   LILY BART (NOW REALLY AFRAID)
>   I must insist on you calling me a cab.
>
>   GUS TRENOR
>   Suppose I won't?
>   What then?
>
>   LILY BART
>   If you force me I shall go upstairs to Judy.
>
>   GUS TRENOR
>   Sit down. I've got a word to say to you.

LILY MAKES A MOVE TO GO AND GUS PUSHES A CHAIR WITH HIS FOOT, SO THAT THE CHAIR CRASHES AGAINST THE CLOSED DOORS OF THE DEN. LILY IS NOW TERRIFIED.

<u>   CUT TO:</u>

<u>CLOSE UP</u> LILY BART

>   LILY BART
> If you have anything to say to me you must say it another time.
> I shall go upstairs to Judy unless you call me a cab at once.

<u>   CUT TO:</u>

<u>CLOSE UP</u> GUS TRENOR

>   GUS TRENOR
>   Go upstairs.
>   Judy isn't there.

<u>   CUT TO:</u>

<u>CLOSE UP</u> LILY BART

>   LILY BART
>   Do you mean that Judy is not in the house?

<u>   CUT TO:</u>

<u>CLOSE UP</u> GUS TRENOR

>   GUS TRENOR
>   She's not even in town.

<u>   CUT TO:</u>

<u>CLOSE UP</u> LILY BART {<u>SLIGHTLY WIDER</u>}.

>   LILY BART (AGHAST)
>   I don't believe you.
>   I'll go up -

THE HOUSE OF MIRTH

GUS TRENOR JOINS HER IN A <u>2 SHOT</u>.

> GUS TRENOR
> My wife is still at Bellomont.

> LILY BART
> If she wasn't coming to town she'd have telephoned.

> GUS TRENOR
> She did.

> LILY BART
> I received no message.

> GUS TRENOR
> I didn't send any.

LILY NOW HORRIFIED.

> LILY BART
> How dare you compromise me in this way.

> GUS TRENOR
> Don't take that high tone with me. I've been patient long enough. After all, the man who pays for the dinner is generally allowed a seat at the table.

> LILY BART
> I don't know what you mean!

GUS TRENOR COMES CLOSER TO HER AND DROPS HIS VOICE TO AN INTIMATE TONE.

> GUS TRENOR
> I didn't begin this business - kept out of the way - but I can tell fast enough when I'm being made a fool of - you've got what you wanted and now Gus isn't needed any more. But that isn't playing fair, Lily, that's dodging the rules of the game - and now you've got to pay.

> LILY BART
> (OUTRAGED)
> Do you mean I owe you money? You told me it was alright.

> GUS TRENOR
> It was alright - it's alright - you're welcome to it, Lily, all of it - I just want to be thanked a little ...

                    LILY BART
         I have thanked you. Or do you wish for payment in kind?

HE GOES TO GRAB AND KISS HER, SHE PUSHES HIM AWAY.

                    LILY BART
             If I owe you money you shall be paid.

                    GUS TRENOR
               You owe me nine thousand dollars.

                    LILY BART
                    (SHOCKED)
                 Nine thousand? (PAUSE)
                    I will pay you.

                    GUS TRENOR
         I suppose you'll go to Selden or Rosedale for it. Unless
         you've settled those scores already and I'm the only one left
                       out in the cold.

                    LILY BART
             What more do you have to say to me?

               GUS TRENOR (AFTER A PAUSE)
                       Go home!

LILY RUNS FROM THE ROOM.
                                                          CUT TO:

49. INT. NIGHT. MRS PENISTON'S HOUSE.

<u>SIDE SHOT</u> OF FRONT DOOR OPENING. LILY COMES IN AND CLOSES THE FRONT DOOR VERY QUIETLY THEN WALKS TO THE FOOT OF THE STAIRS.
<u>PAN WITH HER</u> (<u>R-L</u>)
SHE IS STILL CLEARLY VERY SHOCKED AND SHAKEN. SHE ASCENDS THE STAIRS.
<u>CRANE UP</u> WITH HER.
AS SHE NEARS THE LANDING AT THE TOP OF THE STAIRS, LIGHT FLOODS OUT FROM THE DOOR OF THE UPSTAIRS SITTING ROOM BEING OPENED. LILY STOPS, STARTLED. SHE CONTINUES UP THE STAIRS.

                    MRS PENISTON (VOICE OVER)
              Come here Lily, I wish to speak with you.

                    LILY BART
                (STILL CLIMBING THE STAIRS)
            Aunt Julia it is very late and I am very tired.

THE HOUSE OF MIRTH

> MRS PENISTON (VOICE OVER)
> I must insist Lily.

LILY GOES INTO THE ROOM AND CLOSES THE DOOR.
TRACK AND PAN (R-L) ALONG THE DARK LANDING TO A BEDROOM DOOR AJAR. GRACE STEPNEY BEHIND THE DOOR.
SHE HAS SEEN EVERYTHING. SLOWLY SHE CLOSES THE DOOR.

CUT TO:

50. INT. NIGHT. MRS PENISTON'S SITTING ROOM.

CLOSE UP MRS PENISTON.

> MRS PENISTON
> You're a bad colour, Lily. This incessant rushing about is beginning to tell on you.

CUT TO:

SHOT OF LILY COMING IN AND SITTING DOWN OPPOSITE MRS PENISTON.

> LILY BART
> I don't think it's that.
> I've had other worries.

CUT TO:

CLOSE UP MRS PENISTON.

> MRS PENISTON
> Ah.

CUT TO:

2 SHOT.
SILENCE BETWEEN THEM. LILY IS VERY AWKWARD. SHE STRUGGLES TO IMPART THE WORST OF THE NEWS.

> LILY BART
> The fact is I owe some money.

MRS PENISTON REMAINS SILENT.

> LILY BART
> I ... I have been foolish ... there are bills ... not tradesmen ... that are pressing ... they must be settled.

> MRS PENISTON
> I paid your dressmaker for you last October - but if you owe Madame Celeste another thousand dollars she may send me your account.

LILY BART
It isn't only Madame Celeste. (PAUSE)
I owe a great deal more than a thousand dollars.

CLOSE UP MRS PENISTON.

MRS PENISTON (ALARMED)
A great deal more?
To whom?
Do I know these people?

LILY BART (VOICE OVER)
Some by name, others by reputation.

MRS PENISTON
Then they are of no consequence.

CUT TO:

CLOSE UP LILY BART.

LILY BART
The debts I speak of are different.
(WITH GREAT DIFFICULTY)
The fact is I've been playing cards a good deal ...

CUT TO:

2 SHOT.

MRS PENISTON (OUTRAGED)
It's true then?
You play cards for money?

LILY IS SILENT.

MRS PENISTON
Do you play on Sundays?

LILY BART
You're hard on me Aunt Julia ... I have never really cared for cards but one hates to be thought priggish and one drifts into doing what the others do. I've had a dreadful lesson ...
If you help me out this time I promise ...

MRS PENISTON
You needn't make any promises, it's unnecessary. When I offered you a home I didn't undertake to pay your gambling debts.

CLOSE UP LILY BART.

THE HOUSE OF MIRTH

                    LILY BART (HORRIFIED)
        Aunt Julia! You don't mean that you won't help me?

                                                        CUT TO:

CLOSE UP MRS PENISTON.

                         MRS PENISTON
                          (IMPLACABLE)
        I shall certainly not do anything to give the impression
                 that I countenance your behaviour.

                                                        CUT TO:

CLOSE UP LILY BART.

                          LILY BART
                Aunt Julia I shall be disgraced.

                                                        CUT TO:

CLOSE UP MRS PENISTON.

                         MRS PENISTON
        I consider that you are disgraced, Lily. And now I must ask
          you to leave me, this scene has been extremely painful
                 to me and I have my own health to consider.

PAN (L-R) TO LILY.

                    MRS PENISTON (VOICE OVER)
        And tell Jennings that I wish to see no-one until tomorrow
                afternoon and then only Grace Stepney.

                          LILY BART
                          (STUNNED)
                    Grace? ... Yes Aunt Julia.

LILY RISES WITHOUT SPEAKING AND GOES TO THE DOOR.
PAN WITH HER (R-L).
SHE GOES OUT.
                                                        CUT TO:

51. INT. NIGHT. LANDING. MRS PENISTON'S HOUSE.

LILY COMES OUT STUNNED BY THE INTERVIEW.
SHE STANDS BY THE DOOR FOR A MOMENT COMPLETELY DISTRAUGHT.
THEN A THOUGHT COMES TO HER AND SHE RUNS ANXIOUSLY ALONG THE
LANDING TO GRACE STEPNEY'S ROOM.
PAN AND TRACK WITH HER (R-L).

SHE KNOCKS QUIETLY BUT ANXIOUSLY ON THE DOOR.
GRACE OPENS THE DOOR.

                GRACE STEPNEY
                (URGENT AND QUIET)
  Lily it's after midnight! What will Aunt Julia think?

                LILY BART
         (PUSHING PAST HER AND GOING IN)
  I don't care - I couldn't go to my room - I hate it so.

                                    CUT TO:

52. INT. NIGHT. GRACE STEPNEY'S BEDROOM. MRS PENISTON'S HOUSE.

<u>SHOT OF</u> GRACE CLOSING THE DOOR. THE ROOM IS LIT ONLY BY CANDLES AND A SMALL FIRE.

                GRACE STEPNEY
    Lily, what has happened? Can't you tell me?

                                    CUT TO:

<u>SHOT OF</u> LILY SINKING DOWN BY THE FENDER IN FRONT OF THE FIRE.

              LILY BART (VERY UPSET)
  I came to you because I couldn't bear being alone ...
             not tonight, in the dark.

LILY IS VERY DISTRAUGHT.
                                    CUT TO:

<u>SHOT OF</u> GRACE STILL AT THE DOOR. SILENCE.
THEN SHE MOVES TO LILY.
<u>PAN WITH HER</u> {L-R) TO A <u>2 SHOT</u> <u>OF</u> LILY ON THE FLOOR BY THE FENDER, GRACE SITTING IN AN ARMCHAIR OPPOSITE HER.
SILENCE.
                GRACE STEPNEY
           Tell me. If you can.

THE SILENCE IS BROKEN ONLY BY LILY'S TEARS, THEN SHE MANAGES TO CONTROL HERSELF ENOUGH TO SPEAK.

                LILY BART
  I thought I could manage my own life ... but I have been
  foolish, Grace - foolish to the point of being compromised ...

THE HOUSE OF MIRTH

                GRACE STEPNEY
            By whom? Mr Selden?

                 LILY BART
              No. Not Mr Selden.
                  (PAUSE)
    I've been careless and imprudent about
  money - I'm frightened to think what I owe ...

HER VOICE TRAILS OFF IN TEARS. GRACE IS SILENT.
<u>HOLD</u>.
                                             <u>CUT TO:</u>

<u>CLOSE UP</u> LILY BART.

                 LILY BART
Grace - you know Lawrence - if I asked him to help me, told him why - would he loathe me if I went to him and told him <u>everything</u>?

                                             <u>CUT TO:</u>

<u>CLOSE UP</u> GRACE STEPNEY.

                GRACE STEPNEY
            (NOT LOOKING AT LILY)
           No. You must not do that.
                    (PAUSE)
            He is like other men.
    (UNABLE TO KEEP THE VENOM OUT OF HER VOICE)
They have minds like moral fly-paper. They can forgive a woman almost anything except the loss of her good name. If you wish to keep your reputation intact, Lily, tell him nothing.

                                             <u>CUT TO:</u>

<u>CLOSE UP</u> LILY BART.

                 LILY BART
          (DESPERATE FOR SOME HOPE)
But he must have spoken to you about me - what does he really
                think of me?

                                             <u>CUT TO:</u>

<u>CLOSE UP</u> GRACE STEPNEY.

          GRACE STEPNEY (SMILING AND EVASIVE)
          We've never discussed you - Lily
        I have no idea what Mr Selden thinks.

SILENCE.

                                                                                         CUT TO:

<u>2 SHOT</u>.
LILY BRINGS HERSELF UNDER CONTROL.

                         LILY BART
        I must trust in his good faith. I will
          write to him and ask him to come.

GRACE REMAINS SILENT.
LILY GETS UP AND LEAVES.

                         LILY BART
                    Goodnight Grace.

GRACE WATCHES HER GO.

                       GRACE STEPNEY
                    Goodnight Lily.

THE DOOR IS HEARD CLOSI<u>NG</u>.
<u>HOLD ON</u> GRACE. SHE IS NEAR TO TEARS. SHE SEES HERSELF RETREATING DOWN NEUTRAL-TINTED DULLNESS TO A DULL, LONELY MIDDLE-AGE.

              GRACE STEPNEY (CRYING AND ANGUISHED)
                 Lawrence! Lawrence!

                                                       DISSOLVE TO:

53. INT. DAY. MRS PENISTON'S HOUSE.

<u>SIDE SHOT OF</u> LILY COMING OUT OF HER ROOM CARRYING THE LETTER TO LAWRENCE SELDEN.
<u>TRACK WITH HER</u> (<u>L-R</u>)
SHE PASSES GRACE'S BEDROOM AND THROUGH THE OPEN DOOR SEES THAT IT IS EMPTY.
SHE CONTINUES TO MRS PENISTON'S ROOM.
<u>CONTINUE TO TRACK AND PAN</u> (<u>L-R</u>) WITH HER.
SHE KNOCKS ON THE DOOR OF MRS PENISTON'S ROOM AND GOES IN. IT TOO IS EMPTY.
SHE CONTINUES DOWNSTAIRS.
<u>CRANE DOWN</u> AND <u>PAN WITH HER</u> (<u>L-R</u>)
AS SHE GETS HALFWAY DOWN THE STAIRS, PICK UP IN A <u>2 SHOT</u> LILY AND JENNINGS THE BUTLER WALKING TOWARDS CAMERA.

THE HOUSE OF MIRTH

                          LILY BART
                Is my aunt downstairs Jennings?

CRANE AND PAN STOP WHEN LILY GETS TO THE FOOT OF THE STAIRS.
2 SHOT LILY AND JENNINGS IN THE VESTIBULE.

                          JENNINGS
         No Miss Bart. Mrs Peniston left for Richfield early this
                   morning with Miss Stepney.

                     LILY BART (SHOCKED)
                       Oh ... (RECOVERING)
                         Thank you.

SOUNDTRACK: A CLOCK STRIKES THE HALF HOUR.

                          LILY BART
         Oh Jennings, would you see that the boy delivers this at once
                   to Mr Selden at The Benedick?

                          JENNINGS
                         Yes Miss.

HE MOVES OUT OF SHOT.

                          LILY BART
         And would you serve tea in the downstairs sitting room at
         four, and show Mr Selden in there as soon as he arrives?

                     JENNINGS (VOICE OVER)
                       Yes Miss Bart.

LILY LEAVES SHOT.
HOLD ON THE VESTIBULE AND THE CLOSED FRONT DOOR.
SILENCE.
THEN:
                                                    DISSOLVE TO:

54. INT. DAY HALL. MRS PENISTON'S HOUSE.

SHOT LOOKING FROM THE FRONT DOOR DOWN THE DESERTED HALLWAY
AND STAIRS.
SILENCE.
HOLD.
SOUNDTRACK: A CLOCK STRIKES FOUR.
TRACK DOWN THE HALL TO THE DOWNSTAIRS SITTING ROOM - IT'S
DOORS ARE CLOSED.
                                                    DISSOLVE TO:

55. INT. DAY SITTING ROOM.

CONTINUE TRACKING TOWARDS LILY, SEATED BY THE FIRE IN FRONT OF A TABLE SET FOR TEA. TRACK STOPS WHEN SHE IS IN MID-SHOT. HOLD.
SOUNDTRACK: A CLOCK STRIKES FIVE.
SHE LOOKS COMPLETELY DESOLATE AND DROPS HER HEAD.
HOLD.
THERE IS A KNOCK ON THE DOOR. SHE LOOKS UP, SMILING AND EXPECTANT.

      LILY BART
  (SURPRISED AND DISMAYED BUT TRYING TO HIDE IT).
      Mr. Rosedale!

SHE IS FLUSTERED BUT MANAGES TO POUR SOME TEA WITHOUT LOOKING AT SIM ROSEDALE.

              CUT TO:

CLOSE UP SIM ROSEDALE. HE IS SMILING.

     SIM ROSEDALE (STILL SMILING)
      Pretty well done ...

PAN WITH HIM (R-L) TO FIREPLACE TO 2 SHOT SIM ROSEDALE AND LILY. SHE HANDS HIM HIS TEA AND HE SITS DOWN OPPOSITE HER. LILY IS PUZZLED BUT STILL SILENT.

      SIM ROSEDALE (SMILING)
     ... Yes - very well done.

              CUT TO:

CLOSE UP SIM ROSEDALE.

       SIM ROSEDALE
   Why do you put up this kind of bluff?

LILY DOESN'T RESPOND.

       SIM ROSEDALE
    Why aren't you straight with me?

SILENCE FROM LILY.

              CUT TO:

CLOSE UP LILY. STILL SILENT.

THE HOUSE OF MIRTH

                    SIM ROSEDALE (VOICE OVER)
I know there have been times when you have been worried - a girl like you shouldn't have worries ...

                           LILY BART
You are quite right Mr Rosedale. I have had worries - I have been careless about money.

                                                    CUT TO:

<u>CLOSE UP</u> SIM ROSEDALE.

                    SIM ROSEDALE (QUICKLY)
...I'm offering you the chance to turn your back on them once and for all. Oh I know you're not in love with me - you're not even fond of me - yet ...

                                                  CUT TO:

<u>CLOSE UP</u> LILY BART.

                        LILY BART (QUICKLY)
I'm very much flattered by your offer but I should be selfish and ungrateful if I made the reason for accepting your generosity financial.

                                                CUT TO:

<u>CLOSE UP</u> SIM ROSEDALE.

                           SIM ROSEDALE
Miss Bart, I generally get what I want in life. I have attained a certain social position and I have the means to maintain it. Now all I want is the woman - the right woman - to share both with me.

<u>CLOSE UP</u> LILY BART.
SHE TRIES TO INTERRUPT ROSEDALE BUT HE CONTINUES TO SPEAK OVER HER. BEING SO FORCIBLY SILENCED SHOCKS HER.

                    SIM ROSEDALE (VOICE OVER)
You have a fondness for luxury and amusement, and not to have to settle for it.

                                                  CUT TO:

<u>CLOSE UP</u> SIM ROSEDALE.

                         SIM ROSEDALE
... I can provide you with the style and the means of settling.

                                                  CUT TO:

CLOSE UP LILY BART.

                  LILY BART
You are mistaken on one point Mr Rosedale. Whatever I enjoy I am prepared to pay for.

A LONG PAUSE.

                                            CUT TO:

2 SHOT. LILY RISES AND SO DOES SIM ROSEDALE.

                  SIM ROSEDALE
I've spoken too plainly. I didn't mean to give offence.

            LILY BART (FLATTERED BUT REPELLED)
You must give me time to consider your kindness.

                  SIM ROSEDALE
Goodbye Miss Bart. You will consider my proposal?

                    LILY BART
                    Of course.

SIM ROSEDALE LEAVES.
AND LILY SITS DOWN. WE HEAR THE DOOR CLOSE.
AND LILY DROPS ALL PRETENCE AT POISE.
THE TELEPHONE IS HEARD RINGING AND SHE LOOKS UP QUICKLY, SURE IT IS LAWRENCE SELDEN RINGING.
SHE GETS UP AND RUNS OUT.

                                            CUT TO:

56. INT. DAY VESTIBULE AND HALL.

LILY BART COMES RUNNING OUT OF THE SITTING ROOM, THROUGH THE HALL TO THE DRAWING ROOM.

                                            CUT TO:

57. INT. DAY DRAWING ROOM.

SHOT OF LILY RUNNING INTO THE GLOOMY DRAWING ROOM. SHE PICKS THE RECEIVER UP.

                    LILY BART
                      Yes!

              BERTHA DORSET (VOICE OVER)
                Are you alone Lily?

THE HOUSE OF MIRTH

                    LILY BART
              (PUTTING A BRAVE VOICE ON)
Yes quite alone, Bertha - everyone is gone away - my aunt to
            Richfield ... everyone else to Europe ...

              BERTHA DORSET (VOICE OVER)
      Except Lawrence Selden who's gone to London ...

                    LILY BART
               (STUNNED BUT HIDING IT)
                How unsophisticated of him.

              BERTHA DORSET (VOICE OVER)
       Will you join us then on a cruise to the
                     Mediterranean?

                    LILY BART
            (KNOWING THAT SHE CANNOT REFUSE)
         Well, I am not sure that I am able to ...

                 BERTHA DORSET (V O.)
You'll be doing me a great service. You are always so
attentive to George, listening to all his old stories which
he's been telling since the Civil War - you're the only one
         with enough fortitude to take an interest -

                    LILY BART
            Nonsense - George can be charming -

SHE TURNS AND SEES HER REFLECTION IN THE MIRROR ABOVE THE
MANTELPIECE.
LILY KEEPS LOOKING AT HERSELF REFLECTED IN THE MIRROR.

              BERTHA DORSET (VOICE OVER)
                 Good - you'll come then?

                    LILY BART
           Yes - it sounds delightful. Goodbye.

SOUNDTRACK: INTRO TO THE TRIO FROM ACT I, <u>COSÌ FAN TUTTE</u>.
<u>PAN AND TRACK</u> (<u>R-L</u>) TO THE MIRROR.
<u>HOLD ON</u> THE MIRROR AND LILY'S REFLECTION.
                                          <u>DISSOLVE TO:</u>

THE EMPTY ROOM (INCLUDING THE CHANDELIER) IS REFLECTED IN THE MIRROR.
EVERYTHING IS COVERED IN WHITE DUST SHEETS.

                                          <u>DISSOLVE TO:</u>

58. INT. DAY. BELLOMONT AND OTHER HOUSES.

THE INTERIORS OF THE HOUSES ARE SWATHED IN DUST SHEETS AND COVERED UP.
EMPTY.
THE WEATHER OUTSIDE IS GREY WITH SQUALLY RAIN.
PAN AND TRACK (L-R) TO WINDOWS OVERLOOKING THE TERRACE.

DISSOLVE TO:

59. EXT. DAY. BELLOMONT AND OTHER HOUSES.

SHOT OF TERRACE AND LAWN.
PAN AND TRACK (L-R) DOWN THE LAWN, PAST THE DESERTED TENNIS COURTS, DOWN THROUGH THE WET TREES TO THE SEA, EMPTY EXCEPT FOR SOME BOATS BOBBING ON THE GREY, RAIN SWEPT WATER.
SOUNDTRACK: THE TRIO FROM ACT 1, COSÌ FAN TUTTE, 'SOAVE SIA IL VENTO' ('MAY THE WIND BE GENTLE').

START TRACKING ACROSS THE SURFACE OF THE GREY WATER WHICH IS HEAVING AND STORMY, LASHED WITH RAIN.
SOUNDTRACK: TRIO FROM ACT I, COSÌ FAN TUTTE, 'TRANQUILLA SIA L'ONDA' ('MAY THE WAVE BE CALM').

DISSOLVE TO:

60. EXT. DAY. WATER.

CONTINUE TRACKING ACROSS THE SURFACE OF THE WATER WHICH GRADUALLY CHANGES FROM GREY TO BLUE, DAPPLED WITH MEDITERRANEAN SUNLIGHT.
SOUNDTRACK: TRIO, ACT I, COSÌ FAN TUTTE, 'ED OGNI ELEMENTO BENIGNO RISPONDA AI NOSTRI DESIR' ('AND MAY EVERY BENIGN ELEMENT RESPOND TO OUR WISHES') TRIO ENDS.

CONTINUE TRACKING OVER THE WATER, NOW RIPPLING IN THE SUN.
THEN CRANE UP TO THE PROW OF A YACHT SKIMMING THE WAVES. THE WATER DRENCHED IN SUNLIGHT.
IT IS THE YACHT 'SABRINA', OWNED BY THE DORSETS.
HOLD ON THE SHIMMERING WATER. IT IS THE FOLLOWING SPRING.

TITLE CARD: "THE FRENCH RIVIERA - 1906".

DISSOLVE TO:

61. EXT. DAY. TERRACE. MONTE CARLO CASINO.

SHOT OF LAWRENCE SELDEN STANDING ON THE STEPS WHICH LEAD DOWN FROM THE CASINO.

THE HOUSE OF MIRTH

                CARRY FISHER (VOICE OVER)
                  Mr. Selden do join us!

LAWRENCE SELDEN SMILES AND MOVES DOWN THE STEPS.
<u>PAN WITH HIM</u> (<u>R-L</u>)

TO A <u>GROUP SHOT</u> CONSISTING OF CARRY FISHER, MR AND. MRS JACK STEPNEY, MR AND MRS BRY AND LORD HUBERT DACEY.
<u>PAN ENDS</u> ON THE GROUP SHOT AS SELDEN JOINS IN.
THE SEA SHIMMERING BEYOND THEM.
THE GROUP WALK AWAY TO THE FURTHER END OF THE TERRACE.
<u>TRACK WITH THEM</u>.

              CARRY FISHER (TO LAWRENCE SELDEN)
     We're starving to death because we can't decide where to lunch.

                       MRS BRY
     Of course one gets the best things at The Terrasse, but <u>all</u>
                  the Americans go there now.

                    CARRY FISHER
          The Duchess has taken up Becassin's lately.

                    GWEN STEPNEY
     The aristocracy go to that little place at the Condamine.

                    LORD DACEY
     It's the only restaurant in Europe where they can cook peas.

                      MR. BRY
     <u>Peas</u>? It just shows you what Europe is coming to when a chef
             can make a reputation cooking <u>peas</u>!

                    CARRY FISHER
             What brings you to Monte Carlo?

                  LAWRENCE SELDEN
     I finished my business with a client in London - so I decided
      to come down to renew my objective interest in life.

              CARRY FISHER (SMILING AND CHARMING)
     Ah - so you are not as far removed from being manipulated by
           the strings of society as one might think.

             LAWRENCE SELDEN (CHARMED BY HER CANDOUR)
                  Mrs Fisher - none of us are.

THEY HAVE REACHED THE PARAPET WHICH OVERLOOKS THE HARBOUR.

                    JACK STEPNEY
              I do believe the Dorsets are back.

               LAWRENCE SELDEN (DISQUIETED)
                        So soon?

TRACK PAST THEM TO THE SEA BEYOND, GLITTERING IN THE SUN.
A YACHT RIDES AN ANCHOR.

                    LORD HUBERT (VOICE OVER)
             It's their yacht, 'The Sabrina' - oh yes.

HOLD ON SEA AND YACHT.
                                              DISSOLVE TO:

62. EXT. DAY. AFTERDECK. YACHT.

OVER THE DISSOLVE:
SOUNDTRACK: WE HEAR SOMEONE READING IN FRENCH.
DISSOLVE TO 2 SHOT OF NED SILYERTON AND BERTHA DORSET UNDER THE
AWNING: SHE ON A DAY BED, HE SITTING ON THE FLOOR BESIDE IT.
HE IS READING POETRY.
BERTHA - EYES CLOSED AND SMILING.
PAN (R-L) TO A 2 SHOT OF LILY BART (ON A DAY BED) AND GEORGE
DORSET SITTING ON A DECK CHAIR.

                         GEORGE DORSET
                   (IN A LOW, IRRITATED VOICE)
             He's reading Verlaine to her now - in French!

LILY SMILES THEN CONTINUES TO READ.
GEORGE DORSET GETS UP AND GOES.
LILY STOPS READING FOR A MOMENT AND CLOSES HER EYES TO ENJOY
THE SUN.

SOUNDTRACK: BERTHA DORSET AND NED SILVERTON LAUGHING,
THEN SILENCE EXCEPT FOR THE LAPPING OF THE WATER.
THE YACHT GENTLY DRIFTS AROUND SO THAT LILY IS IN THE SUN.
SHE OPENS HER EYES AND THEN UNFURLS A PARASOL DIRECTLY IN
FRONT OF CAMERA, OBSCURING HER.
HOLD ON PARASOL.

63. EXT. DAY. TERRACE, MONTE CARLO CASINO.

PARASOL UNFURLS TO REVEAL CARRY FISHER AND LAWRENCE SELDEN (LORD
HUBERT, JACK STEPNEY, MRS STEPNEY AND MR AND MRS BRY BEHIND)
TRACK BACK WITH THEM.

THE HOUSE OF MIRTH

                    CARRY FISHER (TO LAWRENCE SELDEN)
        Well what's the use of mincing matters? We all know what
        Bertha brought her abroad for. The Silverton affair is at
         the acute stage. It's necessary that George be distracted
          and I'm certain Lily does distract him. A clever woman
           would know when to play her cards right but Lily's never
              been very clever in that way. I do hope there hasn't
           been a row. Rumour has it that Bertha is very jealous of
                              Lily's success here.

SELDEN DOESN'T REPLY.
HE AND MRS FISHER LEAVE FRAME, AND WE ARE NOW FRAMING LORD
HUBERT AND JACK STEPNEY, WHO HAVE OVERHEARD THE CONVERSATION.
CONTINUE TRACKING BACK.

                              LORD HUBERT
                  The whole situation is a little mixed
              as I see it. Wasn't there an aunt somewhere?

                              JACK STEPNEY
                            She's in New York.

                              LORD HUBERT
               Ah! Pity New York's such a long way off.

PAN (R-L) TO THE SEA SHIMMERING BEYOND WITH THE 'SABRINA'.
SAIL RIDING AT ANCHOR.
HOLD.
THEN IN A LONG DISSOLVE WE GO FROM DAY TO NIGHT. HOLD.
THEN CRANE UP TO THE SKY.
THEN FIREWORKS SHOOT UP INTO THE NIGHT SKY AND EXPLODE.
HOLD ON SKY AND FIREWORKS.
THEN CRANE DOWN TO:

64. EXT. NIGHT. STREET MONTE CARLO.

CONTINUE CRANING DOWN TO 2 SHOT LILY BART AND GEORGE DORSET
AMIDST A LARGE CROWD ENJOYING THE FÊTE. THEY ARE BEING PUSHED
THROUGH THE THRONG.

                              GEORGE DORSET
                   (LOOKING AROUND AND SHOUTING TO LILY)
                         Where the devil are they?

CRANE AND PAN (L-R) OVER THE CROWD TO A SHOT OF A CAB ON THE
EDGE OF THE THRONG.
BERTHA DORSET AND NED SILVERTON GET IN AND THE CAB GOES OFF.

CONTINUE PANNING (L-R) AND CRANING UP TO LAWRENCE SELDEN ON
THE TERRACE OVERLOOKING THE STREET.
HE HAS SEEN BERTHA DORSET AND NED SILVERTON DRIVE OFF ALONE.
HE IS JOINED BY CARRY FISHER AND THE REST AS THEY LOOK AT THE
CROWD AND THE FIREWORKS.
CONTINUE PANNING (L-R) DOWN THE ENTIRE LENGTH OF THE GROUP.
IT IS JOINED BY LILY BART AND GEORGE DORSET.

GENERAL APPROBATION OF LILY. ONLY SELDEN HOLDS BACK AND IS
SILENT.

                        CARRY FISHER
                Oh Lily. You look ten years younger!

LILY BEAMS. SHE BARELY GLANCES AT SELDEN.
THE GROUP MOVES OFF.
PAN WITH IT (L-R).
                                                    DISSOLVE TO:

65. EXT. NIGHT. STREET, MONTE CARLO.

SHOT OF LAWRENCE SELDEN, LILY BART, GEORGE DORSET, CARRY
FISHER, MR AND MRS BRY, MR AND MRS STEPNEY AND LORD HUBERT
WALKING DOWN A SIDE STREET PAST SHOPS STILL LIT.
THE FÊTE IS COMING TO AN END.
THEY ALL WALK THROUGH THE SHOT UNTIL WE SEE SELDEN AND LILY.
HE DETAINS HER IN FRONT OF ONE OF THE SHOPS.
TRACK STOPS.
A CERTAIN COOLNESS BETWEEN THEM.

                          LILY BART
        How did you find London Mr Selden? More agreeable than New York?

                       LAWRENCE SELDEN
        In some ways, yes. Nevertheless, I stopped over to see you -
                 I beg you to leave the yacht.

                          LILY BART
            To leave? What do you mean? What has happened?

                       LAWRENCE SELDEN
         Nothing. But if anything should, why be in the way of it?

                          LILY BART
              How can you think I would leave Bertha?

                       LAWRENCE SELDEN
                You have yourself to think of now.

THE HOUSE OF MIRTH

                    LILY BART
                Nothing will happen.

                  LAWRENCE SELDEN
            (LIGHTER - HE IS NOT AT ALL SURE)
                Of course not, sure!

THEY MOVE OUT OF SHOT.
<u>HOLD ON</u> SHOP FRONT - IT IS A JEWELLERS.
                                                    <u>CUT TO:</u>

66. INT. DAY. YACHT.

<u>SHOT OF</u> OPEN DOOR TO LILY'S CABIN. GEORGE DORSET IN THE DOOR FRAME.

                   GEORGE DORSET
                Have you seen Bertha?

                                                    <u>CUT TO:</u>

<u>SHOT OF</u> LILY FINISHING DRESSING.

                    LILY BART
                        No.
                  Is she not up yet?

                                                    <u>CUT TO:</u>

<u>SHOT OF</u> GEORGE DORSET.

                   GEORGE DORSET
                      (ANGRY)
    Not up yet! Has she gone to bed? Do you know what time she
              came aboard this morning? At seven!

                                                    <u>CUT TO:</u>

<u>SHOT OF</u> LILY. SHE GETS UP AND MOVES TO THE DOOR.
<u>PAN WITH HER</u> (<u>R-L</u>) TO A <u>2 SHOT</u> OF LILY AND GEORGE DORSET.

                    LILY BART
            At seven? Was there an accident?

                   GEORGE DORSET
       There was no accident. I waited for them <u>all</u> night!

                    LILY BART
              (TRYING TO MOLLIFY HIM)
        Why didn't you call me to share your vigil.

                    GEORGE DORSET
                       (GRIMLY)
    I don't think you would have cared for the denouement.

                                                    CUT TO:

CLOSE UP LILY BART.
                      LILY BART
              (TRYING TO MAKE LIGHT OF IT)
    Denouement? Isn't that too big a word for such a small incident?

                                                    CUT TO:

CLOSE UP GEORGE DORSET.
                    GEORGE DORSET
                       Don't!
                       Don't.

SILENCE.
                                                    CUT TO:

CLOSE UP LILY BART.
                      LILY BART
                       (CARING)
              I only want to help you.

                                                    CUT TO:

CLOSE UP GEORGE DORSET.

                    GEORGE DORSET
    You do by being sweet and patient with me. But you can't want
                    to see me ridiculous.
                        (PAUSE)
      If it hadn't been for you I'd have ended it long ago.

SILENCE.
HE MOVES AWAY FROM THE CABIN DOOR.
                                                    CUT TO:

SHOT GEORGE DORSET MOVING DOWN THE COMPANION WAY.

                    GEORGE DORSET
                I'll go to see Selden.

                LILY BART (VOICE OVER)
                        No!

HE TURNS TO LOOK AT HER.
                                                    CUT TO:

THE HOUSE OF MIRTH

<u>GEORGE DORSET'S POV</u> OF LILY AT HER CABIN DOOR.

                         LILY BART
                            No.

                 GEORGE DORSET (VOICE OVER)
     Why not? One lawyer will do just as well as another.

                 LILY BART (FORCING A SMILE)
      Well go and see Mr Selden then. You'll have time
                     before dinner.

                                                                         CUT TO:

GEORGE DORSET WALKS OUT OF SHOT.
<u>HOLD</u>.

                                                                               CUT TO:

67. EXT. DAY. AFTER DECK. YACHT.

<u>WIDE SHOT OF</u> LILY (<u>FRAME LEFT</u>) ON A DAY BED UNDER THE AWNING.
PAUSE.
THEN (<u>FRAME RIGHT</u>) BERTHA DORSET COMES ALONG THE DECK AND
SITS DOWN ON THE DAY BED (<u>FRAME RIGHT</u>) OPPOSITE LILY.
NEITHER SPEAK.

                       BERTHA DORSET
       I suppose I ought to say good morning.

                          LILY BART
       I tried to see you but you weren't up.

                       BERTHA DORSET
  No. I got to bed late. After we separated during the fête we
        thought we ought to wait but we missed you.

                                                                       CUT TO:

<u>CLOSE UP</u> LILY BART.

                  LILY BART (BEWILDERED)
               <u>You</u> missed <u>us</u>?
    But I thought you didn't get back to the yacht
              until this morning.

                                                                     CUT TO:

<u>CLOSE UP</u> BERTHA DORSET.

                    BERTHA DORSET
                  Who told you that?
                                                    CUT TO:

CLOSE UP LILY BART.

                       LILY BART
                        George.
                                                    CUT TO:

CLOSE UP BERTHA DORSET.

                    BERTHA DORSET
             Is that his version? Poor George.
    He's had one of his attacks again. It's very bad for him to
    be worried and whenever anything upsetting happens it always
                    brings on an attack.

                                                    CUT TO:

CLOSE UP LILY BART.

                       LILY BART
                    (REALLY PUZZLED)
                   Anything upsetting?
                                                    CUT TO:

CLOSE UP BERTHA DORSET.

                    BERTHA DORSET
                 (LOOKS CASUALLY AWAY)
    Yes, such as having you so conspicuously on his hands in the
    small hours. You know, my dear, you're rather a responsibility
             in such a scandalous place after midnight.

                                                    CUT TO:

CLOSE UP LILY BART.

                       LILY BART
            (ASTONISHED BUT TRYING TO LAUGH IT OFF)
         Well really - considering it was you who burdened him
                    with the responsibility!

                                                    CUT TO:

CLOSE UP BERTHA DORSET.

THE HOUSE OF MIRTH

                  BERTHA DORSET
A married man should not have the burden of being seen alone with a single woman.

<u>CUT TO:</u>

<u>CLOSE UP</u> LILY BART.

                  LILY BART
Yes we were alone. Is that so dreadful? After all Bertha we lost you as much as you mislaid us.

               BERTHA DORSET (MILDLY)
Oh, so now it is my fault for not having had the superhuman cleverness to find you in that dreadful crowd? Or the imagination to believe that you wouldn't wait for us at the quay until we managed to meet you?

<u>CUT TO:</u>

<u>CLOSE UP</u> LILY BART.

                LILY BART (INDIGNANT)
No - simply by our all keeping together.

<u>CUT TO:</u>

<u>CLOSE UP</u> BERTHA DORSET.

                  BERTHA DORSET
Keeping together? Lily you're not a child to be led by the hand.

<u>CUT TO:</u>

<u>CLOSE UP</u> LILY BART.

                  LILY BART
            (EVEN MORE INDIGNANT)
No - nor to be lectured Bertha.

<u>CUT TO:</u>

<u>CLOSE UP</u> BERTHA DORSET.

                  BERTHA DORSET
Lecture you? Heaven forbid! I was merely trying to give you a friendly hint. But it's usually the other way around isn't it? I'm expected to take hints, not to give them.

CUT TO:

CLOSE UP LILY BART

> LILY BART
> (ANGRY AND SLIGHTLY AFRAID)
> Hints - from me to you?

CUT TO:

CLOSE UP BERTHA DORSET.

> BERTHA DORSET
> Oh negative ones merely - what not to be or to do or to see. Only, my dear, if you'll let me say so, I didn't understand that one of my negative duties was not to warn you when you carried your imprudence too far.

CUT TO:

CLOSE UP LILY BART.
SHE IS STUNNED AND DISTURBED.
PAN AWAY FROM HER (R-L).

THEN DISSOLVE TO

68. INT. NIGHT. BECASSIN'S RESTAURANT.

CONTINUE PANNING (R-L) FROM INSIDE THE RESTAURANT, LOOKING THROUGH THE PLATE GLASS WINDOW.
A LARGE GROUP CONSISTING OF THE DORSETS, THE BRYS, CARRY FISHER THE STEPNEYS, LORD HUBERT, LORD AND LADY SKIDDAW AND, BRINGING UP THE REAR, LAWRENCE SELDEN AND LILY BART.
THEN PAN INTO THE RESTAURANT FOYER.

OUTSIDE IT HAS BEGUN TO RAIN AND THE WIND IS SQUALLY THEY COME IN AND TAKE OFF THEIR CLOAKS ETC.
CONTINUE PANNING (R-L) PAST THEM THROUGH GLASS DOORS AND INTERIOR GLASS PARTITIONS TO A SHOT OF THE ENTIRE GROUP SEATED AT THE TABLE, EATING.
THE DORSETS SIT AT ONE END, LILY BART AT THE OTHER SEATED BETWEEN LAWRENCE SELDEN AND CARRY FISHER.

TRACK IN ON LILY, SELDEN AND CARRY FISHER.
TRACK STOPS ON A 2 SHOT OF SELDEN AND LILY.

> LILY BART
> (QUIETLY TO LAWRENCE SELDEN)
> Did you see George today?

THE HOUSE OF MIRTH

                LAWRENCE SELDEN
                     Yes.

                  LILY BART
            Well? What happened?
            What _will_ happen?

                LAWRENCE SELDEN
  Nothing as yet and nothing in the future I think.

                  LILY BART
                You're sure?

                LAWRENCE SELDEN
    I'm not sure, but I'm a good deal surer.

LILY LOOKS DOUBTFUL.

                LAWRENCE SELDEN
      But assume everything is as usual.

LILY SMILES AND LOOKS DOWN AT THE DORSETS.
                                            CUT TO:

LILY'S POV OF BERTHA AND GEORGE DORSET.
GEORGE HAS CAUGHT LILY'S EYE BUT CANNOT LOOK AT HER AND DROPS HIS EYES AND TOUCHES HIS CUTLERY.
BERTHA IS ALL SMILES AND DOESN'T LOOK AT LILY.
                                            CUT TO:

DORSETS' POV OF LILY.
SHE LOOKS POISED AND RADIANT. SHE IS TALKING TO THE PEOPLE JUST BEYOND CARRY FISHER AND SOMEONE MAKES A JOKE, WHICH WE DON'T HEAR, AND SHE LAUGHS WITH GREAT CHARM.
                                            CUT TO:

CLOSE UP SIDEVIEW OF LAWRENCE SELDEN. HE LOOKS AT LILY FOR A MOMENT.
HOLD.
WITH EVERY MOVEMENT AND GESTURE SHE SEEMS EVER MORE BEAUTIFUL.
                                            CUT TO:

LAWRENCE SELDEN'S POV OF LILY.
WITH EVERY SHOT HER RADIANCE SEEMS TO GROW.
HOLD.
SHE LOOKS AT HIM AND SMILES.
                                            CUT TO:

2 SHOT OF THE BRYS AT THE FAR END OF THE TABLE. THEY EAT AND BLUSTER.

                                                    CUT TO:

2 SHOT OF CARRY FISHER AND LILY.

                    CARRY FISHER
            Before I go I want to leave you the Brys.

                     LILY BART
            It's charming of you to remember me but ....

                    CARRY FISHER
        What you really mean is that you've snubbed the Brys
                  and you know they know it.

                     LILY BART
                       Carry!

                    CARRY FISHER
        If you'd even managed to have them invited to the Sabrina once
                - especially when Royalty was coming.

                     LILY BART
        Stay over and I'll get the Duchess to dine with them.

                    CARRY FISHER
            I shan't stay over - the Gormers
         have paid for my salon-lit and I leave tonight.
         But get the Duchess to dine with them all the same.

HOLD.
                                                    DISSOLVE TO:

69. INT. NIGHT. BECASSIN'S RESTAURANT.

SHOT OF THE DORSETS' END OF THE TABLE.
DINNER NEARLY OVER. THE MEN SMOKE CIGARS, THE LADIES DRINK LIQUEURS. THEY GET UP IN HAPHAZARD ORDER, THE WAITERS HANDING THEM THEIR CLOAKS.
MR. BRY LOOKS DOWN TOWARDS LILY'S END OF THE TABLE.

                      MR. BRY
                     (TO LILY)
         Come on Lily if you're going back to the yacht.

                                                    CUT TO:

THE HOUSE OF MIRTH

LILY BART, LAWRENCE SELDEN AND CARRY FISHER RISE AND GO TO JOIN THE GROUP.

CUT TO:

THE FIRST GROUP INCLUDE THE DORSETS, ALL READY TO LEAVE.

> BERTHA DORSET
> Miss Bart is not going back to the yacht.

CUT TO:

CLOSE UP LILY BART SHE IS STUNNED.
SHE STANDS THERE IN THE SILENCE.

CUT TO:

FIRST GROUP.

> GEORGE DORSET
> Bertha! ... Miss Bart ... there is some misunderstanding ... some mistake ...

> BERTHA DORSET
> Miss Bart remains here.

COMPLETE SILENCE.
AS NO ONE DARES MOVE.

> BERTHA DORSET
> And I think, George, we had better not detain our guests any longer.

SHE TURNS AND GOES, FOLLOWED BY GEORGE AND THE REST.

CUT TO:

WIDE SHOT. LILY WITH THE GUESTS AT HER END OF THE TABLE - ALL OF THEM ARE EXTREMELY EMBARRASSED.

> LILY BART
> (SHOCKED AND STUNNED, SHE JUST ABOUT RECOVERS HERSELF)
> (SMILING)
> I have some business to attend to and it is easier for me to remain ashore for the night.

THE GUESTS NEAR HER ARE NOT CONVINCED, BUT ARE TOO POLITE, TOO EMBARRASSED TO LET ON.
THE GUESTS NEAR HER SHUFFLE OFF IN SILENCE. ONLY LAWRENCE SELDEN STAYS.

                          LILY BART
                     (TO LAWRENCE SELDEN)
            Mr. Selden you promised to see me to my cab.

THE WAITER GIVES LILY'S CLOAK TO SELDEN, WHO PUTS IT ON LILY.

                                                       CUT TO:

SHOT OF ALL THE GUESTS LEAVING IN A SUBDUED MANNER.
                                                       CUT TO:

2 SHOT LILY AND SELDEN STANDING ALONE.

                          LILY BART
                  (QUIETLY, BUT WITH DESPERATION)
                  Do you know a quiet hotel?

                       LAWRENCE SELDEN
                That you can go to alone? Impossible.

                          LILY BART
                Well it's too wet to sleep outside.

                       LAWRENCE SELDEN
              But there must be someone you can go to?

                          LILY BART
                         At this hour?

                       LAWRENCE SELDEN
              Good God! If only you'd listened to me.

                     LILY BART (COWED)
                          Not now.
PAUSE.

                       LAWRENCE SELDEN
             You must go immediately to the Stepneys.

                          LILY BART
          I can't - you mustn't ask me - you don't know Gwen.

                       LAWRENCE SELDEN
             Come - you must appear to go there directly.

                          LILY BART
                      And if she refuses?

THE HOUSE OF MIRTH

                    LAWRENCE SELDEN
                  She won't. Trust me.

HE USHERS HER OUT.
PAN (R-L) WITH THEM. OUTSIDE HEAVY WIND AND RAIN.
                                                CUT TO:

70. EXT. NIGHT. STEPNEY HOUSE. MONTE CARLO.

WIDE SHOT. DOOR OPEN.
THE BACK OF LILY DISAPPEARING INTO THE HOUSE.
JACK STEPNEY AND LAWRENCE SELDEN - FOREGROUND.

                     JACK STEPNEY
            My wife is asleep and can't be disturbed.

HE WAITS FOR LILY TO GO.

                     JACK STEPNEY
         It's understood then - she leaves on the early train
                       tomorrow morning.

AND THE DOOR SLAMS SHUT.
HOLD ON THE DOOR. NIGHT. RAIN. WIND.
PAN AWAY (R-L) FROM THE DOOR INTO DARKNESS. THEN

                                                DISSOLVE TO:
SOUND TRACK (THROUGH THE DISSOLVE):

                   GWEN STEPNEY (VOICE OVER)
              Lily will get everything of course -

                   JACK STEPNEY (VOICE OVER)
              Aunt Julia was always a just woman.

                   GWEN STEPNEY (VOICE OVER)
          Well - it's only about four hundred thousand -

                                                DISSOLVE TO:

71. INT. DAY. MRS PENISTON'S HOUSE. NEW YORK.

CONTINUE PANNING (R-L) AROUND THE PURPLE DRAWING ROOM.
THE BLINDS ARE HALF CLOSED AND SUNLIGHT POURS INTO THE ROOM
BETWEEN THEM, MAKING THE ROOM HOT IN THE SILENCE.
THE DRAWING ROOM IS FILLED WITH MRS PENISTON'S RELATIVES (ALL IN
DEEP MOURNING). THESE INCLUDE MR AND MRS STEPNEY AND GRACE STEPNEY.
LAWYER FRAMED.

                    LAWYER
              (HE BEGINS TO READ THE WILL)
   I, Julia Grace Peniston of 5th Avenue, New York, being of
          sound mind and body, do hereby bequeath ...
                  (HIS VOICE FADES)

CONTINUE PANNING (R-L) PAST JACK AND GWEN STEPNEY.

                 LILY BART (VOICE OVER)
                  How fat Jack's growing ...

WE PAN PAST JACK STEPNEY AND FRAME GWEN STEPNEY. SHE LOOKS
OFF CAMERA AND COOLLY NODS.

                 LILY BART (VOICE OVER)
           I wonder why rich people always grow fat ...

PAN ENDS ON LILY BART. SHE RETURNS GWEN STEPNEY'S NOD.

                 LILY BART (VOICE OVER)
     ... I shall have to be careful of my figure when I inherit ...

                   LAWYER (VOICE OVER)
              And to my niece, Miss Lily Bart,
         I bequeath the sum of ten thousand dollars.

LILY LOOKS UP, SHAKEN FROM HER REVERIE AND STUNNED BY THE
MEAGRENESS OF THE BEQUEST.
                                                    CUT TO:

SHOT OF LAWYER AND THE MOURNERS (LILY'S POV).
THEY ARE AUDIBLY SHOCKED BY WHAT THEY HAVE HEARD

                   LAWYER (VOICE OVER)
       And the residue of my estate I bequeath to my dear niece and
                 namesake, Grace Julia Stepney.
              Given under my hand 22nd May 1906.
                                                    CUT TO:

CLOSE UP LILY TOO SHOCKED TO MOVE FOR A MOMENT. THEN SHE GETS
UP AND GOES TO GRACE.
                                                    CUT TO:

SHOT OF GRACE STEPNEY IN THE MIDST OF A GROUP MOURNERS. SHE
IS CRYING INCONSOLABLY.
LILY JOINS THE GROUP, BUT EVERYONE IN IT AVOIDS MAKING EYE
CONTACT WITH HER.

THE HOUSE OF MIRTH

                LILY BART (TO GRACE)
          My dear Grace, I'm so glad.

GRACE IS TOO UPSET TO RESPOND AND IS LEAD OFF BY MOURNERS, LEAVING LILY ALONE.
SHE WATCHES THEM GO.
                                                CUT TO:

<u>LILY'S POV</u> OF ALL THE MOURNERS DRIFTING AWAY.
THEY GO INTO THE HALL AND OUT OF THE HOUSE, THEIR VOICES TRAILING OFF.
THEN SILENCE.
                                                CUT TO:

<u>SHOT OF</u> LILY ALL ALONE IN THE DRAWING ROOM. SHE STANDS IN THE SILENCE.
HOLD.
                                                CUT TO:

72. INT. DAY. RESTAURANT.

<u>SHOT OF</u> LILY BART AT A TABLE. THE REST OF THE RESTAURANT IS BEHIND HER, INCLUDING SOME INNER DINING ROOMS.

                      LILY BART
                       (BUOYANT)
          What sweet shall we have today?

                                                CUT TO:

<u>SHOT OF</u> CARRY FISHER.

                    CARRY FISHER
                        Lily!
                                                CUT TO:

<u>CLOSE UP</u> LILY BART.

                      LILY BART
My dear Carry, you wouldn't have me let the head waiter see I've nothing to live on but my Aunt Julia's legacy? Think of Bertha Dorset's satisfaction if she came in and found us lunching on cold mutton and tea!

                                                CUT TO:

<u>CLOSE UP</u> CARRY FISHER.

                    CARRY FISHER
   I was horrid to you in Monte Carlo Lily. I'm thoroughly
   ashamed of myself and I've wanted to tell you so ever since,
                    and that's the truth.

                                                      CUT TO:

CLOSE UP LILY BART.

                      LILY BART
                (LAUGHING AND DISMISSIVE)
                     What is truth?
      Where a woman is concerned it's the story that's
                    easiest to believe.
                        (PENSIVE)
   If I'd got the money no-one would dare ignore me. And if they
   did it wouldn't matter. I'd be independent of them. Instead
     of having to flatter I'd have been free forever from the
                humiliations of the relatively poor.
                         (PAUSE)
                      ... But now ...

                                                      CUT TO:

CLOSE UP CARRY FISHER.

                     CARRY FISHER
         Oh Lily, it's so unjust. Grace Stepney
        must <u>feel</u> she has no right to that inheritance.

                                                      CUT TO:

CLOSE UP LILY BART.

                      LILY BART
Anyone who knew how to please Aunt Julia has a right to her money.

                                                      CUT TO:

CLOSE UP CARRY FISHER.

                     CARRY FISHER
                 But she was devoted to you.

                                                      CUT TO:

CLOSE UP LILY BART.

                      LILY BART
   Be honest, Carry, she disapproved of my going with the
           Dorset's and heard of my break with them.

> (QUIETLY)
> After all Bertha did turn me off the yacht.

PAUSE.

> LILY BART
> (WITH REAL CONCERN)
> I must know where I stand, Carry. I must know what is being said of me.

CUT TO:

CLOSE UP CARRY FISHER.

> CARRY FISHER
> (DIPLOMATIC)
> I don't listen.

CARRY CATCHES SIGHT OF SOMETHING BEHIND LILY AND BECOMES UNEASY.

CUT TO:

WIDER SHOT OF LILY AND RESTAURANT.

> LILY BART
> (UNAWARE OF CARRY'S UNEASE)
> One hears such things without listening.

BEHIND HER JUDY AND GUS TRENOR COME OUT OF THE INNER DINING ROOM WITH FRIENDS.
THEY CATCH SIGHT OF CARRY FISHER ONLY, BUT NOT LILY BART.

> MR. AND MRS TRENOR
> Carry how delightful to see you.

THEY KEEP MOVING TOWARDS THE EXIT.

> LILY BART
> Judy! How delightful!

> JUDY TRENOR
> (EMBARRASSED AND NOT STOPPING TO CHAT)
> Oh ... Lily ... what a pleasure it is to see you ...
> (AT A LOSS)
> Gus ...

> GUS TRENOR
> (DISTANT)
> Miss Bart ... I must see the head waiter. Judy.

THEY MOVE OFF OUT OF THE RESTAURANT.

PAN WITH THEM (L-R)
THEY LEAVE.

                     CUT TO:

<u>CLOSE UP</u> LILY BART SHE IS CRESTFALLEN AS SHE REALISES THAT SHE HAS LOST THE TRENORS.

         LILY BART
         (DEFEATED)
  Where Judy leads all the world will follow.

                      CUT TO:

<u>CLOSE UP</u> CARRY FISHER.

        CARRY FISHER
    (TRYING TO RESCUE THE SITUATION)
    Not your real friends.
        (PAUSE)
Meanwhile what do you say to putting a few things in a trunk and spending the summer with me and the Gormers?

                      CUT TO:

<u>CLOSE UP</u> LILY BART.

        LILY BART
  To take me out of my "friends"' way you mean?

                       CUT TO:

<u>CLOSE UP</u> CARRY FISHER.

        CARRY FISHER
    (TRYING TO RAISE LILY'S MORALE)
To keep you out of their sight 'til they realise how much they miss you. Besides, the Gormers have taken a tremendous fancy to you - Oh I know they're not quite your set - they're a kind of social Coney Island - but anyone is welcome who can make a lot of noise and doesn't put on airs.

                      CUT TO:

<u>CLOSE UP</u> LILY BART.

        LILY BART
    (MAKING THE BEST OF IT)
    Yes. I shall come.

THE HOUSE OF MIRTH

SHE PICKS UP THE MENU.

> LILY BART
> (RALLYING)
> Well - what shall it be? Coup Jacques or Pêches à la Melba?

DISSOLVE TO:

73. EXT. DAY. THE GORMERS' HOUSE.

SHOT OF THE SEA AND THE GREENSWARD.
IN THE FOREGROUND LADIES IN WHITE LACE CARRYING PARASOLS, MEN IN TENNIS WHITES. MOTOR LAUNCHES CRISS-CROSS IN THE BACKGROUND.
THE SEA SHIMMERING IN THE SUN.
HOLD.

CUT TO:

74. EXT. DAY. VERANDA. THE GORMERS' HOUSE.

SHOT OF LILY LYING ON A DAY BED IN THE SHADE OF THE VERANDA.
SHE LOOKS OUT TO SEA.
SHE HEARS LAUGHTER AND FOOTSTEPS AND LOOKS TO HER LEFT.

CUT TO:

SHOT OF THE OPEN DOORS LEADING INTO THE HOUSE.
A COUPLE RUN OUT CARRYING RACKETS AND GIGGLING.
FOLLOWED BY MATTIE GORMER, WHO STANDS IN THE DOOR FRAME.

> MATTIE GORMER
> (TO LILY)
> Miss Lily ... Paul Morpeth wants to paint me and I wish to play tennis ... what should I do?

CUT TO:

SHOT OF LILY BART.

> LILY BART
> Pose, dear Mattie. It's too hot for tennis.

LILY LEANS BACK, CLOSES HER EYES.
JUST THE SOUND OF FAR OFF LAUGHING AND THE WATER SURGING.
HOLD.

> CARRY FISHER
> The more I think of my idea of getting you here the better I like it!

LILY OPENS HER EYES AND LOOKS UP.

<u>CUT TO:</u>

<u>SHOT OF</u> CARRY FISHER SITTING DOWN OPPOSITE LILY.

<u>CUT TO:</u>

<u>CLOSE UP</u> LILY BART.

> LILY BART
> (IRONIC)
> More noise, more colour ... more slap-dash sociability.

<u>CUT TO:</u>

<u>CLOSE UP</u> CARRY FISHER.

> CARRY FISHER
> But greater good nature too - less rivalry.

<u>CUT TO:</u>

<u>CLOSE UP</u> LILY BART.

> LILY BART
> (SMILING AND CONCEDING THE POINT)
> Yes that's true.

SHE LOOKS AROUND AND FOR A MOMENT DOESN'T SPEAK.

> LILY BART
> (RATHER SADLY)
> Soon they'll all be leaving ... for Newport and Bar Harbour or Long Island ... and me to an hotel in broiling New York ...

<u>CUT TO:</u>

<u>CLOSE UP</u> CARRY FISHER.

> CARRY FISHER
> (DECISIVE)
> Lily! You must marry as soon as you can!

<u>CUT TO:</u>

<u>CLOSE UP</u> LILY BART.

> LILY BART
> (SHE LAUGHS SLIGHTLY)
> Do you mean to recommend me to 'a good man's love'?

<u>CUT TO:</u>

THE HOUSE OF MIRTH

CLOSE UP CARRY FISHER.

                    CARRY FISHER
No - I don't think either of my candidates would answer to that description.

                                                                CUT TO:

CLOSE UP LILY BART.

                    LILY BART
Either? Are there actually two?

                                                                  CUT TO:

CLOSE UP CARRY FISHER.

                    CARRY FISHER
Well perhaps I ought to say one and a half.

                                                                 CUT TO:

CLOSE UP LILY BART.

                    LILY BART
                    (LAUGHING)
Other things being equal. I think I should prefer half a husband. Who is he?

                                                                  CUT TO:

CLOSE UP CARRY FISHER.

                    CARRY FISHER
George Dorset.

                                                                 CUT TO:

CLOSE UP LILY BART

                    LILY BART
                        Oh!

                                                                 CUT TO:

CLOSE UP CARRY FISHER.

                    CARRY FISHER
Don't fly out at me 'til you hear my reasons. Since they got back from Europe things have been going badly for them. Bertha's behaviour has strained even George's credulity. They're over at their place now but I think the end will come soon.

                                                                 CUT TO:

CLOSE UP LILY BART.

> LILY BART
> The end will never come. Bertha always knows how to get him back whenever she wants him.

CUT TO:

CLOSE UP CARRY FISHER.

> CARRY FISHER
> Lily he wouldn't stay with her ten minutes if he knew ...

CUT TO:

CLOSE UP LILY BART THINKING THAT SOME HOW CARRY KNOWS ABOUT THE LETTERS SHE TURNS SHARPLY TO HER.

> LILY BART
> Knew?

CLOSE UP CARRY FISHER.

> CARRY FISHER
> If he had positive proof, I mean -

CUT TO:

CLOSE UP LILY BART.

> LILY BART
> (EMBARRASSED AND STIFFENING)
> Please, Carry, let us drop this subject. It's too odious to me.

SILENCE.

> LILY BART
> (TRYING TO BE LIGHT)
> And your second candidate? We mustn't forget him.

PAUSE.

> CARRY FISHER (VOICE OVER)
> Sim Rosedale.

LONG PAUSE.

> LILY BART
> (GETTING UP)
> I think, Carry, that I should like to go for a walk.

CUT TO:

2 SHOT OF CARRY FISHER AND LILY BART. CARRY RISES AND LILY EXITS FROM THE VERANDA AND WALKS OFF SCREEN.

THE HOUSE OF MIRTH

CARRY LOOKS AFTER HER FOR A WHLE. THEN PAUL MORPETH AND MATTIE GORMER JOIN HER AND LOOK AFTER LILY.

                    CARRY FISHER
                    She is lovely.

                    PAUL MORPETH
Not the face - too self-controlled. But the rest of her - by God! What a model she'd make!

PAN (L-R) TO A SHOT OF LILY WALKING TOWARDS THE GREENSWARD AND THE SEA BEYOND.
HOLD.
                                                                                  CUT TO:

75. EXT. DAY. SEA AND GREENSWARD.

SIDEVIEW OF LILY WALKING - THE SEA BEYOND.
TRACK WITH HER (L-R). SHE WALKS FOR A WHILE.
THEN

                  GEORGE DORSET (VOICE OVER)
                      Miss Bart!

SHE STOPS DEAD IN HER TRACKS.
                                                                                  CUT TO:

2 SHOT (SIDEVIEW) LILY BART AND GEORGE DORSET. LILY FRAME LEFT. GEORGE DORSET FRAME RIGHT.

                    GEORGE DORSET
             You'll shake hands won't you?

SHE MAKES NO MOVE TO DO SO OR TO SPEAK.
HE STAYS WHERE HE IS.

                    GEORGE DORSET
            I've been hoping to meet you.
         I should've written if I'd dared.

STILL NO REACTION FROM LILY.

                    GEORGE DORSET
             I wanted to apologise ...

                      LILY BART
                    (CUTTING IN)
           Don't let us speak of it.

PAUSE.

CUT TO:

CLOSE UP LILY BART.

> LILY BART
> I was very sorry for you.

CUT TO:

CLOSE UP GEORGE DORSET.

> GEORGE DORSET
> You must let me explain ... I was deceived ...

CLOSE UP LILY BART.

> LILY BART
> I am still more sorry for you then. But you must see that I am not exactly the person with whom the subject can be discussed.

CUT TO:

CLOSE UP GEORGE DORSET.

> GEORGE DORSET
> Why not?
> It's you of all people that I owe an explanation to.

CUT TO:

CLOSE UP LILY BART.

> LILY BART
> No explanation is necessary. The situation was perfectly clear to me.

SHE MAKES TO GO.

CUT TO:

CLOSE UP GEORGE DORSET.

> GEORGE DORSET
> Miss Bart don't turn away from me.

CUT TO:

CLOSE UP LILY BART. SHE STAYS.

> LILY BART
> You must understand that after what has happened we cannot be friends again.
> I wish to be kind. I bear you no ill-will.

                                                        CUT TO:

CLOSE UP GEORGE DORSET.

                        GEORGE DORSET
              Wasn't I punished enough at the at the time?

LILY STILL DOES NOT RESPOND.

                        GEORGE DORSET
                   Is there to be no respite?

                                                        CUT TO:

CLOSE UP LILY BART.

                          LILY BART
         I should have thought you have complete respite in the
             reconciliation which was affected at my expense.

                                                        CUT TO:

CLOSE UP GEORGE DORSET.

                        GEORGE DORSET
                      Don't put it that way.

                                                        CUT TO:

CLOSE UP LILY BART.

                          LILY BART
         I have told you I don't blame you. All I ask you to
       understand is that after the use Bertha made of me - after all
          that her behaviour has since implied - it is impossible that
                        you and I should meet.

                                                        CUT TO:

CLOSE UP GEORGE DORSET.

                        GEORGE DORSET
                         Please help me.

                                                        CUT TO:

CLOSE UP LILY BART.

                          LILY BART
         I'm sorry there is nothing I can do. You must have
                   other friends, other advisors.

                                                        CUT TO:

CLOSE UP GEORGE DORSET.

> GEORGE DORSET
> I never had a friend like you - besides, you're the only person who knows. After all, you were there in Monte Carlo.

CUT TO:

CLOSE UP LILY BART. SHE HAS MADE UP HER MIND NOT TO USE THE LETTERS FOR THE MOMENT.

> LILY BART
> You're mistaken.
> I saw nothing.
> I know nothing.

CUT TO:

2 SHOT LILY BART AND GEORGE DORSET. LILY EXTREME FRAME LEFT. GEORGE EXTREME FRAME RIGHT.

> GEORGE DORSET
> Just say what you know and the way will be clear for us both ...

SHE DOESN'T SPEAK.
SLOWLY TRACK IN ON THE SEA GLITTERING BEYOND THEM.

> GEORGE DORSET (VOICE OVER)
> Just say a word, just say the word ... there will be no publicity ...

SEA FRAMED. HOLD ON THE SEA.

> LILY BART (VOICE OVER)
> I know nothing.

> GEORGE DORSET (VOICE OVER)
> You're sacrificing both of us.

> LILY BART (VOICE OVER)
> I know nothing. Absolutely nothing.

DISSOLVE TO:

76. EXT. DAY. VERANDA. THE GORMERS' HOUSE.

SHOT (FROM THE HOUSE) OF BERTHA DORSET GETTING OUT OF A LIGHT PHAETON AND COMING TOWARDS CAMERA.

THE HOUSE OF MIRTH

                    BERTHA DORSET
                      (SMILING)
                Mrs Gormer? Bertha Dorset.
         I just thought I'd pay you a neighbourly call.

                                              DISSOLVE TO:

77. INT. NIGHT. BEDROOM, CARRY FISHER'S HOUSE.

<u>SHOT OF</u> LILY BART GOING THROUGH BERTHA DORSET AND LAWRENCE
SELDEN'S LETTERS. SHE IS AT HER DRESSING TABLE GETTING READY
FOR BED. THE ROOM IS LIT MAINLY BY THE FIRE IN THE GRATE.
THERE IS A LIGHT KNOCK ON THE DOOR. LILY IS STARTLED. SHE
BUNDLES THE LETTERS INTO HER DRESSING TABLE DRAWER, PICKS UP
A BRUSH AND STARTS TO BRUSH HER HAIR.

                      LILY BART
                      Come in.

                                                 CUT TO:

<u>SHOT OF</u> CARRY FISHER COMING INTO THE BEDROOM.

                     CARRY FISHER
    May I come in and have a cigarette by your fire? If we talk in
              my room we shall disturb the child.

<u>PAN WITH HER</u> (<u>R-L</u>) TO A CHAIR BY THE FIRE.
SHE SITS DOWN AND LIGHTS A CIGARETTE, LEANS BACK AND ENJOYS IT.

                     CARRY FISHER
         It's such a blessing to have a quiet few weeks here.

                                                 CUT TO:

<u>CLOSE UP</u> LILY BART.
                      LILY BART
                  (BRUSHING HER HAIR)
                It's a well earned rest.

SILENCE AS LILY CONTINUES BRUSHING HER HAIR AND CARRY SMOKES.

                      LILY BART
       Thank you for inviting me, Carry, I love it here at Tuxedo.

                 CARRY FISHER (VOICE OVER)
                Yes, it's a pleasant house.

SILENCE.

> LILY BART
> How are the Brys?

CUT TO:

SHOT OF CARRY FISHER.

> CARRY FISHER
> Louisa Bry is a stern task-master.
> Talk about love making people jealous -
> it's <u>nothing</u> to social ambition.

SILENCE.
LILY CONTINUES TO BRUSH HER HAIR, CARRY TO SMOKE.

> CARRY FISHER
> Your hair is wonderful, Lily. So light and alive ...
> Paul Morpeth wants to paint you ...

CUT TO:

CLOSE UP LILY BART.

> LILY BART
> (NEVER MISSING A STROKE)
> I think not.

SILENCE.

CUT TO:

CLOSE UP CARRY FISHER.

> CARRY FISHER
> (CAUTIOUSLY)
> By the way ... I had a visit from Mattie Gormer the other day ...
> she turned up with Bertha Dorset of all people!

CUT TO:

CLOSE UP LILY BART - BACK OF HER HEAD. A SLIGHT PAUSE, THEN SHE CONTINUES BRUSHING HER HAIR FROM BROW TO NAPE.

> LILY BART
> No doubt the rabbit always thinks it is fascinating the anaconda.

CUT TO:

CLOSE UP CARRY FISHER.

> CARRY FISHER
> Now that they're fast friends I think Mattie will sacrifice anything for her.

THE HOUSE OF MIRTH

                                                        CUT TO:

CLOSE UP LILY BART

                        LILY BART
                    Including me?

                                                        CUT TO:

SHOT OF CARRY FISHER.
PAUSE.

                        CARRY FISHER
                    (WITH QUIET FEELING)
                My dear the world is vile.

PAN (R-L) TO THE FIRE.
HOLD ON THE FIRE.

                                                    DISSOLVE TO:

78. INT. LATE AFT. AUTUMN. DRAWING ROOM, CARRY FISHER'S HOUSE.

SHOT OF FIRE. CONTINUE TO PAN (R-L) PAST SIM ROSEDALE AND
CARRY FISHER'S CHILD TALKING AND LAUGHING QUIETLY TOGETHER.
CONTINUE PANNING (R-L) TO A 2 SHOT OF LILY AND CARRY ON THE
THRESHOLD.
CARRY PUSHES LILY FORWARD SLIGHTLY AND MOUTHS 'GO ON!'
BUT LILY IS HESITANT.

                        CARRY FISHER
                  (CLAPPING HER HANDS TOGETHER)
                    Come along!

                                                        CUT TO:

2 SHOT SIM ROSEDALE AND CHILD.
THE CHILD LOOKS UP AND SIM ROSEDALE GETS UP AND STANDS WITH
HIS BACK TO LILY AND CARRY, CLEARLY EMBARRASSED.

                        CARRY FISHER
                 You ought to be in bed!

                            CHILD
                       Yes mother.

THE CHILD RUNS OFF.

                                                        CUT TO:

WIDE SHOT LILY BART, CARRY FISHER AND CHILD RUNNING OUT OF
THE ROOM.

                        CHILD
                Goodnight Miss Bart.

                     LILY BART
                Goodnight Edith.

CARRY EXITS TOO.
SILENCE.

                     LILY BART
             Where are the others?

                                                     CUT TO:

WIDE SHOT OF SIM ROSEDALE, WHO TURNS AROUND.

                    SIM ROSEDALE
       I am your only fellow guest Miss Lily.

                                                       CUT TO:

WIDE 2 SHOT.

                     LILY BART
       (COMING TO THE HEARTH AND SITTING DOWN)
       I think Carry was trying to be subtle.

SIM ROSEDALE SITS TOO.
AN AWKWARD SILENCE.

                    SIM ROSEDALE
                You look tired.

                     LILY BART
            I've been sleeping badly.

SILENCE. STILL VERY AWKWARD.

                    SIM ROSEDALE
  In fact, Miss Lily, I came especially to see you ... on a
      delicate matter ... I hope you believe that.

                                                     CUT TO:

CLOSE UP LILY BART

THE HOUSE OF MIRTH

                          LILY BART
         Thank you Mr Rosedale I do believe what you say ...
                          (QUIETLY)
         ... and I am ready to marry you whenever you wish.

                                                          CUT TO:

CLOSE UP SIM ROSEDALE.
HE IS COMPLETELY ASTONISHED.

                          SIM ROSEDALE
                       But Miss Lily ...
                                                          CUT TO:

CLOSE UP LILY BART
                          LILY BART
                   (QUIETLY INTERRUPTING HIM)
         For I suppose that is what you do wish. And though I was unable
         to consent when you spoke to me before I am ready, now that I
         know you so much better, to trust my happiness to your hands.

                                                          CUT TO:

CLOSE UP SIM ROSEDALE.
HE IS STILL COMPLETELY STUNNED. THEN HE LETS OUT A SHORT
LAUGH, OPENS HIS CIGARETTE CASE AND SMOKES A CIGARETTE.

                          SIM ROSEDALE
         My dear Miss Lily, but you made me feel that my suit was so
         hopeless that I really had no intention of renewing it.

                                                          CUT TO:

CLOSE UP LILY BART
IT IS NOW HER TURN TO BE ASTONISHED - AND HUMILIATED.

                   LILY BART (WITH SOME DIGNITY)
         I have no-one to blame but myself if I gave you the impression
                       that my decision was final.
                       (WITH A TINGE OF SADNESS)
         Before we bid each other goodbye, I want at least to thank you
                  for having once thought of me as you did.

                                                          CUT TO:

CLOSE UP SIM ROSEDALE.

                          SIM ROSEDALE
                Why do you talk of saying goodbye?
             Can't we still be good friends all the same?

                                                          CUT TO:

CLOSE UP LILY BART.

>LILY BART
>(SMILING)
>What is your idea of being 'good friends'? Seeing me without asking me to marry you?

CUT TO:

CLOSE UP SIM ROSEDALE.

>SIM ROSEDALE
>Well - that's about the size of it.

CUT TO:

CLOSE UP LILY BART.

>LILY BART
>(SMILING)
>I like your frankness, but I am afraid our friendship can hardly continue on those terms.

SHE MAKES TO GET UP AND GO.

>SIM ROSEDALE (VOICE OVER)
>Miss Lily ...

SHE REMAINS SEATED.

>SIM ROSEDALE (VOICE OVER)
>What I mean is ...

>LILY BART
>What you mean to say is that I am not as desirable a match as once you thought me.

CUT TO:

CLOSE UP SIM ROSEDALE.

>SIM ROSEDALE
>Yes. That's what I do mean. I don't believe the stories about you, but my not believing them isn't going to alter the situation.

CUT TO:

CLOSE UP LILY BART.

>LILY BART
>If they are not true doesn't that alter the situation?

THE HOUSE OF MIRTH

                                                        CUT TO:

CLOSE UP SIM ROSEDALE.

                        SIM ROSEDALE
            You know as well as I do that last year you wouldn't
              look at me; now you appear willing to do so.
            What's changed in the interval? Your situation.
                  Then you thought you could do better.

                                                        CUT TO:

CLOSE UP LILY BART.

                          LILY BART
                           (IRONIC)
                       You think you can?

                                                        CUT TO:

CLOSE UP SIM ROSEDALE.

                        SIM ROSEDALE
                          Yes I do.
     I've done very well. I've placed Wall Street under obligations
       which only 5th Avenue can repay. And I know the quickest way
       to queer oneself with the right people is to be seen with the
                             wrong ones.
                     I want to avoid mistakes.

                                                        CUT TO:

CLOSE UP (LOOSER) LILY BART.

                          LILY BART
                         I understand.

SHE GETS UP.
CRANE UP WITH HER.

                          LILY BART
                    Goodbye Mr Rosedale.

PAN WITH HER (R-L).
AFTER A MOMENT, BUT BEFORE SHE GETS OUT OF THE ROOM.

                    SIM ROSEDALE (VOICE OVER)
              Why don't you use those letters of hers?

LILY STOPS DEAD IN HER TRACKS, COMPLETELY STUNNED. SLOWLY SHE
TURNS AROUND TO FACE SIM ROSEDALE.

                                                              CUT TO:
WIDER SHOT.
SIM ROSEDALE AT THE HEARTH.

                          SIM ROSEDALE
              Don't ask how I know you bought them.
                              I know.
          And I don't suppose you bought those letters simply because
                     you're collecting autographs.

                                                              CUT TO:

WIDE SHOT OF LILY BART (SIM ROSEDALE'S POV)
SHE IS AT A COMPLETE LOSS FOR WORDS.
                                                              CUT TO:

WIDE SHOT OF SIM ROSEDALE (LILY'S POV).

                          SIM ROSEDALE
      You see I know where you stand - you have Bertha completely
       in your power. You wish to be rehabilitated socially and you
      have the means for your redemption. In a deal like this nobody
         comes out with perfectly clean hands, but if you're going
        to fight Bertha don't inflict an open injury - reduce it to a
                         private transaction.

                                                              CUT TO:

CLOSE UP LILY BART.

                            LILY BART
                           (DISGUSTED)
                    'Give and take' you mean?

                                                              CUT TO:

CLOSE UP SIM ROSEDALE.

                          SIM ROSEDALE
                       Yes - as in business.

                                                              CUT TO:

CLOSE UP LILY BART

                            LILY BART
                           Or politics.

                                                              CUT TO:

SIM ROSEDALE (LILY'S POV).

THE HOUSE OF MIRTH

                    SIM ROSEDALE
   You see how simple it is? There's no point in frightening
   Bertha into line - you have to keep her there. That's my share
              in the business. That's what I'm offering you.

                                                           CUT TO:

LOOSER CLOSE UP LILY BART

                        LILY BART
       To reconcile with Bertha and then you'll marry me?

                                                           CUT TO:

CLOSE UP SIM ROSEDALE.

                      SIM ROSEDALE
                  What do you say, Miss Lily.

                                                           CUT TO:

CLOSE UP LILY BART.

                        LILY BART
   You are mistaken in both the facts and what you infer from them.

                                                           CUT TO:

CLOSE UP SIM ROSEDALE.

                      SIM ROSEDALE
                       (ASTOUNDED)
                    Well I'll be damned!
       I suppose it's because the letters are to him?

SILENCE.
                      SIM ROSEDALE
               I thought we understood each other?

                                                           CUT TO:

CLOSE UP LILY BART.
                        LILY BART
                        We do now.

PAN WITH HER (R-L) OUT OF THE ROOM.

                                                      DISSOLVE TO:

79. INT. DAY. LATE AUTUMN, DRAWING ROOM. MRS PENISTON'S HOUSE.

CONTINUE PANNING (R-L) TO GRACE STEPNEY AT THE WINDOW -
BLINDS DRAWN HALF WAY DOWN.
PAN STOPS ON A WIDE SHOT OF GRACE AT THE WINDOW.

> LILY BART (VOICE OVER)
> How are you Grace?

> GRACE STEPNEY
> (NEAR TO TEARS)
> Her memory is everywhere ... the whole house ...

SHE REGAINS HER COMPOSURE.

> GRACE STEPNEY
> And you, Lily how are you? You look dreadfully tired.

CUT TO:

SHOT OF LILY (SHE SITS DOWN).

> LILY BART
> I don't sleep at night.

CUT TO:

SHOT OF GRACE STEPNEY. SHE SITS DOWN NEAR THE WINDOW.

> GRACE STEPNEY
> (CONCERNED)
> Since when?

CUT TO:

CLOSE UP LILY BART

> LILY BART
> I don't , I can't remember.

SILENCE.

> LILY BART
> There are other worries ... dreadful things ...

> GRACE STEPNEY (VOICE OVER)
> What things?

> LILY BART
> Poverty. I don't know anything more dreadful, do you?

CUT TO:

SHOT OF GRACE STEPNEY.
GRACE DOESN'T KNOW WHAT TO SAY.

CUT TO:

THE HOUSE OF MIRTH

<u>CLOSE UP</u> LILY BART.

                            LILY BART
        I can't go on in this way much longer.

STILL NO ANSWER FROM GRACE.
SILENCE.
                            LILY BART
  Do you have any idea when the legacies will be paid?

                                                        CUT TO:

<u>SHOT OF</u> GRACE STEPNEY.

                          GRACE STEPNEY
   No, Lily. No-one has received them yet. Not even me.

SILENCE.
                                                       CUT TO:

<u>CLOSE UP</u> LILY BART.

                            LILY BART
                 (WITH GREAT DIFFICULTY)
  The truth is ... I need money ... Grace ... would you be
      willing to advance the amount of my legacy?

                                                        CUT TO:

<u>SHOT OF</u> GRACE STEPNEY.

                    GRACE STEPNEY (QUIETLY)
   You must be patient. Remember how beautifully patient
                 Aunt Julia always was.
                                                     CUT TO:

<u>CLOSE UP</u> LILY BART.

                            LILY BART
But you will have everything Grace it would be so easy for you
     to borrow ten times the amount I'm asking for.

                                                        CUT TO:

<u>SHOT OF</u> GRACE STEPNEY.

                        GRACE STEPNEY
                            (APPALLED)
                             Borrow?
                                                        CUT TO:

CLOSE UP LILY BART

                    LILY BART
         Grace I'm at the end of my tether.

                                            CUT TO:

SHOT OF GRACE STEPNEY.

                  GRACE STEPNEY
              (FULL OF RECTITUDE)
     Do you imagine for a moment that
I would raise money on my expectations from Aunt Julia?
                    (PAUSE)
Why, Lily, if you must know the truth it was the idea of your
     being in debt that brought on her last illness.

                                            CUT TO:

CLOSE UP LILY BART.

                    LILY BART
                (HUMBLED)
        You won't help me then?

                                           CUT TO:

SHOT OF GRACE STEPNEY.

                  GRACE STEPNEY
If I can do anything to make you realise the folly of your
course and how deeply <u>she</u> disapproved of it, I shall feel it
   is the truest way of making up to you for her loss.

SILENCE.

                                             CUT TO:

WIDE 2 SHOT. GRACE STANDS UP. OBVIOUSLY THE INTERVIEW IS OVER. LILY STANDS.

                    LILY BART
     Thank you Grace. It was good of you to see me.
                     Goodbye.

SHE GOES OUT.
PAN WITH HER (R-L) TO THE DRAWING ROOM DOORS. SHE GOES THROUGH THEM.

                                             CUT TO:

THE HOUSE OF MIRTH

80. EXT. DAY. LATE AUTUMN. MRS PENISTON'S HOUSE.

<u>SHOT OF</u> THE FRONT DOOR CLOSING.
<u>PAN</u> (<u>R-L</u>) TO LILY. SHE LOOKS AT THE HOUSE FOR A MOMENT THEN MOVES ACROSS THE ROAD TO THE PARK SIDE OF 5TH AVENUE.

CUT TO:

81. EXT. DAY. LATE AUTUMN. PARK AVENUE.

<u>SHOT OF</u> LILY (<u>SIDEVIEW</u>) WALKING ALONG THE PAVEMENT, THE PARK BEYOND HER. SHE IS VERY UPSET.
<u>TRACK WITH HER</u> (L-R)
SHE IS DEEP IN THOUGHT WHEN LAWRENCE SELDEN COMES OUT OF THE PARK AND FALLS IN ALONGSIDE. SHE IS SURPRISED BUT GLAD TO SEE SELDEN.
<u>TRACK DOES NOT STOP</u>. DO <u>TWO TRACKS</u> - BOTH <u>POVS</u>.

LILY BART
Mr. Selden.

LAWRENCE SELDEN
I haven't seen you since you got back from Europe.

LILY BART
Why are we perpetually missing each other?

LAWRENCE SELDEN
You seem to have been absorbed by the Gormers.

LILY BART
That intimacy is at an end. The Trenors too. Bertha's influence is everywhere. Even my aunt got her revenge for my perceived waywardness.

LAWRENCE SELDEN
I know. You were treated abominably.
But I was sorry to hear of Mrs Peniston's death.

THEY WALK IN SILENCE.

LAWRENCE SELDEN
I meant to write ... I mean to be sympathetic ...

LILY BART
There are other ways of showing sympathy.

HE DOESN'T REPLY.

LILY BART
And your support was always a comfort.

LAWRENCE SELDEN
Though you exaggerate the importance of anything
I could do for you - you can't exaggerate my readiness to
do it - if you ask me to.

A SILENCE BETWEEN THEM AS THEY CONTINUE TO WALK.
CONTINUE TRACKING (L-R)

LAWRENCE SELDEN
And how is life?

LILY BART
Unaffordable. I shall have to look for work - you see I am
rather hard-up at the moment.

LAWRENCE SELDEN
(DISTURBED)
Surely not as hard-up as all that.

LILY BART
You think we live on the rich? We live with them but it's a
privilege we have to pay for. Every luxury has its tax - and
beggars mustn't be choosers.

LAWRENCE SELDEN
(WORRIED)
What will you do?

LILY BART
(LAUGHING)
Oh don't look so worried - it hasn't come to the employment
agencies just yet. Carry Fisher is using all her resourcefulness
to discover a working vein for the vague wealth of my talents.
Her inexhaustible good nature is adept at creating an artificial
demand far in excess of any actual supply.

LAWRENCE SELDEN
It doesn't sound very amusing.

LILY BART
It isn't.
(MOMENTARILY DISGUSTED)
And I'm sick of it!
(IMMEDIATELY REGAINING HER COMPOSURE)

THE HOUSE OF MIRTH

Oh I'll find something to tide me over.
I think Carry has found me somebody to whom I can be a sort of social secretary.
You know how good I am with the helpless rich.

                LAWRENCE SELDEN
                May I come to see you?

                LILY BART
           Of course. That would be delightful
              (SHE HANDS HIM HER CARD)
'Miss Lily Bart - C/O Mrs Norma Hatch, Emporium Hotel'.

LAWRENCE SELDEN STOPS - LILY DOES SO TOO.
<u>TRACK STOPS</u>.

                LAWRENCE SELDEN
                  (SHOCKED)
              But she's divorced!

                LILY BART
            You're shocked Mr Selden.

                LAWRENCE SELDEN
            Let us say 'surprised'.

THEY SHAKE HANDS.
                LILY BART
            Come to see me anyway.

<u>PAN AWAY</u> WITH HER.
<u>HOLD</u> AS SHE WALKS AWAY.
                                                      CUT TO:
<u>SHOT OF</u> LAWRENCE SELDEN.
HE WATCHES HER GO. HE LOOKS AT THE CARD THEN TEARS IT UP IN DISGUST. HE DROPS THE BITS INTO THE GUTTER.
<u>PAN DOWN</u> TO SEE THE BITS RUN IN WATER ALONG THE GUTTER TO THE STORM DRAIN.
<u>TRACK IN</u> ON THE STORM DRAIN AND BLACKNESS.

                      DISSOLVE OUT OF BLACKNESS TO:

82. INT. DAY. EMPORIUM HOTEL, LILY'S ROOM.

<u>SHOT OF</u> LILY IN BED - AWAKE BUT LUXURIATING IN A LARGE SOFT BED. SHE MAKES NO ATTEMPT TO GET UP.
<u>HOLD</u>.
                                                      CUT TO:

SHOT OF LILY'S ROOM (LILY'S POV).
A FIRE IN THE GRATE, A BREAKFAST TABLE. BUT THE FURNITURE IS
LARGE AND VULGAR.
SUDDENLY THE DOOR OPENS AND MRS HATCH COMES RUNNING IN
WITHOUT KNOCKING.

>   MRS HATCH
>   Lily!

CUT TO:

CLOSE UP LILY BART.

>   LILY BART
>   (SHOCKED)
>   Mrs Hatch! I'm not dressed!

CUT TO:

SHOT OF MRS HATCH.

>   MRS HATCH
>   Oh Lily! It doesn't matter. This is the twentieth century,
>   not the Dark Ages.
>   As soon as you've eaten come to my rooms -
>   we've just got to go through my schedule.
>   I'm leaving in twenty minutes so please be quick!

SHE EXITS JUST AS QUICKLY AS SHE CAME IN.

CUT TO:

83. INT. DAY. CORRIDOR/LOBBY, EMPORIUM HOTEL.

2 SHOT MRS HATCH AND LILY BART.
TRACK BACK WITH THEM AS THEY WALK QUICKLY ALONG A CORRIDOR
FROM MRS HATCH'S SUITE OF ROOMS TO THE HOTEL LOBBY.

>   MRS HATCH
>   (BREATHLESSLY)
>   I cannot find my prescription Lily - do you have it?
>   I'm always losing them

>   LILY BART
>   (WRITING IN A LARGE ENGAGEMENT DIARY AS THEY WALK)
>   You usually leave them on your dressing table Mrs Hatch.

>   MRS HATCH
>   Of course I do! Get it filled for me today, Lily, if I don't
>   have my Chloral at night I never sleep ... and I have to see
>   my beauty doctor today otherwise I cannot face society ...

THE HOUSE OF MIRTH

The manicure will have to wait until tomorrow. I'm just not up to it today ... so put her off ... don't look sour Lily, she won't mind ... she <u>never</u> minds ...
After lunch I shall go to Sherrys for tea then I'm playing bridge with my lawyer this evening ... eight I think ... I'll try to go for my dress fitting in the morning but only if it doesn't interfere with the art exhibition at four ... then supper ... no, the theatre first and then supper ...

SHE STOPS. SO DOES LILY. THEY ARE NOW IN THE LOBBY.
<u>TRACK STOPS</u>.

LILY BART
But Mrs Hatch if you don't tell me in advance of these changes how shall I be able to keep your diary accurately?

MRS HATCH
(CHARMING)
Lily, engagements are <u>made</u> to be broken - especially with trades people - they expect it.

LILY BART
(DEFEATED)
Yes Mrs Hatch.

MRS HATCH WALKS OUT OF SHOT TO THE DOOR.
                                              CUT TO:
<u>SHOT OF</u> MRS HATCH (<u>LILY'S POV</u>).

MRS HATCH
(TURNING AROUND AS SHE LEAVES)
Oh - and by the way - on Friday I'm dining with Melville Stancy and some people called 'The Gormers' ...

                                              CUT TO:
<u>CLOSE UP</u> LILY BART.
LILY BART
(STUNNED BY THIS LAST BIT OF NEWS)
Yes Mrs Hatch.

MRS HATCH (VOICE OVER)
...And don't forget my prescription Lily ... it's on the dressing table ...

SHE HALF TURNS AND IS SHOCKED BY WHAT SHE SEES.
                                              CUT TO:

<u>SHOT OF</u> LAWRENCE SELDEN.

                    LAWRENCE SELDEN
        Carry Fisher was anxious to know how you were getting on.

                                                            CUT TO:

SHOT OF LILY BART. PAN WITH HER (R-L) TO A 2 SHOT WITH
LAWRENCE SELDEN.

                        LILY BART
        (TRYING TO CONCEAL HER SURPRISE AT SEEING SELDEN)
            Why didn't she look me up herself then?

                     LAWRENCE SELDEN
            She was afraid of being importunate.
                        (SMILING)
            You see no such scruple restrained me.

                        LILY BART
            Then you have come to be of use to me?

                     LAWRENCE SELDEN
                            Yes.

                        LILY BART
                        (LIGHTLY)
                So - what am I to do with you?

                     LAWRENCE SELDEN
                You could talk things over with me.

                        LILY BART
        What makes you think I have anything in particular to talk about?

                     LAWRENCE SELDEN
            My initiative doesn't go beyond putting myself at your
                disposal. I shouldn't have come if I had thought
                        I could be of no use to you.

SILENCE.
                                                            CUT TO:
CLOSE UP LAWRENCE SELDEN.

                     LAWRENCE SELDEN
                    (QUIETLY OUTRAGED)
                Do you know where you are?

                        LILY BART
                Of course I know where I am!

THE HOUSE OF MIRTH

PAUSE.

      LAWRENCE SELDEN
  You must let me take you away from here.

CUT TO:

CLOSE UP LILY BART, NO LONGER LISTENING.
PAN WITH HER (R-L)

      LILY BART
  (ANGRY AND WALKING TO THE WINDOW)
 If you have come here to say disagreeable things
    about Mrs Hatch ...

CUT TO:

CLOSE UP LAWRENCE SELDEN.

      LAWRENCE SELDEN
    (INTERRUPTING HER)
It is precisely your relationship with her that concerns me.

CUT TO:

CLOSE UP LILY BART.

      LILY BART
  (TURNING TO HIM, COLDLY)
 My relationship to Mrs Hatch is one I have no reason to
be ashamed of. She has helped me earn a living when my old
   friends were quite content to see me starve.

CUT TO:

CLOSE UP LAWRENCE SELDEN.

      LAWRENCE SELDEN
 Nonsense! Starvation is not the only alternative.
  I know that your aunt's legacy could make you
     modestly independent.

CUT TO:

CLOSE UP LILY BART.

      LILY BART
 What you don't happen to know is that I owe
   every penny of that legacy!

CUT TO:

CLOSE UP LAWRENCE SELDEN.

                    LAWRENCE SELDEN (SHOCKED)
                          Good God!

                                                          CUT TO:

CLOSE UP LILY BART.

                            LILY BART
                             (HEATED)
Every penny! And more besides. I have no money except my small
income and I need to earn money in order to keep myself alive.

SILENCE.

                                                          CUT TO:

CLOSE UP LAWRENCE SELDEN.

                         LAWRENCE SELDEN
                I should be happier to see you out of
                    this particular 'employment'.

                                                          CUT TO:

CLOSE UP LILY BART.

                            LILY BART
                         But I should not.

                                                          CUT TO:

WIDE 2 SHOT.
ANGRY SILENCE.
LILY LOOKS OUT OF THE WINDOW.
SELDEN REMAINS SILENT FOR A WHILE.

                         LAWRENCE SELDEN
              I simply wish to point out to you the false position
                        you have placed yourself in.

                            LILY BART
                            (SMILING)
        I suppose by that you mean my being on the outside of
        society? But I have long been excluded from it and I
        remember your once telling me that it was only those on
            the inside who took the difference seriously.

                         LAWRENCE SELDEN
          The question is: Mrs Hatch's desire to be inside may put
                   you in the position I call false.

                                                          CUT TO:

CLOSE UP LAWRENCE SELDEN.

THE HOUSE OF MIRTH

      LAWRENCE SELDEN
    You cannot want this!

                CUT TO:

CLOSE UP LILY BART.

       LILY BART
  You have already told me that the sole object of my upbringing was to teach me to get what I want. Why not assume that that is precisely what I am doing now?

                CUT TO:

CLOSE UP LAWRENCE SELDEN.

      LAWRENCE SELDEN
  I have never thought of you as a successful example of that kind of upbringing.

                CUT TO:

CLOSE UP LILY BART
       LILY BART
      (A HARD LAUGH)
  Give me a little more time! I may still do credit to my training!

                CUT TO:

CLOSE UP LAWRENCE SELDEN.

      LAWRENCE SELDEN
    That was undignified.

                CUT TO:

CLOSE UP LILY BART.

       LILY BART
  Where does dignity end and rectitude begin?

                CUT TO:

WIDE 2 SHOT.

      LAWRENCE SELDEN
    Good day Miss Bart.

       LILY BART
    Good day Mr Selden

HE LEAVES. SHE TURNS AND LOOKS OUT OF THE WINDOW AND WATCHES HIM GO. THEN SHE WALKS SLOWLY OUT OF THE LOBBY.

                CUT TO:

84. INT. DAY. EMPORIUM HOTEL.

SHOT OF LILY COMING INTO MRS HATCH'S SUITE OF ROOMS.
PINK DAMASK EVERYWHERE. THE FURNITURE IS LARGE, ORNATE AND EXPENSIVELY VULGAR.
MRS HATCH'S CLOTHES LIE ALL OVER THE ROOMS AND LILY WALKS THROUGH THE SUITE AT A LOSS AMIDST SO MUCH CHAOS AND WASTE.
SHE GOES TO THE DRESSING TABLE TO SEARCH FOR THE PRESCRIPTION.
SHE FINDS A HALF FILLED CHLORAL BOTTLE BUT NOT THE PRESCRIPTION.
SHE LOOKS INTO THE DRAWER AND TO HER SURPRISE SEES TWO PRESCRIPTIONS WITHOUT DATES ON THEM.
SHE PAUSES FOR A MOMENT THEN WRITES THE DATE ON ONE PRESCRIPTION - 21ST JANUARY 1907 - BUT FOLDS THE OTHER PRESCRIPTION UP AND PUTS IT INSIDE HER DRESS.
SHE PICKS UP THE HALF-FILLED BOTTLE OF CHLORAL AND GOES TO HER OWN ROOM.

CUT TO:

85. INT. DAY. LILY BART'S ROOM. EMPORIUM HOTEL.

SHOT OF LILY COMING IN AND GOING TO BED.
SHE LIES DOWN, STILL HOLDING THE CHLORAL.
SHE SEEMS DEFEATED AND VERY TIRED.
SHE TAKES A DOSE OF CHLORAL.
THEN, LITTLE BY LITTLE. SHE FALLS ASLEEP.
WHEN SHE IS ASLEEP PAN AWAY FROM HER (R-L) TO THE WINDOW AND THE GATHERING DARK.

SOUNDTRACK: THE VOICES SEEM FAR OFF.

1ST GIRL (VOICE OVER)
... The one with the green paradise? It'll be ready right off ...

2ND GIRL (VOICE OVER)
How'd I know? I told her he'd never look at her again and he didn't ...

DISSOLVE TO:

86. INT. LATE AFTERNOON WORK ROOM. MDE REGINA'S MILLINERY SHOP.

SHOT OF WINDOW. OUTSIDE, THE DREARY MARCH TWILIGHT.
HOLD ON THE WINDOW.

SOUNDTRACK:

3RD GIRL (VOICE OVER)
... Five dollars and her picture in the paper ...

THE HOUSE OF MIRTH

CRANE DOWN FROM THE WINDOW AND PAN (R-L) TO:
A GIRL LIGHTS ONE OF THE LAST GAS JETS WHICH HANG TWO-BY-TWO DOWN THE LENGTH OF THE WORKROOM.
CRANE FINISHES ON A SHOT OF LILY WORKING ON A HAT.
WE HEAR THE QUIET HUB-BUB OF TWENTY GIRLS ALL WORKING.
LILY STOPS WORK FOR A MOMENT AND LOOKS AT THEM. THEIR TALK SEEMS ABSTRACT AND FAR AWAY.
LILY LOOKS AS IF SHE WILL SWOON FROM A SORT OF SPIRITUAL FATIGUE. SHE LOOKS AT THE GIRLS WITH A KIND OF NUMB INCOMPREHENSION.
                                                    CUT TO:

LILY'S POV OF THE WORKROOM.
ABOUT TWENTY GIRLS WORK AROUND A LARGE RECTANGULAR TABLE MAKING AND FINISHING HATS.
THEY ALL TALK QUIETLY AS THEY WORK.

SOUNDTRACK:

                    4TH GIRL
        ... She sent for me to alter the blue tulle ...

                    5TH GIRL
                  That Virot hat?

                    6TH GIRL
        ... She's tall - with her hair frizzed out ...

AT ONE END OF THE ROOM IS A SMALL GLASS-PANELLED OFFICE - MDE REGINA'S OFFICE.
MDE REGINA IS SEATED AT HER DESK. STANDING IN FRONT OF THE DESK IS A TALL FOREWOMAN - MISS HAINES. SHE IS SHOWING A HAT TO MDE REGINA.
THEY BOTH LOOK IN LILY'S DIRECTION.
                                                    CUT TO:

SHOT OF LILY. SHE LOOKS AS IF SHE'LL SWOON THEN SHE LOOKS DOWN AND CONTINUES TO WORK, FINISHING A HAT.
HOLD. THEN

                    MISS HAINES (VOICE OVER)
             Look at these spangles Miss Bart ...

LILY LOOKS UP.
                                                    CUT TO:

SHOT OF MISS HAINES.

>   MISS HAINES
>   (HOLDING A HAT)
>   ... Every one of 'em sewed on crooked.

                                                        CUT TO:

CLOSE UP LILY BART.

>   LILY BART
>   I'm sorry. I'm afraid I'm not well.

                                                        CUT TO:

SHOT OF MISS HAINES.

>   MISS HAINES
>   (UNSYMPATHETIC)
>   If you can't do better I'll give the hat to Miss Kilroy.

SHE DOES SO.
>   MISS HAINES
>   (AS SHE WALKS AWAY)
>   Go back to binding edges.

                                                        CUT TO:

SHOT OF LILY. SHE LOOKS COMPLETELY DEMORALISED AND
GOES BACK TO BINDING.
HOLD ON HER.

                                                    DISSOLVE TO:

87. INT. LATE AFTERNOON WORK ROOM, MDE REGINA'S MILLINERY SHOP.

LONG SHOT (FROM THE OFFICE END OF THE WORKROOM)
A BELL IS HEARD AND ALL THE GIRLS STOP WORKING AND START
TOWARDS THE DOOR. THE WORK DAY IS OVER.
LILY IS ONE OF THE LAST.
AS SHE PASSES THE OFFICE, MDE REGINA CALLS THROUGH THE HALF-
OPEN DOOR. SHE IS SEATED AT HER DESK.

>   MDE REGINA
>   Miss Bart!

LILY GOES INTO THE OFFICE AND CLOSES THE DOOR.

                                                        CUT TO:

88. INT. LATE AFTERNOON WORK ROOM. MDE REGINA'S OFFICE.

2 SHOT MDE REGINA SITTING (FRAME RIGHT) LILY STANDING
(FRAME LEFT).

MDE REGINA
Miss Bart I must draw your attention to the fact that your work is poor and your attendance irregular.

LILY BART
Miss Haines is right - I am clumsy and slow to learn, but I have been indisposed lately.
I shall try to improve.

CUT TO:

CLOSE UP MDE REGINA.

MDE REGINA
It's too late for that. I took you on as an untrained apprentice as a favour to Mrs Fisher but against my better judgement. As the season is nearly over I'm afraid I must dispense with your services.

CUT TO:

CLOSE UP LILY BART
SHE SEEMS NEITHER SURPRISED OR RELIEVED, JUST RESIGNED.
SILENCE.

CUT TO:

2 SHOT.

MDE REGINA
(STANDING)
I trust you will find a position more suited to your skills.

SHE HANDS LILY HER WAGES.
LILY TAKES THEM AND LEAVES.

LILY BART
Thank you.

CUT TO:

88. EXT. TWILIGHT. MDE REGINA'S MILLINERY SHOP.

THE LAST FEW GIRLS COME OUT INTO THE DREARY MARCH TWILIGHT.
LILY FOLLOWS AND CROSSES THE STREET TO 6TH AVENUE.
PAN WITH HER (L-R) AS SHE WALKS AWAY.

CUT TO:

89. EXT. TWILIGHT. 6TH AVENUE.

SHOT OF CORNER OF THE STREET WITH A DRUGGIST'S SHOP ON THE CORNER. LILY STANDING LOOKING INTO THE WINDOW.
SHE SEEMS VERY NERVOUS. SHE WAITS FOR A WHILE THEN GOES IN.

CUT TO:

90. INT. TWILIGHT. DRUGGIST'S SHOP.

SHOT OF A VERY NERVOUS LILY COMING TO THE COUNTER. A CLERK COMES OUT AND WAITS ON HER.
SHE DOESN'T MOVE FOR A MOMENT.

      CLERK
    Can I help?

SHE TAKES A PAPER FROM HER DRESS AND HANDS IT TO HIM.
HE UNFOLDS THE PRESCRIPTION.

      CLERK
    Mrs Hatch?

      LILY BART
    (CHOKING WITH NERVES)
    Yes.

HE GOES TO FILL THE PRESCRIPTION.
SHE WAITS IN THE SHOP WITH MOUNTING ANXIETY.
THE CLERK COMES BACK OUT OF THE DISPENSARY.
HE HANDS HER THE PHIAL.

      CLERK
  You mustn't increase the dose. Mrs Hatch.

      LILY BART
    Of course not.

LILY NODS AND QUICKLY LEAVES THE SHOP.

      CLERK
    (CALLING AFTER HER)
  It's Chloral remember. Be careful

CUT TO:

92. EXT. TWILIGHT. STREET AND ELEVATED RAILWAY.

SHOT OF LILY BART WALKING UNDER THE ELEVATED RAILWAY TOWARDS CAMERA.
A TRAIN ROARS OVERHEAD.
SHE STOPS FOR A MOMENT AT THE FOOT OF THE STAIRS WHICH LEAD DOWN FROM THE PLATFORM.
CROWDS OF PEOPLE AND THE DEAFENING SOUND OF THE TRAIN RATTLING OVERHEAD.

THE HOUSE OF MIRTH

SIM ROSEDALE (LOOKING PROSPEROUS) COMES DOWN THE STEPS TO THE STREET.

>   SIM ROSEDALE
>   Miss Lily!

SHE TRIES TO RECOVER HERSELF.

>   SIM ROSEDALE
>   What's the matter?
>
>   LILY BART
>   I'm a little tired - it's nothing.
>   Stay with me a moment, please.

ANOTHER TRAIN SHRIEKS OVERHEAD AND THEY WAIT FOR IT TO PASS.

>   SIM ROSEDALE
>   We can't stay here. Let me take you to The Longworth
>   for some tea.

<u>PAN WITH THEM</u> (<u>L-R</u>) AS THEY CROSS THE STREET AND ENTER THE LONGWORTH HOTEL.
>   CUT TO:

93. INT. TWILIGHT LONGWORTH HOTEL.

<u>CLOSE UP</u> LILY BART.

>   SIM ROSEDALE (VOICE OVER)
>   Take your tea strong.

SHE SIPS HER TEA PUTS IT DOWN ON THE TABLE AND LEANS BACK IN UTTER LASSITUDE.
SHE LOOKS HAGGARD.
>   CUT TO:

<u>CLOSE UP</u> SIM ROSEDALE.
AN AWKWARD SILENCE.

>   SIM ROSEDALE
>   I haven't seen you for ages ...

SILENCE.

>   SIM ROSEDALE
>   I didn't know what had become of you ...
>
>   CUT TO:

<u>CLOSE UP</u> LILY BART.

> LILY BART
> I have joined the working classes.
> I was trying to learn to become a milliner.

CUT TO:

<u>CLOSE UP</u> SIM ROSEDALE.
HE LOOKS AT HER IN DISBELIEF.

> SIM ROSEDALE
> You're not serious.

CUT TO:

<u>CLOSE UP</u> LILY BART.

> LILY BART
> Perfectly serious.

<u>CLOSE UP</u> SIM ROSEDALE.

> SIM ROSEDALE
> But I understood you were with Mrs Hatch.

CUT TO:

<u>CLOSE UP</u> LILY BART.

> LILY BART
> She dismissed me two months ago – after she h<u>a</u>d got into society it seemed my reputation was a social liability. Since then I've been obliged to work for my living.

CUT TO:

<u>2 SHOT</u> (<u>SIDEVIEW</u>) SIM ROSEDALE AND LILY BART. SILENCE.
HE IS EMBARRASSED AND FIDDLES WITH THE TEA THINGS.

> SIM ROSEDALE
> It was no place for you any how.

SHE ROUSES HERSELF AND HALF RISES TO GO.

> LILY BART
> I must go ...

> SIM ROSEDALE
> No. Rest a little longer.

THE HOUSE OF MIRTH

SHE DOES SO.

                      SIM ROSEDALE
What on earth did you mean when you said you were learning to be a milliner?

                      LILY BART
Just what I said. I am an apprentice at Madame Regina's ...

PAUSE.

                      LILY BART
... I *was* an apprentice at Madame Regina's

                      SIM ROSEDALE
But I understood that you got a legacy from your aunt.

                      LILY BART
I got ten thousand dollars. But it is not paid until Spring and anyway I owe it already.

                      SIM ROSEDALE
The whole ten thousand?

                      LILY BART
Every penny.

SHE PAUSES TO GATHER HER STRENGTH.

                      LILY BART
I think Gus Trenor spoke to you once about having made some money for me in stocks -

ROSEDALE NODS.

                                                         CUT TO:

<u>CLOSE UP</u> LILY BART.

                      LILY BART
He made me about nine thousand dollars. I knew nothing about business and I thought he was investing my own money. In fact what he had made he had 'given' me. It was meant in kindness but it was not the sort of obligation I could remain under.
I was incredibly stupid and I had spent the money before I realised my mistake. And so my aunt's legacy will have to go to pay it back.
That is why I must now work.

                                                            CUT TO:

<u>CLOSE UP</u> SIM ROSEDALE.

>   SIM ROSEDALE
>   But that will clean you out altogether.

CUT TO:

<u>CLOSE UP</u> LILY BART.

>   LILY BART
>   Altogether. Yes.

CUT TO:

<u>2 SHOT</u> (<u>SIDEVIEW</u>) SIM ROSEDALE AND LILY BART.

>   SIM ROSEDALE
>   (AFTER A PAUSE)
>   Miss Lily if you want my backing ...

SHE STANDS TO GO.

>   LILY BART
>   Thank you. Your tea has given me tremendous backing –
>   I feel equal to anything now.

SIM ROSEDALE STANDS.

>   SIM ROSEDALE
>   Let me walk you home.

THEY LEAVE.
<u>PAN</u> (<u>L-R</u>) WITH THEM.

CUT TO:

94. EXT. TWILIGHT. STREET AND BOARDING HOUSE.

<u>2 SHOT</u>.
<u>CONTINUE PANNING</u> WITH THEM (<u>L-R</u>) AS THEY APPROACH THE BOARDING HOUSE. IT IS A LARGE SHABBY, GENTEEL BROWNSTONE.

>   SIM ROSEDALE
>   This isn't the place?

>   LILY BART
>   Yes. I room and board here.
>   I have lived too long on my 'friends'.

THEY GO IN.

CUT TO:

THE HOUSE OF MIRTH

95. TWILIGHT. BOARDING HOUSE.

THE PARLOUR - MORE SPARSE SHABBINESS.
ON ONE SIDE OF A MAIN HALL AND STAIRCASE. ON THE OTHER SIDE A DINING ROOM - A COUPLE OF PEOPLE STILL EATING.
THROUGHOUT LILY RETAINS THE LAST VESTIGES OF DIGNITY.
SHOT OF THEM COMING IN THROUGH THE DOOR.
AS THEY COME TOWARDS CAMERA, SIM ROSEDALE GOES TO GO INTO THE DINING ROOM, BUT LILY MOTIONS HIM INTO THE PARLOUR.
2 SHOT (SIDEVIEW) SHE SITS DOWN. HE REMAINS STANDING.

>SIM ROSEDALE
>(LOOKING AROUND)
>You can't go on living here.

>LILY BART
>I have gone over my expenses very carefully and I rather think I shall be able to manage it.

>SIM ROSEDALE (SITTING)
>That's not what I mean.

>LILY BART
>It's what I mean.

SILENCE.

>LILY BART
>I'm out of work now.

>CUT TO:

CLOSE UP SIM ROSEDALE.

>SIM ROSEDALE
>(REALLY MOVED)
>What a way for you to talk. You being in a place like this ...

>CUT TO:

CLOSE UP LILY BART.

>LILY BART
>My situation is nothing exceptional.

>CUT TO:

CLOSE UP SIM ROSEDALE.

>SIM ROSEDALE
>(HEATED)
>But you are!

SILENCE.

                     SIM ROSEDALE
                   It's an outrage.
LONG SILENCE.

                     SIM ROSEDALE
     Look here - I know it's none of my business but you must
                 accept help from somebody ...

                                                      CUT TO:

CLOSE UP LILY BART.
SHE DOESN'T RESPOND.
                                                      CUT TO:

CLOSE UP SIM ROSEDALE.

                     SIM ROSEDALE
       You spoke to me of the debt to Gus Trenor - well -
              I'll lend you the money to pay him ...
                     (HE STIFLES HER OBJECTION)
       Let me finish - it'll be purely a business arrangement.
              How can you have anything against that?

                                                      CUT TO:

CLOSE UP LILY BART.

                      LILY BART
       Only this: that is exactly what Gus Trenor proposed.
         Once the debt is paid I shall have no security.
         I was compromised once, I cannot be so again.

                                                      CUT TO:

CLOSE UP SIM ROSEDALE.
HE SEEMS GENUINELY HURT BY WHAT SHE'S SAID.
                                                      CUT TO:

CLOSE UP LILY BART.
SHE IS AWARE SHE HAS HURT HIM.

                      LILY BART
                    (WITH KINDNESS)
       I am very grateful for your kindness ... but ... it is
                 impossible ... you must see that ...

                                                      CUT TO:

2 SHOT (SIDEVIEW) SIM ROSEDALE AND LILY BART. HE DOESN'T SEE
AT ALL.

THE HOUSE OF MIRTH

                SIM ROSEDALE
We must try and think of your future.

                LILY BART
If you only knew how little difference that makes now.

ROSEDALE DOES NOT KNOW WHAT TO DO OR SAY.

                SIM ROSEDALE
At least let me tell Selden where you're living.

SHE STANDS AND SO DOES ROSEDALE.

                LILY BART
            It will do no good.

                SIM ROSEDALE
                Please.

                LILY BART
Very well. You may tell him if you wish.

LONG SILENCE

                SIM ROSEDALE
If only you would let me help you, you could wipe your feet on them.

SHE SMILES AT HIM AND IS VISIBLY MOVED BY HIS CLUMSY KINDNESS. SHE PROFFERS HER HAND AND HE SHAKES IT. THEN GOES OUT.

                                  CUT TO:

<u>CLOSE UP</u> LILY BART.
SHE IS STILL VERY MOVED BUT SHE REFUSES TO CRY. SHE TURNS AND WALKS UPSTAIRS.
                                  CUT TO:

96. INT. NIGHT. BOARDING HOUSE.

<u>SHOT OF</u> LILY BART COMING UP THE STAIRS AND ONTO THE LANDING. GOING TO HER ROOM THEN GOING IN.
                                  CUT TO:

97. INT. NIGHT. LILY'S ROOM. BOARDING HOUSE.

<u>SHOT OF</u> LILY BART COMING INTO THE LONG NARROW ROOM. SHE SITS ON THE BED IN THE DARK. THEN SHE REMEMBERS SHE HAS THE CHLORAL.

SHE PUTS IT ON THE SIDE TABLE.
SHE SITS FOR A MOMENT IN THE DARK.

SOUNDTRACK:

> SIM ROSEDALE (VOICE OVER)
> Why don't you use the letters? ... It would be so simple ... it is so simple ...

THEN SHE TAKES A DOSE OF CHLORAL AND LIES BACK ON THE BED.
TRACK IN ON HER TO CLOSE UP.
SHE LIES IN THE DARK LISTENING TO THE NOISES OF THE HOUSE AND STREET.

> LILY BART (VOICE OVER)
> Use them ... use them ...

SHE SLIDES INTO A TROUBLED SLEEP.
TRACK AND PAN (R-L) AWAY FROM HER TO THE WINDOW.
IT IS NIGHT.
HOLD ON THE WINDOW.
THEN IN A LONG DISSOLVE IT BECOMES THE NEXT AFTERNOON. A COLD SPRING DAY (BUT WITH SUN).

98. AFTERNOON. LILY'S ROOM, BOARDING HOUSE.

LILY BART AT HER BEDSIDE GOING THROUGH HER TRUNK.
SHE IS PUTTING THE DRESSES THAT SHE HAS MANAGED TO KEEP ON TO THE BED. THE LAST DRESS - THE ONE SHE WORE AS MRS LLOYD FOR THE TABLEAU VIVANT - IS THE LAST TO GO ON THE BED.
SHE GOES ON LOOKING FOR SOMETHING - THEN SHE FINDS IT - THE LETTERS OF BERTHA DORSET.
SHE PUTS THEM INSIDE HER DRESS AND LEAVES. SHE HAS FINALLY DECIDED TO USE THEM.

                                                    CUT TO:

99. EXT. AFTERNOON. STREET OUTSIDE THE BOARDING HOUSE.

SHOT OF LILY - FULL OF RESOLVE - LEAVING THE BOARDING HOUSE.
THE WEATHER HAS TURNED. IT IS NOW WINDY, DARK AND THREATENING RAIN.
TRACK AND PAN WITH HER (L-R) TO A SIDE STREET. SHE WALKS DOWN IT.
BASEMENT SHOPS TO HER LEFT - THEIR SIGNS BLOWING IN THE GUSTY WIND.
TRACK WITH HER FROM BEHIND.
AS SHE WALKS DOWN THE STREET A CROWDED STREETCAR COMES INTO SHOT AND STOPS JUST AHEAD OF HER. SHE GETS ON AND IT MOVES OFF.

                                                DISSOLVE TO:

THE HOUSE OF MIRTH

100. EXT. LATE AFTERNOON. STREETCAR.

<u>SHOT OF</u> LILY INSIDE THE STREETCAR LOOKING OUT OF THE WINDOW. SHE HOLDS THE LETTERS.
<u>TRACK WITH HER</u> (<u>R-L</u>)
SHE LOOKS UP AT THE FACADES OF THE FASHIONABLE HOUSES - HOUSES WHERE ONCE SHE WAS AN HONOURED GUEST.

                                                                        DISSOLVE TO:

101. EXT. LATE AFTERNOON 5TH AVENUE.

<u>LILY'S POV</u> OF THE FASHIONABLE MANSIONS AS THEY DRIFT PAST.
<u>TRACK</u> PAST THEM (<u>L-R</u>)

                                                                        DISSOLVE TO:

102. EXT. LATE AFTERNOON 5TH AVENUE.

<u>SHOT OF</u> LILY AT THE STREETCAR WINDOW. HER RESOLVE SEEMS TO BE WEAKENING.
<u>TRACK</u> WITH THE STREETCAR (<u>R-L</u>). THE STREETCAR STOPS.
<u>TRACK AROUND</u> TO A <u>SIDEVIEW</u> OF THE STREETCAR.
LILY GETS OFF AND MOVES ACROSS THE ROAD TOWARDS BERTHA DORSET'S HOUSE.
<u>TRACK WITH HER</u> TO BERTHA'S FRONT DOOR. THE HOUSE IS IN DARKNESS.
<u>TRACK STOPS</u> WHEN LILY REACHES THE FRONT DOOR AND RINGS THE BELL. SILENCE.
SHE RINGS A SECOND TIME AND THE DOOR IS OPENED BY A BUTLER.

                        LILY BART
              (TRYING TO MUSTER SOME DIGNITY)
Will you please inform Mrs Dorset that Miss Lily Bart
                 wishes to speak with her.

                        BUTLER
           Mrs Dorset is not at home, Miss Bart.

                        LILY BART
            (HER RESOLVE WEAKENING BY THE SECOND)
      Then I should like to speak with Mr Dorset.

                        BUTLER
I'm sorry, Miss Bart, but Mr and Mrs Dorset left for the
               country two days ago.

                        LILY BART
            (COMPLETELY CRUSHED BY THIS)
                        Oh ...

                    BUTLER
            Shall I take a message?

                    LILY BART
        (THE LAST DREGS OF HER RESOLVE DRAINING AWAY)
            No ... no message.

THE BUTLER CLOSES THE DOOR.
LILY STANDS THERE FOR A MOMENT, COMPLETELY AT A LOSS AS TO
WHAT TO DO.
THEN SHE MOVES TO THE SIDEWALK.
PAN WITH HER (R-L).
SHE STARTS TO WALK SLOWLY, AIMLESSLY, ALONG THE STREET.
TRACK WITH HER FROM BEHIND.

                                            DISSOLVE TO:

103. EXT./INT. LATE AFTERNOON. THE BENEDICK.

SIDE VIEW OF LILY WALKING.
TRACK WITH HER (R-L).
IT STARTS TO RAIN BUT SHE DOES NOT HURRY, DESPITE GETTING
COMPLETELY SOAKED.
SHE LOOKS UP AT THE BUILDING AND REALISES THAT IT IS LAWRENCE
SELDEN'S APARTMENT BUILDING.
TRACK WITH HER TO THE ENTRANCE.
SHE STOPS FOR A MOMENT, THEN RUNS INTO THE LOBBY.
TRACK WITH HER (FROM BEHIND) AS SHE GOES TO THE STAIRS THEN
GOES UP.
PAN UP WITH HER.

                                               CUT TO:

104. INT. LATE AFTERNOON. THE BENEDICK.

THE LANDING LEADING UP TO LAWRENCE SELDEN'S APARTMENT.
SHOT OF LILY COMING UP THE STAIRS.
WHEN SHE GETS TO THE TOP PAN WITH HER {L-R) TO LAWRENCE
SELDEN'S DOOR.
SHOT ENDS WITH THE CAMERA IMMEDIATELY BEHIND HER.
SHE HESITATES A MOMENT THEN KNOCKS LIGHTLY.
LAWRENCE SELDEN OPENS THE DOOR AND TRIES TO CONCEAL HIS
SURPRISE WITH A SMILE AND MOTIONS HER TO COME IN.
SHE ENTERS.
TRACK IN WITH HER.

105. INT. DAY. LAWRENCE SELDEN'S APARTMENT.

THE AFTERNOON IS LENGTHENING AND GETTING DARK, AND THE ROOM
LOOKS COSY AND SAFE.

THE HOUSE OF MIRTH

OUTSIDE IT IS STILL RAINING.
SHE GOES TO THE FIREPLACE BUT STILL DOESN'T SPEAK OR TURN AROUND

<u>CUT TO:</u>

FRONT VIEW OF LILY, LAWRENCE SELDEN IN THE BACKGROUND. HE COMES TOWARDS HER AND STANDS BEHIND THE ARMCHAIR. SILENCE BETWEEN THEM, THEN AFTER A SHORT WHILE:

            LILY BART
       (WITH HER BACK TO HIM)
I came to tell you that I was sorry for the way we parted ...
         (SHE TURNS TO HIM)
... for what I said to you that day at Mrs Hatch's ...

        LAWRENCE SELDEN
      I was sorry too ...

SILENCE.

        LAWRENCE SELDEN
  I can recommend the armchair ...

SHE REMAINS STANDING.

        LAWRENCE SELDEN
  ...You look so tired ... do sit down.

AS SHE DOES SO HE PUTS A CUSHION BEHIND HER.
SILENCE.

        LAWRENCE SELDEN
You're drenched. Let me make you some tea ...

           LILY BART
             No -
       (SHE STARTS TO CRY)
   I must go in a moment ...

HE COMES AND SITS DOWN BY THE FIRE OPPOSITE HER.
<u>TRACK IN</u> ON LILY.
LONG SILENCE.

           LILY BART
      I must go ...

BUT SHE MAKES NO MOVE TO DO SO.
<u>TRACK ENDS</u> IN <u>CLOSE UP</u>

                    LILY BART
I may not see you again for a long time and I wanted to tell
you that I have never forgotten the things you said to me at
Bellomont, that they have helped keep me from becoming what
                many people thought me to be.

                                                      CUT TO:

CLOSE UP LAWRENCE SELDEN.

                  LAWRENCE SELDEN
                     (QUIETLY)
      I'm glad - but nothing I have said has really made the
          difference. The difference is in yourself.

                                                      CUT TO:

CLOSE UP LILY BART.

                     LILY BART
                 Oh don't say that!
      That is all I have lived on! Don't take it from me now!
                 (WITH GREAT DIFFICULTY)
We resist the great temptations but it is the little ones that
                  eventually pull us down ...
         ... I remember your saying that such a life could never
satisfy me and I was ashamed to admit that it could - that was
               what I wanted to thank you for ...
                       (TEARS)
              ... I have tried ... tried hard ...
                     (MORE TEARS)
             But life is difficult and I am
    a useless person ... and now I'm on the rubbish heap ...
                (BREAKS DOWN COMPLETELY)

                                                      CUT TO:

CLOSE UP LAWRENCE SELDEN.

                  LAWRENCE SELDEN
                    (VERY MOVED)
              Lily - can I help you?

                                                      CUT TO:

CLOSE UP LILY BART.

                     LILY BART
    You told me once that you could help me only by loving me.

THE HOUSE OF MIRTH

    Well ... you did love me for a moment and it helped me ...
        But the moment is gone ... and I let it go.
               (IN COMPLETE ANGUISH)
           And one must go on living ...

                                                                           CUT TO:

<u>CLOSE UP</u> LAWRENCE SELDEN.

                  LAWRENCE SELDEN
                   (DEEPLY MOVED)
Lily you mustn't speak in this way. Things may change ... but
      ... you can never go out of my life.

                                                                             CUT TO:

<u>CLOSE UP</u> LILY BART.

                        LILY BART
Let us be friends. Then I shall feel safe ... whatever happens ...

                                                                           CUT TO:

<u>CLOSE UP</u> LAWRENCE SELDEN.

                  LAWRENCE SELDEN
               (NOW VERY CONCERNED)
    What do you mean? What is going to happen?

                                                                           CUT TO:

<u>SLIGHTLY WIDER SHOT OF</u> LILY BART.

                       LILY BART
                (TRYING TO SMILE)
Nothing ... nothing at all ... but I should like some tea now ...

HE WALKS PAST HER AND SHE SITS LOOKING AT THE FIRE.
THE ROOM SEEMS VERY, VERY COMFORTING AND SAFE.
SHE LOOKS AT THE FIRE THEN TOUCHES HER DRESS AND BRINGS OUT
THE BERTHA DORSET LETTERS.
SHE LOOKS AT THEM THEN MOVES TOWARDS THE HEARTH.
<u>PAN</u> (<u>R-L</u>) DOWN HER ARM TO HER HAND HOLDING THE LETTERS. THEN
SHE SLIPS THEM GENTLY INTO THE FIRE.
<u>HOLD ON</u> THE FIRE AS THEY BURN.
THEN <u>PAN</u> (<u>L-R</u>) TO SELDEN COMING BACK INTO THE ROOM.
HE PLACES LILY'S TEA ON THE TABLE BESIDE THE ARMCHAIR.
HE STANDS AND LOOKS AT HER.
SILENCE.
                                                                           CUT TO:

<u>SHOT OF</u> LILY AT THE WINDOW (<u>HIS POV</u>).

OUTSIDE IT IS STILL RAINING.
SHE IS LOOKING OUT OF THE WINDOW (BACK TO SELDEN AND CAMERA).
HOLD.
SILENCE.
SHE TURNS TO LOOK AT HIM.

                        LILY BART
                    Goodbye Lawrence.

PAN WITH HER (L-R) TO A 2 SHOT WITH SELDEN.
SHE KISSES HIM.
THEN RUNS FROM THE ROOM.
TRACK IN ON DOORWAY. THEN

                                            DISSOLVE TO:

106. INT. LATE AFTERNOON. LILY'S ROOM, BOARDING HOUSE.

LONG SHOT OF LILY'S LONG, DARK NARROW ROOM.
TRACK IN ON IT.
KNOCKING IS HEARD.
TRACK STOPS AS LILY OPENS IT AND THE LANDLADY GIVES HER AN
ENVELOPE. SHE CLOSES THE DOOR AND OPENS THE ENVELOPE.
A LETTER AND A CHEQUE.
SHE GOES TO HER DESK AND SITS DOWN, PUTTING THE LETTER AND THE
CHEQUE ON THE DESK.

                                                       CUT TO:

SHOT OF THE CHEQUE AND LETTER. IT IS THE PAYMENT OF HER
AUNT'S LEGACY. THE CHEQUE IS FOR TEN THOUSAND DOLLARS.

                                                       CUT TO:

CLOSE UP LILY BART.
SHE KEEPS LOOKING AT THE CHEQUE.

                        LILY BART
                        (QUIETLY)
                Ten thousand dollars ...
                Ten thousand dollars ...

HOLD.
THEN SHE WRITES.
SLOWLY PAN DOWN TO THE DESK.
SHE HAS WRITTEN OUT TWO ENVELOPES - ONE TO HER BANK, WHICH
SHE SEALS, AND ONE TO CHARLES AUGUSTUS TRENOR, FOR A CHEQUE
FOR TEN THOUSAND DOLLARS, WHICH SHE DOES NOT SEAL.

                                                       CUT TO:

WIDE SHOT OF LILY BART.
SHE GOES TO THE WINDOW AND PULLS THE BLIND DOWN. RAIN OUTSIDE.
SHE IS STILL CARRYING BOTH ENVELOPES.
SHE GOES TO HER BED, PLACES BOTH ENVELOPES ON HER BEDSIDE
TABLE AND PICKS UP THE CHLORAL.
SHE DRINKS FROM THE BOTTLE.
SHE LIES BACK ON THE DRESSES WHICH ARE STILL ON TOP OF THE BED.
TRACK IN ON HER.
TRACK STOPS WHEN SHE IS IN CLOSE UP.
HOLD.
SHE STARTS TO GET DROWSY.
SHE HALF STARTS AWAKE THEN STARTS TO SLIDE INTO HER FINAL SLEEP.
HOLD.
HER BREATHING BECOMES REGULAR BUT HEAVY.
PAN DOWN TO HER HAND HOLDING THE BOTTLE OF CHLORAL.
THE BOTTLE SLIPS FROM HER FINGERS AND THE LIQUID CHLORAL
SPILLS OUT OVER THE DRESS SHE WORE AT THE TABLEAU VIVANT.
IT STAINS THE DRESS LIKE BLOOD.
CONTINUE PANNING DOWN. THEN

DISSOLVE TO:

107. INT. DAY. LAWRENCE SELDEN'S APARTMENT. 'THE BENEDICK'.

CONTINUE PANNING TO THE FIREPLACE - THE GRATE.
ASHES AND THE HALF-BURNT PACKET OF BERTHA DORSET LETTERS.
HOLD.
PAN (L-R) TO LAWRENCE SELDEN IN ARMCHAIR, DRINKING TEA.
HE FINISHES HIS TEA THEN NOTICES THE HALF-BURNT LETTERS.
HE BENDS DOWN TO EXAMINE THEM.
STAY ON HIS FACE AS IT GRADUALLY DAWNS ON HIM WHAT THEY ARE
AND WHAT LILY HAS DONE FOR HIM.

LAWRENCE SELDEN
Oh Lily!

HE RUSHES FROM THE ROOM.

CUT TO:

108. INT. DAY. BOARDING HOUSE.

SHOT OF LAWRENCE SELDEN RUNNING UP THE STAIRS TO THE LANDING.
THEN RUNNING DOWN TO LILY BART'S DOOR.

CUT TO:

109. INT. DAY. LILY'S ROOM. BOARDING HOUSE.

SHOT OF LAWRENCE SELDEN AS THE DOOR OPENS. CAMERA INSIDE THE ROOM.

>   LAWRENCE SELDEN
>   Lily?! ... Miss Bart? -
>
>   LANDLADY (VOICE OVER)
>   (FROM INSIDE THE ROOM)
>   It's a great mercy.

SHE COMES OUT AND SELDEN STANDS THERE OVERWHELMED.

>   LAWRENCE SELDEN
>   May I see her - alone?
>
>   LANDLADY
>   Will it take long?
>
>   LAWRENCE SELDEN
>   It won't take long.

TRACK BACK WITH SELDEN AS HE ENTERS THE DARK ROOM.
HE CLOSES THE DOOR AND MOVES TOWARDS THE WINDOW.
PAN WITH HIM (L-R).
HE PULLS UP THE BLIND - SUN COMES POURING INTO THE ROOM.
HE LOOKS TOWARDS THE BED.

                                                         CUT TO:

SHOT OF LILY DEAD ON THE BED. NOW NO LONGER BEAUTIFUL - JUST
A GREY CORPSE IN A SHABBY ROOM.

                                                         CUT TO:

SHOT - FROM THE OTHER SIDE OF THE BED - LILY IN THE FOREGROUND.
SELDEN COMES AND KNEELS AT HER BEDSIDE.

SOUNDTRACK: SLOW MOVEMENT, MARCELLO OBOE CONCERTO.

HE KNEELS DOWN AND LOOKS AT HER, THEN SEES THE TWO ENVELOPES
ON HER BEDSIDE TABLE.
HE PICKS UP THE GUS TRENOR ENVELOPE AND TAKES OUT THE CHEQUE
AND SMLLES.
HE LOOKS DOWN AT HER.

>   LAWRENCE SELDEN
>   Oh - Lily!

HE STARTS TO WEEP
AND BURIES HIS HEAD IN THE DRESSES ON WHICH LILY IS LYING.
HOLD.
THEN HE LOOKS UP AT HER AND LEANS CLOSER TO HER.

THE HOUSE OF MIRTH

                    LAWRENCE SELDEN
                      (WHISPERING)
                  Lily ... I love you ...

THEN HE STARTS TO SOB AGAIN AND BURIES HIS HEAD IN THE BED
CLOTHES.
                                                  DISSOLVE TO:

2 SHOT - SELDEN'S BACK TO CAMERA.
HE IS STILL CRYING.

SOUNDTRACK: SLOW MOVEMENT, MARCELLO OBOE CONCERTO CONTINUES
HOLD.
THEN IN A LONG DISSOLVE THIS SHOT TURNS INTO AN OLD SEPIA-TYPE
PRINT.
HOLD.

SOUNDTRACK: MARCELLO CONCERTO

TITLE: 'NEW YORK 1907'
                                                    FADE TO:

CLOSING TITLES.
RUN MUSIC UNDER TITLES TO END.

                         THE END.

2/3/09

FADE UP ON:

INT. FLAT. DAY.

A SITTING ROOM OF A FURNISHED FLAT IN THE DARK.

SHOT OF THE DOOR TO THE FLAT. A TOWEL HAS BEEN WEDGED UNDER THE DOOR.

HOLD

S/T. GAS FIRE/HISSING LOUDLY

DISS TO:

WINDOW. THE CURTAINS DRAWN THOUGH IT IS STILL LIGHT OUTSIDE.

HOLD

S/T. GAS FIRE/HISSING LOUDLY

DISS TO:

SHOT OF A SHAPE LYING ON THE FLOOR IN FRONT OF A GAS FIRE WHICH IS NOT LIT.

TRACK IN ON IT

S/T GAS FIRE/HISSING LOUDLY

TRACK STOPS ON THE UNLIT GAS FIRE

The Deep Blue Sea (2011): first draft, opening scene. (© The Terence Davies Estate, held by the Terence Davies Archive at Edge Hill University)

THE DEEP BLUE SEA (2011)

The Deep Blue Sea (2011): Rachel Weisz as Hester Collyer.

The Deep Blue Sea
Shooting script – 24 September 2010 (Locked)

Cast and crew of *The Deep Blue Sea* include:

HESTER COLLYER	Rachel Weisz
FREDDIE PAGE	Tom Hiddleston
SIR WILLIAM COLLYER	Simon Russell Beale
JACKIE JACKSON	Harry Hadden-Paton
MRS ELTON	Ann Mitchell
LIZ JACKSON	Sarah Kants
MR. MILLER	Karl Johnson
PHILIP WELCH	Jolyon Coy
COLLYER'S MOTHER	Barbara Jefford
HESTER'S FATHER	Oliver Ford Davies
Written and Directed by	Terence Davies
From the play by	Terence Rattigan
Producers	Sean O'Connor
	Kate Ogborn
Director of Photography	Florian Hoffmeister
Editor	David Charap
Production Designer	James Merifield
Costume Designer	Ruth Myers
Casting Director	Jane Arnell
Music Director	Ian Neil
Composer	Samuel Barber
	Violin Concerto (1939)

A Camberwell/Fly Film (2011) production with:
UK Film Council / FilmFour / Protagonist Pictures / Lypsync Productions / Artificial Eye.

THE DEEP BLUE SEA

by
TERENCE DAVIES

Adapted from the play by
TERENCE RATTIGAN

LOCKED SHOOTING SCRIPT

24/09/10

AN INTRODUCTION.

The theme of *The Deep Blue Sea* is an ancient, almost elemental one - the undefinable nature of love. The three main characters - Hester, her lover and her husband – all offer and expect love from each other. But each has a different definition of both the word 'Love' - and the emotion. It is this confusion that leads to Hester's crisis which is at the heart of this film.

The context of Hester's dilemma is early post-war Britain, a world of bomb-sites and privation, set in a victorious nation now bankrupt and exhausted. In many ways, the challenges faced by Hester reflect the broader changes in British identity in the wake of the Second World War. The moral certainties and conventions of the 1930s have been exploded and each of the characters are attempting to come to terms with their new post-war identities. For Hester, the changing (indeed liberating) times have allowed her to engage in both her sexuality and her rage.

As in *Brief Encounter*, I have filtered the whole story through Hester's consciousness. Like Laura (Celia Johnson), Hester articulates her story to the audience in partial voice over, inviting a sense of intimacy with the audience. This is *her* story, *her* journey. *The Deep Blue Sea* is not a linear narrative, but a patchwork of memory and real-time. And in some ways, the film attempts to investigate another age-old theme - the mystery of personality. What provokes Hester to behave the way she does? What are the impulses that drive us to abandon, to love - even to death?

As a passionate cinema-goer in the 1950s, I was fascinated by the great female dramas of the period - popular stories that articulated the dreams and desires of a generation of women - *Letter from an Unknown Woman* (1948), *All That Heaven Allows* (1955), *The Heiress* (1949), *It Always Rains on Sunday* (1947) and, of course, *Brief Encounter* (1945).

Hester's is such a story of a passionate, but ordinary, woman in crisis. In this film, I hope to play homage to these great melodramas, but refracted through twenty-first century eyes.

                                                                  Terence Davies

                                                    FADE UP ON
1. A LONDON STREET. NIGHT.

Large grand houses that have been converted into flats. The houses have a shabby, faded grandeur and have obviously come down in the world.

FADE UP TITLE

> **'THE DEEP BLUE SEA'**
> **London**
> **Around 1950**

                                                    FADE TITLE

Then the 2nd Movement of the Barber Violin Concerto is heard.

TRACK BACK down the street.

A crisp Autumn evening. September. After rain.

Halfway down the street we continue TRACKING BACK but PAN (R-L) to the opposite side of the street.

A bomb-site, then the houses which have survived The Blitz come into view.

TRACK AND PAN stops on one particular boarding house.

TRACK IN ON the ground floor flat and front door.

PHILIP WELCH is finishing a cigarette between the house and the railings.

On the ground floor, the curtains have been drawn closed. MRS ELTON (the landlady) is putting out empty milk bottles, then goes back inside closing the front door.

CRANE UP to first floor front. At the window, MR MILLER - a middle-aged man in his pyjamas and dressing gown drinks a cup of cocoa.

Continue CRANING UP to second floor front. CRANE STOPS on this window.

HESTER COLLYER looking out. HOLD on her.

> HESTER'S VOICE OVER
> My darling Freddie. A moment ago I knew exactly what I wanted to say to you.
> I have run through this letter in my mind so very often and I wanted to compose something eloquent but the words just don't seem to be there. I think that's because this time I really do want to die ...

She closes the curtains.

                                                    DISSOLVE TO:

2. INT. SITTING ROOM. HESTER'S FLAT. NIGHT.

HESTER at the window but the curtains now drawn.

She turns and goes into the body of the room.

She goes to the table.

She opens a bottle of aspirins and methodically takes them- sipping from a glass of water on the table.

Over a chair - a towel.

She takes the towel to the door of the flat and wedges the towel between the floor and the bottom of the door.

She then locks the door.

HESTER'S VOICE OVER
... You'll want to know why and I'd like to make you understand because if you understood you might forgive me ... just accept that it isn't your fault ... you can't help being as you are - I can't help being as I am ...

She goes to the mantelpiece.

She puts a letter (addressed to 'FREDDIE') on the mantle and picks up several shillings.

She kneels down in front of the gas fire and puts the money into the gas meter which is to her left. Then switches it on.

DISSOLVE TO:

Gas fire.

SOUNDTRACK: Gas hissing loudly.

HOLD

Then TRACK AND PAN (R-L) around to HESTER who is lying in the foetal position covered by a rug in front of the gas fire.

SOUNDTRACK: Gas fire hissing.

HESTER'S VOICE OVER
... Forgive me ... Oh Freddie I'm so sorry ...

SOUNDTRACK: Gas fire hissing loudly. Then the Barber violin concerto is heard swelling above the hissing gas fire.

HOLD ON HESTER

She is staring straight ahead.

HOLD on her.

Then her eyes begin to droop as the gas takes effect.

DISSOLVE TO:

THE DEEP BLUE SEA

3. INT. SIR WILLIAM COLLYER'S HOUSE. NIGHT.

CLOSE UP of HESTER.

She is sitting by the fire drinking an after dinner coffee. The room is lit only by the fire.

She stares at the fire then looks at COLLYER. She's near to tears but doesn't cry.

                                                                                   CUT TO:

CLOSE UP WILLIAM COLLYER

He is sitting on the sofa listening (like HESTER) to the Barber on the wireless. He too is absorbed by the music.

                                                                                 CUT TO:

CLOSE UP HESTER

She keeps looking at COLLYER.

                        HESTER'S VOICE OVER
   What made William choose Sunningdale that summer? ... he wanted the golf ... I wasn't keen, I remember ... I'd have preferred the sea ...

SOUNDTRACK: The Barber continues.

                        HESTER'S VOICE OVER
   I didn't even think you were particularly good looking ...

She looks back at the fire ...

PAN (L-R) to fire.

Then HOLD on fire.

                                                           DISSOLVE TO:

4. EXT. GOLF CLUB. DAY.

A verandah on which HESTER is sitting - on a lounger enjoying the sun. She is half asleep.

SOUNDTRACK: Barber violin concerto continues.

FREDDIE is standing at the end of the lounger.

HESTER opens her eyes.

                        HESTER'S VOICE OVER
   I'd seen you several times at the club but never paid much attention to you ...

FREDDIE sits down on the lounger and touches HESTER'S arm.

> HESTER'S VOICE OVER
> Then suddenly you touched my arm ...
>
>   CUT TO:

CLOSE UP of FREDDIE doing just that.

> HESTER'S VOICE OVER
> And said something quite conventional ...
>
>   CUT TO:

> FREDDIE
> I really mean it. It's not just a line. I really think you're the most attractive girl I've met ...
>
>   CUT TO:

HESTER

> HESTER'S VOICE OVER
> For a change you didn't use that irritating RAF slang ... 'He does it for effect' William once said ...
>
>   CUT TO:

5. EXT. LINCOLN'S INN. DAY.

HESTER and COLLYER walking through the Inn towards COLLYER'S chambers.

> HESTER'S VOICE OVER
> About a week later William and I had just had lunch and I was walking him back to his chambers in Lincoln's Inn ...

HESTER and COLLYER exchange polite kisses. He goes into his chambers and she towards the Chancery Lane exit.

> HESTER'S VOICE OVER
> ... and I saw you quite by accident.
>
>   CUT TO:

6. EXT. CHANCERY LANE EXIT, LINCOLN'S INN. DAY.

HESTER comes out and goes down Chancery Lane.

                                                          CUT TO:

7. EXT. EDE AND RAVENSCROFT SHOP, CHANCERY LANE. DAY.

HESTER and FREDDIE meet.

THE DEEP BLUE SEA

> HESTER'S VOICE OVER
> I ran into you outside Ede & Ravenscroft ... you invited me for a drink ... I don't usually drink during the day, as you know, it makes me sleepy ... but I accepted all the same ...

<u>CUT TO:</u>

8. INT. CITY PUB. DAY. CROWDED.

HESTER sitting in a corner with FREDDIE - she's clearly a fish out of water.

FREDDIE has had a few and is ebullient yet slightly aggressive.

> FREDDIE
> I survived the Battle of Britain old fruit, old darling! ... SURVIVED! ... mixture of fear and excitement ... nothing like it ... excitement and fear ... irresistible combo ...

They look at one another.

A clear sexual attraction.

> FREDDIE
> (less aggressive, more quietly intimate)
> ... we were doing something <u>important</u> - for dear old Blighty ...

They lean forward and kiss each other.

> FREDDIE
> ... old fruit, old darling ...

> HESTER'S VOICE OVER
> One thing led to another ... above all I didn't want to hurt William ...

<u>DISSOLVE TO:</u>

9. INT. COLLYER'S MOTHER'S HOUSE. GUEST BEDROOM. EVENING.

HESTER and COLLYER come into the bedroom at COLLYER'S MOTHER'S house in the country. CUT TO <u>their POV</u>. Twin beds.

<u>CUT TO:</u>

HESTER and COLLYER.

> HESTER
> Twin beds. <u>Again</u>!

COLLYER
(smiling)
Mother has an ... arcane view of married life.

HESTER
How were you conceived then? Willpower?

COLLYER
(smiling)
Don't be vulgar Hester ... we are talking about mummy.

HESTER sighs at the thought of spending time with his mother.

COLLYER
It's not that bad. Don't let her rile you.

CUT TO:

10. INT. COLLYER'S MOTHER'S HOUSE. DINING ROOM. EVENING.

COLLYER'S mother at the head of the table. She is a <u>real</u> dowager.
COLLYER and HESTER on either side of her.
The atmosphere is stiff.
HESTER and COLLYER's mother clearly do not get on.
Silence.

COLLYER
Will you be going to Wimbledon this year, mother?

MOTHER
No. Since your Father died I've not been able to enjoy tennis. I'm thinking of giving up our seats.

COLLYER
But they're on the Centre Court?

MOTHER
Yes. There is that.
(To HESTER)
Do you play?

HESTER
Tennis?

MOTHER
Anything.

                    HESTER
                    (riled)
        I occasionally play a hand at canasta.

                    MOTHER
                    (sharp)
        Cards are a pastime. I meant a sport.

                    HESTER
              (trying to contain herself)
   I've always thought of sport as one of the more pointless of
                    human activities.

                    MOTHER
            That was almost offensive.

                    COLLYER
         (trying to pour oil on troubled waters)
      I'm sure Hester didn't mean to be impolite, mother.

Silence.
                    MOTHER
          I take it you don't play then?

                    HESTER
Occasionally. I just find it very difficult to be passionate about it.

                    MOTHER
Beware of passion, Hester. It always leads to something ugly.

                    HESTER
         What would you replace it with?

                    MOTHER
     (taking a moment) A guarded enthusiasm. It's safer.

                    HESTER
              But much more dull.
                                                    CUT TO:

11. EXT. COLLYER'S MOTHER'S HOUSE. TERRACE AND GARDEN. DAY. GLORIOUS WEATHER.

MOTHER and HESTER sitting at a table in the sun.

                    HESTER
                  (sincerely)
           Oh, the garden is glorious!

                        MOTHER
    Yes. It's my one unalloyed pleasure. So much safer than
                    people, don't you think?

HESTER'S heart sinks.

                        HESTER
                 No. Not in the long run.
Silence.
COLLYER joins them. He carries a tray with tea and cakes on it and puts it on the table then sits down between them.

                        MOTHER
                        Ah, tea!
COLLYER goes to pour.

                        MOTHER
        No darling! Hester will pour, won't you, dear?

                        HESTER
                      (grudgingly)
                      If you wish.

                        COLLYER
            The garden is really lovely, mother!

                        MOTHER
            Yes. Even Hester has been admiring it ...
                    almost passionately.

HESTER stiffens.

COLLYER picks this up. HESTER pours then hands him his cup <u>first</u>. Then mother's.

                        COLLYER
                Would you like a cake, mother?

                        MOTHER
          Oh yes! The Battenburg. It's a pleasure I've
                       never outgrown.

He gives her the cake.

                        MOTHER
                       (to HESTER)
        Is there anything <u>you</u> haven't outgrown, Hester?

                        HESTER
    Yes. Insensitivity. I've never been able to forgive it.

THE DEEP BLUE SEA

Before MOTHER can reply HESTER gets up quickly, kisses COLLYER and runs into the house.

> HESTER
> I'm going in to pack, darling. I'd like to get an early start back to town.

CUT TO:

12. INT. COLLYER'S MOTHER'S HOUSE. GUEST BEDROOM. DAY.

HESTER sitting on one of the single beds. The single bed opposite her has a half packed open suitcase on it.

She is on the telephone; back to camera.

When she speaks it is both low and secretive.

> HESTER
> Yes ... Freddie, of course ... I'm hoping we'll be leaving for London soon ... no, not there ... I'll meet you at Jackie Jackson's as soon as I can, Freddie ... (laughs) yes, darling ... me too ...

COLLYER has come quietly into the bedroom and unseen, stands at the door.

> COLLYER'S VOICE OVER
> And who else do you call 'darling'?

HESTER spins around very startled. She doesn't speak but clearly looks guilty.

> COLLYER
> I assume this means what I think it means?

HESTER doesn't speak.

> COLLYER
> Well - how long?

> HESTER
> William ... I ...

> COLLYER
> How long has this been going on?

> HESTER
> Some months.

> COLLYER
> I see.

She goes to speak.

                    COLLYER
I'll meet you at the car after I've said goodbye to mother. I
don't want her upset unnecessarily, that way, at least, our
                dignity will remain intact.
                                                  DISSOLVE TO:

13. INT./EXT. HALL AND FRONT DOOR OF BOARDING HOUSE. DAY.

The front door is open and FREDDIE and HESTER come
towards it then come into the hallway. FREDDIE carries
one suitcase.

                    FREDDIE
          Morning Mrs E! Still doing post duty?
                                                     CUT TO:

MRS ELTON is at a table near the foot of the stairs.
She is sorting post out for her tenants and laying them in
separate piles.

                    MRS ELTON
It saves time. Especially in the mornings. My tenants can pick
          up their letters on their way out to work.
                                                     CUT TO:

FREDDIE and HESTER

                    FREDDIE
              You're a treasure Mrs E!
                                                     CUT TO:
MRS ELTON

                    MRS ELTON
                  (clearly charmed)
      It's all part of the service ... go right up ...

                                                     CUT TO:

FREDDIE and HESTER going up the stairs. FREDDIE at a run.
HESTER more slowly.

                    FREDDIE
                    (to HESTER)
          Second floor front. Bit of a hike ...
                                                     CUT TO:

MRS ELTON at the bottom of the stairs.

THE DEEP BLUE SEA

          MRS ELTON
          (to HESTER)
      Some post Mrs Page.

CUT TO:

HESTER doesn't respond.

CUT TO:

MRS ELTON

          MRS ELTON
          Mrs Page!

CUT TO:

HESTER

          HESTER
          (startled)
          Yes?

CUT TO:

MRS ELTON

          MRS ELTON
          Your post.

CUT TO:

          HESTER
          (still hesitant)
          Oh yes ...

She comes back down and takes the post.

          HESTER
          Thank you.

Then goes upstairs.

CUT TO:

14. INT. SITTING ROOM. HESTER'S FLAT. DAY.

FREDDIE and HESTER come in. He puts her suitcase down.

FREDDIE goes to the window and draws back the curtains to reveal just how dreary and shabby the room is.

          FREDDIE
          (trying to be positive)
      You'll make it look cosy in no time.

CUT TO:

HESTER. She looks around the room, her heart sinking and tries to smile.

DISSOLVE TO:

15. INT. BEDROOM. HESTER'S FLAT. NIGHT.

<u>TRACK IN</u> ON HESTER and FREDDIE in bed making love very passionately. (NB These sex scenes are <u>not</u> explicit)

HOLD

SOUNDTRACK: The Barber violin concerto is heard.

DISSOLVE TO:

HESTER and FREDDIE in bed immediately after they have both climaxed but still very passionate.

HOLD

SOUNDTRACK: The Barber violin concerto is heard.

DISSOLVE TO:

HESTER and FREDDIE after sex. He lies on his side with his back to her.

HOLD

SOUNDTRACK: The Barber violin concerto starts to fade.

HESTER turns towards FREDDIE and strokes his back. She leans forward. She licks the nape of his neck.

> HESTER'S VOICE OVER
> The rest you know ...

DISSOLVE TO:

16. INT. SITTING ROOM. HESTER'S FLAT. DAY.

HESTER lying in front of the gas fire. The sound of knocking on the door.

> PHILIP WELCH'S VOICE OVER

Mrs Elton! There's escaping gas I think it's coming from here!

The sound of the flat door being forced.

> MRS ELTON'S VOICE OVER
> Mrs Page! Mrs Page!

HOLD on HESTER throughout this scene until other shots are indicated.

> WELCH'S VOICE OVER
> Don't light a match! How do you switch it off?

> MRS ELTON'S VOICE OVER

It's already off! The meter must have run out ... she isn't dead is she?

> WELCH'S VOICE OVER
> Help me get her to the window.

THE DEEP BLUE SEA

<u>TRACK AND PAN</u> (R-L) <u>HOLDING</u> on HESTER as she is lifted from the floor and taken to a chair by the window.

The curtains are thrown back (we see this reflected on HESTER as the light floods in). We hear the window being opened.

      WELCH'S VOICE OVER
    (softly) Mrs Page ... Mrs Page ...

HESTER doesn't respond.

      WELCH'S VOICE OVER
    We should get a doctor.

      MRS ELTON'S VOICE OVER
I'll get Mr Miller from downstairs ... he'll know what to do ...

      WELCH'S VOICE OVER
     Is he a doctor?

      MRS ELTON'S VOICE OVER
 Mr Miller! Can you come up please! It's urgent!

HESTER starts to come round but she is still groggy.

       HESTER
     (half conscious)
 Freddie? ... where's Freddie? ... We hear someone come in.

      WELCH'S VOICE OVER
  There was an empty aspirin bottle beside her.

Suddenly HESTER'S face is slapped hard and her eyes open. MR MILLER stands before her.
              <u>CUT TO:</u>
MR MILLER

       MR MILLER
  (holding the empty bottle in front of HESTER'S face)
      How many?
              <u>CUT TO:</u>
HESTER

She closes her eyes and Miller slaps her again.

      MILLER'S VOICE OVER
      How many?!

HESTER starts to come round to almost consciousness.

>   HESTER
>   Twelve.

Then her eyes close again.

She is picked up and taken into the bedroom and laid on the bed.

16A. INT. BEDROOM. HESTER'S FLAT. DAY.

<u>TRACK IN</u> <u>TWO SHOT</u>.
                                                            <u>CUT TO:</u>

>   MILLER
>   (to Mrs Elton)
>   Get me a bowl.

MILLER prepares an injection from a bag he's brought with him.
                                                            <u>CUT TO:</u>

<u>TWO SHOT</u>

MRS ELTON and MILLER

>   MILLER
>   Hold it to her mouth.

MRS ELTON does so.
                                                            <u>CUT TO:</u>

MILLER and HESTER. He gives her an injection.
                                                            <u>CUT TO:</u>

MRS ELTON and HESTER.

HESTER vomits into the bowl.
                                                            <u>CUT TO:</u>

WELCH at the bedroom door.

>   WELCH
>   Is there anything we can do?
                                                            <u>CUT TO:</u>

MILLER

>   MILLER
>   There's nothing you can do.
                                                            <u>CUT TO:</u>

MRS ELTON

>   MRS ELTON
>   You don't mean she's dying?
                                                            <u>CUT TO:</u>

THE DEEP BLUE SEA

MILLER

> MILLER
> On the contrary.

CUT TO:

MRS ELTON

> MRS ELTON
> But she did try to kill herself didn't she?

CUT TO:

MILLER

> MILLER
> It would seem so.

CUT TO:

MRS ELTON

> MRS ELTON
> She'll recover?

CUT TO:

MILLER

> MILLER
> Sixty grains of aspirin are hardly enough to kill a healthy child and the symptoms of gas poisoning are very slight.

CUT TO:

WELCH

> WELCH
> Do you think she'll try again doctor?

CUT TO:

MILLER

> MILLER
> I'm not a doctor. But I will say she will probably try again, yes.

CUT TO:

WELCH

> WELCH
>
> Isn't attempted suicide a crime? Don't people go to gaol for it?

CUT TO:

> MILLER
> People go to gaol for all sorts of reasons.

CUT TO:

WELCH

                    WELCH
          Should we call the police?

                                          CUT TO:

MILLER

                    MILLER
                (emphatically)
                      No!

                                          CUT TO:

MRS ELTON

                  MRS ELTON
             (equally emphatically)
                      No!

HESTER becomes more and more awake. She gets up and feels in one of the pockets of her dressing gown, takes out a packet of cigarettes and matches from it and lights a cigarette.

                    WELCH
      Don't you think you should go back to bed?

                    HESTER
        No I just feel a bit dopey, that's all.

She moves to the bedroom door and politely ushers out WELCH, MILLER and MRS ELTON.

                    HESTER
     I'm terribly sorry for all the trouble I've caused.

                                          CUT TO:

17. INT. SITTING ROOM. HESTER'S FLAT. DAY.

All four come out of the bedroom - WELCH, MILLER and MRS ELTON go to the door of the flat.

HESTER goes to the mantelpiece.

                    WELCH
          Are you sure you're alright?

HESTER by the mantelpiece looking for something.

                    HESTER
              Yes. Thank you.

THE DEEP BLUE SEA

She finds the letter addressed to 'FREDDIE' and puts it in the other pocket of her dressing gown.

MILLER and WELCH leave. MRS ELTON stays.

> MRS ELTON
> Oh Mr Miller - I don't like to ask - but could you come down later and see Mr Elton. He's bad again.

MR MILLER just nods yes.

> HESTER
> (to MRS ELTON)
> Please don't say anything to Mr Page about my idiotic accident. I don't want to alarm him.

> MRS ELTON
> If that's the way you want it.

> HESTER
> That's the way I want it.

MRS ELTON leaves.

HESTER looks for a cigarette then lights it.

She sits on the sofa then lies down on it, smoking her cigarette.

She stares ahead. Smoking and thinking.

CUT TO:

CLOSE UP HESTER

HOLD

TRACK AWAY from her R to L

DISSOLVE TO:

18. INT. NATIONAL GALLERY. DAY.

Continue TRACKING R to L over paintings. Stopping at a Braque Picture.

> FREDDIE'S VOICE OVER
> It looks like bits of crockery.

CUT TO:

FREDDIE and Hester.

> HESTER
> It's a Braque.

FREDDIE
(laughing)
Bric-a-Braque!

HESTER smiles weakly.

FREDDIE
That was a joke.

HESTER
So I gathered.

FREDDIE
(irked)
We can't all be 'cultured'.

HESTER
We can't all be childish, either.

FREDDIE
(getting more and more angry)
Listen, it was childish people like me that saved people like you from invasion!

HESTER
(equally angry)
That's beside the point! No one's questioning your bravery - just your mind.

FREDDIE
(really riled)
There's nothing wrong with my mind!
FUBAR!

HESTER
What the hell do you mean by that?!

FREDDIE
You're the clever one! You work it out! He walks angrily away from her.

HESTER follows him, grabs his arm and spins him around to her.

HESTER
What did you mean by that?!

FREDDIE
FUBAR. Acronym. 'Fucked Up Beyond All Recognition.'

FREDDIE walks away from her furious. He doesn't care where he is, neither does she.

> HESTER
> Where are you going?!

> FREDDIE
> To the impressionists!

CUT TO:

19. INT. BOARDING HOUSE. DAY.

HESTER comes in the front door then closes it. She sees MRS ELTON then puts on a smile.

CUT TO:

MRS ELTON coming up the hall towards the front door.

> MRS ELTON
> Oh! I thought you were the second delivery.

CUT TO:

HESTER

> HESTER
> (smiling)
> More misdeliveries?

CUT TO:

MRS ELTON

> MRS ELTON
> (Showing a clutch of letters to HESTER)
> Wagstaff & Quinn - undertakers! They're at the other end of the street! So are Hawkes & Guyler! Bleeding postman!
>
> (Showing one particular letter to HESTER)
> 'Lady Collyer', I ask you! What would she need with a ration book?

CUT TO:

HESTER

> HESTER
> (her smile fading)
> Oh ... that's mine.

CUT TO:

MRS ELTON

MRS ELTON
I beg your pardon?

CUT TO:

HESTER

HESTER
It's for me.

CUT TO:

MRS ELTON

MRS ELTON
And Mr Page ... ?

CUT TO:

HESTER

HESTER
Is not my husband.

Silence.

HESTER (cont'd)
I'd rather you continued to think of me as 'Mrs Page'.

Pause.

CUT TO:

MRS ELTON

MRS ELTON
Alright. But I run a respectable house here and I don't want any kind of trouble.

CUT TO:

HESTER

HESTER
Of course not, Mrs Elton.

CUT TO:

MRS ELTON

MRS ELTON
What people do in private is best left there. I neither condone nor condemn.

CUT TO:

HESTER

HESTER
(taking the ration book)
Thank you, Mrs Elton. That's very generous of you.

MRS ELTON goes back down the hall and HESTER continues upstairs.

CUT TO:

THE DEEP BLUE SEA

20. INT. SITTING ROOM. HESTER'S FLAT. DAY.

HESTER comes in and closes the door.

She looks across at the sofa and sees FREDDIE lying on it.

                                                          CUT TO:

Her POV of FREDDIE on the sofa.

HESTER ENTERS SHOT and kneels down behind his head.

> FREDDIE
> (contrite)
> Forgive me?

> HESTER
> (lovingly)
> I'd rather die.

They both smile.

She kisses him lightly on the mouth.

> HESTER
> Why did you go to the impressionists?

> FREDDIE
> I only did it for the Monet.

They both cringe at the pun.

Pause.

She slides her hands down inside his shirt and they kiss very passionately.

HOLD ON THEM

                                                          CUT TO:

21. INT. LOCAL PUB. NIGHT.

JACKIE JACKSON and FREDDIE doing a double act.

> JACKIE JACKSON
> (imitating an upper class accent)
> Stop! That man there!

FREDDIE stops and comes to attention.

> FREDDIE
> (imitating JACKIE JACKSON)
> Just got back from giving Jerry a damn good thrashing, sir

JACKIE JACKSON
Good show Page.

FREDDIE
Had to ditch the crate in the drink though ... no fuel, no
ammo left but it was still a wizzo prang, sir!

JACKIE JACKSON
Carry on!

FREDDIE
(Mrs Mopp from ITMA)
Can I do you now sir?

CUT TO:

LIZ and HESTER

LIZ
(long suffering)
They'll do the navy now.

CUT TO:

TWO SHOT of FREDDIE and JACKIE JACKSON.

They continue doing their double act in upper class voices.

JACKIE JACKSON
Range Two Thousand and closing fast, number One!

FREDDIE
Stand by torps!

JACKIE JACKSON
Torps ready sir!

FREDDIE
Fire one!

JACKIE JACKSON
Fire one!

FREDDIE
Fire two!

JACKIE JACKSON
Fire two! We've hit her a mid-ships, sir!

FREDDIE
Very good! Stand by to pick up survivors!

CUT TO:

THE DEEP BLUE SEA

<u>TWO SHOT</u> of LIZ and HESTER.

The two women get on and clearly like one another.

> LIZ
> (to JACKIE JACKSON and FREDDIE)
> Alright you two! Come down to earth.

> JACKIE JACKSON
> (in a 'hurt' Terry-Thomas voice)
> Oh ... I say ... Kitten!

> LIZ
> (to Hester)
> Oh humour them, for God's sake otherwise we'll get a replay of the entire war!

FREDDIE and JACKIE JACKSON start making explosion noises.

> LIZ
> That's all we need - sound effects!

> FREDDIE
> (imitating JACKIE JACKSON)
> Oh! You've gawn all frosty, Kitten!

> LIZ
> Oh, is it agony? One does hope so! Well if it gets too cold you could always rub two boy scouts together. Drinks gentlemen! The ladies are thirsty.

> HESTER
> Parched!

<u>CUT TO:</u>

<u>SHOT</u> of JACKIE JACKSON and FREDDIE going to the bar. <u>TRACK WITH THEM</u> from behind.

Then <u>TRACK</u> AROUND (<u>L to R</u>) over a dissolve to a FRONT <u>SHOT</u> of FREDDIE and JACKIE JACKSON carrying drinks on a tray and sitting down opposite LIZ and HESTER.

<u>TRACK BACK WITH</u> THEM.

<u>SOUNDTRACK</u>: During and over this.

> ALL
> (singing)
> 'See the pyramids along the Nile,/Watch the sunrise on a tropic isle/Just remember darling all the while/You belong to me'.

FREDDIE and JACKIE JACKSON are singing.

They sit down putting the drinks on the table.

>   ALL (cont'd)
>   (singing)
> 'See the marketplace in old Algiers/Send me photographs and souvenirs/Just remember when a dream appears/You belong to me'.

PAN (L to R) to TWO SHOT of LIZ and HESTER.

LIZ is singing and HESTER is radiant - enjoying herself in this impromptu happiness.

>   ALL (cont'd)
>   (singing)
> 'I'll be so alone without you/Maybe you'll be lonesome too and blue'.

PAN AWAY from them (L to R)

DISSOLVE TO:

22. INT. CLUB. SMALL DANCE FLOOR. NIGHT.

PAN (L to R) to HESTER and FREDDIE on the dance floor. JACKIE and LIZ in the background.

SOUNDTRACK: Jo Stafford (on record) singing the rest of the song.

>   JO STAFFORD VOICE OVER
>   (from record)
> 'Fly the ocean in a silver plane/See the jungle when it's wet with rain/Just remember 'til you're home again/You belong to me'.

PAN (L to R) and

DISSOLVE TO:

23. EXT. STREET. NIGHT. THE FOUR WALKING HOME.

PAN (L to R) to TWO SHOT of LIZ and HESTER.

FREDDIE and JACKIE JACKSON just behind them.

>   HESTER
>   (quietly to LIZ)
> I'd only say this to you but I'm not very good at being alone.

>   LIZ
> But I've always thought of you as very self-sufficient.

THE DEEP BLUE SEA

> HESTER
> (smiling)
> Appearances can be deceptive. 'We live in an age of surfaces'.

FREDDIE and JACKIE JACKSON have caught up with them.

> FREDDIE
> Who said that?

> HESTER
> Oscar.

> FREDDIE
> Oscar who?

> HESTER
> Wilde, of course.

> LIZ
> Who did you think she meant? Oscar Homolka?

> LIZ, JACKIE JACKSON & FREDDIE
> (singing)
> 'And Regis Toomey'!

> LIZ
> (to HESTER)
> Do you think they'll ever grow up?

> HESTER
> Probably not.

They stop when they get to where LIZ and JACKIE JACKSON live.

> LIZ & JACKIE JACKSON
> We'll say good-night.

> FREDDIE
> Be good! And if you can't be good ...

> ALL FOUR
> Be careful!

LIZ & JACKIE JACKSON go in.

HESTER & FREDDIE just stand there. Then they embrace passionately and kiss passionately, HESTER rubbing herself against FREDDIE.

                        HESTER
                   Oh, I love you so!
                                                CUT TO:

The house where JACKIE JACKSON & LIZ live.

The front door opens and JACKIE JACKSON pops his head out and sees them kissing passionately.

                     JACKIE JACKSON
                        (shouting)
                 And we'll have less of that!
                                                CUT TO:

HESTER & FREDDIE
                        FREDDIE
                 They can't ration everything!

FREDDIE & HESTER look at each other simply happy in each others arms.

                        FREDDIE
                   Come on, let's go home.
                                            DISSOLVE TO:

24. INT. SITTING ROOM. HESTER'S FLAT. DAY.

HESTER lying on the sofa smoking. She finishes her cigarette, gets up and goes idly to the window and stares out.
                                                CUT TO:

25. EXTERIOR OF WINDOW. DAY.

HESTER looking out.

SOUNDTRACK: Barber violin concerto is heard but as if on the radio.
                                                CUT TO:

26. INT. SITTING ROOM. HESTER'S FLAT. DAY.

CLOSE UP of HESTER standing at the window.

SOUNDTRACK: The Barber violin concerto is heard.
                                                CUT TO:

FREDDIE comes into the flat. He throws down his golf clubs and sits down, taking off his driving gloves.

                        FREDDIE
         How's tricks Hes? Just done ninety-three down The Great
         West. Alvis - smashing job. Jackie Jackson gave me a lift.

THE DEEP BLUE SEA

He switches on a lamp.

> FREDDIE (cont'd)
> Let's have a bit of light on the subject.

Starts to redial the radio programme.
The Barber ends abruptly.

> FREDDIE (cont'd)
> Oh Christ! Let's have something with a bit of life in it ... He turns the dial until he gets the BBC Light programme. It is an edition of 'Educating Archie'.

CUT TO:

HESTER still at the window. Still not looking at FREDDIE.

> HESTER
> Did you have a good weekend?

CUT TO:

FREDDIE

> FREDDIE
> Not bad. Won both my matches. Took a fiver off Jackie – he was livid. Then it started raining. Golf – kaput!

CUT TO:

HESTER

> HESTER
> (still not looking at him)
> How much did you win altogether?

CUT TO:

FREDDIE

> FREDDIE
> Seven.

CUT TO:

HESTER

> HESTER
> (still not looking at him)
> Can I have some of it for the rent?

CUT TO:

FREDDIE

> FREDDIE
> Oh hell! Alright you can have three. I need the rest for lunch. Job prospect. South American. The DFC and Bar seems to have impressed him.

CUT TO:

HESTER

                    HESTER
    (finishing her cigarette but still not looking at him)
                What South American?

                                                    CUT TO:
FREDDIE
                    FREDDIE
    Bloke I met at golf. Do you know you've not looked at me
                    since I came in?

                                                    CUT TO:
HESTER
                    HESTER
        (curt but still not looking at him)
            I know what you look like Freddie.

Silence.

                                                    CUT TO:
FREDDIE
FREDDIE switches off the wireless.

                    FREDDIE
            I've done something haven't I?

Silence.
HESTER still doesn't look at him.

                    FREDDIE (cont'd)
            Oh my God! Many happy returns!

She still doesn't look at him.

                    FREDDIE (cont'd)
            Had you arranged something special?

                                                    CUT TO:
HESTER
                    HESTER
            Just steak and a bottle of claret.

He goes to her and puts his arms around her waist.
She has her back to him.
TWO SHOT
                    FREDDIE
                    (wheedling)
    Come on ... I'm sorry ... I can't say anymore can I?

                    HESTER
                (beginning to melt)
                No - you can't.

                    FREDDIE
                Still love me?

                    HESTER
                I still love you.

He kisses her neck and HESTER turns around to him and responds with
great passion, the kiss being prolonged by her. He breaks from her
a little and moves behind her again. His arms around her waist.

                    FREDDIE
                I need a cigarette.

He reaches inside both pockets of her dressing gown. Takes
out a packet from one pocket and the letter from the other.

                    HESTER
                (seeing the letter)
                Give me that!

                    FREDDIE
                (slightly puzzled)
                But it's addressed to me.

FREDDIE lets go of her and walks into the middle of the room.
He opens the letter and begins reading it.

                    HESTER
                Freddie, give me the letter!

                    FREDDIE
                (still reading)
It was addressed to me! He reads it - becoming more and more
   furious. He puts the letter in his pocket and storms out.

                    HESTER
                Freddie! Freddie!

She takes off her dressing gown as quickly as possible, runs
into the bedroom and returns with her coat and shoes. She
quickly puts the shoes on but before she can put her coat on
there's a light tap on the door. She drops her coat and runs
to the door and opens it.
                                                    CUT TO:

27. INT. LANDING OUTSIDE FLAT. DAY.

HESTER opens the door but doesn't speak for a moment.
                                                    CUT TO:

Her POV. WILLIAM COLLYER and MRS ELTON on the landing.

              HESTER'S VOICE OVER
           How did you know I was here?

                    COLLYER
            Your landlady telephoned me.

                   MRS ELTON
     I'm sorry but I was worried about you ...

                    COLLYER
(coming into the flat softly as he passes HESTER)
                Tell her to go.

                    HESTER
      It's alright Mrs Elton. Thank you.

MRS ELTON goes downstairs.

                                              CUT TO:

28. INT. SITTING ROOM. HESTER'S FLAT. LATE AFTERNOON.

COLLYER and HESTER stand for a moment in silence.

                    HESTER
            How did she find you?

                    COLLYER
I'm still in the telephone book. I assume she used her initiative.

                    HESTER
          I'm flattered you came.

                    COLLYER
  Don't be. My motives were entirely selfish. I was hoping
                   to gloat.

They look at each other for the first time with genuine affection.
                 COLLYER (cont'd)
              Are you alright?

Before she can answer MILLER comes in without knocking and comes up to HESTER.
                    MILLER
   You ought to be in bed. Let me look at you.

THE DEEP BLUE SEA

(He feels her pulse)
Tongue.
(She extends it)
You should live to a ripe old age.

COLLYER
(concerned but angry)
Are you her doctor?

MILLER
No.

COLLYER
What are you then?

HESTER
Shall we just say that he is a 'philanthropist'.

COLLYER
(to MILLER)
A little more respect might not come amiss.

MILLER
I give my respect to those who've earned it. To everyone else I'm civil.

MILLER leaves.

COLLYER
I take it he's not a qualified medical practitioner?

HESTER
You take it quite correctly.

COLLYER
(really concerned)
What happened?

HESTER
I must be careful what I say. Attempted suicide is a crime, isn't it?

COLLYER
(shocked)
Yes.

HESTER
And I am speaking to a judge.

COLLYER
(angry)
You're speaking to your husband.

Silence.

COLLYER (cont'd)
Why didn't you let me know you were back in London?

HESTER
The last time I saw you, you said you never wanted to hear from me again.

COLLYER
The last time I saw you I didn't know what I was saying.

Silence.

COLLYER (cont'd)
How long have you been back from Canada?

HESTER
Three or four months. Freddie lost his job in Ottawa. Neither of us liked it anyway.

Pause.

COLLYER
Has he deserted you?

HESTER
No. He's just got back. He's been playing golf at Sunningdale ...
(realising what she's just said)
Do you still play?

COLLYER
I don't go to Sunningdale anymore ...

HESTER
But you used to love golf. What do you do for exercise?

COLLYER
I play tennis with David, occasionally.

HESTER
(an attempt to lighten the atmosphere)
Has he become very pompous since being made Solicitor-General?

THE DEEP BLUE SEA

                    COLLYER
    All Solicitors-General are pompous. It helps their game.

Silence.

                    COLLYER (cont'd)
          Is he being unfaithful to you?

                    HESTER
                      No.

                    COLLYER
               He still loves you?

                    HESTER
          As much as he did ten months ago.

                    COLLYER
             And you still love him?

                    HESTER
           Yes William, I still love him.

Silence.

                    COLLYER
                 Is it money?

HESTER doesn't respond.

                    HESTER
        Sit down Bill. It's nice to see you again.

She extends her arm. On her wrist a bracelet.
COLLYER joins her and takes her hand.

                    COLLYER
              (still holding her hand)
           I'm glad you still wear it.

She doesn't speak. Both sit down on the sofa.

                    COLLYER
    As yet I've taken no steps - so you can have the divorce
                 if you still want it?

                    HESTER
                   (smiling)
           That's generous of you Bill.

COLLYER
(smiles sadly)
Can I do anything to help?

She shakes her head.

COLLYER (cont'd)
Well, at least I found you again.

HESTER
Did you look very hard?

COLLYER
No. You see I rather foolishly thought that my indifference would hurt your vanity.
(Concerned)
Did you really try to kill yourself?

HESTER
(nods)
'Whilst the balance of my mind was disturbed', isn't that the legal phrase?

COLLYER
What disturbed that balance?

HESTER
Anger. Hatred. Shame. Of myself. Of being alive.
(Pause)
Are you still angry?

COLLYER
At Page?

HESTER
At both of us?

COLLYER
Yes. He betrayed my friendship. You betrayed my trust.
(Pause)
But anger fades and is replaced by regret.
(Pause)
You said just now his feelings for you hadn't changed.

HESTER
They haven't. But zero minus zero is still zero.

COLLYER
How long have you known this?

> HESTER
> From the beginning.

> COLLYER
> But how, in the name of reason, can you go on loving a man who can give you nothing?

> HESTER
> Oh but he does give me something from time to time.

> COLLYER
> What?

> HESTER
> Himself.

Silence.

> COLLYER
> For someone like myself whose profession is the study of human nature I'm very inexperienced in matters of this kind.

> HESTER
> So am I Bill. So am I.
> (Pause)
> Blame my conventional upbringing – you see I was brought up to think that in cases of this kind it was more proper for the man to do the loving.

Silence.

> COLLYER
> I wish you'd try to find a way I could help you.

She stands. So does COLLYER.

> HESTER
> I'll try to find a way.

They shake hands rather awkwardly and stand there looking at each other.

COLLYER goes to the door.

> COLLYER
> (turning)
> Oh ... many happy returns of yesterday.

> HESTER
> (smiling)
> Thank you.

COLLYER leaves.

HESTER goes to the window and looks out. It is starting to get dark.

HESTER's POV of COLLYER'S Rolls Royce. It drives away.

                                                            CUT TO:

HESTER quickly puts on her coat and runs out.

SOUNDTRACK: Barber violin concerto is heard.

                                                            CUT TO:

29. INT. HALL. EARLY EVENING.

HESTER running downstairs.

                                                            CUT TO:

30. INT. HALL AND FRONT DOOR. EARLY EVENING.

HESTER in hall. She comes flying down the stairs opens the front door and runs out leaving the front door open.

Outside a steady drizzle.

                                                            CUT TO:

31. EXT. STREET. EARLY EVENING.

TRACK with HESTER running down the street (side view of her L to R).

                                                            CUT TO:

Another street.

TRACK as above.

                                                            CUT TO:

32. EXT. ALLEY. EARLY EVENING. A LONG, NARROW ALLEY.

HESTER comes running down it towards a pub - halfway down. She pauses for breath then walks down the alley and into the pub.

SOUNDTRACK: The Barber violin concerto mixes to the people in the pub singing 'Any time'.

                                                            CUT TO:

THE DEEP BLUE SEA

33. INT. LOCAL PUB. EVENING.

We see HESTER come in, clearly looking for FREDDIE.

The pub is crowded and a sing-song in progress.

>   ALL
>   (singing)
>   'Any time you're feeling lonely
>   Any time you're feeling blue
>   Any time you're thinking 'bout me
>   That's the time I'll be thinking of you.
>   So any time you say you want me back again
>   That's the time I'll come right back to you'.

Immediately they go into the next song, 'How you gonna' keep 'em down on the farm?'

During the singing FREDDIE is seen (<u>HESTER'S POV</u>) carrying drinks above his head as he weaves his way through the crowd to join his friend JACKIE JACKSON.

He and JACKIE sing along as well.

HESTER joins them.

JACKIE JACKSON nods to HESTER.

FREDDIE ignores her. He just keeps on drinking.

HESTER tries to take FREDDIE'S arm but he pulls it violently away from her.

She looks at JACKIE JACKSON nearby and mouths 'Please Jackie' and indicating towards outside.

JACKIE JACKSON takes FREDDIE by the arm and says something to him but we cannot hear it above the noise of the pub.

Then FREDDIE and JACKIE JACKSON go to the exit followed by HESTER.

<u>CUT TO:</u>

34. EXT. LOCAL PUB. EVENING.

The three of them outside. FREDDIE seething.

>   FREDDIE
>   (to JACKIE JACKSON)
>   Just because I forgot her bloody birthday!

JACKIE JACKSON tries to look conciliatory.

HESTER says nothing.

FREDDIE (cont'd)
My God! If all the men who forgot their wives' birthdays were to come home to suicide notes the line would stretch from here to the Shetlands!

An angry silence.

HESTER
Can I have the letter?

FREDDIE
WHY?!

HESTER
It belongs to me.

FREDDIE
It had my name on it!
(Exploding)
My God! Aren't women the end?!
(Pointing to HESTER)
Marries the first man who asks her and falls in love with the first man who gives her the eye.

Silence.
JACKIE JACKSON still tries to be conciliatory.

JACKIE JACKSON
By the way, how did it go with Lopez?

FREDDIE
(Still seething)
Am I boring you? Just say so and we'll have a nice little chat about the weather.

JACKIE JACKSON
Look Freddie. I think you two ought to talk ... I'll disappear ...

FREDDIE
I've got a whole bloody lifetime to talk to her! <u>Stay</u>!

HESTER
(calmly)
Come on Freddie, come home.

FREDDIE
Oh that cool, calm and collected act –
(to JACKIE JACKSON)

THE DEEP BLUE SEA

You see it ... it always works so bloody well, because it's always so bloody lethal!

      HESTER
     (getting angry now)
No one's blaming you for God's sake!

      FREDDIE
(exploding again and taking the letter from his pocket, reads extracts from it in a fury)
'... I know that I'm going to die ... just accept that it isn't your fault - it really isn't Freddie ... you can't help who you are - I can't help what I am'. Well I'm not carrying the can for this old darling! <u>No dice</u>! I'm not the villain of the piece.

      HESTER
No one's saying you are!

      FREDDIE
I was the one who wanted to wait for the divorce - you didn't - you jumped that particular fence ... I never gave myself a big build up - you knew exactly what you were getting!

      HESTER
     (equally angry)
I knew the risk I was taking and I took it - for you!

An angry lull.

      FREDDIE
   (his anger flaring up again)
My God, how I hate being tangled up in other people's emotions. I've tried to avoid them all my life yet it always happens to me ... <u>always</u>!

    (Slightly calmer)

You've always said I don't really love you in the way you love me ... but <u>that's</u> not my fault.

    (To JACKIE JACKSON)

I'll give you a case, Jack and Jill ... Jill loves Jack but Jack doesn't love Jill in the same way ... Jack never asked to be loved ...

      HESTER
     (fuming)
And what about Jill?

> FREDDIE
> (incandescent with rage)
> That's Jill's hard luck!

Silence.

> FREDDIE (cont'd)
> I can't be bloody Romeo all the time.

Silence.

> JACKIE JACKSON
> (trying to patch things up)
> Come on you two - let's go inside and have a drink.

> FREDDIE
> (looking in his pocket for change and then to JACKIE JACKSON)
> Have you got a shilling?

> JACKIE JACKSON
> What?

> FREDDIE
> Have you got a shilling!

JACKIE JACKSON looks in his pocket, finds one and gives it to FREDDIE.

> FREDDIE
> (tossing it to HESTER)
> For the gas meter. In case I'm late for supper!

HESTER is stunned for a moment.

<u>SOUNDTRACK</u>: Barber violin concerto is heard (end of the first movement).

Then she gathers herself.

> HESTER
> (more conciliatory)
> Freddie darling ... come home ... please ...

> FREDDIE
> (morose but still angry)
> No ... you'll start talking ... and pleading ...

> HESTER
> No ... I won't ... I promise I won't ... I swear I won't try to make you stay ... I won't even talk if you don't want me to ... trust me Freddie, ... I swear ...

FREDDIE doesn't respond.

THE DEEP BLUE SEA

> JACKIE JACKSON
> Freddie, be reasonable ... she's given her word for God's sake!

FREDDIE goes back inside the pub.

> FREDDIE
> (to JACKIE JACKSON as he does so)
> Will you get my wash things from the flat for me ... I'll collect the rest of my stuff when I can face it ...

He goes inside the pub.

> HESTER
> (to JACKIE JACKSON)
> It's alright Jackie. He knows me too well.

> JACKIE JACKSON
> But you gave your word!

> HESTER
> He knew perfectly well I had no intention of keeping it ... that's why he wouldn't come ... I just wanted to be with him for a while longer.

HESTER starts to walk away from the pub. JACKIE JACKSON walks back with her.

> JACKIE JACKSON
> At least it's stopped raining.

<u>TRACK BACK</u> with them as they walk.

> HESTER
> How long have you been with him?

> JACKIE JACKSON
> Since six.

> HESTER
> He can do a lot of talking in three hours, especially when he's drunk.

> JACKIE JACKSON
> At least what he says makes sense.

> HESTER
> Does it?

                    JACKIE JACKSON
        Freddie was very frank with me, so I know the
                      whole situation.

                         HESTER
                         Do you?

                     JACKIE JACKSON
        We've all been in love ... but there are other aspects that
              are just as important, maybe more so ...

                         HESTER
                    Like spiritual values?

JACKIE just nods.

                         HESTER
        You have exactly the same expression on your face as my
           father had when he talked about the pettiness of the
        physical. Then he suggested that I go to Lyme Regis to
                      'think things over'.

They walk a little way in silence.

                     JACKIE JACKSON
        Look Hester - I'll get Freddie back to my place and calm
           him down ... give me and Liz a ring once you've got back
           home. Who knows, you may still be able to work things out.

                         HESTER
                     Thanks Jackie.

                     JACKIE JACKSON
                    And you'll be fine?

                         HESTER
                      I'll be fine.

They smile at one another and JACKIE JACKSON goes back towards the pub.
                                                        CUT TO:

35. EXT. STREET NEAR LOCAL PUB. NIGHT.

HESTER continues her way back home alone.
<u>SOUNDTRACK</u>: The Barber violin concerto continues.
                                                        CUT TO:

THE DEEP BLUE SEA

35A. EXT. PARADE OF SHOPS. NIGHT.

HESTER stops in front of a parade of shops. She pauses for a moment then takes out a packet of cigarettes from her pocket, lights one and takes a drag on it. She catches her reflection in the window of one of the darkened shops.

CUT TO:

35B

HESTER'S POV of the shop and window.

Then

DISSOLVE TO:

36. INT. EDE & RAVENSCROFT. DAY.

We are in the INTERIOR of Ede & Ravenscroft looking out of the window. Day.

HESTER is looking into the shop (from Chancery Lane) and is clearly anxious.

She enters the shop.

COLLYER is with an assistant but doesn't acknowledge her.

She stands just behind COLLYER.

Tension in the quiet of the shop.

Silence.

They don't speak.

The ASSISTANT comes back in and hands the wig box to COLLYER.

     COLLYER
    Thank you.

     ASSISTANT
    (to COLLYER)
Shall we send everything to your chambers Sir William?

     COLLYER
    Yes ...
  (giving the assistant a business card)
... at Lincoln's Inn ... but I'll take the wig box with me now.

     ASSISTANT
   Good day, Sir William.

CUT TO:

SHOT of window (looking out towards Chancery Lane and the exit door).

COLLYER leaves followed by HESTER.

TRACK IN on window.

                                                    DISSOLVE TO:

37. INT. ROLLS ROYCE. NIGHT.

Continue TRACK into HESTER & COLLYER on the back seat.

TRACK STOPS IN TWO SHOT.

        COLLYER
   (not looking at HESTER but his anger is very
     controlled - like black ice)
   Do you realise what you're doing?

        HESTER
        (calmly)
   Yes William. I do.

        COLLYER
   It's just a sordid little affair.

        HESTER
   No. It's not. I love him.

        COLLYER
   It's infatuation! There's more to love than ... physicality.

        HESTER
   There isn't for me anymore.

        COLLYER
   I won't consent to a divorce.

        HESTER
   Bill ...

        COLLYER
   I intend to make it as difficult as possible for you.

        HESTER
   You sound just like my father.

        COLLYER
   What do you mean?

                    HESTER
    That tone of voice. That same mixture of irritation
    and sanctimoniousness. It's hard enough to take it
    when it comes from a vicar, when it comes from you
                    it's insufferable.

Pause.
                    HESTER
                (trying to smile)
    I'm sorry William, I didn't mean for that to sound as
                spiteful as it did.

A tense silence.
                    COLLYER
    How can you throw away so much for so little.

                    HESTER
    I didn't think it was going to be easy.

                    COLLYER
    Is it so hard to stay and continue?

                    HESTER
    Yes William ... it is ...

Then.
COLLYER leans forward and slides the glass panel which separates the chauffeur from himself and HESTER.

                    COLLYER
    You can drop me here, Flitton.

                FLITTON'S VOICE OVER
                Very good, sir.

The car draws to a halt.

                    HESTER
    Shall I come into dinner with you?

                    COLLYER
    In the circumstances I think not.

HESTER goes to touch his arm.

                COLLYER (cont'd)
    I'll never give you a divorce! I never want to see you again!

COLLYER leans forward.

                    COLLYER (cont'd)
    You may call for me at about 10.45, Flitton. You may take
       Lady Collyer to where ever it is she wishes to go.

COLLYER gets out of the car.

HESTER turns away in despair.

                                                    DISSOLVE TO:

38. INT. CHURCH. DAY.

HESTER is standing in front of the pews on the right. Her back to the altar.

Her FATHER - is moving along the pews on the left hand side and placing hymnals on the pews at the aisles end.

He moves away from her.

                    FATHER'S VOICE OVER
                    (over the DISSOLVE)
        Do the right thing - go back to your husband.

CLOSE UP HESTER

                          HESTER
            Father, I came to you for advice ...

CLOSE UP FATHER

                          FATHER
                    I've given it to you.

CLOSE UP HESTER

                          HESTER
       ... for support then ... from you, from your heart ...

CLOSE UP FATHER

                          FATHER
    St. Paul tells us that we are bound by the law - both
    spiritual and temporal ... you have a husband, your first
                        loyalty is to him..

CLOSE UP HESTER

                          HESTER
    Oh for God's sake father, the last thing I need is for
       you to start quoting from St. Paul's epistle to the
                        Beverly sisters!

THE DEEP BLUE SEA

<u>CLOSE UP</u> FATHER

>> FATHER
>> Romans.

<u>CLOSE UP</u> HESTER

>> HESTER
>> Oh does it matter?!

<u>CLOSE UP</u> FATHER

>> FATHER
>> Yes Hester. It does.

<u>CLOSE UP</u> HESTER – she looks wretched.

<u>HOLD</u> on her.

>> THEN DISSOLVE TO:

HESTER'S reflection in the window of the darkened shop.

>> DISSOLVE TO:

38A (NB: THIS IS THE REVERSE SHOT OF 35B)

We see HESTER from <u>INSIDE</u> the darkened shop standing on the pavement looking at us.

She drops her cigarette.

>> CUT TO:

39. INT. TELEPHONE BOX. EVENING.

HESTER enters the telephone booth, puts her money in, dials and waits until it's answered. She then presses button A and is connected.

>> HESTER
>> Oh hello Liz – have Jackie and Freddie got back yet? Oh ...
>> may I speak to Freddie ...

> (a long pause)

Darling, it's Hester – don't ring off! No scene I promise, I promise ... I only wanted to know about the job, that's all ... did you see the man? ... good, good ... well done ... how soon? As soon as that? Oh Freddie ...

> (a pause)

> (really crestfallen)

> Will you stay with Liz and Jackie until you leave? ...
> No, don't tell me if you don't want to ...
>
> (very hard for her)
>
> ... look Freddie I want you to do one last thing for me. Will you come and collect your things yourself? Just to say goodbye ... that's all ... surely there's no harm ...

The line goes dead.

She looks for a moment at the receiver then replaces it.

CUT TO:

40. INT. TUBE STATION PLATFORM. NIGHT.

HESTER comes down a set of stairs. She comes down quickly as if she is impatient for something.

CUT TO:

41. INT. TUBE STATION PLATFORM. NIGHT.

She comes onto the platform and moves towards the platform's edge then stops.

Pause.

She stands there for a moment.

SOUNDTRACK: The sound of a tube train is heard rumbling in the tunnel as it comes towards the station platform.

CUT TO:

HESTER'S feet. She inches towards the platform's edge.

CUT TO:

CLOSE UP OF HESTER.

She looks towards the tunnel from which the tube train will emerge and we hear it rumbling louder and louder as it gets nearer and nearer.

PAN AWAY (R to L) from

HESTER to the tunnel and the black hole beyond.

SOUNDTRACK: The rumbling of the train changes into the dull but loud sound of bombs falling above during the Blitz.

Instead of the train emerging from the tunnel white dust billows out caused by the bombs.

THE DEEP BLUE SEA

<u>TRACK BACK DOWN</u> along the length of the platform which is now crammed with men, women and children sheltering from an air raid in 1940.

<u>SOUNDTRACK</u>: A man's voice.

>   MAN
>   (sings solo)
>   'In Dublin's fair city
>   Where the girls are so pretty
>   'twas there that I first met sweet Molly Malone
>   As she wheeled her wheel-barrow
>   Through streets broad and narrow ... '

Everyone only joins in on the refrain, but softly.

>   ALL
>   (singing)
>   'Crying "Cockles and mussels
>   Alive, alive oh"
>   Alive, alive oh,
>   Alive, alive oh.
>   Crying "Cockles and mussels alive
>   Alive oh"'

CONTINUE <u>TRACKING BACK</u>

<u>SOUNDTRACK</u>: MAN singing

>   MAN
>   'Now she was a fishmonger
>   And sure 'twas no wonder
> For so were her mother and father before And they each wheeled
>   their barrow Through streets broad and narrow ... '

>   ALL
>   (singing)
>   'Crying "Cockles and mussels
>   alive Alive oh"'.

<u>TRACK</u> STOPS and <u>PAN AROUND</u> <u>R to L</u> to <u>TWO SHOT</u> of COLLYER & HESTER holding one another.

<u>SOUNDTRACK</u>: Man singing

>   MAN
>   (sings solo)
>   'She died of a fever
>   and no one could save her
>   And that was the end of sweet Molly Malone
>   Now her ghost wheels her barrow
>   Through streets broad and narrow ... '

                             ALL
                  'Crying "Cockles and mussels
                         alive Alive oh"'
                                                    DISSOLVE TO:

42. INT. TUBE STATION. NIGHT.

HESTER on the platform.

The tube train rushes by [This will be an effect, not an actual train].

She stands there for a moment then leaves.
                                                         CUT TO:

43. EXT. STREET. NIGHT.

HESTER walks down the street on which she lives.

SOUNDTRACK: Barber violin concerto continues.

As she nears the front steps of the house a black Rolls Royce draws up and stops.

COLLYER gets out and stands by the car door.

                           HESTER
                         (seeing him)
                 This is a surprise. No Flitton?

                           COLLYER
             No. I decided to drive myself. I thought it best.

                           (Pause)

I was worried about you ... please get in ... out of the chill ...

HESTER goes to him but does not enter the car.

Silence.

COLLYER hands her a wrapped present.

                           COLLYER
                    A belated birthday gift.

                           HESTER
                    Oh thank you Bill.
                       (She unwraps it)
         Oh, The Sonnets! Thank you! I've always loved them!

                           COLLYER
                       Where is he?

THE DEEP BLUE SEA

HESTER
Drinking with a friend.

COLLYER
In the old days he hardly ever touched alcohol. He said it impaired his judgement.

HESTER
(almost to herself)
It didn't tonight.

Pause.

COLLYER
What's happened to you Hester?

HESTER
Love Bill, that's all.

COLLYER
And it's driven you to attempt suicide?

HESTER
No Bill. I drove myself. Love, it would seem, drives all sorts of things.
What's the quote about love? 'It comforteth like sunshine after rain ...

COLLYER
(finishing the quote)
... and lust's effect is tempest after sun.'

HESTER
One can't go on living on a flat plane - not after discovering something more ... more ...

COLLYER
Primitive?

HESTER
Shall we say 'natural'?

COLLYER
(not cruelly)
In sober truth Hester, isn't it lust?

HESTER
(angrily)
Oh Bill, do you think I can tell you in sober truth what I feel for Freddie? Lust isn't the whole of life - and

> Freddie is, you see, for me the whole of life - and death. Put a label on that if you can?

They look at each other for a moment.

> HESTER (cont'd)
> His life stopped in 1940. He loved 1940. He's never been really happy since the war.
> (Slight pause)
> He once told me how he envied you - a brilliant lawyer ...

> COLLYER
> That sounds too spontaneous to be sincere.

> HESTER
> No. He meant it. He said he envied you for other reasons besides your career ... I knew then - in that tiny moment - I had no power to resist. No power at all.

> COLLYER
> During those months, why didn't you talk to me about it?

> HESTER
> It would have made no difference.

> COLLYER
> Meaning that I would have made no difference.

> HESTER
> That's not what I said.

Just then FREDDIE turns the corner, sees the Rolls and starts to walk towards it. He's still drunk and still aggressive.

> FREDDIE
> (as he gets to the car)
> Ah, the noble judge! Hung any good Christians lately?

He stops at the car.

> FREDDIE (cont'd)
> (To COLLYER)
> You heard about her little 'accident'?

COLLYER doesn't reply.

> FREDDIE (cont'd)
> Did you ever forget her birthday?

COLLYER doesn't reply.

THE DEEP BLUE SEA

FREDDIE (cont'd)
No. You're not the forgetful type.

HESTER
You're drunk! You'd better go inside!

FREDDIE
(Saluting HESTER)
Yes squadron leader!

(To COLLYER)
You see how I'm bullied? Bet you were never bullied like this?

HESTER and COLLYER just look at him with disdain.

FREDDIE
Am I being uncouth? 'Yes Freddie, you're being very uncouth'.

He turns and walks to the steps and then turns around.

FREDDIE (cont'd)
(To COLLYER)
Come round again - some time soon - when I've got my self respect back! You'll know we're in - I'll leave mother burning in the window for you ...

Shouting as he goes to the front door.

FREDDIE
Still love her, M'Lord?

FREDDIE goes into the boarding house.
HESTER and COLLYER stood at the car.

COLLYER
The answer to that is yes.

HESTER very moved. So is COLLYER.

HESTER
Please Bill, don't ...

COLLYER
Hester, don't you see what I'm offering you?

HESTER
And don't you know how difficult it is for me to refuse?

> COLLYER
> Is there nothing I can say?

> HESTER
> No. But we'll see what the future brings.

> COLLYER
> Our future?

> HESTER
> No. Just the future.

She kisses him suddenly.

COLLYER gets into the car and closes the door.

He looks at HESTER. He is very close to tears but not crying.

HESTER looks at him - near to tears but not crying.

COLLYER looks at her for a moment longer then the car drives off.

HESTER watches it go then goes into the boarding house.

> CUT TO:

44. INT. HALLWAY. BOARDING HOUSE. NIGHT.

HESTER comes in and goes to go upstairs.

> MRS ELTON'S VOICE OVER
> (from the end of the hall)
> Oh Mrs Page ... Do you have a minute?

> HESTER
> (stopping)
> Yes of course, what is it?

> CUT TO:

<u>HESTER'S POV</u> of MRS ELTON standing at her flat door.

> MRS ELTON
> On your way up could you ... ?

There is a crash and someone shouting out in pain.

MRS ELTON disappears into her flat.

HESTER runs down the hall - sees the flat door is still open and runs in.

> CUT TO:

45. INT. MRS ELTON'S FLAT. NIGHT.

SHOT of HESTER running in through the dark sitting room to the bed room.

CUT TO:

46. INT. THE ELTON'S BEDROOM. NIGHT.

Interior of MR & MRS ELTON'S bedroom. SHOT of MRS ELTON trying to get MR ELTON back into bed.

HESTER goes to the other side of the bed and helps

MRS ELTON to get MR ELTON into an upright position. They both hold him as

MRS ELTON plumps up the pillows and they ease him back against them.

MRS ELTON soothes his forehead. He is very weak. His breathing becoming more steady.

                MRS ELTON
       There we are ... safe as houses ...

                MR ELTON
                (very weak)
   I can face anything as long as you're there ...

                MRS ELTON
      I'll always be here Frank ...
                (pause)
      ... you handsome devil! ...
                (pause)
    You were a real dish weren't you?

                MR ELTON
           (smiling weakly)
     Yes ... I was a real dish ...

CUT TO:

HESTER. She just looks at them both.

CUT TO:

HESTER'S POV. TWO SHOT of MR & MRS ELTON.

She strokes his forehead and he quietly goes to sleep.

PAN DOWN to a SHOT of her hand holding his, gently. We see on the bedside table a photo of when MR ELTON was a young seaman in the Royal Navy.

CUT TO:

47. INT. THE ELTON'S FLAT. SITTING ROOM. NIGHT.

Interior of MRS ELTON'S flat. The darkened sitting room.

HESTER and MRS ELTON come out into the body of the room and go towards the door ... as they do so ...

> MRS ELTON
> Thanks, dear. For the hand.

HESTER just smiles, then MRS ELTON stops in the middle of the room and looks straight at HESTER.

> MRS ELTON (cont'd)
> But I don't want a repeat of that nonsense this morning ... d'you hear ...

HESTER doesn't answer for a moment.

> HESTER
> Sometimes it's difficult to judge - when you're caught between the devil and the deep blue sea.

> MRS ELTON
> Listen. A lot of rubbish is talked about 'love'. D'you know what real love is? It's wiping someone's arse or changing the sheets after they've wet themselves but never letting them lose their dignity so that you can <u>both</u> go on ... suicide? No one's worth it.

They get to the flat door.

> MRS ELTON
> Oh, by the way - on your way up will you ask Mr Miller to pop down to have a look at Frank?

> HESTER
> Yes, of course.

CUT TO:

48. INT. BOARDING HOUSE HALL/STAIRS/LANDING. NIGHT.

HESTER comes back along the hall then goes upstairs.

HESTER gets to the landing on which MILLER'S flat is. As she does so he opens the door to his flat.

> MILLER
> How are you tonight, Mrs Page?

THE DEEP BLUE SEA

HESTER
Well. Thank you. Could you let me have some sleeping tablets?

MILLER
No. I've been involved enough with the police - whether you live or die is your choice.

HESTER
How can anyone live without hope?

MILLER
Quite easily. Most people have to. To live without hope can mean living without despair.

HESTER
What is there beyond hope?

MILLER
There's life.

HESTER
That's what I can't face.

MILLER
Everyone must find a purpose to go on living. Go to bed and don't let it be a moment too long.

She goes to protest.

MILLER (cont'd)
Voices carry on the stairs.

HESTER
Like mine and Freddie's? All the respectable tenants saying there's that kept woman and her drunken boyfriend ... serves her right ...

MILLER
I didn't say that. But then I may not be a respectable tenant.

MRS ELTON'S voice from the hall.

MRS ELTON'S VOICE OVER
Oh, Mr Miller! Mr Elton's ready now!

MILLER
I'll be down in five minutes!

                        (To HESTER)
    You're not the only one to have been too close to the gas fire.
                        (Almost to himself)
                    And he wasn't worth it either.
                        (To HESTER)
                    I hope you've learnt your lesson.

He goes downstairs.

HESTER continues upstairs to her flat.

                            HESTER
                    Yes. I've learnt my lesson.

                            MILLER
                        Now - live!

                            HESTER
                    By the skin of my teeth?

                            MILLER
            Or by the skin of somebody elses.

HESTER laughs for the first time.

                        MILLER (cont'd)
                        (smiling)
        A sense of humour - that's a good sign. Hold on to it.
                It's worth it's weight in gold.

                                                        CUT TO:

49. INT. LANDING BOARDING HOUSE. NIGHT.

The landing where the flat is.

HESTER goes to open the flat door but it is locked.

                            HESTER
                    Freddie let me in ...

No response.

                        HESTER (cont'd)
            Freddie don't be childish ... let me in ...

The door is unlocked and HESTER goes in and closes the door.

                                                        CUT TO:

50. INT. SITTING ROOM. HESTER'S FLAT. NIGHT.

FREDDIE sullen but contrite sits down in a chair. The atmosphere is quiet but tense.

>HESTER
>Where were you most of the day?

>FREDDIE
>Seeing a man about a job.

>HESTER
>What man?

>FREDDIE
>Lopez. South America. He made me an offer.

>HESTER
>What kind of offer?

>FREDDIE
>Test pilot.

>HESTER
>But you've said a hundred times that you'd never go back to it ... you told me that you had no nerve or judgement left ...

>FREDDIE
>I know what I said. I'm accepting it anyway. (Pause) Don't worry about my nerve or my judgement. A month or two on the wagon and I'll be the old ace again ...

>HESTER
>Whereabouts in South America?

>FREDDIE
>Rio.

>HESTER
>When do we go?

>FREDDIE
>We don't. I'm going alone. That's what I wanted to tell you.

Silence.

>HESTER
>(at length
>Why Freddie?

FREDDIE
Today - the letter ... the suicide attempt ... we're lethal to each other.
(Pause)
You can't expect a bloke to go on after he's driven someone to suicide ... much as he loves her ...

HESTER
Do you think leaving me will drive me away from it?

FREDDIE
That's a risk we'll both have to take.

HESTER
You're scaring me Freddie.

FREDDIE
No scare. It's on the level. I don't enjoy hurting you, I'm not a sadist ... but it's on the level.

Silence.

FREDDIE (cont'd)
I'll leave now.

HESTER
Stay with me tonight, Freddie ... just one more night.

FREDDIE
No ... you'll start talking and I'll be lost, both of us will be lost.

HESTER
Don't be cruel ... how can you be so cruel?

FREDDIE
It's over Hes.

HESTER
That isn't true. It isn't.

FREDDIE
It's over ... it ended today ... I'm sorry Hes ... don't look at me like that ... you don't know what it does to me.

Pause.

HESTER
You've got all your things here. You've got to pack.

He remains silent.

THE DEEP BLUE SEA

>   HESTER (cont'd)
> I won't speak. I won't argue. But don't leave me alone
>   tonight ... not tonight ... don't leave me alone tonight ...

FREDDIE is as wretched as HESTER.

>   DISSOLVE TO:

51. INT. BEDROOM. HESTER'S FLAT. DAY.

HESTER in bed. She wakes up and realises that FREDDIE is not beside her. She turns towards the door.

>   CUT TO:

HESTER'S POV.

SHOT of FREDDIE'S stockinged feet disappearing out of the bedroom door.

HESTER gets up, puts on her dressing gown and goes to the bedroom door and opens it softly.

>   CUT TO:

52. INT. SITTING ROOM. HESTER'S FLAT. DAY.

HESTER at the bedroom door.

>   CUT TO:

HESTER'S POV.

FREDDIE on tip toe goes to the sofa carrying his shoes.

The sitting room is in semi-darkness. Only one curtain has been drawn back slightly.

FREDDIE at the sofa finishing packing. They look at each other for a moment.

>   HESTER
>   You look very smart.

>   FREDDIE
>   The old blue serge ... will it pass?

>   HESTER
>   It'll pass. But your shoes need a clean.

>   FREDDIE
>   Yes.

Silence.

She comes to the back of the sofa and takes FREDDIE'S shoes from him, goes to the table and goes to put the shoes on it.

FREDDIE
(quickly)
Don't put shoes on a table! ... it's bad luck ... or so they say ...

HESTER
(putting the shoes on the table and sitting down)
Do they?

Silence as she buffs his shoes. When she finishes she goes to the back of the sofa and gives the shoes to FREDDIE who puts them on.

HESTER
Had any breakfast?

FREDDIE
Just a black coffee. No 'hair of the dog'.

He smiles half-heartedly.
HESTER does the same.

HESTER
When exactly are you off to Rio?

FREDDIE
Thursday. I told you.

HESTER
Yes. Of course you did. By boat?

FREDDIE
No. Flying. London - West Africa - then across to Natal.

HESTER
Sounds exciting.

Pause.

FREDDIE
Oh, by the way - about the rent. My golf clubs will fetch thirty or forty quid. That'll take care of the rent and some odd bills ...

Silence.

FREDDIE (cont'd)
What'll you do, Hes?

HESTER
I'm not quite sure. Get the divorce out of the way - tidy things up ...

THE DEEP BLUE SEA

> FREDDIE
> Good idea. It's never too late to begin again. Isn't that what they say?

> HESTER
> Yes. That's what they say.

FREDDIE picks up his case from the sofa, goes to the door, takes his mac from a hook on the door, then turns back to look at HESTER.

There is just as much sorrow in his face as in hers.

They are both close to tears.

> FREDDIE
> Good bye Hes.

> HESTER
> Good bye Freddie.

Silence.

> FREDDIE
> I'm going to miss you ...

She is unable to speak.

> FREDDIE (cont'd)
> (with great difficulty)
> Thanks - for everything.

> HESTER
> (with great difficulty)
> Thank you.

> FREDDIE
> Be safe.

> HESTER
> Be Good.

He leaves quickly. She stands alone for a moment.

<u>SOUNDTRACK</u>: The Barber violin concerto is heard.

She notices that FREDDIE has left his driving gloves on the sofa.

She picks them up and as she does so she sees - lying next to them - the book of sonnets which COLLYER gave her as a birthday present the night before.

Holding both of them she goes to the window and looks out of the partially drawn curtains.

SOUNDTRACK:

                COLLYER'S VOICE OVER
                 (reading sonnet 143)
    'Lo, as a careful housewife runs to catch
     One of her feathered creatures broke away,
  Sets down her babe, and makes all swift despatch
      In pursuit of the thing she would have stay;
  Whilst her neglected child holds her in chase,
     Cries to catch her whose busy care is bent
    To follow that which flies before her face.
    Not prizing her poor infant's discontent; ...'

                                    DISSOLVE TO:

53. EXT. HESTER'S FLAT/WINDOW. DAY.

EXTERIOR SHOT of HESTER at the window. (As if watching FREDDIE walking down the street).

                COLLYER'S VOICE OVER
  'So runneth thou after that which flies from thee,
     Whilst I thy babe chase thee afar behind;
    But if thou catch thy hope, turn back to me,
   And play the mother's part, kiss me, be kind;
  So I will pray that thou mayest have thy will,
   If thou turn back, and my loud crying still.'

She begins to weep.

                                    DISSOLVE TO:

54. INT. HESTER'S FLAT/WINDOW. DAY.

INTERIOR SHOT of HESTER at the window. Weeping into FREDDIE'S gloves in which she has buried her face.

SOUNDTRACK: The Barber violin concerto continues.

Her sobbing reaches its climax as she walks towards the mantelpiece. She gets to the fireplace and kneels down in front of the gas fire and looks at it for a moment. She switches the gas fire on.

SOUNDTRACK: Hissing of the gas fire is heard. She keeps looking at the gas fire.

SOUNDTRACK: A man's voice singing solo as if from a long way away.

                        MAN
                   (sings solo)
      ' ... Crying "Cockles and mussels.
         Alive Alive oh ... "'

THE DEEP BLUE SEA

Then she strikes a match and lights the gas fire.

CLOSE UP HESTER.

The flames of the gas fire are reflected on her tear stained face.

But now she is calm.

She has decided to live.

HOLD.

SOUNDTRACK: The Barber violin concerto continues.

She gets up CRANE UP with her, then PAN & TRACK R to L with her to the window. She draws the curtains back fully and the September sunlight streams in.

She stands at the window - calm now.

DISSOLVE TO:

55. EXT. BOARDING HOUSE. WINDOW. DAY.

HESTER is seen at the window.

HOLD.

SOUNDTRACK: The Barber violin concerto continues over all subsequent shots to the end credits.

Then.

CRANE DOWN from HESTER'S window past MR MILLER'S flat. He is standing in a dressing gown drinking coffee and looking out of the window.

Continue CRANING DOWN to ground floor flat and front door.

MRS ELTON opens the front door, picks up the milk and post and goes back inside but leaves the front door open. PHILIP WELCH exits as if off to work.

TRACK & PAN (L to R) away from the house then into the middle of the street.

TRACK UP middle of street.

SOUNDTRACK: The Barber violin concerto swells then finishes.

FADE TO BLACK

THE END

12/1/02   MINISTER   160.

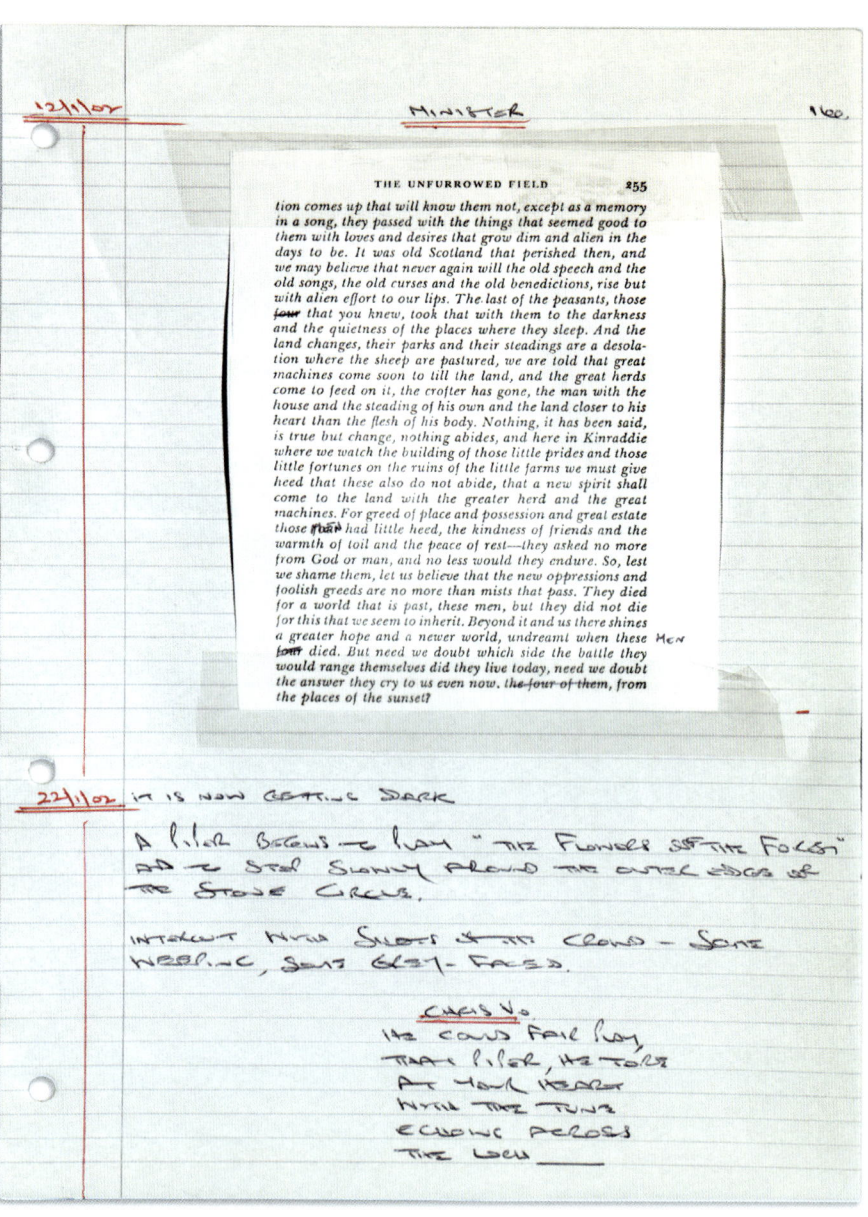

> THE UNFURROWED FIELD   255
>
> tion comes up that will know them not, except as a memory in a song, they passed with the things that seemed good to them with loves and desires that grow dim and alien in the days to be. It was old Scotland that perished then, and we may believe that never again will the old speech and the old songs, the old curses and the old benedictions, rise but with alien effort to our lips. The last of the peasants, those ~~four~~ that you knew, took that with them to the darkness and the quietness of the places where they sleep. And the land changes, their parks and their steadings are a desolation where the sheep are pastured, we are told that great machines come soon to till the land, and the great herds come to feed on it, the crofter has gone, the man with the house and the steading of his own and the land closer to his heart than the flesh of his body. Nothing, it has been said, is true but change, nothing abides, and here in Kinraddie where we watch the building of those little prides and those little fortunes on the ruins of the little farms we must give heed that these also do not abide, that a new spirit shall come to the land with the greater herd and the great machines. For greed of place and possession and great estate those ~~that~~ had little heed, the kindness of friends and the warmth of toil and the peace of rest—they asked no more from God or man, and no less would they endure. So, lest we shame them, let us believe that the new oppressions and foolish greeds are no more than mists that pass. They died for a world that is past, these men, but they did not die for this that we seem to inherit. Beyond it and us there shines a greater hope and a newer world, undreamt when these MEN ~~four~~ died. But need we doubt which side the battle they would range themselves did they live today, need we doubt the answer they cry to us even now. ~~the four of them,~~ from the places of the sunset?

22/1/02   IT IS NOW GETTING DARK

A PIPER BEGINS TO PLAY "THE FLOWERS OF THE FOREST" AND TO STEP SLOWLY AROUND THE OUTER EDGE OF THE STONE CIRCLE.

INTERCUT WITH SHOTS OF THE CROWD — SOME WEEPING, SOME GREY-FACED.

            CHRIS V.O.
       HE COULD FAIR PLAY,
       THAT PIPER, HE TORE
       AT YOUR HEART
       WITH THE TUNE
       ECHOING ACROSS
       THE LOCH ___

Sunset Song (2015): First draft, closing scene. (© The Terence Davies Estate, held by the Terence Davies Archive at Edge Hill University)

SUNSET SONG (2015)

Sunset Song (2015): Agyness Deyn as Chris Guthrie.

Sunset Song
February 2004 (Second Draft)

Cast and crew of *Sunset Song* include:

CHRIS GUTHRIE	Agyness Deyn
EWAN TAVENDALE	Kevin Guthrie
JOHN GUTHRIE	Peter Mullan
WILL GUTHRIE	Jack Greenlees
MARGET GUTHRIE	Daniela Nardini
CHAE STRACHAN	Ian Pirie
LONG ROB	Douglas Rankine
REVEREND GIBBON	Mark Bonnar

Written and Directed by	Terence Davies
From the novel by	Lewis Grassic Gibbon
Producers	Roy Boulter
	Sol Papadopoulos
	Nicolas Steil
Director of Photography	Michael McDonough
Editor	David Charap
Production Designer	Andy Harris
Costume Designer	Uli Simon
Casting Directors	John Hubbard and Ros Hubbard
Composer	Gast Waltzing

A Hurricane Films (2015) production with:
Iris Productions / SellOut Pictures / BFI / Creative Scotland /
BBC Scotland / Luxembourg Film Fund

SUNSET SONG

A screenplay
by Terence Davies

Based on the novel
by Lewis Grassic Gibbon

2ND DRAFT FEBRUARY 2004

Developed with the assistance of
Scottish Screen

"THE SONG OF THE EARTH"

It is thirty years ago now.

When the Sunday night serial on BBC1 went out in ancient Black & White.

Sunset Song by Lewis Grassic Gibbon was one of them and its grandeur has stayed with me.

It is a dark and brooding novel about the Scottish peasantry, about the land in general and one family – The Guthries – in particular. They are subsistence farmers extracting a meagre living from the earth.

It is a novel about the power and cruelty of both family and Nature, about the enduring presence of the land and the courage of the human spirit in the face of hardship. Against this background – but of equal stature – is the story of the daughter of the family Chris Guthrie and her evolution from schoolgirl to wife to mother to widow, then finally becoming a symbol for Scotland itself. The novel is both symbolic and rhapsodic.

It is a work of epic intimacy set before, during and after The Great War.

Yet it is delicate.

A filigree of the music of the seasons together with the more modest music of pipes and accordion, played at weddings with the Scottish voices singing the melancholy airs of the old times – "THE FLOWERS OF THE FOREST" and "AULD ROBIN"; songs to pull the heartstrings, to make you remember the long-dead, making you wish for the longed-for happiness which we all need – content and secure in the knowledge that we will <u>never</u> die... for we are young and in our prime.

But time is cruel and so is the land which gives life its harsh beauty, as well as its moments of epiphany beside the lamp or in the firelight at gloaming.

The song is yours and mine, of all who feel and have suffered or been happy. It is the song heard with quiet courage in the face of death. Or life.

But Chris has a deeper insight, an innate wisdom. Chris sings the Song of the Earth for humanity, a rhapsody for us all as she charts the eternal cycle of birth, marriage and death. As the song explores the timeless mysteries of land, home and family – this last one being the greatest mystery of all. For the family contains all our greatest ecstasies and all our cherished terrors.

The book is suffused with a lyrical melancholy, a quiet threnody for the mystery of life ... for life is a mystery contained within an enigma.

SUNSET SONG

How can we bear time or subdue nature?

We cannot.

We can only endure.

At the end of the work a remembrance parade and service is held in an attempt to heal all suffering. At the end of this great work time and the land endure beyond war, beyond human suffering even beyond life itself.

It is a story which deserves to be told.

It is a film which has to be made.

Terence Davies

Sunset Song (2015): Terence Davies directing Agyness Deyn.

FADE UP ON:

1. EXT. DAY.

HIGH SHOT of North Sea glittering under a blazing sun.

TRACK across it. Silence except for the sound of the water and the cry of the gulls and sea birds. The water ripples and slides as a gentle wind sweeps over its surface.

                                                                                          DISSOLVE TO:

2. EXT. THE LAND AROUND ECHT - DAY.

Continue TRACKING (in HIGH SHOT) across it.

The fields empty and baking in the heat. The wind gently rippling across the crops. Sun and cloud in the electric heat.

Silence except for birdsong.

                                                                                           DISSOLVE TO:

3. EXT. SKY - DAY.

Cloudless in high summer - immense.

The sun blazing down from centre frame.

Then a head comes into frame but we cannot see who it is - silhouetted as it is against the sun.

                                           TRACK DOWN AND AROUND TO:

4. EXT. FIELD - DAY

We FRAME a 15 year old girl - CHRIS GUTHRIE sitting amongst the crops in the sun.

Silence.

                            MOTHER (VOICE OVER)
          To my dawlie Chris. Trust in God and do the right.

SOUNDTRACK: A school bell is heard tolling the children to school.

                                                                                        DISSOLVE TO:

5. EXT. ECHT SCHOOL - DAY.

WIDE SHOT of school. It stands alone surrounded by fields.

SOUNDTRACK: Bell tolling fades into:

                          INSPECTOR (VOICE OVER)
              Say "o-oo, o-oo, o-oo butin."

SUNSET SONG

> ENTIRE CLASS (VOICE OVER)
> "O-oo, o-oo, o-ooo – butin."

CUT TO:

6. INT. CLASSROOM - DAY.

<u>WIDE SHOT</u> of entire class of girls. CHRIS GUTHRIE seated amongst them. Sitting beside her, her friend MARGET STRACHAN.

> ENTIRE CLASS
> "O-oo – o-oo – o-oo Butin."

> INSPECTOR (VOICE OVER)
> No. Put your mouths as though you were going to whistle.
> (Pronounce it "weesel")

The class do so.

> INSPECTOR (VOICE OVER) (CONT'D)
> But don't do it.

They all look puzzled.

CUT TO:

7. INT. CLASSROOM - DAY.

<u>2 SHOT</u>. INSPECTOR (CFR) slightly behind him MRS HEMANS the class teacher.

> INSPECTOR
> Say "o-oo, o-oo, o-oo".

They do so. He looks crestfallen.

> INSPECTOR (CONT'D)
> Mrs Hemans, is there <u>one</u> pupil who is proficient in <u>any</u> way with the French language?

> MRS HEMANS
> Chris Guthrie is one of my best, especially in Latin.

> INSPECTOR
> Let her come forward.

CUT TO:

8. INT. CLASSROOM - DAY.

<u>SHOT</u> of CHRIS getting up, very embarrassed. <u>SHOT</u> of MARGET winking encouragement at her.

                    INSPECTOR
            Now - "o-oo - ooo - Butin."

                     CHRIS
                o-oo - ooo - Butin.

CHRIS does it perfectly.

                    INSPECTOR
             I hope your Latin is as good.
                                                CUT TO:

9. EXT. SCHOOL - DAY.

SHOT of INSPECTOR in a gig moving off (R-L).

              MRS HEMANS (VOICE OVER)
         Chris, run after the Inspector man with his bag.

We see CHRIS do so.
                     CHRIS
                   (Shouting)
                    Whist!!

The gig stops.
                                                CUT TO:

10. EXT. SCHOOL - DAY.

CHRIS comes up to gig and gives him his bag.

                    INSPECTOR
                     Thanks.
He drives off.
CHRIS looks after him.
HOLD on her.

                CHRIS (VOICE OVER)
          So that was Chris and her reading and schooling.

                                                CUT TO:

11. EXT. SCHOOL - DAY.

CHRIS POV of gig. The INSPECTOR driving away into the distance.
HOLD.
                CHRIS (VOICE OVER)
         Yes, she sat for her bursary - and got it.

                                                CUT TO:

SUNSET SONG

12. EXT. SCHOOL - DAY.

<u>SHOT</u> of CHRIS taking an exam. We see her through the window. <u>HOLD</u>. She is looking out of window directly at camera.

>   CHRIS (VOICE OVER)
>   But two Chrisses there were that fought for her heart.

She continues to look out.

>   CHRIS (VOICE OVER) (CONT'D)
>   She hated the land and the coarse speak of the folk and
>   learning was brave and fine one day ...

She looks away.

CUT TO:

13. INT. SCHOOLROOM - DAY.

<u>SHOT</u> of CHRIS looking from outside and straight ahead and looks at the rest of the class engaged in the exam.

>   CHRIS (VOICE OVER)
>   ... and the next she'd waken with the peewits crying across
>   the hills, deep and deep, crying in the heart of her ...

She looks close to tears.

>   CHRIS (VOICE OVER) (CONT'D)
>   ... and the smell of the earth in her face, almost made
>   her cry for the beauty of it and the sweetness of the
>   Scottish land and skies ...

CUT TO:

14. INT. CLASSROOM - DAY.

CHRIS <u>POV</u> of the rest of the class. At the front, on a dais, the INVIGILATOR sits.

He looks up and catches CHRIS daydreaming and makes an irritable gesture with his hand for her to continue working.

CUT TO:

15. INT. CLASSROOM - DAY.

<u>SHOT</u> of CHRIS. She drops her eyes and continues with the exam. <u>HOLD</u>.

                    CHRIS (VOICE OVER)
    And the next minute that passed from her and she was
    English, back to the English words so sharp and clean
    and true ... for a while, for a while till they slid so
    smoothly from her throat she knew that they could never
             say anything worth the saying at all.

                                                    CUT TO:

16. INT. KIRK AT ECHT - DAY.

WIDE SHOT of PREACHER in pulpit amidst congregation.

                    MINISTER'S (VOICE OVER)
           "Cast thy Bread Upon the waters;
          For thou shalt Find it after Many days ...
          As thou knowest not The way of the spirit
     Thou knowest not the Works of God who Maketh all."

SHOTS of congregation listening to sermon.

Final 2-SHOT on CHRIS and WILL. SHOT Of MARGET and CHAE
STRACHAN in pews.

                                                    CUT TO:

17. INT. KIRK AT ECHT - DAY.

SHOT of CHRIS, WILL (her elder brother), JOHN GUTHRIE (father),
MOTHER (very pregnant) and two smaller siblings in pew.

                    MINISTER'S (VOICE OVER)
            "In the morning Sow thy seed
        And in the evening Withold not thine Hand.
         Truly the light is Sweet, and a pleasant Thing
            it is for the Eyes to behold the sun;
           Therefore remove Sorrow from thy Heart;
             and put away Evil from thy flesh:
              For childhood and youth Are vanity.
                Thus sayeth the Lord God Jehovah."
         I take as my text "The Song of Solomon".

                                                    CUT TO:

18. EXT. KIRK - DAY.

SHOT of the GUTHRIE family together with CHAE and MARGET STRACHAN
leaving the church with the rest of the congregation.

The GUTHRIE family (except CHRIS) lags behind with MARGET as
CHAE joins JOHN.

SUNSET SONG

> CHAE STRACHAN
> Well preaching like that's a fine way of having your bit of pleasure by proxy ... I prefer to take mine more private-like.
>
> CUT TO:

19. EXT. ROAD - DAY.

The GUTHRIES and CHAE walk ahead.

CHRIS and MARGET saunter behind in the oppressive heat.

PAN (L-R) from first group to 2-SHOT - CHRIS and MARGET, then TRACK BACK with them.

> CHRIS
> Folks say there hasn't been a drought like this since '83.

> MARGET
> Well they can't blame this on Gladstone, anyway.

Both smile.

> CHRIS
> But the ministers are praying for rain.

> MARGET
> In between the bit about the army and the Prince of Wales' rheumatics.
>
> CUT TO:

20. EXT. ROAD - DAY.

A car driving directly towards the group which makes no attempt to clear the road. The car is forced to stop as the group stops and blocks the road.

The LADY PASSENGER winds down the window.

> LADY PASSENGER
> You're causing an obstruction, my man.
>
> CUT TO:

21. EXT. ROAD - DAY.

CLOSE UP JOHN.

> JOHN GUTHRIE
> I'm not your man, thank God! If I was I'd have your face scraped with a muck-rake.
>
> CUT TO:

22. EXT. ROAD - DAY.

SHOT of LADY and CHAUFFEUR.

                   LADY PASSENGER
            James <u>make</u> them move!

The CHAUFFEUR - none too bravely - makes to get out of the car.

                      CHAUFFEUR
     Yes, madam. Keep your damn children off the road.

                                        CUT TO:

23. EXT. ROAD - DAY.

2-SHOT JOHN and CHAE. They move towards CHAUFFEUR.

                    JOHN GUTHRIE
      You keep a civil tongue in your head!

                    CHAE STRACHAN
      What the hell d'you think you're up to?
The CHAUFFEUR quickly gets back into car and shuts the door.

              CHAE STRACHAN (CONT'D)
                       (to LADY)
      The revolution will sweep you all away!

The CHAUFFEUR starts the car and drives off.

                   LADY PASSENGER
                  (as it does so)
      You've not heard the last of this!

                    JOHN GUTHRIE
               (to ALL, smiling)
       That's the way to treat gentry!

They all walk home.

                                        CUT TO:

24. INT. KITCHEN CAIRNDHU AT ECHT DUSK - EARLY EVENING

MOTHER and JOHN sit in front of the fire and lit by it. WILL sits at the table with CHRIS. She is reading aloud by the light of the paraffin lamp. Whilst she reads CLOSE UPS of MOTHER, JOHN, WILL.

                              CHRIS
     "And when the first reformation came some folk cried
       "Whiggam!" and some cried "Rome!" and some cried "the
        King!" The Kinraddies sat them quiet and decent and
         peaceable in their castle. Then Dutch William came and
          the Kinraddies were all for the Covenant. Then John
           Kinraddie went south and became a great man in the
           Court. But by then it was an ill time for the Scottish
           gentry for the poison of the French Revolution came over
            the seas and the new Laird of Kinraddie became a Jacobin
                  and joined the Jacobin Club in Aberdeen ... "

<u>2-SHOT</u> MOTHER and JOHN.

                              MOTHER
                       (reminiscing out loud)
                    There's no land like Aberdeen ...

                          JOHN AND MOTHER
                          (an old shared joke)
                    ... or folks so fine that bide there.

They both smile gently.
                                                              <u>CUT TO:</u>
<u>CLOSE UP</u> MOTHER.
                              MOTHER
                            (to CHRIS)
       Oh Chris my lass, there are better things than your
         books or studies or loving or bedding, there's the
          countryside your own, you it's, in the days when you're
                        neither bairn nor woman.

                                                              <u>CUT TO:</u>
<u>CLOSE UP</u> JOHN.
                           JOHN GUTHRIE
                             (gently)
                 Peace, Jean, peace. She'll do us credit.
                            (to CHRIS)
                     Go on Chris, read us more ...

                                                              <u>CUT TO:</u>
<u>CLOSE UP</u> CHRIS.
                              CHRIS
          And there at Aberdeen he was nearly killed in rioting
              for liberty, and equality and fraternity ... "

                                                              <u>CUT TO:</u>

CLOSE UP WILL.

        WILL
    Equality should begin at home.
                CUT TO:

CLOSE UP JOHN GUTHRIE in a fury, about to speak but before he can ...
                CUT TO:

CLOSE UP WILL.

        WILL (CONT'D)
      (gets up and leaves)
 Don't tell me! I know where the barn is! A tense silence.
                CUT TO:

25. INT. STABLE/BARN. CAIRNDHU AT ECHT - DUSK.

SHOT of CHRIS at barn/stable door. She looks at WILL and smiles. She carries a Latin grammar.

        CHRIS
      Amo, amas.
                CUT TO:

26. INT. STABLE/BARN. CAIRNDHU AT ECHT - DUSK.

SHOT of WILL watering the horse - BESS.

        WILL
      I love a lass!

They both giggle. He leads the horse from drinking into her stall and begins curry-combing her.

        WILL (CONT'D)
    Clever enough to be a teacher.
                CUT TO:

27. INT. STABLE/BARN. CAIRNDHU AT ECHT - DUSK.

SHOT of CHRIS.
        CHRIS
      Clever enough.

She continues to look at him grooming BESS.
                CUT TO:

28. EXT. BARN - DUSK.

SHOT of JOHN GUTHRIE passing the barn door. He stops and listens.

                                                        CUT TO:

29. INT. BARN/STABLE. CAIRNDHU AT ECHT - DUSK.

WIDE SHOT. CHRIS in FRAME LEFT.
HORSE and WILL filling rest of FRAME.
Silence.
>   WILL
>   (Finishing grooming Bess)
>   Come over Jehovah!

And hits her flank.

                                                        CUT TO:

30. INT. BARN/STABLE. CAIRNDHU AT ECHT - DUSK.

SHOT of JOHN GUTHRIE running in, in a fury.
PAN WITH HIM (R-L) to FRAME all three at first.
JOHN GUTHRIE begins to beat WILL very badly.
TRACK IN on them as WILL falls below the legs of BESS.

                                                        CUT TO:

31. INT. BARN/STABLE. CAIRNDHU AT ECHT - DUSK.

SHOT of CHRIS horrified at the beating. Runs out.

                                                        CUT TO:

32. INT. BARN/STABLE. CAIRNDHU AT ECHT - DUSK.

CLOSE SHOT of WILL beneath the hooves of BESS. The beating stops. BESS calm.

WILL lies still.

CRANE UP OR CUT to JOHN GUTHRIE standing over WILL.

>   JOHN
> And mind, my mannie, if I ever hear you again take your
>   Maker's name in vain, I'll libb you. Mind that. I'll
>   libb you like a lamb.

                                                        CUT TO:

33. INT. BEDROOM. CAIRNDHU AT ECHT - NIGHT.

WILL and CHRIS are in bed together.

Silence in the dark.

Then:

      WILL
    I hate him ...

      CHRIS
    Oh Will.

      WILL
    (Smiling)
    I hate him.

SOUNDTRACK: The sound of JOHN GUTHRIE and his wife, JEAN, moving around their bedroom next door.

     MOTHER (VOICE OVER)
    Four in a family's fine.

    JOHN GUTHRIE (VOICE OVER)
    Fine?

     MOTHER (VOICE OVER)
    There'll be no more.

    JOHN GUTHRIE (VOICE OVER)
 We'll have what God in His mercy may send to us, woman.
    See you to that!

Scuffling. Silence.

Then the rhythmic sound of silent, forced sex.

CHRIS and WILL listen.

      WILL
    I hate him.

SOUNDTRACK: MOTHER screaming.

              CUT TO:

34. INT. COTTAGE. CAIRNDHU AT ECHT - NIGHT.

SHOT of DOCTOR at top of stairs.

      DOCTOR
    (Shouting)
  Man it's a fair tough case -

SUNSET SONG

MOTHERS screams get worse.

> DOCTOR (CONT'D)
> I'll need your help ...

CUT TO:

35. INT. KITCHEN. COTTAGE CAIRNDHU AT ECHT - NIGHT.

<u>CLOSE UP</u> JOHN GUTHRIE in front of fire.

> JOHN GUTHRIE
> (To himself)
> God forgive me for my lusts
> (Almost crying)
> It's her bonny hair ...

He looks up.

CUT TO:

36. INT. KITCHEN. COTTAGE CAIRNDHU AT ECHT - NIGHT.

<u>SHOT</u> of CHRIS at door.

She is terrified of the screaming.

> JOHN GUTHRIE
> (Raging)
> Get into the parlour and get the doctor an egg for breakfast. <u>Now</u>!

She exits.

> DOCTOR (VOICE OVER)
> Guthrie, man, do you hear me?

> JOHN GUTHRIE
> I'm not deaf!

Goes upstairs.

CUT TO:

37. INT. PARLOUR COTTAGE CAIRNDHU AT ECHT - NIGHT.

<u>2-SHOT</u> CHRIS and WILL sitting at table set for breakfast.

MOTHER's screams unbearable in the silence.

> WILL
> She's far too old for that. She shouldn't be having another baby. It's him, it's the beast.

Screams continue.

>   CHRIS
> What has Father to do with it?

>   WILL
> Don't you know you fool? What's a bull to do with a calf?

Screams continue.

>   WILL (CONT'D)
> But don't worry. His friend Jehovah will
>   see to it all.

There is another terrible scream.

They both stand in the silence.

>   DOCTOR (VOICE OVER)
> Hot water, jugs of it. Pour me a basin of water,
>   Chris, and put plenty of soap near by it.

>   CHRIS
>   (In a whisper)
>   Ay doctor.

>   DOCTOR (VOICE OVER)
>   D'you hear me?

>   WILL
>   (Shouting)
> Ay doctor only she's feared.

>   DOCTOR (VOICE OVER)
> She'll have a damned sight more to fear when she's having a
>   bairn of her own. Pour out that water quick!

>   CUT TO:

38. INT. COTTAGE CAIRNDHU AT ECHT - NIGHT.

<u>SHOT</u> of DOCTOR washing his hands of blood etc. He wipes them and sits down to the table. Silence.

<u>SHOT</u> of WILL. <u>SHOT</u> of CHRIS - still terrified. Silence.

>   CHRIS
>   There's your egg, doctor.

>   DOCTOR
>   (Beginning to eat)
>   It's twins.

SUNSET SONG

                                                                CUT TO:

39. INT. PARENTS' BEDROOM. COTTAGE CAIRNDHU AT ECHT - DAY.

<u>SHOT</u> of MOTHER in bed. Her family around her, CHRIS, WILL and the smaller siblings, ALEC and DOD. MOTHER holds the twins in her arms.

She is frail, exhausted but still with lustrous hair.

> MOTHER
> (Looking up)
> We'll need more rooms.

                                                                CUT TO:

40. INT. PARENTS' BEDROOM. COTTAGE CAIRNDHU AT ECHT - DAY.

<u>SHOT</u> of JOHN GUTHRIE at foot of bed. He is quietly proud.

> JOHN GUTHRIE
> (Gruff but loving)
> More rooms? D'ye think we're gentry?

                                                                CUT TO:

41. INT. PARENTS' BEDROOM. COTTAGE CAIRNDHU AT ECHT - DAY.

<u>SHOT</u> of MOTHER.

> MOTHER
> (Quietly loving)
> Well, well, we're to bide here then?

                                                                CUT TO:

42. INT. PARENTS' BEDROOM. COTTAGE CAIRNDHU AT ECHT - DAY.

<u>SHOT</u> of JOHN GUTHRIE.

> JOHN GUTHRIE
> (Very loving)
> Content yourself. I'll find a place.

                                                            DISSOLVE TO:

43. EXT. COTTAGE. CAIRNDHU AT ECHT - TWILIGHT.

<u>WIDE SHOT</u>. The cottage stands out alone against a great immensity of sky. Two horse-drawn carts loaded with the Guthrie possessions stand <u>FRAME LEFT</u> of it and some cattle.

Silence.

Then distant rolling thunder and rain clouds scudding across the sky as the light begins to fail. Then rain in the distance.

SUPERIMPOSE TITLE
"SUNSET SONG"

CUT TO:

44. EXT. COTTAGE CAIRNDHU AT ECHT - TWILIGHT.

SHOT of cottage door. The whole family coming out.

JOHN GUTHRIE last of all. He bangs the front door shut and leaves FRAME.

HOLD on door.

Then the rain falling against the door.

CUT TO:

45. EXT. COTTAGE. CAIRNDHU AT ECHT - TWILIGHT.

SHOT of the two carts moving off away from Echt. Gathering dark. Rain getting heavier.

DISSOLVE TO:

46. EXT. ROAD TO KINRADDIE - NIGHT.

SHOT of the two carts coming TOWARDS CAMERA. Very heavy rain.

JOHN GUTHRIE leading his horse and cart through mud and rain.

WILL and CHRIS (sitting under a tarpaulin) driving theirs. The going is very heavy. JOHN's horse stops - stuck in mud. WILL and CHRIS's cart stops but they don't get down.

JOHN pulls his horse but it won't budge. He runs to the back of his cart and stops and looks at WILL and CHRIS sitting on their cart.

JOHN GUTHRIE
Have you no sense you brats? Get down!

CUT TO:

47. EXT. ROAD TO KINRADDIE - NIGHT.

SHOT of WILL and CHRIS getting down and joining JOHN. Heavy rain.

CUT TO:

SUNSET SONG

48. EXT. ROAD TO KINRADDIE - NIGHT.

SHOT of back of JOHN's cart.

A tarpaulin. It is lifted quickly to reveal MOTHER breast-feeding one twin and holding the other: ALEC and DOD either side of her. They are lit from a hanging lantern inside the tarpaulin.

> MOTHER
> We'd better loosen up at Portlethen then and not try the slug this night.

CUT TO:

49. EXT. ROAD TO KINRADDIE - NIGHT.

3-SHOT. JOHN, WILL and CHRIS.

> JOHN GUTHRIE
> (in a fury)
> Damn't to hell. D'you think I'm made of silver?

CUT TO:

50. EXT. ROAD TO KINRADDIE - NIGHT.

SHOT of JEAN GUTHRIE - MOTHER.

> MOTHER
> (Weary)
> No, we're not made of silver - but maybe we'll all die of the night.

The tarpaulin is dragged down by JOHN.

PAN (R-L) with JOHN as he goes to the horse and starts pulling it through the mud and rain. It begins to move as does the cart.

> JOHN GUTHRIE
> Come on then lass ... come on ...

Horse and cart on the move again.

> JOHN GUTHRIE (CONT'D)
> Fine ... Clyde ... fine.

CUT TO:

51. EXT. ROAD TO KINRADDIE - NIGHT.

SHOT of WILL and CHRIS leading their horse and cart through the mud and rain.

PAN with it (R-L). The little procession trudges on through the terrible weather.

                                                                                   CUT TO:

52. EXT. WIDE SHOT KINRADDIE - NIGHT.

The little procession trudging wearily from (R-L) across the FRAME through the wind and rain towards the house extreme FRAME LEFT.

The procession stops. They all go into the house.

HOLD on house and skyscape.

                            CHRIS (VOICE OVER)
So that was how we came to Blaewearie - Oh my heart - Oh Kinraddie.

                                                        DISSOLVE TO:

53. EXT. HOUSE AT KINRADDIE - DAY.

WIDE SHOT. Brilliant sunshine.

                      JOHN GUTHRIE (VOICE OVER)
                            (Shouting)
Get out and get on with the breakfast and get your work done else I'll warm your lugs for you!

HOLD on WIDE SHOT.

The sound of gunshots in the distance followed by a flock of birds flying across the sky. Then silence. Heat.

                                                          CUT TO:

54. INT. HOUSE - DAY.

SHOT of JOHN at hearth. He is cleaning his gun. He finishes then hangs the gun over the fireplace, counts the pellets in a tin and puts the tin in the inglenook.

                                                          CUT TO:

55. INT. HOUSE - DAY.

SHOT of the rest of the family eating breakfast.

                                                          CUT TO:

56. INT. HOUSE - DAY.

WIDE SHOT of JOHN finishing his breakfast.

SUNSET SONG

>   JOHN GUTHRIE
>   I'm off to the mart at Laurencekirk.

JOHN leaves.

Pause.

WILL goes to hearth and takes down the gun.

CUT TO:

57. INT. HOUSE - DAY.

CLOSE UP CHRIS.

>   CHRIS
>   (Afraid)
>   No other soul must handle the gun but Father.

CUT TO:

58. INT. HOUSE - DAY.

CLOSE UP WILL.

>   WILL
>   (Smiling)
>   Aye.

He takes the pellets and goes out.

CUT TO:

59. INT. HOUSE - DAY.

SHOT of CHRIS and the family. They eat in silence.

The sound of the gun being fired.

Silence.

Then MOTHER gives a strange little smile and laugh.

CUT TO:

60. EXT. HOUSE - DAY.

SHOT of WILL having reloaded the gun, lifts it up to fire directly at CAMERA.

He pulls the trigger.

CUT (ON THE BANG) TO:

61. EXT. DUNCAIRN COLLEGE - DAY.

CLOSE UP Heraldic beast.

PAN AND TRACK (R-L) to class of girls sitting on chairs in the playground drawing the beast.

CHRIS and MARGET STRACHAN sit together.

SOUNDTRACK: VOICE OVER as we PAN AND TRACK.

>   MR. KINLOCH (VOICE OVER)
>   Noo ... that's not quate right ...

MR. KINLOCH in vision now near CHRIS and MARGET.

>   MR. KINLOCH (CONT'D)
>   More like the head of one of Chrissie's father's pigs
>   than an heraldic animal, I'm afraid.

Continue PANNING and TRACKING (R-L) to pick up
MR. MURGETSON's class of boys walking towards the school.

>   BOYS
>   (all)
>   Moo! Moo!

>   MR. MURGETSON
>   (In French)
>   Silence!
>   (Looks at MR. KINLOCH)
>   Canaille? Eh?

>   BOYS
>   (All
>   May-swee!

>   MR. MURGETSON
>   (Disgusted)
>   Les bêtes!

Continue PANNING (R-L) and

                                                    DISSOLVE TO:

62. EXT. LANE LEADING TO KINRADDIE - DAY.

PAN stops on 2-SHOT - CHRIS and MARGET. They walk home through the summer heat of late afternoon.

TRACK with them.

>   CHRIS
>   Is your father really a Socialist?

                        MARGET
     Yes. Chae says all should be equal - rich and poor, men
     and women - He wants me to learn so that I'll be ready
                     for the revolution ...

                         CHRIS
                  And if it doesn't come?

                        MARGET
     Then I'll train to be a doctor and cut up the bodies of the
     paupers - so take care you don't die a pauper, Chris. I'd hate
     some day to be standing there with the scalpel in my hand looking
     into your queer dead face and crying "But this is Chris Guthrie!"

                         CHRIS
                       (Shocked)
                    Marget Strachan!

MARGET runs away laughing and whooping.

                        MARGET
                (Full of the joy of life)
       Oh Chrissie, Chrissie, only fools love being alive!

CHRIS waves and smiles back then runs home.

<u>PAN away</u> from her (<u>R-L</u>) then

                                                    DISSOLVE TO:

63. INT. HOUSE AT KINRADDIE - EVENING.

<u>SHOT</u> of CHRIS running into house and stopping abruptly.

                                                    CUT TO:

64. INT. HOUSE AT KINRADDIE - EVENING.

<u>WIDE SHOT</u> of JOHN and MOTHER at hearth. JOHN counting the pellets.

                                                    CUT TO:

65. INT. HOUSE AT KINRADDIE - EVENING.

<u>CLOSE UP</u> WILL.

                                                    CUT TO:

66. INT. HOUSE AT KINRADDIE – EVENING.

2-SHOT. MOTHER AND JOHN.

A very tense silence.

MOTHER laughs that strange laugh again.

                    MOTHER
  You and your guns, what harm was in Will that he used it?

JOHN gets to his feet – catlike.

                  JOHN GUTHRIE
               (With quiet menace)
    Come out to the barn with me, Will.

                                        CUT TO:

67. INT. HOUSE AT KINRADDIE – EVENING.

CLOSE UP WILL. He looks at CHRIS.

                                        CUT TO:

68. INT. HOUSE AT KINRADDIE – EVENING.

CLOSE UP CHRIS.

                    CHRIS
               (To Father)
          Father, you can't.

                                        CUT TO:

69. INT. HOUSE AT KINRADDIE – EVENING.

CLOSE UP JOHN.

                  JOHN GUTHRIE
     Be quiet else I'll take you as well.

                                        CUT TO:

70. INT. HOUSE AT KINRADDIE – EVENING.

WIDE SHOT of all four. WILL goes out followed by JOHN.

                                        CUT TO:

71. INT. BARN AT KINRADDIE – EVENING.

2-SHOT. WILL drops his trousers and bends over.

SUNSET SONG

JOHN takes his belt from his trouser and begins to flog WILL.

<u>HOLD</u>.

WILL does not cry out.

<u>CUT TO:</u>

72. INT. BEDROOM - NIGHT.

<u>SHOT</u> of WILL lying (back to CAMERA) in CHRIS's arms, "Pieta."

<u>PAN UP</u> from his body as CHRIS strokes his torn skin trying to soothe both him and it. He is crying.

<u>PAN</u> stops on CHRIS.

WILL's crying subsides into sleep. She continues to stroke him then looks up at CAMERA.

>   MARGET (VOICE OVER)
> Men! Women! What fools they are below their clothes!

CHRIS stops stroking the sleeping WILL. She is both mystified and disquieted.

>   CHRIS (VOICE OVER)
>   (Speaking softly)
> There are lovely things in the world lovely that don't endure,
>   and the lovelier for that.

<u>CRANE UP</u> from them and:

<u>DISSOLVE TO:</u>

73. EXT. STRACHAN'S FARM - DAY.

<u>CRANE UP</u> on CHRIS and MARGET.

>   MARGET
>   (Her voice blending with CHRIS's)
>   And the lovelier for that ...

As the <u>CRANE UP</u> gets to waist height MARGET slips her arms around CHRIS.

<u>CRANE</u> stops on <u>CLOSE UP</u> <u>2-SHOT</u>.

>   MARGET (CONT'D)
> Wait till you find yourself in the arms of your lad, in the
>   harvest time and he'll stop joking ...

She pulls CHRIS closer.

                    MARGET (CONT'D)
              ... he'll take you like this ...

CHRIS half struggles to get free.

                    MARGET (CONT'D)
          ... there's not a body to see us! And hold you like this,
                    with his hands held so,
               (She cups Chris's face in her hands)
                    and kiss you like this!

She does.
                                                          CUT TO:

74. INT. BEDROOM - NIGHT.

<u>CLOSE UP</u> CHRIS. She blushes at the memory.
CHRIS and WILL "Pieta" on the bed in darkness and silence.

                         CHRIS
                      (Whispering)
                    Nothing endures.

Yet she smiles through tears.
<u>CLOSE UP/WIDE SHOT</u> of CHRIS and WILL in darkness... (PIETA)

                    CHRIS (CONT'D)
                        (Softly)
            Nothing endures ... not even friends ...

                                                          CUT TO:

75. EXT. STATION - DAY.

MARGET STRACHAN, CHAE STRACHAN and CHRIS on platform.

                         CHRIS
                         (Sad)
                     But Aberdeen.

                         MARGET
         It's a better place for a scholar and I'll be trained
                     all the sooner.

                      CHAE STRACHAN
              Ay, Marget lass, you'll do fine ...

The train pulls out and MARGET is gone.

SUNSET SONG

                    JOHN GUTHRIE (VOICE OVER)
        Friends? Stick to your lesson and lets see you make a
            name for yourself, you've no time for friends.

                                                          CUT TO:

76. EXT. FIELD - DAY.

<u>WIDE SHOT</u> of JOHN sowing followed by WILL carrying corn and CHRIS carrying pails of corn.

<u>TRACK BACK</u> with them.

                        JOHN GUTHRIE
                (half sings, half whistles as he sows)
        "Bonny wee thing Canty wee thing Lovely wee thing Wert
                         thou mine ... "

CHRIS stops and looks up listening to the larks and drops her pails. JOHN and WILL stop.

                    JOHN GUTHRIE (CONT'D)
                  (Turning round with a grin)
            Damn't to hell. Are you a fair fool?

CHRIS grins and picks up the pails.

They continue sowing. <u>TRACK BACK</u> with them.

                    JOHN GUTHRIE (CONT'D)
                 (Half whistling, half singing)
        "I would clasp thee in my bosom, Lest my jewel I should tyne ..."

                                                          CUT TO:

77. EXT. HOUSE AT KINRADDIE - DAY.

<u>WIDE SHOT</u>. Piles of blankets and tubs.

CHRIS - in a tub - trampling the blankets. She has rolled her knickers up but is still very hot. As she tramples the blankets in the tub she takes off her petticoat and skirt and continues. MOTHER comes out of the house.

                            MOTHER
            God, you've stripped! You'd make a fine lad, Chris.

MOTHER continues washing.

                                                          CUT TO:

78. EXT. HOUSE AT KINRADDIE - DAY.

SHOT of JOHN and WILL leading the horses in.

JOHN sees CHRIS.

                    JOHN GUTHRIE
Get out of that at once, you shameful limmer, and get on your clothes!

                                            CUT TO:

79. EXT. HOUSE AT KINRADDIE - DAY.

SHOT of CHRIS jumping out of tub and running into the house.

PAN to MOTHER (R-L).

                    JOHN GUTHRIE (VOICE OVER)
                          (Angry)
What would folks say if they saw her near naked?

                          MOTHER
If your neighbours haven't seen a naked lass they must have fathered their own bairns with their breeks on.

                                      DISSOLVE TO:

80. INT. HOUSE AT KINRADDIE - EVENING.

SHOT from inside kitchen looking out.

JOHN sharpening a hoe is joined by REV. GIBBON.

                    REV. GIBBON
Well, you'll be my neighbour Guthrie, man?
                    JOHN GUTHRIE
                        (Tart)
Ay, and you'll be the new minister Mister Gibbon.

                    REV. GIBBON
                    (Chastened)
You've a fine-kept farm, Mr. Guthrie, trig and trim, though I hear you've sat down a bare six months.

JOHN smiles.

                    JOHN GUTHRIE
            This is my daughter Chris.
                                          CUT TO:

SUNSET SONG

81. EXT. HOUSE AT KINRADDIE - EVENING.

SHOT of CHRIS at table studying by the light of a paraffin lamp. She looks up and smiles.

                REV. GIBBON (VOICE OVER)
I hear you're right clever, Chrissie and go up to the Duncairn College. How do you like it?

                CHRIS
                (Smiling)
                Fine, sir.

                                              CUT TO:

82. INT. HOUSE AT KINRADDIE - EVENING.

2-SHOT JOHN and REV. GIBBON.

                REV. GIBBON
         And what are you to be?

                                              CUT TO:

83. EXT. HOUSE AT KINRADDIE - EVENING.

CLOSE UP CHRIS.

                CHRIS
           A teacher, sir.

                                              CUT TO:

84. INT. HOUSE AT KINRADDIE - EVENING.

2-SHOT JOHN and REV. GIBBON.

                REV. GIBBON
    Well there's no profession more honourable.

They walk away from the house talking about the land.

                                              CUT TO:

85. EXT./INT. HOUSE AT KINRADDIE - EVENING.

SHOT of CHRIS resuming her studies.

HOLD. Then PAN (L-R) to MOTHER.

When MOTHER is FRAMED she is seen just standing there - a vacant look on her face, which is deathly white.

                                              CUT TO:

86. INT. HOUSE AT KINRADDIE - EVENING.

<u>SHOT</u> of CHRIS. (MOTHER'S <u>POV</u>) CHRIS looks at MOTHER.

CHRIS very distressed runs to MOTHER.

<u>CUT TO:</u>

87. INT. HOUSE AT KINRADDIE - EVENING.

<u>2-SHOT</u>. CHRIS throwing her arms around MOTHER.

                  CHRIS
                (Crying)
  Oh Mother I didn't mean to vex at the washing.

                 MOTHER
Not you Chris, just life. I cannot tell you a thing or advise - you'll have to face men for yourself. When the time comes, there's none can stand and help you.

CHRIS clings tightly to her. MOTHER kisses CHRIS.

               MOTHER (CONT'D)
 Mind that for me sometime if I cannot suffer it longer.

They hold in a fast embrace.

Silence.

Then we hear the twins crying.

               MOTHER (CONT'D)
               (Laughing)
     We're daft the two of us ...

<u>DISSOLVE TO:</u>

88. EXT. LOCH - EVENING.

The loch still in the warm, soft evening air. The sun reflected in its glass-like surface.

<u>DISSOLVE TO:</u>

89. EXT. LOCH - DAY.

CHRIS'S reflection seen in the surface of the water.

<u>DISSOLVE TO:</u>

SUNSET SONG

90. EXT. STANDING STONES - DAY.

The sun moves around the stones and the shadow it throws moves slowly around with it.

>   DOD/ALEC (VOICE OVER)
>   (Calling but distant and faint)
>   Chris! Chrissie!

<u>TRACK IN</u> on CHRIS lying in the grass. Her arms, her hair, her long body lying in the grass near the stones.

<u>SOUNDTRACK</u>: The snipes calling.

>   DOD/ALEC (CONT'D)
>   (Their voices getting closer)
>   Chrissie!

CHRIS stands up from the grass and looks towards the calling children.

>   CUT TO:

91. EXT. STANDING STONES - DAY.

<u>LONG SHOT</u> (CHRIS'S <u>POV</u>) of DOD and ALEC waving at the bottom of the brae.

>   DOD/ALEC (VOICE OVER)
>   (Anxious)
>   Chris-ssie!

>   CUT TO:

92. EXT. STANDING STONES - DAY.

<u>MID CLOSE UP</u> CHRIS. She smiles, her face suffused with happiness. She runs downhill.

<u>PAN WITH HER</u> (<u>R-L</u>).

>   DOD/ALEC (VOICE OVER)
>   The doctor's come Chrissie!

>   CUT TO:

93. INT. HOUSE AT KINRADDIE - DAY.

All three come running into the kitchen flushed from running and CHRIS looking worried.

>   CUT TO:

94. INT. KITCHEN AT KINRADDIE - DAY.

JOHN hunched over the fire.

CUT TO:

95. INT. KITCHEN AT KINRADDIE - DAY.

2-SHOT. DOCTOR and WILL at window. WILL crying.

CUT TO:

96. INT. KITCHEN AT KINRADDIE - DAY.

CHRIS CLOSE UP

                CHRIS
            What is it?

                WILL
            It's Mother!

She makes to go upstairs.

CUT TO:

97. INT. KITCHEN AT KINRADDIE - DAY.

2-SHOT. DOCTOR and CHRIS. He bars her way.

                DOCTOR
    She's poisoned herself - and the two bairns.

CHRIS is too stunned to speak.

                CHRIS
            (In shock)
        Why did she do it?
                DOCTOR
She was pregnant again and it unbalanced her. You'd better fetch Mistress Munro.

              JOHN GUTHRIE
No - I'll write to my sister Janet in Aucterless - she'll come.

DISSOLVE TO:

98. INT. KITCHEN AT KINRADDIE - DAY.

SHOT of kitchen door leading upstairs. AUNTIE JANET comes in.

SUNSET SONG

> AUNTIE JANET
> She's ready now. You can go up and see her.

CUT TO:

99. INT. KITCHEN AT KINRADDIE - DAY.

<u>WIDE SHOT</u>.

All go upstairs. CHRIS last of all.

> AUNTIE JANET
> You'll be leaving college now, I'll warrant. You'll find little time for education and dreaming when you're keeping house here.

CUT TO:

100. INT. KITCHEN AT KINRADDIE - DAY.

<u>CLOSE UP</u> CHRIS.

She doesn't answer.

CUT TO:

101. INT. BEDROOM - DAY.

<u>SHOT</u> of door. DOD, ALEC and WILL are already there. The two children too shocked except to stare. WILL overcome with grief. CHRIS enters. She stands and looks for a moment then she too breaks down.

CUT TO:

102. INT. BEDROOM - DAY.

MOTHER laid out in a nightgown.

JOHN kneeling by bed. Silence.

Then he leans forward touches her hair then kisses MOTHER.

> JOHN GUTHRIE
> (Softly)
> Jean ... Jean ...

CUT TO:

103. EXT. KINRADDIE HOUSE - DAY.

<u>WIDE SHOT</u>. The funeral procession walks slowly away (<u>R-L</u>).

The two small coffins preceding MOTHERS coffin, the mourners following.

All the mourners are men. No women.

> CHRIS (VOICE OVER)
> The June of the year it was when Mother had poisoned herself and the twins ...
> So long as that and so near as that but the world went on and you with it and you'd never be the same again.

HOLD.

They exit.

PAN UP to the immensity of the sky.

HOLD.

DISSOLVE TO:

104. INT. KITCHEN AT KINRADDIE - DAY.

JOHN at the fire.
JANET and her husband at the table, near them DOD and ALEC.
On the other side of the table WILL and CHRIS. Silence.

> AUNTIE JANET
> (To DOD/ALEC)
> You're to come to Aucterless with your uncle and me.

They just look.

> JOHN GUTHRIE
> So you'd like to steal my flesh from me?

> AUNTIE JANET
> Aye John - just as you asked when you wrote. We've never a bairn of our own though, God knows it's not for want of trying.

> JOHN GUTHRIE
> Ill blood breeds ill.

> AUNTIE JANET
> Aye, but it'll be long 'ere I'll have to kill myself because my man beds me like a breeding sow.

> JOHN GUTHRIE
> You dirty bitch.
> (He looks at DOD/ALEC)
> They won't go back to school -
> (In a fury)
> Why won't you go back?!

                    WILL
                 (Standing)
          Why should they go back? I wouldn't!

JOHN jumps up in a fury.

                  JOHN GUTHRIE
          And where do you wander each night?!

WILL doesn't answer.

CHRIS pushes the table between them. To separate them.

                    DOD
              (Quietly, very scared)
          They say "Whose mother was a daftie?"

                    ALEC
                  (Quiet)
              "Daftie! Daftie!" They say.

                  AUNTIE JANET
     Well that's past now. You're to come to live at Aucterless
                with your uncle and me.

JOHN sits down. WILL goes out.

Silence.

CHRIS follows WILL outside.

                                                    CUT TO:

105. EXT. KINRADDIE – DAY.

WILL and CHRIS bring the cattle home as they walk.

                    WILL
          Chris, don't let father make a damned slave of you, as
                he'd like to. We've our own lives to lead.

                    CHRIS
          What else can I do but bide at home now.

They bring the cattle into the barn, then settle into silence.

                    WILL
          If I saved long enough I could go to Canada. A man is
                    his own master there.

                    CHRIS
          Oh, Will, and could you send for me as your housekeeper?

Pause.

>   WILL
>   (He slaps one of the cattle)
>   Ay maybe ... but maybe it would hardly suit you.

Silence.

She is crestfallen.

He gets up and gets the bicycle leaning outside the barn and mounts.

>   CHRIS
>   Drumlithie?

>   WILL
>   (Smiles)
>   Aye.
>   He rides off.

She watches him go and turns towards the house.

>   CUT TO:

106. EXT. BARN AND HOUSE - EVENING.

JOHN GUTHRIE is watching WILL go. JOHN is in a quiet fury.

The back of CHRIS moving towards the house.

<u>TRACK</u> with her.

<u>TRACK</u> stops when she gets to JOHN.

>   JOHN GUTHRIE
>   If you've tended the cattle get off to your bed.

She goes in.

<u>HOLD</u> on JOHN.

>   CUT TO:

107. INT. BEDROOM - EVENING.

CHRIS kneeling by her trunk which is open. She is wrapping up all her school books and putting them into the trunk.

>   CHRIS (VOICE OVER)
>   Something died in her heart and went down with Mother to
>   lie in Kinraddie Kirkyard. The child in her heart had
>   died then and Chris of the books and dreams died with
>   it and the dark quiet corpse that was her childhood was
>   folded in the tissue paper and was laid away forever.

SUNSET SONG

She finishes putting her books in the trunk, then closes the lid.

Pause for a moment then she hears her FATHER come softly up the stairs and stand by her door.

She is both puzzled and frightened.

                                                                                                    CUT TO:

The door.

The latch is lifted, held a moment, then dropped and we hear JOHN pad away upstairs.

                                                                                                     CUT TO:

<u>CLOSE UP</u> CHRIS.

<u>HOLD</u> on her.

                                                                                                     CUT TO:

108. EXT. FIELD – DAY.

JOHN at the edge of the field, cutting a 'road' around the edge of the field of corn. He scythes his way slowly round.

                                                                                                     CUT TO:

109. EXT. FIELD – DAY.

CHRIS goes to the parks and sees the harvest yellow and ripe and lush. She moves through the fields and meets WILL.

They both walk together through the ripening fields of corn. They come across JOHN.

He finishes scything and walks up to an old mechanical reaper at the edge of the field. Horses yoked to it.

                       JOHN GUTHRIE
     I got it at Echt. We'll cut the corn quicker now.

                            WILL
  I'd be the fool of Kinraddie driving a thing like that.

                       JOHN GUTHRIE
                        (laughing)
If Kinraddie's laughter can make you a bigger fool than nature made you it'll be a miracle. Don't fret, I'll do the driving.

JOHN GUTHRIE gets up on the reaper and starts cutting.

                                                                                                     CUT TO:

110. EXT. FIELDS NEAR THE HOUSE - DAY.

JOHN GUTHRIE singing hymns as he drives the mechanical reaper through the corn.

WILL and CHRIS following behind it binding the stalks. This continues for a long time.

Then they stop to drink. All three hot and tired from the work.

>   TINK (VOICE OVER)
>   Is there work?

They look to the TINK.

                                                    CUT TO:

111. EXT. FIELD - DAY.

Their POV of TINK, dark, gypsy-like and strong.

HOLD.

                                                    CUT TO:

112. EXT. FIELD - DAY.

CLOSE UP JOHN.

>   JOHN GUTHRIE
>   Maybe, maybe. Let's see the work that you've in you first.

                                                    CUT TO:

113. EXT. FIELD - DAY.

CLOSE UP TINK.

>   TINK
>   Ay - fine that.

He joins them.

                                                    CUT TO:

114. EXT. FIELD - DAY.

JOHN starts driving the reaper again.

CHRIS, WILL and TINK running behind binding the stalks.

This continues for a long time, then CHRIS looks quickly at TINK.

                                                    CUT TO:

115. EXT. FIELD - DAY.

<u>Her POV</u> of TINK. He winks at her and smiles.

CUT TO:

116. EXT. FIELD - EARLY EVENING.

The reaper stops. All stop exhausted by the work.
They drink.

>   JOHN GUTHRIE
>   (to TINK)
>   I'll take you on for a day or so, if the weather holds.

JOHN GUTHRIE takes CHRIS aside.

>   JOHN GUTHRIE (CONT'D)
>   (quietly)
>   Go up to the house and see to the supper - no idling
>   mind - I won't have him in the kitchen - he's all lice -
>   he can have a shake down in the barn.

CHRIS goes off.

CUT TO:

117. INT. BARN - NIGHT.

<u>SHOT</u> of CHRIS coming into barn with TINK's supper.
She moves through the semi-darkness but can't see him. She stops.

>   CHRIS
>   (Not a little afraid)
>   I'd have you eat in the house if it hadn't been for Father.

>   TINK (VOICE OVER)
>   (From the dark)
>   I'm as little anxious for his company as he is for mine.

She stands there not knowing where he is. Silence.

CUT TO:

118. INT. BARN - NIGHT.

<u>SHOT</u> of two arms slithering around her legs.

CUT TO:

119. INT. BARN - NIGHT.

<u>CLOSE UP</u> CHRIS. Rigid with fear.

<u>HOLD</u>.

She breathing hard, almost scarcely at all.

                                                                        <u>CUT TO:</u>

120. INT. BARN - NIGHT.

The top half of TINK's body wraps around the bottom part of her legs. He begins to kiss and lick her feet and legs.

                            TINK
                    (Soft and caressive)
   Oh - oh that's a sore waste of hot blood like yours ...

                                                                         <u>CUT TO:</u>

121. INT. BARN - NIGHT.

<u>CLOSE UP</u> CHRIS. Both scared and excited.

                        TINK (VOICE OVER)
                    ... a sore waste ...

She steps backwards.

                                                                          <u>CUT TO:</u>

122. INT. BARN - NIGHT.

<u>SHOT</u> of TINK still with his arms around her legs, still kissing them.

                            TINK
    I'll be here, mind - if you want me I'll be here.

                                                                            <u>CUT TO:</u>

123. INT. BARN - NIGHT.

<u>WIDE SHOT</u>. CHRIS and TINK. She puts his supper down. She runs out. He leans back in to the straw.

                                                                             <u>CUT TO:</u>

124. EXT. BEDROOM WINDOW. KINRADDIE - NIGHT.

SHOT of CHRIS opening window and smelling the earth. Moonlight. She looks towards the barn.

                                                                                  CUT TO:

125. EXT. BARN - NIGHT.

The half-open barn doors and the spill of a paraffin lamp light. TINK begins to whistle.

                                                                                   CUT TO:

126. INT. BEDROOM - NIGHT.

SHOT of CHRIS (in nightgown) turning from the window and catching her reflection in the long mirror.

TINK stops whistling.

She drops the nightgown and looks at her own nakedness - with both pleasure and innocence. She touches herself below the left breast then runs her hand over her skin. She smiles. Then she extends her hand and moves towards her reflection in the mirror and touches it.

                                                                       DISSOLVE TO:

127. EXT. ROAD TO DRUMLITHIE - DAY.

SHOT of CHILDREN splashing and playing in the river.

                                                                   PAN (R-L) TO:

128. EXT. ROAD TO DRUMLITHIE - DAY.

SHOT of CHRIS - hot, radiant and walking with a purpose. PAN (R-L) from her then:

                                                                      DISSOLVE TO:

129. EXT. YARD. DRUMLITHIE - DAY.

Continue PANNING (R-L) to 2-SHOT. GALT (FACING CAMERA) and CHRIS back to it. He is loading berries into her basket.

                                      GALT
And how's Will? We haven't seen much of him here of late.

CHRIS doesn't answer.

GALT sees someone approaching from behind her.

                    GALT (CONT'D)
Faith - the roses are fair fading from Mollie Douglas's cheeks.

A cycle bell is heard. CHRIS turns round.

                        CHRIS
                          Oh!

                                                          CUT TO:

130. EXT. YARD. DRUMLITHIE - DAY.

A girl rides her bicycle to them then stops by CHRIS. Silence between them.

                        CHRIS
                      (To GALT)
   And I'll have two pounds of your blackberries too.

He loads her basket.

                                                            CUT TO:

131. EXT. STREET. DRUMLITHIE - DAY.

<u>2-SHOT</u> - CHRIS/MOLLIE. They walk together in silence.

<u>TRACK BACK</u> with them.

                        CHRIS
           You'll be Mollie Douglas?

                        MOLLIE
      Yes. You're Will Guthrie's sister?

                        CHRIS
                          Aye.

                        MOLLIE
             (Almost in tears)
 You must tell Will to ride over this night, I can't bear it any longer! I don't care if I'm shameless or not! (Now crying)

CHRIS stops and so does MOLLIE.

<u>TRACK STOPS</u>.

                   MOLLIE (CONT'D)
                    (Horrified)
  Oh you think that! Like all of them. But it isn't true!

SUNSET SONG

CHRIS is ashamed and does not speak.

>   MOLLIE (CONT'D)
>   (Quietly)
> It's not that at all, only I love him so sore I can't live if
>   I don't see Will.
>   (She wheels her bicycle away)
>   Ta, ta.

                                                        CUT TO:

132. INT. KITCHEN AT KINRADDIE - EVENING.

<u>CLOSE UP</u> WILL. He is eating his supper. He suddenly looks like a grown man - mature and handsome.

                                                        CUT TO:

133. INT. KITCHEN AT KINRADDIE - EVENING.

<u>CLOSE UP</u> CHRIS. She looks at him with new eyes.

                                                        CUT TO:

134. INT. KITCHEN AT KINRADDIE - EVENING.

<u>SLIGHTLY WIDER SHOT</u> of WILL. He finishes eating then gets up and loiters from door to window idly whistling.

                                                        CUT TO:

135. INT. KITCHEN AT KINRADDIE - EVENING.

<u>SLIGHTLY WIDER SHOT</u> of CHRIS (WILL'S <u>POV</u>)

>   CHRIS
> I met Mollie Douglas at Drumlithie today. She asked me to ask
>   you to go down and see her.

                                                        CUT TO:

136. INT. KITCHEN AT KINRADDIE - EVENING.

<u>SHOT</u> of WILL. He stands stock still and stops whistling.

>   CHRIS (VOICE OVER)
>   Will!

>   WILL
> I hear. What's the good? I haven't even a fee/wages.

                                                        CUT TO:

137. INT. KITCHEN AT KINRADDIE - EVENING.

CLOSE UP CHRIS.
        CHRIS
  Maybe she doesn't want your money, just you.
      Do love her, Will?

Silence.

        CHRIS (CONT'D)
  You're biding away from her now - is she with baby
       to you?
               CUT TO:

138. INT. KITCHEN AT KINRADDIE - EVENING.

CLOSE UP WILL.
        WILL
  You needn't be feared for that, I'd soon as cut my own
      throat as do hurt to her.
               CUT TO:

139. INT. KITCHEN AT KINRADDIE - EVENING.

2-SHOT. CHRIS gets up and goes to WILL at window. They put their arms around one another.

Silence as they look out of window.

        WILL
     (Seeing something)
  Whin burning - they're burning the whins up Drumlochty
  Way. Come up to the moor and have a try at ours. They're
      damned sore in need of it.

        CHRIS
   But I've got jelly to make, you gowk!

        WILL
   Oh to Hell with your jelly - come on.

They both run out.
               CUT TO:

140. EXT. YARD. AT KINRADDIE - EVENING.

As they run out JOHN is coming home.

SUNSET SONG

                     JOHN GUTHRIE
What's this I hear about you and some bitch in
                      Drumlithie?

                             WILL
                        (Sarcastic)
               She's no a virgin neither!
                                             CUT TO:

141. EXT. FIELD - NIGHT.

<u>SHOT</u> OF CHRIS and WILL with torches. As they run they set fire to the whins so that the whole field is ablaze.

                 CHRIS'S (VOICE OVER) OVER DISSOLVE
The harvest was gathered in; then it was time for the
    Threshing Dinner at Peesies Knapp and the whole of
                      Kinraddie came.
                                       DISSOLVE TO:

142. INT. PEESIES KNAPP BARN - NIGHT.

The barn ready for the Threshing Dinner.

<u>WIDE SHOT</u>. Trestle tables filled with the villagers eating and talking. The women (including CHRIS) serving soup: FAST ALONG the length of the tables. The tables piled high with extra food.

More and more VILLAGERS enter barn.
                                                       CUT TO:

143. INT. PEESIES KNAPP BARN - NIGHT.

<u>SHOT</u> of CHRIS moving down a trestle table and serving. At the table are seated JOHN GUTHRIE, CHAE, LONG ROB, MUNRO and ALEC MUTCH, who has very large ears.

                          ALEC MUTCH
                          Ay Chris!
                                                     CUT TO:

CHRIS who barely acknowledges him and keeps moving down the table and serving.
                                        CUT TO TRESTLE TABLE.

                             MUNRO
                      (to JOHN GUTHRIE)
Losh man, she's fair an expert getting, the daughter.
     The kitchens more her style than college.

                                                    CUT TO:

CHRIS, who looks at him with contempt. Some of the VILLAGERS laugh.

JOHN GUTHRIE doesn't react, he just goes on eating. CHRIS continues down the trestle table serving.

                                                    CUT TO:

TRESTLE TABLE.

                    ALEC MUTCH
     Education ... most of it is a coarse thing; learning ...
        just teaching your children a lot of damned nonsense
         that put them above themselves and give you their lip
                      soon as look at you.

                                                    CUT TO:

CHAE.

                    CHAE STRACHAN
   Damn't, man, you're clear wrong to think that. Educations the
   thing if the working man wants to put him up level with the rich.

                                                    CUT TO:

LONG ROB.
                     LONG ROB
     I'd have thought a bit balance in the bank would do that.

Laughter.

                                                    CUT TO:

CHAE.

                    CHAE STRACHAN
      The more education, the more sense. And less Kirks and
                          Ministers.

                                                    CUT TO:

MUNRO.
                      MUNRO
     Well, well, we'll hear nothing coarse of religion.

                                                    CUT TO:

LONG ROB.
                     LONG ROB
   Well, well Munro we'll turn to the mentally afflicted in
   general, not just in particular. How's that Foreman of yours
         getting on? Is he still keeping up his shorthand?

Lots of laughter (including JOHN GUTHRIE).

                                                    CUT TO:

CHRIS (she has smiled as well).

CONTINUE with her down the table.

                                                                              CUT TO:

144. INT. PEESIES KNAPP BARN - NIGHT.

SHOT of table.

2-SHOT of WILL and EWAN TAVENDALE. They drink their soup. EWAN'S head stays down so that we do not see his face.

                              WILL
              Hello Chris. How have you gotten on?

                                                       CUT TO CHRIS.

                              CHRIS
                      Fine. How've you?

                                                       CUT TO WILL.

CLOSE UP WILL.

                              WILL
  Well, God, my back would feel a dammned sight easier if
      I'd spent the day in my bed. Eh Tavendale?

PAN (L-R) to EWAN, head still down.

                      WILL (VOICE OVER) (CONT'D)
              This is Ewan Tavendale, Chris.

He looks up for the first time at CHRIS. He is stocky and dark. Not conventionally good looking but very attractive. He looks at CHRIS, clearly drawn to her. He half smiles.

                                                    CUT TO CHRIS.

She is half drawn to him, half not. But it is clear an attraction immediately is between them. She doesn't know whether to smile or not.

HOLD on her.

                    WILL (VOICE OVER) (CONT'D)
           The wind's still up and a fine frost.

She only half hears him.

                            CHRIS
                 (still looking at EWAN)
        I'm back to Blaewearie ... the milking ...

                                                      CUT TO:

145. EXT. ROAD LEADING TO BLAEWEARIE - NIGHT.

SHOT of CHRIS coming along it in the crisp night air. She pulls her shawl about herself, then laughs and runs away up road.

HOLD on her.

>   CHRIS (VOICE OVER)
>   Sweet breath he had ... and when she fell asleep she dreamed
>   of him ...

PAN UP to the star filled, cold night sky and HOLD.

>   CHRIS (VOICE OVER) (CONT'D)
>   ... an awful dream that made her blush even while she knew
>   she slept ...

Sparks enter the FRAME blown quick by the wind.

PAN/CRANE down to Peesies Knapp barn ablaze.

                                                              CUT TO:

146. INT. BLAEWEARIE - NIGHT.

Bedroom door. It opens. WILL comes out.

>   WILL
>   (shouting)
>   Father! Chris! See that light down there in the Knapp?

JOHN, WILL rush downstairs, CHRIS following dressing as she goes downstairs.

>   CHRIS
>   Wait for me. I'm coming as well.

>   WILL
>   Alright, but for Christ's sake hurry!

                                                              CUT TO:

147. EXT. PEESIES KNAPP - NIGHT.

Barn ablaze. VILLAGERS arriving, running and in gigs.

A line of MEN and WOMEN handing pails of water down a line then throwing the water onto the fire, trying to douse the flames.

                                                              CUT TO:

JOHN GUTHRIE. JOHN is banging on the house door.

SUNSET SONG

>   JOHN GUTHRIE
>   (shouting)
>   Damn't to hell! Do you want to be roasted?

No answer. He smashes the window in. Then breaks the door down.

CHAE, his WIFE and CHILDREN come running out of the house. Smoke billowing out. CHAE dressed only in trousers. WILL helps with the water. CHRIS comforts CHAE'S WIFE.

>   CHAE'S WIFE
>   Oh my sampler!

JOHN GUTHRIE runs back inside house.

                                              CUT TO:

148. INT. CHAE'S HOUSE - NIGHT.

Smoke filled. JOHN GUTHRIE comes running in, sees sampler on the wall, grabs it and runs out.

                                              CUT TO:

149. EXT. CHAE'S HOUSE - NIGHT.

JOHN, coughing, gives sampler to CHAE'S WIFE.

                                              CUT TO:

150. INT. BARN - NIGHT.

LONG ROB, CHAE, WILL and JOHN. They run into the barn and get some of the animals out. The animals are terrified. But the barn is ablaze.

The men rush out and the roof collapses in on the remaining animals. Their screams can be heard.

                                              CUT TO:

151. EXT. BARN - NIGHT.

LONG ROB and WILL drag a blackened carcass of a pig - roasted alive. JOHN and CHAE join them and look.

>   CHAE STRACHAN
>   We're all to hell.

All three (and the VILLAGERS) watch the barn blaze. The sparks fly up in the night sky. CRANE UP with them.

                    CHRIS (VOICE OVER)
        So that was the burning of Peesies Knapp. Outside it was
                          hard and cold ...

HOLD on sky.

                    CHRIS (VOICE OVER) (CONT'D)
         ... starless but clear as though the steel of the ground
                       glowed faintly of itself ...

HOLD on sky.

The sparks DISSOLVE INTO snowflakes. A flurry at first then strong snow and a wind.

                                                    CRANE DOWN TO:

152. EXT. BARN AT KINRADDIE - NIGHT.

SHOT of CHRIS and WILL coming out of the barn into a fierce snow storm. WILL carries a lantern. They run towards the house.

                                                           CUT TO:

153. INT. KITCHEN AT KINRADDIE - NIGHT.

SHOT of CHRIS and WILL coming into the kitchen which is warm and snug. They sit down.

Silence.

                              CHRIS
                        (very embarrassed)
                   How's your friend Ewan Tavendale?

                              WILL
                      So he caught your eye then?

CHRIS half smiles, blushes, but doesn't say anything.

                           WILL (CONT'D)
                            (smiling)
         Be careful of that brute, Chrissie, he's a terror with
                  the ladies ... Sarah Sinclair will vouch.

Silence.
                              CHRIS
                  Why haven't you gone to see Mollie tonight?

                              WILL
             Listen to the wind! It'll blow the damn place down!

SUNSET SONG

>   (Smiling)
>   I'll go tomorrow - isn't that enough?

He exits. CHRIS goes to work: baking.

                                                    CUT TO:

154. INT. BARN - NIGHT.

SHOT of JOHN feeding the cattle with turnips.

Silence except for the lowing of the cows and the snort and thump of beasts in their stalls.

Silence except for the soft murmuring of the animals in the warm barn.

                                                    CUT TO:

155. INT. HOUSE. KITCHEN AT KINRADDIE - NIGHT.

JOHN by the fire reading paper. CHRIS at table kneading dough. WILL on the far side of the room lost in thought.

Silence.

Then the peal of the parlour clock striking midnight echoing through the house. CHRIS looks at JOHN. WILL looks at JOHN.

>   JOHN GUTHRIE
>   (Stops reading and looks into fire)
>   God, I wonder why Jean left us?

                                                    CUT TO WILL.

He goes to speak to JOHN. WILL'S eyes fill with tears and pity. He tries desperately to say something comforting to JOHN but cannot. He looks down and is silent.

                                                    CUT TO CHRIS.

She looks away from JOHN, silent tears coursing down her face as she hides from them; neither man seeing her cry.

Then suddenly.

                                                    CUT TO:

156. INT. KITCHEN AT KINRADDIE - NIGHT.

SHOT of door. A loud bang on it.

Then it opens to reveal LONG ROB standing there - the storm raging behind him.

                    LONG ROB
            Happy New Year! Am I the first?

                   JOHN GUTHRIE
    Ay, man, you're fairly that - out of that coat of yours.

LONG ROB takes off his coat. JOHN hands him a hot toddy.

                                                  CUT TO:

SHOT of the door, it opens, CHAE STRACHAN is there.

                  CHAE STRACHAN
        Happy New Year. I'm the first foot in am I not?

Comes in and slips and goes down onto the floor. Much laughter.

                    LONG ROB
    (To CHAE) God Almighty, Chae, you can't sleep there ...

CHAE is hoisted into a chair.
                                                  CUT TO:

JOHN smiling, LONG ROB, CHAE begin singing.
                                                  CUT TO:

WILL half smiling.
                                                  CUT TO:

CHRIS after her tears, suffused with a quiet happiness.

                                              DISSOLVE TO:

157. EXT./INT. CHRIS'S BEDROOM - NIGHT.

She comes to the window and looks out. The storm has stopped just the quiet gentle snowflakes dropping down.
                LONG ROB (VOICE OVER)
           Losh man they're queer beasts, horses.

CHRIS looks down at him and smiles.

                CHAE STRACHAN (VOICE OVER)
        Damn't if you want a canty beast there's nothing
                       like a camel.

Laughter.
                                                  CUT TO:

158. EXT. HOUSE AT KINRADDIE - NIGHT.

<u>2-SHOT</u>. CHAE and LONG ROB (CHRIS'S <u>POV</u>) walking home through the snow - singing.

<u>TILT UP</u> to <u>WIDE SHOT</u> of Kinraddie village swaddled in snow.

<u>DISSOLVE TO:</u>

159. EXT. SKY - DAY.

The sky huge. Spring. Wonderful spring weather.

<u>SOUNDTRACK</u>: The sound of the peewits.

              LONG ROB (VOICE OVER)
     There is no God! And if there is He's a fool!

<u>PAN DOWN TO:</u>

160. EXT. LONG ROB'S MILL - DAY.

<u>2-SHOT</u>. LONG ROB and CHAE STRACHAN.

                CHAE STRACHAN
  No, man, you're fair wrong there. And man, Rob, you'll
          burn in Hell for that y'know.

                    LONG ROB
  Damn the fears, that's nothing but an old wife's babble
            for fearing the bairns.

                CHAE STRACHAN
    But something is up there; Rob, man, there's no
              denying that.

                    LONG ROB
   If I thought that I'd cut my throat this minute.

<u>PAN AWAY</u> (<u>L-R</u>) from LONG ROB and CHAE to pick up CHRIS walking through the shade.

When CHRIS is in <u>CLOSE UP</u> <u>TRACK BACK</u> with her.

She smiles at both men.

            LONG ROB (VOICE OVER) (CONT'D)
       Is it about the bruised corn, Chris?

She nods.

>   LONG ROB (VOICE OVER) (CONT'D)
>   Tell Will I'll do it tonight.

She nods and waves.

Continue TRACKING with her then PAN AWAY from her (L-R). Then

                                              DISSOLVE TO:

161. EXT. FARM AT KINRADDIE - DAY.

Continue PANNING (L-R) to FRAME MID-SHOT of JOHN and WILL coming towards CHRIS.

>   JOHN GUTHRIE
>   (To WILL, provocatively)
>   I'm thinking to have down the hay with a scythe this
>   year. The reaper's making you soft.
>
>   WILL
>   (To JOHN, not rising to the bait)
>   All right.
>   (He starts to whistle)
>
>   JOHN GUTHRIE
>   Hold your damn whistle, you'll need all your breath.

As they pass CHRIS, JOHN doesn't speak but WILL winks and smiles at her and starts to hum.

Continue PANNING (L-R) and FRAME CHRIS.

She looks after the two men.

                                              CUT TO:

162. EXT. FARM AT KINRADDIE - DAY.

CHRIS (POV) of JOHN and WILL walking away. WILL starts to sing "Up in the Morning".

                                              CUT TO:

163. INT. KITCHEN AT KINRADDIE - DAY.

SHOT of CHRIS baking. Kitchen very hot. She wears just a vest and petticoat.

HOLD on her.

She lifts a cake from oven to table then starts.
                    CUT TO:

164. INT. KITCHEN AT KINRADDIE - DAY.

SHOT of EWAN TAVENDALE at door watching her.

He holds his gaze.

Silence.

         EWAN
    (Half embarrassed, half not)
    Hello - is Will about?

                    CUT TO:

165. INT. KITCHEN AT KINRADDIE - DAY.

SHOT of CHRIS. She holds her gaze on him.

Silence.

         CHRIS
    No - Drumlithie I think.

Silence.

She catches some sweat running down her neck.
                    CUT TO:

166. INT. KITCHEN AT KINRADDIE - DAY.

SHOT of EWAN. His shirt slightly open. His tanned face but white throat and chest.

He still gazes at her for a moment then drops his eyes.

                    CUT TO:

167. INT. KITCHEN AT KINRADDIE - DAY.

CLOSE UP CHRIS. She drops her eyes.

HOLD on her.
                    CUT TO:

168. INT. KITCHEN AT KINRADDIE - DAY.

CLOSE UP EWAN. He looks at her again.

         EWAN
  Well, I was hoping I'd see him in case he should leave
       us sudden - like.
                    CUT TO:

169. INT. KITCHEN AT KINRADDIE - DAY.

CLOSE UP CHRIS.

       CHRIS
      (Shocked)
  Leave? Who said Will was leaving?

               CUT TO:

170. INT. KITCHEN AT KINRADDIE - DAY.

CLOSE UP EWAN.

       EWAN
  Oh I was heard he was trying for a job in Aberdeen.
    Tell him I called. Ta-ta.

He moves away from the door.

               CUT TO:

171. INT. KITCHEN. KINRADDIE. - DAY.

CLOSE UP CHRIS

       CHRIS
    (sitting down slowly)
    Ta-ta.

             DISSOLVE TO:

172. EXT. SKY - DAY.

A red sun hanging in the sky. Birds. The sound of the sea beyond the house.

             DISSOLVE TO:

173. EXT. FIELDS - DAY.

The fields ready for hay-making.

            CUT/DISSOLVE TO:

174. INT. KITCHEN AT KINRADDIE - DAY.

SHOT of JOHN, WILL, CHRIS at table. Breakfast.

       WILL
  (Eating his porridge. To JOHN)
  I'm off to Aberdeen today.

JOHN doesn't speak. CHRIS is stunned. JOHN finishes his porridge, gets up, lights his pipe and goes out of the house.

>   WILL (CONT'D)
>   (Looking after him)
>   The old fool thinks he can frighten me still.

Silence.

>   WILL (CONT'D)
>   (With passion to CHRIS)
>   Chris - Lord, I wish you were coming as well!

>   CHRIS
>   (Staring - amazed)
>   What - up to Aberdeen? I'd like it fine but I can't.

Silence.

>   CHRIS (CONT'D)
>   (Quietly)
>   Hurry and dress, else you'll miss your train.

He goes upstairs. She just sits there sadly. PAN AWAY from her (L-R) to stairs.

HOLD ON empty stairs.

CUT TO:

175. INT. KITCHEN AT KINRADDIE - DAY.

CLOSE UP CHRIS at foot of stairs.

>   CHRIS
>   (Calling)
>   Are you having a sleep before you set out!

>   WILL (VOICE OVER)
>   (Shaky)
>   All right, I'll soon be down.

She goes back into kitchen. And turns as she hears his footsteps on the stairs.

CUT TO:

176. INT. FOOT OF STAIRS - DAY.

SHOT of WILL coming into kitchen. He wears his Sunday best.

>   WILL
>   (Quietly)
>   Well, will I do?

CUT TO:

177. INT. KITCHEN - DAY.

CLOSE UP CHRIS.

                CHRIS
              (Quietly)
      You look fair brave.

                                       CUT TO:

178. INT. KITCHEN - DAY.

CLOSE UP WILL. He moves to door.
PAN WITH HIM.
He gets to the door then stops. His eyes full of tears.

                                       CUT TO:

179. INT. KITCHEN - DAY.

CLOSE UP CHRIS. She looks at WILL. Her eyes full of tears.

                                       CUT TO:

180. INT. KITCHEN - DAY.

WIDE 2-SHOT. WILL And CHRIS. He runs towards her weeping. They embrace and kiss. Weeping.

                WILL
          Oh, to Hell!

Exits.
PAN (L-R) to door. TRACK IN on open door.
WILL running away - getting smaller and smaller.

                                       CUT TO:

181. EXT. KITCHEN AT KINRADDIE - DAY.

CLOSE UP CHRIS. She watches him go and she weeps.

                                DISSOLVE TO:

182. INT. PARLOUR AT KINRADDIE - EVENING.

SHOT of parlour clock with its loud tick tock.

                                DISSOLVE TO:

183. INT. KITCHEN AT KINRADDIE - EVENING.

<u>SHOT</u> of the window of kitchen by the door, open in the warm evening. A slight breeze. The honeysuckle tapping lightly against the window pane. Sheep bleating in the distance. The sound of JOHN GUTHRIE'S gun.

DISSOLVE TO:

184. EXT. HAYRICK YARD AT KINRADDIE - EVENING.

JOHN setting up the hayricks in the corn yard.

CUT TO:

185. EXT. KITCHEN AT KINRADDIE - EVENING.

<u>SHOT</u> of CHRIS at window/door enjoying the soft evening air.

Then she hears a strange sound and runs into yard. She stops suddenly.

CUT TO:

186. EXT. YARD AT KINRADDIE - EVENING.

<u>SHOT</u> of JOHN fallen amongst the hayricks. He is having a kind of fit and blood trickles from his mouth.

CHRIS enters <u>SHOT</u> and kneels beside him cradling his head in her hands and lap.

> JOHN GUTHRIE
> (Slurred)
> All right Jean lass.

CHRIS, frantic, strokes his head and face. Then he recognises her and pushes her away.

> JOHN GUTHRIE (CONT'D)
> (Slurred but very angry)
> Get into the house you white faced bitch!

She runs away.

<u>HOLD</u> ON JOHN as he tries to get up, but can't.

CUT TO:

187. INT. BEDROOM. KINRADDIE - NIGHT.

<u>SHOT</u> of DOCTOR by bed examining JOHN.

                    DOCTOR
            What's this? What's wrong with you now?

                    JOHN GUTHRIE
                      (slurred)
            That's for you to find out. What the hell do you think
                      you're paid for?

The DOCTOR grins.

                    DOCTOR
            Chris, help me strip him.
                                                    CUT TO:

188. INT. KITCHEN - NIGHT.

                    DOCTOR
            It's a stroke, Chris.

                    CHRIS
            Yes, Doctor.

                    DOCTOR
            He'll need a lot of looking after.

The DOCTOR goes. CHRIS sits down worn out.
                                                    DISSOLVE TO:

189. INT. KITCHEN - DAY.

SHOT of CHRIS asleep in chair.

She wakes to find the post has been delivered.

She picks up the letter and reads it.

She looks upset. She goes upstairs.
                                                    CUT TO:

190. INT. BEDROOM - DAY.

SHOT of JOHN in bed. Side view. CHRIS facing camera.

                    CHRIS
            Will's married Mollie Douglas.

Silence.

                    CHRIS (CONT'D)
            They've sailed from Southampton to the Argentine.

SUNSET SONG

Silence.

He doesn't respond.

She takes a whistle from her pocket, but holds it in her hand.

> CHRIS (CONT'D)
> Just blow the whistle when you need me.

HOLD.

    CUT TO:

191. INT. BEDROOM - DAY.

SHOT of JOHN in bed. CHRIS POV He tries to speak but cannot find the words.

PAN DOWN to his right hand.

He moves it across to CHRIS's lap (PAN), and catches hold of her hand which holds the whistle.

He grabs both firmly then tightens his hold.

    CUT TO:

192. INT. BEDROOM - DAY.

CLOSE UP CHRIS as he squeezes her hand. She winces in pain, but doesn't make a sound.

    CUT TO:

193. INT. BEDROOM - DAY.

CLOSE UP JOHN. He stares intently at her but doesn't speak.

> JOHN GUTHRIE (VOICE OVER)
> (whispering)
> You're my flesh and blood - I can do with you what I will ...

    CUT TO:

194. INT. KITCHEN - NIGHT.

SHOT of CHRIS sitting in the kitchen lit only by the fire.

She looks upwards and around listening to every creak of the house. As she looks up she hears a scraping sound.

    CUT TO:

195. INT. JOHN'S BEDROOM - NIGHT.

SHOT of JOHN dragging himself with great difficulty from his bed.

CUT TO:

196. INT. KITCHEN - NIGHT.

WIDE SHOT. CHRIS moves quietly towards the door leading to the stairs and quickly runs up.

CUT TO:

197. INT. CHRIS'S BEDROOM - NIGHT.

She comes in and locks the door and sits down on her bed.

> JOHN GUTHRIE (VOICE OVER)
> (whispering)
> Come to me Chris, do you hear ...

She hears him struggling out of bed and coming towards her door.

CUT TO:

198. INT. CHRIS'S BEDROOM - NIGHT.

HOLD on latch.

We hear JOHN struggling to get to the door.

Silence.

Then the latch is tried but the locked door won't open.

> JOHN GUTHRIE (VOICE OVER)
> (whisper)
> Chris ... Chris ...

CUT TO:

199. INT. CHRIS'S BEDROOM - NIGHT.

She listens to him go back to his own room.

> CHRIS
> (frightened whisper)
> I wont, I wont ...

HOLD on her.

There is the sound of JOHN falling heavily, then silence.
She brings the bedclothes around herself and listens.

DISSOLVE TO:

200. INT. CHRIS'S BEDROOM - DAY.

SHOT of CHRIS still in the same position as the previous shot.
She wakes up and then goes to the door.
PAN WITH HER. She opens the door.

CUT TO:

201. INT. OUTSIDE BEDROOM DOOR - DAY.

CHRIS POV JOHN lying dead on landing.

CUT TO:

202. INT. OUTSIDE BEDROOM DOOR - DAY.

CLOSE UP CHRIS. She looks and knows.

CUT TO:

203. EXT. CHRIS'S BEDROOM WINDOW - DAY.

She looks out to the fields.

CUT TO:

204. EXT. FIELDS - DAY.

In the distance CHAE STRACHAN singing.
HOLD.

CUT TO:

205. EXT. CHRIS'S BEDROOM WINDOW - DAY.

She hangs a white sheet from it.

CUT TO:

206. INT. KITCHEN - DAY.

SHOT of CHRIS just sitting there.
HOLD.

CUT TO:

207. INT. KITCHEN - DAY.

CHRIS <u>POV</u> of door. CHAE comes running up

                CHAE
      Chris, lass, what's wrong?

CUT TO:

208. INT. KITCHEN - DAY.

<u>SHOT</u> of CHRIS.

               CHRIS
     Chae, my Father's dead.

CUT TO:

209. INT. PARLOUR - DAY.

<u>WIDE SHOT</u> of parlour packed with people from the village.

              LONG ROB
           (to REV. GIBBON)
    You'll have a dram, Rev. Gibbon?

            REV. GIBBON
              Spirits?

            UNCLE TAM
  Och, aye, it's the custom, isn't it?

            REV. GIBBON
    Yes, thank you. I'll have a drop.

The drink is poured. REV. GIBBON sips it in the silence broken only by the odd cough and the loud ticking of the parlour clock.

<u>HOLD</u>.

CUT TO:

210. INT. KITCHEN - DAY.

Packed with people, more villagers, mostly women, including CHRIS and her AUNTIE JANET.

The UNDERTAKER comes in.

                             UNDERTAKER
                              (to CHRIS)
            Would you like to see him before he's screwed down?

CHRIS followed by AUNTIE JANET, exits.
                                                              CUT TO:

211. INT. BEDROOM - DAY.

SHOT of JOHN in coffin.
                                                              CUT TO:

212. INT. BEDROOM - DAY.

CHRIS, AUNTIE, UNCLE, LONG ROB, CHAE and UNDERTAKER looking down at JOHN. Silence.

                                CHAE
                Well, well goodbye, Blaewearie man.

                              LONG ROB
                              (choked)
                       He was a fine neighbour.

UNDERTAKER looks at AUNTIE JANET.

                            AUNTIE JANET
                             (To CHRIS)
             They're to screw it down now, kiss your Father.

                                CHRIS
                         (shaking her head)
                            Goodbye Father.

She leaves.
                                                              CUT TO:

213. INT. PARLOUR - DAY.

The coffin is carried through towards the kitchen.
                                                              CUT TO:

214. INT. KITCHEN - DAY.

The coffin is carried through and out of the house.
                                                              CUT TO:

215. EXT. KINRADDIE YARD - DAY.

A squally wind - threatening rain. The funeral procession. LONG ROB, CHAE and the other MEN carry the coffin.

Behind it, CHRIS. Behind her, EWAN and the VILLAGERS.

CHRIS is the only woman at the funeral.

CUT TO:

216. EXT. KINRADDIE YARD - DAY.

SHOT of CHRIS joined by EWAN.

Rain starts to fall - a fine drizzle.

CUT TO:

217. EXT. KIRKYARD GRAVESIDE - DAY.

Wind heavy and driving drizzle.

REV. GIBBON tries to keep his bible dry.

>REV. GIBBON
>Ashes to ashes, dust to dust ... etc.

CUT TO:

218. EXT. KIRKYARD GRAVESIDE - DAY.

The SEXTON offers a shovel of earth to CHRIS.

She takes a handful and throws it onto the coffin now inside the grave. The earth is red.

PAN UP to her face.

CUT TO:

219. EXT. KIRKYARD GRAVESIDE - DAY.

SHOT of grave, red earth being shovelled over it.

CUT TO:

220. EXT. KIRKYARD GRAVESIDE - DAY.

CLOSE UP CHRIS as rain streams down her face.

CUT TO:

221. EXT. KIRKYARD - DAY.

CHRIS coming out of Kirkyard. People shaking her hand in condolence.

SUNSET SONG

Last of all is EWAN. He takes her hand, then puts his other hand over both his and hers.

CUT TO:

222. INT. KITCHEN. KINRADDIE - DAY.

SHOT of AUNTIE JANET and CHRIS.

AUNTIE JANET begins taking off CHRIS'S wet things.

              AUNTIE JANET
  God be here, it's you that'll be next in your grave.

CUT TO:

223. INT. CHRIS'S BEDROOM - DAY.

SHOT of CHRIS in bed. Snug.

She begins to cry, then buries her face in the bedclothes.

              CHRIS (VOICE OVER)
She was no longer afraid ... only sad for the Father she never helped and forgot to love.

CUT TO:

224. INT. PARLOUR. KINRADDIE - DAY.

The LAWYER - MR. SEMPLE - reading the will.

During the reading SHOTS of CHRIS (astonished), UNCLE TAM (shocked) and AUNTIE JANET (mortified).

              MR. SEMPLE
  "I, John Guthrie of Blaewearie, being of sound mind and body do hereby leave and bequeath to my daughter Christine all my possessions, in silver and belongings to be hers without let or condition. I also appoint Peter Semple as my daughters guardian in such law matters as needs one. But she is to control the goods and gear as she may please. The monies amounting to three hundred pounds I also bequeath to her. Give under my hand etc, etc ... "

He snaps his briefcase shut.

              MR. SEMPLE (CONT'D)
  So think it well over Miss Guthrie.

                    CHRIS
               Oh I'll do that.

                  UNCLE TAM
             (a long deep breath)
      Not a word of Will or his two motherless boys.

                 AUNTIE JANET
                    (piqued)
      For shame, Tam, how can they be motherless now that
                   I've got them?

Silence.
              AUNTIE JANET (CONT'D)
                   (to CHRIS)
       And you'll come up to live with us when you've sold
              Blaewearie's furnishings Chris.

                    CHRIS
                  (getting up)
                   Ay, maybe.

MR. SEMPLE stands.

                 CHRIS (CONT'D)
               I'll see you out.

And she exits with him.

                 CHRIS (CONT'D)
                   (to AUNTIE)
         I'll go down and bring home the cattle.

                                              CUT TO:

225. EXT. BLAEWEARIE - DAY.

MR. SEMPLE and CHRIS come out.

MR. SEMPLE gets into a gig.

                    CHRIS
               Thank you Mr Semple.

He drives off.

                 CHRIS (CONT'D)
                    Goodbye!

She watches him go, then looks up at the sky which is dark and lowering. She shivers slightly in the cold.

SUNSET SONG

PAN UP to sky. Rain threatening.

                                                                                                PAN DOWN TO:

226. EXT. FIELD - LATE AFTERNOON.

SHOT of CHRIS walking through the fields, above her the immense sky.

                          CHRIS (VOICE OVER)
She saw the trail of the mists coming south on the wind to Forfar, down the wide Howe, past the drenched harvests past Brechin and on ...

                                                                                                                 CUT TO:

227. EXT. FIELD AND WALL - LATE AFTERNOON.

A SHOT of the cattle huddled together by the wall and CHRIS among them herding them home.

                          CHRIS (VOICE OVER)
And a queer thought came to her ... nothing endured but the land.

                                                                                                                            CUT TO:

228. INT./EXT. BARN. BLAEWEARIE - TWILIGHT.

She has stalled the cattle and come out of the barn.

                        CHRIS (VOICE OVER)
... sea, sky and the folk who lived they were but a breath ...

                                                                                                                            CUT TO:

229. EXT. BLAEWEARIE - TWILIGHT.

WIDE SHOT of house. The lamps have been lit.
BACK VIEW of CHRIS going towards the house.

                        CHRIS (VOICE OVER)
But the land endured ...

She goes into the house. HOLD on house.

                      CHRIS (VOICE OVER) (CONT'D)
... and ... at that moment ... she felt in the gloaming ... that she was the land.

                                                                                                                    CUT TO:

230. INT. BLAEWEARIE - DAY.

SHOT of CHRIS putting on her coat as she comes into the kitchen.

                  AUNTIE JANET
             Where are you going?

                    CHRIS
I'm away to Stonehaven to see Mr Semple. Can I bring you anything?

                  UNCLE TAM
What are you jaunting there for? I'll transact any business you have.

                    CHRIS
               (going to door)
I'll transact my own business fine.

She leaves. JANET and TAM struck dumb with disapproval.

                                                CUT TO:

231. INT. MR. SEMPLE'S OFFICE CORRIDOR - DAY.

SHOT of CHRIS coming down a long passage towards Mr SEMPLE'S office.

                                                CUT TO:

232. INT. MR. SEMPLE'S OFFICE - DAY.

It is crowded with papers, boxes on shelves making it seem very cramped.

                  MR. SEMPLE
            (pointing to a chair)
Sit down this is fine and comfortable.

SHOT of CHRIS sitting.

              MR. SEMPLE (CONT'D)
Well, well it's Miss Guthrie come up; you've been thinking about the will, no doubt?

                    CHRIS
Yes. Just that. I'm going to live on at Blaewearie a while and not roup the gear at once. Could you see to that with the factor?

                    MR. SEMPLE
                     (shocked)
           But you can't live there alone!

                      CHRIS
      I've no such intention. Could you get me some woman to
      come live with me, some old body who'd be glad of the
                        work?

                    MR. SEMPLE
            Oh God there are plenty of them!

                      CHRIS
      It'll only be for a month or two. Just til I'm settled.

                    MR. SEMPLE
       Just? Well that's cool. There's Mistress Melon. I'll
               send her down in the morn.

CHRIS gets up.

                      CHRIS
              Thank you. Goodbye. She exits.
                                                     CUT TO:

233. EXT. STONEHAVEN STREET - DAY.

<u>SHOT</u> of street clogged with sheep. CHRIS literally can't move for sheep, dogs and drovers.

A gig WIPES <u>FRAME</u> and EWAN jumps from it.

They look at each other from opposite sides of the street, separated by sheep. They "wade" through the animals and meet in the middle of the road, completely surrounded by sheep.

                      EWAN
                Are you up for the day?

                      CHRIS
      Och, aye, just that. I'm going up to the Inn for dinner.

                      EWAN
              Maybe we can eat together?

                      CHRIS
                     (smiling)
              So you're in no hurry to be back.

                              EWAN
         Not unless you should be. They walk away from us surrounded
              by sheep which are being driven towards the camera.

                                                              CUT TO:

234. EXT. DUNNOTTAR CASTLE - DAY.

SHOT of both CHRIS and EWAN walking down the steep rocks away from camera, towards the castle.

PAN UP to Dunnottar Castle perched high on the rock, the sea beyond.

SOUNDTRACK: Seagulls and the voices of CHRIS and EWAN reading the following text:

                          CHRIS (VOICE OVER)
            "Here lyes John Stott, James Atchison, James Russell
                        and William Broun ...

CROSS MIX TO:

                           EWAN (VOICE OVER)
         "... William Broun and one whose name we have not gotten and
              two women whose names also we know not ... "

CROSS FADE TO:

                          CHRIS (VOICE OVER)
              "... also we know not. All died prisoners in
                Dunnottar Castle; Anno 1685; for the adherence
              to the word of God and Scotland's covenanted work
                            of Reformation."

                                                              CUT TO:

235. INT. LONG ROOM. DUNNOTTAR CATLE - DAY.

CHRIS and EWAN are standing in the long, dark cell where the Covenanters were imprisoned and killed. Behind them an open window overlooking the sea. They stand in the silence and semi-darkness, just the crying of the seagulls.

                              EWAN
                           (whispering)
                Let's get out of this. Come down to the sea;
                          I know a nook.

                                                              CUT TO:

236. EXT. SANDY COVE BEACH - DAY.

CHRIS sitting upright, EWAN by her side leaning on one arm, peels an orange. CHRIS takes off her hat. She looks at EWAN.

CHRIS'S POV EWAN. He looks out to sea, eats a bit of orange, then looks at CHRIS and smiles.

CHRIS smiles back.

>   EWAN
>   Chris, do you like me a bit?
>
>   CHRIS
>   (smiling)
>   Can't suffer you at all ... that's why we're out lazing in
>   this place together ...

He blushes, smiles and offers her a piece of orange which she takes and eats.

Calm together they look at the sea.

                                                                                                                         CUT TO:

237. EXT. SEA - DAY.

A boat tacks and flashes. Gulls cry and wheel.

                                                                                                                        CUT TO:

238. EXT. SANDY COVE BEACH - DAY.

2-SHOT, CHRIS and EWAN.

Pause.

>   CHRIS
>   Ewan ... was it true that story they told about you and
>   old Sarah Sinclair?

EWAN doesn't answer.

>   CHRIS (CONT'D)
>   Answer my question.
>
>   EWAN
>   Put a question with some sense in it then.
>
>   CHRIS
>   Did you lie with her?

```
                            EWAN
                (more to himself than CHRIS)
        They were all so anxious that I should ... like they all had!
        ... I'd like to knock their teeth down their damned throats!

                            CHRIS
                      Did you love her?

                            EWAN
                      That old trollop!?

                            CHRIS
        You bedded that old trollop ... what does that make you?

                            EWAN
                 Am I to stand your lip as well?

                            CHRIS
                   Is what I've been hearing true?

                            EWAN
                      (in a sudden fury)
                         Aye! Aye!

He reaches out and grips her arm tightly.

                            CHRIS
                         (frightened)
                    Oh! I don't want to know!

                            EWAN
        Damn, well listen now that you've asked me ... I bedded
                         her like a sow!

CHRIS pulls away from him.

                        EWAN (CONT'D)
                          (shouting)
        Like a sow! And that was what she wanted, she liked being a
        sow! Now you're frightened, frightened that a woman should
           feel like that, maybe someday you'll feel it yourself.

She gets up on her feet.

                            CHRIS
           Maybe I will, but when I do I'll get a better man than
                          you to serve me!

She runs away.
                                                            CUT TO:
```

239. EXT. CLIFF TOP. BEACH – DAY.

HIGH SHOT of EWAN near the cove.

> EWAN
> Chris! Chrissie!

He runs towards the cliffs and begins to climb.

CUT TO:

240. EXT. CLIFF TOP. BEACH – DAY.

SHOT of CHRIS coming up over the cliff top and standing.

HOLD on her. She looks down, then she kneels down and extends her hand and smiles.

PAN L-R to EWAN who takes her hand and smiles back at her. He comes to her on the cliff top. In the background Dunnottar Castle on its rock, the sea swirling around it.

They walk away hand in hand.

CUT TO:

241. INT. TRAIN – EARLY EVENING DAY.

They sit opposite each other in an empty compartment. (Gas light - semi-dark)

Silence.

> EWAN
> Tired, Chrissie?

> CHRIS
> (leaning forward and touching his hand)
> Losh, no, and my name is "Chris," Ewan.

He blushes. She looks at him with love.

CUT TO:

242. EXT. FIELD – NIGHT.

A great storm. Rolling thunder and sheet lightning. The lightning strikes the barbed wire fence and runs along it making the whole thing "live."

The horses rear up in terror.

CUT TO:

243. INT. BEDROOM/LANDING - NIGHT.

CHRIS comes running out of her bedroom in just her underclothes and rushes downstairs.

> AUNTIE JANET
> (at bedroom door)
> Are you alright Chrissie?

> CHRIS
> (tearing downstairs)
> Yes fine.

The thunder and lightning continues.

CUT TO:

244. INT. KITCHEN - NIGHT.

CHRIS comes running into the kitchen, pulls on one of her Father's old coats, some shoes, lights a lamp, then runs to bottom of stairs. The storm continues.

> CHRIS
> Uncle Tam! Uncle Tam! We must take in the horses!

> AUNTIE JANET (VOICE OVER)
> He's feared at the lightning.

CHRIS rushes out, with the lantern.

CUT TO:

245. EXT. FARM - NIGHT.

Terrific thunder and lightning and now torrential rain.

CHRIS comes out and sheet lightning lights up farm and village. She runs to the barn.

CUT TO:

246. INT. BARN - NIGHT.

The cows lowing in the stalls terrified by the storm.

CHRIS checks them then leaves.

CUT TO:

247. EXT. FIELD - NIGHT.

The storm rages. CHRIS running through field with lantern, suddenly falls against something.

CUT TO:

248. EXT. FIELD - NIGHT.

One of the horses - BOB - struck by lightning lies dead.

CUT TO:

249. EXT. FIELD - NIGHT.

The other two horses, Bess and Clyde come out of the darkness to CHRIS and stand beside her whinnying with fear.

CUT TO:

250. EXT. SECOND FIELD - NIGHT.

A flash of lightning lights up the field. Two figures momentarily seen.

CUT TO:

251. EXT. FIELD - NIGHT.

SHOT of CHRIS between the horses, they drag her forward and she drops the lantern.

Complete darkness. Thunder. Rain.

CUT TO:

252. EXT. SECOND FIELD - NIGHT.

Two swinging lanterns. Two MEN emerging from the darkness, CHAE and EWAN.

> CHAE AND EWAN
> (shouting)
> Chris! Chrissie!

CUT TO:

253. EXT. FIELD - NIGHT.

SHOT of CHRIS between the two horses.

> CHRIS
> (shouting)
> I'm here!

They join her.

> CHAE
> (to EWAN)
> Damn't man, take that ...

Gives EWAN the lantern.

>   CHAE (CONT'D)
>   And take the lass and run for my house. I'll see to
>   the horses.

Lightning, thunder, rain.

CUT TO:

254. INT. CHAE'S HOUSE. KITCHEN - NIGHT.

CHRIS and EWAN enter.

>   EWAN
>   Bide here and I'll be off to help Chae.

He leaves. She stands by the kitchen fire. The kitchen is snug and warm. A clock ticks. She looks around the quiet, warm kitchen.

Silence.

Then CHAE and EWAN come bursting in.

>   CHAE
>   (to CHRIS)
>   Damm't Chris, get out of that coat, you must be fair soaked.

He banks up fire.

>   CHRIS
>   (quietly to EWAN)
>   Ewan, I've nothing on below.

EWAN is very embarrassed.

>   CHAE
>   What nothing at all?

>   CHRIS
>   Well, not very much Chae.

He takes one of his wife's coats from the back of the door and gives it to CHRIS.

>   CHAE
>   You can slip into that.

>   CHRIS
>   But Mistress Strachan ...

>   CHAE
>   The old wife's in bed. She'd sleep through a hundred storms.

He points to the parlour beyond.

                    CHAE (CONT'D)
Get out of your things, Chris lass and bring them to dry. I'll have something warm for you and Ewan to drink.

CHRIS goes into the parlour.

                                              CUT TO:

255. INT. PARLOUR. CHAE'S HOUSE - NIGHT.

<u>SHOT</u> of CHRIS coming in.

She leaves the door slightly ajar to use the light from the fire to see by. She stands behind the door and quickly undresses, puts on CHAE'S wife's coat and takes her things into the kitchen.

                                              CUT TO:

256. INT. KITCHEN. CHAE'S HOUSE - NIGHT.

<u>SHOT</u> of the three of them around the fire, drinking toddies. CHRIS'S underwear drying in front of the fire.

Silence except for the storm outside.

                      CHAE
Damn't Chris, was that all you had on?

CHRIS nods.

                      EWAN
You'll have your death of cold. Sit closer.

She moves closer to the fire and EWAN.

<u>HOLD</u>.

                                        DISSOLVE TO:

257. INT. KITCHEN. CHAE'S HOUSE - NIGHT.

<u>SHOT</u> of CHRIS coming out of parlour with her Father's coat on.
<u>PAN WITH HER</u> RIGHT to LEFT to EWAN and CHAE.
EWAN picks up a lantern. CHAE yawning.

                    EWAN
I'll see you back to Blaewearie.

They exit.

CUT TO:

258. INT. FARMYARD. BLAEWEARIE - NIGHT.

<u>SHOT</u> of CHRIS with EWAN, leading the horses towards barn. The storm over but a wind blowing.

They go in to the barn.

CUT TO:

259. INT. BARN. BLAEWEARIE - NIGHT.

<u>SHOT</u> of CHRIS and EWAN coming in with the horses.
They stall them. They stand looking at one another.
CHRIS holds the lantern.
Pause.

>   EWAN
> Are you warm enough?

>   CHRIS
>   (laughs)
>   Fine.

His arms go around her inside her coat. He bends down to kiss her.

>   CHRIS (CONT'D)
> (turning her head slightly away)
>   Oh! Don't ...

He's still so close. She puts the lantern down and they begin to kiss and fondle each other, shyly at first, then passionately.

>   CHRIS (CONT'D)
>   Wait, Ewan.

He immediately stops kissing her but still holds her.

>   CHRIS (CONT'D)
> Come down and see me tomorrow evening.

>   EWAN
> Chris, will you marry me?

CHRIS gives a very big yawn.
EWAN lets her go - offended - then he yawns too.

SUNSET SONG

They both laugh!

CUT TO:

260. INT. BEDROOM BLAEWEARIE - DAY.

A knock on the door.

> UNCLE TAM (VOICE OVER)
> Come away now, there's a fire to light and your Auntie wants her tea.

CHRIS slowly awakes.

> CHRIS
> All right Uncle Tam.

She gets out of bed - naked - and walks to the window and the sun floods in. She smiles to herself and slowly begins to hum and dress.

CUT TO:

261. INT. KITCHEN. BLAEWEARIE - NIGHT.

SHOT of CHRIS, UNCLE TAM and AUNTIE JANET at breakfast.

CHRIS humming softly to herself.

> UNCLE TAM
> You're in fine tune this morning.

> CHRIS
> Aye, Uncle, I'm that.

Breakfast continues.

> UNCLE TAM
> There's no sign of a horse this morn.

> CHRIS
> You couldn't have looked in the stable.

> AUNTIE JANET
> How did they come to be there?

> CHRIS
> Ewan Tavendale helped me.

> UNCLE TAM
> Ah well, it's plain you've no use for relatives here.

>AUNTIE JANET
>I only pray you don't come to disaster.

AUNTIE JANET is on the verge of tears.

>CHRIS
>There's nothing to cry about yet Auntie Janet. Ewan and I haven't lain together. We'll wait till we're married.

>AUNTIE JANET
>(shocked)
>He's to marry you then?

>CHRIS
>I hope so. But you never know.

AUNTIE JANET eats her breakfast with renewed hostility.

CUT TO:

262. INT. KITCHEN. BLAEWEARIE – DAY.

<u>SHOT</u> of CHAE coming in door.

>CHAE STRACHAN
>I'll drive you both to the station.

CUT TO:

263. EXT. BLAEWEARIE – DAY.

<u>SHOT</u> of AUNTIE JANET and UNCLE TAM, CHAE and CHRIS walking towards gig.

>CHAE
>(as they drive off)
>I'll bring Mistress Melon back!

CHRIS waves them off. She stands in the sun and turns towards the house.

>CHRIS
>You're mine ... MINE!

She goes back in.

<u>TRACK IN</u> with her from behind.

As we get inside the camera does 180 degree turn, without a dissolve, to frame MISTRESS MELON and CHAE coming from the gig.

SUNSET SONG

> MISTRESS MELON
> (as she comes in)
> Where'll I put my box, Mem?

> CHRIS
> Maybe Chae will carry it in for us? You'll stay to dinner Chae?

> CHAE
> Oh aye, fine that.

DISSOLVE TO:

264. INT. KITCHEN. BLAEWEARIE - DAY.

SHOT of the three of them eating with relish.

> CHAE
> God that was right fine, Chris. Is there more on the go?

She serves him.

> CHAE (CONT'D)
> (as she does so) Lord, Chris, they'll right soon be after you, the lads, with your eyes like that.

She smiles.

> MISTRESS MELON
> How'll we partition the work Mem?

> CHRIS
> You do the cooking and cleaning and I'll see to the rest.

> MISTRESS MELON
> (nods)
> Yes Mem.

> CHRIS
> (smiling)
> And my name's Chris. We're no gentry.

They both smile.

DISSOLVE TO:

265. INT. PARLOUR. BLAEWEARIE - NIGHT.

WIDE SHOT of parlour. Lit only by the fire. CHRIS sits in a chair by hearth. Silence except for the ticking of the clock. There is a light tap on the door. CHRIS stands up and catches her reflection in the long parlour mirror opposite her.

CUT TO:

266. INT. PARLOUR. BLAEWEARIE - NIGHT.

Her reflection, no longer a girl but a maturing woman. She looks at herself a moment then goes to the door and EWAN comes in. She closes the door and EWAN sits down in chair and pulls her onto his lap. They kiss quietly and gently.

Then fall silent and look at the fire.

                        EWAN
            We'll have to wait to be married.

Silence.
                        EWAN (CONT'D)
            I have no more than a hundred pound saved.

                        CHRIS
I have three hundred, - no credit to me, it was Father's saving.

Pause.
                        CHRIS (CONT'D)
 If we marry fair soon you can take over the Blaewearie lease.

EWAN looks at her with great tenderness.

                        EWAN
            That would be fine then.

And they hold each other in the silence and the firelight.

PAN AWAY from them at the fireside (L-R)

                                              DISSOLVE TO:

267. INT. PARLOUR - NIGHT.

CONTINUE PANNING (L-R) to table at which CHRIS and EWAN are sitting writing out wedding invitations.

                        EWAN
      We'll have the whole of Kinraddie here when we wed.

                        CHRIS
  Yes. Most of the folk will be free to come on new years eve.

Silence and they continue to write.

                        CHRIS (CONT'D)
  I had a letter from Auntie Janet and Uncle Tam. They say it's
   too soon after father's death to wed. So they won't come.

SUNSET SONG

                    EWAN
    Damn it you're only married once as a general rule and it
            won't hurt the old man in Kinraddie Kirkyard.

MISTRESS MELON comes in.

                    MISTRESS MELON
              Is this the list for the food?

                    CHRIS
                    Yes.

                    MISTRESS MELON
    Oh such extravagance! You've ordered enough food to
                    feed the French!

CHRIS and EWAN smile. MISTRESS MELON exits.

                    MISTRESS MELON (CONT'D)
              You'll have no silver left!

Pause.
                    EWAN
              I'll put up the banns tomorrow.

CHRIS continues writing and EWAN looks at her with love. She
finishes writing, she goes to him and they embrace and kiss.
Silence.
                    EWAN (CONT'D)
    I'll bide at Upperhill the day before the marriage.

They go (in an embrace) to the Parlour door.

                    CHRIS
    Reverend Gibbon will say "it seems strange to give such
            a display so close to Mr Guthrie's death."

                    EWAN
        And I'll say "the service I want is a wedding,
                    not a sermon."

He spits into the fire.
They get to the Parlour door still in each others arms.

                    CHRIS
              Look after yourself.

He leaves and she sits down in the firelight.
Silence except for the loud tick of the Parlour clock.
                                              CUT TO:

268. INT. BLAEWEARIE - DAY.

TRACK through Parlour and into kitchen. Everywhere upside down as CHRIS and MISTRESS MELON scrub, polish and clean everything and everywhere.

                                                                TRACK ENDS IN:

269. INT. KITCHEN. BLAEWEARIE - DAY.

LONG ROB and CHAE come to the kitchen door which is open. They carry wedding presents.

LONG ROB two biscuit barrels. CHAE bed linen.

CHRIS turns to them as they come in and put down the presents.

                             CHRIS
                          Thank you!

Then suddenly:

                        CHRIS (CONT'D)
       The barn! It isn't half spruce for the dance!

                      CHAE STRACHAN
    Leave it to us Chris lass. Just tell us what you want.

                                                                   CUT TO:

270. INT. BARN - DAY.

CHAE and LONG ROB come in with ladders. CHRIS and MISTRESS MELON carrying decorations.

                         LONG ROB
            And where's your musician?

                           CHRIS
                      (shocked)
                We fair forgot!

                    CHAE STRACHAN
      It doesn't matter. I'll bring my melodeon

                       LONG ROB
And I'll bring my fiddle and if that doesn't content folk they're looking for a church parade of the Gordons, not a wedding.

                                               DISSOLVE TO:

271. INT. BARN - NIGHT.

LONG SHOT the barn now decorated for the big day.

CUT TO CHRIS:

She comes in and looks at it.

          CHRIS
It's like a picture book.

          CHAE STRACHAN
This time in the morn you'll be a married woman, Chris. Sleep sound tonight.

          CHRIS
         (laughs)
Oh fine that!

          LONG ROB
      (near to tears)
If I'd ever thought of getting married I'd think it fine to sleep with a lass like yourself.

He kisses her.

          CHAE STRACHAN
     (smiling but moved)
Away Rob ... much sleep you'd give her.

CHAE kisses her too. They say their "goodnights" and leave. She stands alone looking suddenly sad and lonesome. She walks slowly down and out of the barn.

CUT TO:

272. INT. HOUSE. BLAEWEARIE - NIGHT.

She wanders from room to room at a loss what to do. All the rooms glistening and pristine, clean as a whistle in preparation for the wedding. She sits down in the parlour. Silence except for the loud tick of the parlour clock.

MISTRESS MELON comes in.

          MISTRESS MELON
For God's sake lass get to your bed! If you don't lie down you'll look more like a bull for the butcher than a bride in the morn!

CHRIS smiles and goes upstairs.

CUT TO:

273. INT. CHRIS'S BEDROOM. BLAEWEARIE - NIGHT.

She sits by the window and looks out.
CUT TO:

Her POV of sky and village. The sky is clear, the Milky Way shining clear.

> CHRIS (VOICE OVER)
> Strange and eerie it was sitting there ...

CRANE DOWN to SHOT of Village. A hoar frost over the whole of Kinraddie.

> CHRIS (VOICE OVER) (CONT'D)
> That this marriage of hers was nothing ... that it would pass on and forward into days that had long forgotten it ...

One by one the lights go off in the Village.

> CHRIS (VOICE OVER)(CONT'D)
> ... and the face of the land change and change again till the last lights sank away from it in the coming of the seasons and the centuries ...

CUT TO:

CLOSE UP of CHRIS at window.

> CHRIS (VOICE OVER)(CONT'D)
> And all her love and tears for Ewan not even a ripple on that flood of water remain in the time to be ... strange to think that tomorrow and all the tomorrows Ewan would share her room and her bed with her.

The parlour clock stikes two and she jumps into bed and lies there.

PAN (R-L) to window. The clock strikes, three, four, five, six, seven throughout PAN.

PAN ends on window.

HOLD.

DISSOLVE TO:

274. INT. BEDROOM - MORNING.

SHOT of window. Outside it's snowing.

CHRIS goes to window and looks out. The houses of Kinraddie under snow. The peewits crying.

SUNSET SONG

<u>CONTINUE PANNING</u> (<u>R-L</u>) to open trunk with CHRIS'S bridal outfit laid on top of it.

> MISTRESS MELON (VOICE OVER)
> How do you feel on your marriage morn Chris?

> CHRIS (VOICE OVER)
> Fine.

<u>CONTINUE PANNING</u> (<u>R-L</u>) over room.

> MISTRESS MELON (VOICE OVER)
> I hope you'll be awful happy and soon have three bairns.

> CHRIS (VOICE OVER)
> You never know.

<u>CONTINUE PANNING</u> (<u>R-L</u>) to <u>FRAME</u> CHRIS in her bridal outfit, looking at herself in the mirror.

> CHRIS (CONT'D)
> If only mother could be here.

And she starts to weep.

> CHRIS (CONT'D)
> (shaking her head)
> Oh don't be a fool!

She looks at herself once more and smiles, content. There is a light tap on the door and she turns and looks towards it.

CUT TO:

<u>SHOT</u> of bedroom door. CHAE opens it.

> CHAE STRACHAN
> (whisper)
> Ready then Chris?

CUT TO:

275. INT. PARLOUR - DAY.

<u>SHOT</u> of CHAE and CHRIS coming in and stopping.

CUT TO:

<u>Their</u> <u>POV</u>. The whole parlour packed with people. REVEREND GIBBON by the window. EWAN and his best man, McIVOR facing REVEREND GIBBON but backing to CAMERA. Everyone stands.

CUT TO:

CHAE taking CHRIS to stand by EWAN.

                                                                                   CUT TO:

2-SHOT EWAN and CHRIS. She looks at him. He doesn't look at her.

                    REV. GIBBON (VOICE OVER)
   (reading the Marriage Service but it sounds far away.)

                                                                                    CUT TO:

CLOSE UP EWAN. He looks at her for the first time.

                              EWAN
                            I will.

                                                                                   CUT TO:

CLOSE UP CHRIS.

                             CHRIS
                            I will.

                                                                                    CUT TO:

Their hands clasped and he puts the ring on her finger.

                         REV. GIBBON
    Let us pray ... Dear God bless this union, give them
    courage and strength for the difficulties that the years
     might bring to them, make fruitful their marriage and
     make their love as pure and enduring in its fulfilment as
                     in its conception.

Each pair of hands clasp over the others.

2-SHOT CHRIS and EWAN. They kiss.

                                                                                  CUT TO:

276. INT. PARLOUR - DAY.

Full of tables now spread with Wedding Breakfast. CHRIS and EWAN sitting at the head of the table. In the centre a wedding cake.

CHRIS and EWAN stand to cut the cake. Applause. Then everyone starts to eat and drink.

                        CHAE STRACHAN
                          (toasting)
                   Here's to you Chris!

They all toast her.

EWAN blushes. CHRIS smiles.

                    CHAE STRACHAN (CONT'D)
   Fill up your glasses folks the Best Man has a toast.

SUNSET SONG

>   McIVOR
>   (standing, bows to CHRIS)
> I've never seen a sweeter bride or known a better friend than
> the groom. I wish them long and lovely days from the summer to
>   the winter of their lives. The bride!

>   ALL
>   Good luck to her!

They all drink.

>   LONG ROB
>   The night's near on us. Who's game for a dance at
>   Chris's wedding?

They all roar approval.

CUT TO:

277. INT. BARN. NIGHT.

They are all lined up then begin to dance "Strip The Willow."
CHAE and LONG ROB tuning up then playing.

>   CHAE STRACHAN
>   "Strip the Willow!"

A brazier lit well away from the straw. MISTRESS MELON comes
in (while the GUESTS dance) with a jug of hot toddy which she
places between CHAE and LONG ROB. "Strip the Willow" finishes
and LONG ROB and CHAE take drinks from the jug.

>   CHAE STRACHAN
>   (to LONG ROB)
>   Here's to you man!

>   LONG ROB
>   (to CHAE)
>   Same to you!

They both begin playing a Schottische.

CUT TO:

CHRIS dancing with REVEREND GIBBON who is very good at
dancing and shouts "Hooch!" every now and then.

CUT TO:

EWAN dancing with MISTRESS GORDON.

CUT TO:

CHRIS laughing as she is spun around by REVEREND GIBBON. Then:

CUT TO:

CHRIS and EWAN. A "Petronella" is struck up and they begin to dance amongst the other guests. Then he draws her from the dance.

CUT TO:

A quiet dark corner near the bar.
2-SHOT CHRIS and EWAN.

     EWAN
    Well Chris?

     CHRIS
    Fine.

     EWAN
  You're the bonniest thing ever seen in Kinraddie,
    Long Rob was right.

Then they kiss and kiss and kiss ...

CUT TO CHAE:

The "Petronella" finishes.

    CHAE STRACHAN
  Where's the bride and groom? Damn't they're lost!

CUT TO:

CHRIS and EWAN coming from their hiding place. GUESTS laugh and applaud them.

CUT TO CHAE:

   CHAE STRACHAN (CONT'D)
  Can anyone else play the melodeon?

    JOCK GORDON
    Ay!

CHAE gives him the instrument then goes and grabs CHRIS.

    CHAE STRACHAN
    (to EWAN)
  Away you greedy brute, wait a while til she's
    yours forever.

SUNSET SONG

He takes CHRIS away to the middle of the dance floor. A slow dance has started and then move about the floor.

<u>2-SHOT</u> CHRIS and CHAE (<u>TRACK WITH THEM</u>)

                CHAE STRACHAN
Never doubt your Ewan Chris or never let him know that you do. Praise him and tell him he's fine and he'll want to cuddle you till the day he dies.

They stop dancing for a moment.

                      CHRIS
                  (near to tears)
              I'll try. And thank you.

                CHAE STRACHAN
And fifty years on he'll blush at the sight of you
                as he does now.

            (as they resume dancing)

    Och it must be the whisky speaking ...

A quicker dance is struck up and CHAE and CHRIS whirl so fast that they stumble away from the other dancers and crash into a piece of sacking hanging from a beam in front of an animal stall.

It comes down only to reveal REVEREND GIBBON on the floor with a young girl. CHRIS is horrified and runs off.

CHAE quickly puts the "screen" back up.

                        <u>CUT TO MISTRESS MELON:</u>

                MISTRESS MELON
                  Supper!
                                  <u>CUT TO:</u>

<u>WIDE SHOT</u> of all GUESTS moving towards tables laid with food at the back of the barn.

The WOMEN fix their hair as they chat and eat. The MEN take food to the barn door and smoke as they talk. Outside the barn a carpet of snow.

                                            <u>CUT TO:</u>

WOMEN in the barn talking quietly.

                                            <u>CUT TO:</u>

MEN at barn door slowly coming back in.

                              <u>CUT TO LONG ROB:</u>

                          LONG ROB
                    Who's for a dance again?

LONG ROB and CHAE strike up a lively jig. GUESTS dancing
including CHRIS and EWAN.

                                                    CUT TO:

WOMEN including MISTRESS MELON, two other WOMEN. CHRIS join
them flushed from dancing.

                       MISTRESS MELON
                       Och! The bride!

                     FIRST FEMALE GUEST
     It's fine to be young and married and maybe he'll treat
     you all right but mine has was a fair bull of a man and
                    not only on the first night ...

                       MISTRESS MELON
           She'll be fine, her lad's both blithe and kind.

                    SECOND FEMALE GUEST
     Take things easy in married life, Chris, but not over
     easy, that's been my ruin. Don't let Ewan saddle you
     with a house full of bairns, don't let him Chris ...

                       MISTRESS MELON
              Are you trying to frighten the lass?

                     FIRST FEMALE GUEST
          They're all the same men; you belong to yourself,
                           mind that.

LONG ROB joins them and stops.

                          LONG ROB
       Don't mind them Chris. It's been the curse of the human
                    race listening to advice.

                            CHRIS
            I'm listening to yours, Rob, now aren't I?

All laugh.
                          LONG ROB
                          (solemn)
       Oh you've your head screwed on and you'll manage fine.

                                              CUT TO CHAE:

SUNSET SONG

                CHAE STRACHAN
         Rob what about a song?

CUT TO LONG ROB:

                LONG ROB
          I'll manage that fine.

He takes his coat off and goes and stands next to CHAE and he begins to sing "Ladies Of Spain".

All listen then applaud.

                CHAE STRACHAN
                 (singing)
     "... the lass who made the bed for me."

Again applause.

CUT TO:

MISTRESS MELON: She sings "Auld Robin Gray." It is sad and the mood has changed to sadness.

CUT TO:

CHRIS and EWAN as MISTRESS MELON sings. CHRIS near to tears. MISTRESS MELON finishes.

                LONG ROB
         A song from the bride!

Silence. CHRIS stands up next to LONG ROB and CHAE and sings "The Flowers of the Forest". Everyone is moved, especially EWAN. She finishes. A rapt silence.

                CHAE STRACHAN
    Let's have another dance! It'll soon be a quarter to
         twelve and we must all be off.

They dance. The dance ends.

                LONG ROB
           It's new year!

They all sing "Auld Lang Syne". They finish, some shaking hands, some kissing. Then they begin to drift home from the barn. Until finally everyone is gone and only CHRIS and EWAN are left.

They walk slowly to the house through the snow.

DISSOLVE TO:

278. INT. BEDROOM - NIGHT.

The bridal bed has been decorated and a fire in the grate blazes.

CUT TO:

CHRIS and EWAN naked. They move to the bed.

                CHRIS
               (softly)
       Put out the light, Ewan.

He does so. They are lit only by the fire. They embrace. He lifts her and she puts her legs around his waist and they move to the bed and consummate the marriage.

        CHRIS (VOICE OVER) (CONT'D)
  So that was her marriage, not like waking from a dream,
       but like going into one.

TRACK from them into the fire. HOLD on fire.

        CHRIS (VOICE OVER) (CONT'D)
  And she wasn't sure, not for days what things they had
     dreamt and what actually done.

DISSOLVE TO:

279. INT. BEDROOM - MORNING.

Still on fire, now out, in grate.

CUT TO:

280. INT. BEDROOM - MORNING.

MISTRESS MELON comes in with tea for them. Places it near them. They are still drowsy.

           MISTRESS MELON
    I'm back to Stonehaven today.

                CHRIS
       Oh, I'll miss you.

           MISTRESS MELON
        (near to tears)
        Ay ... fine.

She goes to the door.

SUNSET SONG

> MISTRESS MELON (CONT'D)
> Fare thee well.

Leaves.

CUT TO:

281. INT. BEDROOM - MORNING.

Quite dark. EWAN gets out of bed followed by CHRIS. They dress quickly in the freezing cold.

CUT TO:

282. INT. KITCHEN - EARLY MORNING.

Still dark and cold. EWAN gets the fire going and CHRIS prepares their breakfast.

CUT TO:

283. EXT. HOUSE - EARLY MORNING.

CHRIS comes out to the dairy. Still very dark and very cold. Little lights in the village and fields beyond. A lantern glows from the barn and stable.

CUT TO:

284. INT. STABLE/BARN - EARLY MORNING.

EWAN feeding the cattle turnips, the cattle's breath hang in the cold morning air.

CHRIS comes in and begins milking. EWAN touches the back of her neck.

> CHRIS
> Your hand's freezing!

> EWAN
> Away woman, you're still asleep. Up in the morning, that's the thing!

He begins to whistle as he leaves the stable. The horses stamp and neigh. CHRIS carries the milk back to the house.

CUT TO:

285. INT. KITCHEN - MORNING.

Still dark but warmer now that the fire's going.

EWAN and CHRIS eating porridge close to the fire and each other. They finish eating.

EWAN gets up and gets JOHN GUTHRIE'S gun down from above the hearth and goes out smiling and whistling.

                                                                                                    CUT TO:

286. EXT. BLAEWEARIE YARD - DAY.

Light now. EWAN in the cart pulled by CLYDE. EWAN drives off for corn.

                                                                                                    CUT TO:

287. EXT. KITCHEN DOOR - DAY.

CHRIS watches him go.

                                                                                                    CUT TO:

288. EXT. HOUSE - DAY.

CHRIS <u>POV</u> of EWAN driving away. He waves then is gone.

                                                                                                  CUT TO:

289. INT. KITCHEN - DAY.

CHRIS looks crestfallen as she wanders aimlessly around the kitchen. Then she sits down at a loss what to do.

                                                                          DISSOLVE TO:

290. INT. BEDROOM - DAY.

CHRIS asleep on the bed. A loud banging is heard. She wakes and runs downstairs.

                                                                                                   CUT TO:

291. INT. KITCHEN - DAY.

EWAN is back. CHRIS runs to him and they embrace, kiss and laugh.

                                    CHRIS
                   I missed you! I missed you!

EWAN smiles with embarrassment and pleasure.

                                    EWAN
  I forgot to unyoke Clyde - we might well have more sense.

They hug each other.

                                                                           DISSOLVE TO:

292. EXT. FIELDS. SPRING - EARLY MORNING.

The fields are shrouded in mist. A fog-horn - far away in Todhead is heard - mournfully. Then the mist begins to lift. Clouds of gulls are heard then the sun is up.

CRANE DOWN to see EWAN ploughing in the field.

Continue CRANE DOWN AND PAN AWAY TO SHOT of all other fields being ploughed by teams of horses and men. Some burning going on.

                                                                                         CUT TO:

293. EXT. BARN - DAY.

CHRIS herding the cattle towards the hayfield. Some of the steers break away and she runs after them.

                                                                                         CUT TO:

294. INT. KITCHEN - DAY.

The kitchen heaped and cluttered with gear and tackle.

                        CHRIS
          Look at my hands! Red with the scrubbing.

                        EWAN
     You're daft. The place is fine. What more do you want?

                        CHRIS
          Less dirt! Maybe you like it but I don't.

                        EWAN
        Well, maybe I do. I like you right well.

They exchange smiles.

                                                                                       CUT TO:

295. INT. BARN - DAY.

SHOT of EWAN winnowing and smoking. He looks up.

                                                                                         CUT TO:

296. INT. BARN - DAY.

EWAN's POV of CHAE (in oil skins) coming into the barn out of the torrential rain.

                          CHAE
        I haven't seen rain like this since I was in Alaska.

                          EWAN
        Damn Alaska! When will it clear in Blaewearie?

                                                        CUT TO:

297. INT. BARN - DAY.

<u>Their POV</u> of the rain outside.

<u>TRACK IN</u> on it.

                                                     DISSOLVE TO:

298. INT. BEDROOM - MORNING.

<u>SHOT</u> of window - lovely sunshine. <u>TRACK BACK</u> to shot of EWAN and CHRIS in bed together - wide awake.

                          EWAN
        Damn Blaewearie! Let's have a holiday today, Chris.

                          CHRIS
                 I can't! I'm cleaning!

                          EWAN
                      (mock anger)
        Are you to spend all your days cleaning? You'll be old
            and wizened. Off on a holiday we'll go today!

CHRIS runs her hand down over his naked body then below the sheets.

                       EWAN (CONT'D)
        You're a shameless limmer for sure - and not yet nineteen.

They kiss.
                       EWAN (CONT'D)
              Come on let's get out and get off!
                                                        CUT TO:

299. EXT. ROAD - DAY.

<u>SHOT</u> of EWAN and CHRIS in a gig driving very fast.

<u>TRACK</u> with them. (<u>L-R</u>)

Then A SERIES OF <u>SHOTS</u> as they drive through: Bervie, Drumlithie, Arbuthnott, Fordoun, Drumlochty and the roads and countryside all around ending at Edzell Castle.

                                                        CUT TO:

SUNSET SONG

300. EXT. GARDENS EDZELL CASTLE - DAY.

The heraldic beasts, the old walls, the perfect flowers and lawns, dead stone beasts. (SHOOT LIKE FLORIST SHOP IN 'VERTIGO'.)

Everything lush, over-ripe and terribly oppressive.

<u>TWO-SHOT</u> of EWAN and CHRIS walking through garden.

> CHRIS (VOICE OVER)
> Folk blythe and young as themselves, had once walked, talked and taken their pleasure there - and they were gone, they had no name or remembered place, even in the lands of death they were maybe forgotten, for maybe the dead died once again - and she tried to tell Ewan of her daft fancy but all he said was -

> EWAN
> Aye.

CHRIS laughs and turns from him.

<u>HOLD</u> on her.

> CHRIS (VOICE OVER)
> And once she had thought there wouldn't be a thing they wouldn't understand together.

CUT TO:

301. EXT. ROAD. EARLY EVENING - DAY.

EWAN and CHRIS in gig returning home but slowly this time. (<u>R-L</u>)

They drive in silence. A wind - EWAN looks at the sky behind them.

CUT TO:

302. EXT. SKY. EARLY EVENING - DAY.

<u>SHOT</u> of the sky - heavy clouds full of rain. It starts to pour in the distance getting closer all the time.

CUT TO:

303. EXT. ROAD - EARLY EVENING.

<u>SHOT</u> of the gig. They begin to drive faster but the wind and rain catch up with them drenching them both.

CUT TO:

304. EXT. BLAEWEARIE - EARLY EVENING.

They drive the gig to the house and jump down completely soaked. CHRIS runs into the house and EWAN takes the horse into the barn.

HOLD ON EXT. Then CRANE UP to the trees. The trees creak in the wind and rain. HOLD.

DISSOLVE TO:

305. EXT. TREES - DAY.

EXACTLY AS THE PREVIOUS SHOT but a bright, hot May day. Sunshine.

BEGIN TO CRANE DOWN to a SHOT overlooking the fields which lie beyond Blaewearie - static in the heat.

> EWAN (VOICE OVER)
> (seeming far away)
> Chris! - Chris!

CONTINUE CRANE DOWN until CHRIS is framed lying in the garden below the beech trees. All around her the quiet rustling of the leaves and the lazy buzz of insects.

HOLD ON HER. Then PAN down her body to her stomach. Her hand begins to hold and stroke her belly.

> CHRIS (VOICE OVER)
> And then the old Chris crept out from the place below the beech trees where the new Chris lay and went into the quiet of the afternoon - the new Chris heard her go and she came back to Blaewearie never again. But she would not tell Ewan, not then, not just then for it was she and only she that felt and knew the wonder of God.

She turns and looks directly to camera.

CUT TO:

306. INT. BEDROOM - DAY.

CHRIS'S POV OF EWAN in bed next to her asleep.

> CHRIS (VOICE OVER)
> And then she knew she hated him ... and loved him all at once and there was nothing to be done ... nothing ... though her heart stirred and melted and froze again in the long dark hours of love and the fruitage of that love as the sower slept all unaware.

CUT TO:

307. INT. KITCHEN - DAY.

CHRIS slow at her work. EWAN comes in.

> EWAN
> (Half-angry, half-laughing)
> Damn't Chris, are you still asleep?

Without replying she goes out to the dairy but slowly. EWAN follows.

CUT TO:

308. EXT. HOUSE - DAY.

EWAN following CHRIS.

> EWAN
> What is wrong? What's up?

She looks at him with barely disguised hostility.

> EWAN (CONT'D)
> What are you glowering for?

> CHRIS
> (calmly)
> For God's sake, must you be an old wife and come trailing after me wherever I go?

> EWAN
> (hurt)
> You're out of the bed the wrong side this morning.

He leaves her.

She moves to go after him - sorry for the hurt she caused him but as EWAN gets in the middle of the close, he shouts back over this shoulder.

> EWAN (CONT'D)
> And I'd like my breakfast before the night comes down.

She runs after him in a fury and spins him round to her.

> CHRIS
> Speak like that to me? Do think I'm your servant? You're mine, mind that, living off my meal and my milk, you Highland pauper!

She slaps him hard in the face. He turns on her in a fury and punches her to the ground.

>   EWAN
>   Get up! Get up! You damn bitch - say that to me!
>   Damn you, get up!

She shields herself from him as he stands over her - apoplectic with rage.

>   CHRIS
>   (as she rises)
>   No - no -

She runs away.

>   EWAN
>   (his anger subsiding)
>   Chris - Chris - come back -

She continues to run away from him.

                                                        CUT TO:

309. EXT. LOCH AND STANDING STONES - DAY.

CHRIS runs through the circle of stones and falls to the ground weeping into the earth. She looks up at the whistling of the broom then sinks down again weeping bitterly.

                                                    DISSOLVE TO:

310. EXT. LOCH AND STANDING STONES - LATE AFTERNOON.

SHOT OF CHRIS. She raises her head - no longer crying and gets up and moves to the rim of the stone circle. She is calm now.

                                                        CUT TO:

311. EXT. LOCH - LATE AFTERNOON.

EWAN calling and searching for her.

                                                        CUT TO:

312. EXT. STANDING STONES - LATE AFTERNOON.

SHOT OF CHRIS.

>   CHRIS
>   (calling softly)
>   Ewan -
>   (now shouting)
>   Ewan! -

He sees her and comes to her.

> CHRIS (CONT'D)
> I didn't mean it. Stay by me, Ewan.

They hold one another - at last - contented.

> EWAN
> Bide you quiet.

He picks her up and carries her home.

CUT/DISSOLVE TO:

313. INT. BEDROOM - LATE AFTERNOON.

OVER DISSOLVE:

> DR. MELDRUM (VOICE OVER)
> What's this you've been doing Chris Guthrie?

DR. MELDRUM taking CHRIS'S pulse. EWAN concerned.

> DR. MELDRUM (CONT'D)
> Well, well, that's fine. Let's see a bit more of you Mistress Tavendale.

He begins his examination.

> DR. MELDRUM (CONT'D)
> And you tell me you didn't know what this thing was, Chris Tavendale?

> CHRIS
> (quietly)
> Oh yes.

> DR. MELDRUM
> (quietly)
> But not Ewan?

She shakes her head.

> DR. MELDRUM (CONT'D)
> (to EWAN)
> You're going to be a father Blaewearie, man. What do you think of that?

EWAN - astonished - tries to speak but cannot.

> DR. MELDRUM (CONT'D)
> Away and make me a cup of tea while Chris and I go into more intimate details –

EWAN just stands there.

> DR. MELDRUM (CONT'D)
> You needn't bide. She's safe enough with an old man, bonny though she be.

EWAN leaves running downstairs.

> DR. MELDRUM (CONT'D)
> (to CHRIS)
> Let's see if everything's right.

CUT TO:

314. INT. KITCHEN - LATE AFTERNOON.

EWAN comes in very happy and puts the kettle on to boil. He begins to sing.

CUT TO:

315. INT. BEDROOM - LATE AFTERNOON.

> DR. MELDRUM
> Damned easy for him to sing Chris, eh? But you'll sing yourself then this bairn of yours comes into the world. You'll have no trouble so you needn't fret.
>
> But look after yourself, eat vegetables and be still and kind to Ewan as the wear of the months will let you be. Good for him and good for you.

CUT TO:

316. INT. PARLOUR - DAY.

CHRIS's pregnancy is now very noticeable. She looks at herself in the mirror - her hands rounding her rounded stomach.

> CHRIS (VOICE OVER)
> I'm safe as a cow but, God, I hope I don't look like one.

> EWAN (VOICE OVER)
> You look fine. Bonnier than ever.

CUT TO:

317. EXT. FIELD - DAY.

CHRIS carrying a basket of food to EWAN who is hoeing potatoes. She runs to EWAN.

> EWAN
> Don't run!

> CHRIS
> (sinking down)
> Don't blether!

He finishes hoeing and sits down with her. She cradles his head on her lap and they eat.

> CHRIS (CONT'D)
> (cheerful)
> Things are changing for the better all round.

CUT TO:

318. EXT. FIELD - DAY.

<u>Their POV</u> of CHAE STRACHAN. He is riding in his gig towards the village and waving a newspaper.

> CHAE STRACHAN
> (shouting to EWAN and CHRIS)
> There's a war on! Britain is to war with Germany!

He goes off.

CUT TO:

319. EXT. FIELD - DAY.

<u>CLOSE UP</u> EWAN and CHRIS.

> EWAN
> (as she bends to kiss him)
> Damn the fears!

CUT TO:

320. EXT. SKY FRANCE - PRE-DAWN.

A huge artillery barrage. It is still quite dark but the shells light up the pre-dawn sky.

<u>HOLD</u>.

CUT TO:

321. INT. KITCHEN - EVENING.

EWAN settling his accounts with LONG ROB. LONG ROB gives some honeysuckle to CHRIS.

                LONG ROB
This'll be for the son, eh, Chris? And when are you having him born?

                CHRIS
Late September, early October.

EWAN sits down beside her and takes her hand in his.

                EWAN
Aye, there'll soon be a family Blaewearie way.

Silence.
LONG ROB picks up the newspaper from the table.

                LONG ROB
              (looking at paper)
They're aye daft devils fighting about something or other. It's a lot of damned nonsense!

                EWAN
They can fight themselves black and blue for all I care.

                CHRIS
              (smiling)
For all we care.
                                DISSOLVE TO:

322. EXT. FIELDS - DAY.

EWAN cuts the corn with the binder, pulled by the two horses, CLYDE and BESS. The corn flying, the teeth of the machine whirring, the corn bound and sorted.
                                        CUT TO:

323. EXT. HOUSE. BLAEWEARIE - DAY.

CHRIS, heavily pregnant coming out of the house, slow and careful.
                                          CUT TO:

324. EXT. FIELDS - DAY.

EWAN finishes binding corn, stops the binder and walks towards the house.

                                                          CUT TO:

325. EXT. BLAEWEARIE CLOSE - DAY.

Late September but still sunny. CHRIS goes to meet EWAN in the close, but before they meet CHRIS doubles up with pain.

                         CHRIS
                         Ewan!

She falls but he catches her.

                    CHRIS (CONT'D)
                  (shaking him free)
      It'll be a long time yet, but get Chae to drive for
      Dr. Meldrum - he'll bring a nurse with him from Bervie.

EWAN just stands there.

                    CHRIS (CONT'D)
       Hurry - though I'm fine. He kisses her and runs off.

                                                          CUT TO:

326. INT. KITCHEN - DAY.

CHRIS comes in as the labour pains get worse. She walks up and down.

                                                          CUT TO:

327. INT. STAIRS - DAY.

She climbs the stairs, the labour pains getting very bad.

                                                          CUT TO:

328. INT. BEDROOM - DAY.

She goes to the bed and in agony collapses on to it and screams and screams.

                                                      DISSOLVE TO:

329. INT. BEDROOM. NIGHT.

SHOT of EWAN at door. CHRIS screaming.

                        EWAN
                Chris - lie still.

DOCTOR MELDRUM and NURSE come in.

                      DR. MELDRUM
              Go downstairs, Ewan.

EWAN leaves.

                   DR. MELDRUM (CONT'D)
  Don't grip yourself up like that Mistress Tavendale,
    slacken and its easy. Wish it to come, there's a
                    brave girl.

CHRIS continues to scream and scream.

                                                    CUT TO:

330. INT. KITCHEN - NIGHT.

EWAN comes in and sits down. CHRIS screamings heard. He sits there terrified and anxious. The screams seem to go on forever. Then they stop. An awful silence. Then the baby is heard crying and EWAN cries also.

                                                    CUT TO:

331. INT. BEDROOM - NIGHT.

EWAN and CHRIS. She holds the baby and EWAN kisses its forehead.

                      EWAN
      He'll be good like his mother.

                    CHRIS
    He'll be quick of temper like you.

                    EWAN
  God, maybe you're right! You could hardly be wrong in a
   thing after bringing a bairn like that into the world.

                    CHRIS
      But you helped a little.

He blushes.

SUNSET SONG

                CHRIS (CONT'D)
     We'll call him 'Ewan' after his father.
CUT TO:

SOUNDTRACK: An OFFICER'S whistle is heard.

332. EXT. TRENCH IN FRANCE - DAY.

SHOT inside the trench.

MEN going over the top.

CRANE UP with them, then CRANE FORWARDS in HIGH SHOT as they move forward across "No-Man's Land." Machine gun fire and a lot of SOLDIERS are mown down.
DISSOLVE TO:

333. EXT. SKY - DAY.

WIDE SHOT of sky white and blue.

                CHRIS (VOICE OVER)
  Spring, rain and seeding, harvests and winter and spring
     again since the day young Ewan was born ...

DISSOLVE AND CRANE DOWN TO:

334. EXT. FIELDS - DAY.

The harvest done, haystacks standing in the sun. Voluptuous and still.

                CHRIS (VOICE OVER)
  Maybe there was war and bloodshed and that was awful ...
    but far off also ... you'd hear it like the north sea
    cry in the morning, a crying and a thunder that became
    unending as the weeks went by, part of life's plan ...

DISSOLVE TO:

335. EXT. BLAEWEARIE - DAY.

SHOT of the house and trees. A gentle rain.

HOLD.

                CHRIS (VOICE OVER)
  But Chris didn't care sitting there at Blaewearie with
   her bairn and her man by her side ... and the grain a
   fine price ... so the farming folk did well ... The rain
      dies away and sunshine after the rain.

CUT TO:

336. INT. KITCHEN – EARLY EVENING. 1916.

<u>SHOT</u> of CHAE at open kitchen door dressed in a soldier's uniform.

> CHAE STRACHAN
> Aye, folk are you in?

CHRIS gasps.

> CHAE STRACHAN (CONT'D)
> God, Chris, I'm not a ghost yet!

EWAN and CHRIS gasp at CHAE dressed as a soldier.

> EWAN
> You're havering man, you don't mean it!

> CHAE STRACHAN
> Damn't aye, that I do! I've enlisted in the North Highlanders ... I'm off to Perth tonight.

> CHRIS
> Oh Chae!

EWAN and CHRIS sit down clearly distressed.

> CHRIS (CONT'D)
> Who'll win?

> CHAE STRACHAN
> If the Germans do there'll be an end to peace forever.

> EWAN
> Oh to hell with them!

CHAE goes to the cot and looks at the baby.

> CHAE STRACHAN
> (tickling baby's toes)
> I mind the day he was born, just yesterday it was. The spring of life, eh, Chris? Sing it and cherish it, 'twill never come again. You've brought out a fine bairn between you.

Silence.

> CHAE STRACHAN (CONT'D)
> Every man might have to fight for bairn and wife ere this war is over.

SUNSET SONG

                        EWAN
                 (serious to CHAE)
So you don't think I should join up, Chae?

CHRIS almost in tears.

                 CHAE STRACHAN
             (seeing CHRIS is upset)
There are fools enough in the fight as it is.

                      CHRIS
                (near to tears)
What a blether about a war.

                      EWAN
              (tenderly to CHRIS)
Och, I was asking only.

They give CHAE a dram of Glenlivet. They sit in subdued silence.

                                                   CUT TO:

337. INT. KITCHEN - EARLY EVENING.

<u>SHOT</u> of LONG ROB at kitchen door.

                     LONG ROB
                     (to EWAN)
Aye, man.

                      EWAN
Aye, man.

LONG ROB goes and shakes <u>CHAE's</u> hand.

                     LONG ROB
Chae Strachan, you're an exception!

They all smile frail smiles.

                LONG ROB (CONT'D)
Oh man, I'd go back with you in the morn if only ...

                 CHAE STRACHAN
If only what, man?

                     LONG ROB
If only I wanted to be easy ... easy and a liar. But I'm damned if I'll begin for any bit war.

Silence.

> LONG ROB (CONT'D)
> Have you seen the casualty lists, Chae? Have you?

CHAE silent.

> LONG ROB (CONT'D)
> 50,000 poor bastards blown to hell for a couple of yards of Belgian mud - men gassed, men mutilated and blinded ...

> CHAE STRACHAN
> But those were brave men.

> LONG ROB
> Or stupid.

Pause.

> CHAE STRACHAN
> They're saying you're cowards.

> EWAN
> Better a coward than a corpse.

Silence.

> CHAE STRACHAN
> I believe in the war, it'll bring good to the world ... It'll bring the days of Socialism to the common folk.

> LONG ROB
> The common folk. When they're not sheep they're swine.

Silence. CHAE finishes his whisky and shakes hands.

> CHAE STRACHAN
> Goodbye then.

They are all moved. Especially CHRIS. CHAE leaves.

CUT TO:

338. INT. KITCHEN - EARLY EVENING.

SHOT of CHAE going out through the door and walking away.

TRACK forward with him (from behind) as he walks out into the Gloaming.

SOUNDTRACK: Glasgow Orpheus Choir singing "All In The April Evening".

DISSOLVE TO:

339. EXT. NO-MAN'S LAND - EARLY EVENING.

CRANE forward in HIGH SHOT of the SOLDIERS now crawling across No-Man's Land. A hail of machine gun fire.

SOUNDTRACK: "All In The April Evening" continues.

DISSOLVE TO:

340. EXT. FIELD'S AROUND BLAEWEARIE - EARLY EVENING.

TRACK forward and across the fields, lush and ripe.

SOUNDTRACK: "All In The April Evening" continues.

DISSOLVE TO:

341. EXT. FIELDS/LANES - EARLY EVENING.

TRACK forward with all the VILLAGERS and the whole of Kinraddie goes to church.

SOUNDTRACK: "All In The April Evening" continues.

DISSOLVE TO:

342. EXT. KIRKYARD - EARLY EVENING.

TRACK forward with the VILLAGERS as they stream into the Kirkyard.

SOUNDTRACK: "All In The April Evening" continues.

DISSOLVE TO:

343. INT. KIRK - EARLY EVENING.

TRACK forward in HIGH SHOT above the seated congregation towards the pulpit. The congregation is tense and silent.

SOUNDTRACK: "All In The April Evening" ends when REVEREND GIBBON is framed in pulpit. A hush falls.

                        REV. GIBBON
    As you know, we are now at war with Germany. This new
    Babylon has as many corruptions as the old one. It has
    been sent as a plague on the world - by God - because

of its sins, because the world has grown wicked and lustful. How long it will rage only God in his wisdom and anger will know.

But it's a chastisement - by blood and fire - that the nations must arise and prevail against this enemy - and Scotland - not least of these in its ancient health and humility to tread again the path of peace and courage that will ultimately lead to our victory.

The congregation nod and murmur in agreement.

>   REV. GIBBON (CONT'D)
> Their King - which they call "Kaiser" - is the anti-Christ and a foul evil upon the earth which must be swept away by the righteous and those who will not fight to defend their country must be exposed for that they truly are - cowards! - And pro-German cowards at that!

CUT TO:

344. INT. KITCHEN - EARLY EVENING.

A stone comes smashing through the window. CHRIS is terrified and EWAN is angry.

>   A VOICE OUTSIDE
> Where's the Kaiser's cronies?

EWAN grabs the gun from the hearth and flings open the door to reveal A GROUP OF MEN.

>   MAN
>   (who threw stone)
> Take care man. Put down that gun.

>   EWAN
>   (apoplectic with anger)
> Smash my windows will you, you scum!

He fires at them and they scatter. He fires again. Other shots are heard in the distance.

<u>HOLD</u> on EWAN at the door fuming with anger and a frightened CHRIS.

CUT TO:

345. EXT. FIELDS - EARLY EVENING.

LONG ROB comes running up to EWAN and CHRIS. LONG ROB carries a gun.

                    LONG ROB
                    What's up?

                    EWAN
                They smashed my windows.

                    LONG ROB
                    Aye, mine too.

                    EWAN
        But they've run off like rats in a barn when they
                    saw us both.

                    LONG ROB
                    (smiling)
        Och ... no so bad for a couple of pro-Germans!

They both laugh but their laughter is tinged with fear.

                                                    CUT TO:

346. INT. KITCHEN - EARLY EVENING.

CHRIS, EWAN and LONG ROB come back into the kitchen.

                    EWAN
                  (to CHRIS)
            Content yourself, they've gone.

They all sit. A second stone comes smashing through
the window.

                MAN'S (VOICE OVER)
                You pro-German bastards!

EWAN gets up angrily but LONG ROB restrains him.

                    LONG ROB
                  Let them be.

EWAN sits down.

CHRIS picks up the second stone which was thrown through
the window. It has and envelope tied to it. She unties the
envelope and three white feathers drop out of it.

                    CHRIS
                  (to LONG ROB)
            What does it mean, Rob?

> LONG ROB
> They send white feathers to the cowards.
> I've already had mine.

> EWAN
> They're all Government men ... ready to die for the King any day of the week ...

> LONG ROB
> And twice on Sundays.

LONG ROB laughs but cannot shift the sad atmosphere.

Silence.

A long silence.

> CHRIS
> They say Parliament's to pass a Conscription Act.

> EWAN
> That means if we don't volunteer they'll make us go anyway.

> LONG ROB
> (laughs)
> It'll be a bit of a jaunt!

> CHRIS
> Will you both be taken?

> EWAN
> Aye.

Silence.

> CHRIS
> But you've been excused before. They don't take folk who farm their own land.

EWAN takes papers from his pocket and gives them to her.

> EWAN
> I'm to report to Aberdeen.

> CHRIS
> (near to tears as she reads)
> Oh Ewan.

> LONG ROB
> It's only for assessment. *I'm* going too. We'll go together.

CHRIS is very upset.

> LONG ROB (CONT'D)
> Don't worry lass they'll have to carry us to the front.

CLOSE UP CHRIS. She stares straight ahead, worried sick.

> CUT TO:

LONG ROB getting up and going to door. CHRIS goes to him and kisses him. He leaves and she watches him go.

> CUT TO:

Her POV of him walking away in the gloaming.

HOLD on him. He begins to whistle then sing "Ladies Of Spain". He gets further and further away until he is gone.

SPECIAL F/X: A train window. In the window EWAN and LONG ROB. The train moves off. It is packed with soldiers and civilians. It moves through the frame. It is endless. It seems to have no end.

> DISSOLVE TO:

347. INT. KITCHEN - DAY.

CHRIS bathing young EWAN, now a toddler. She is singing.

JOHN BRIGSON, their farmhand, comes to the door.

> JOHN BRIGSON
> Faith, mistress, you're light of heart.

EWAN pushes past him into the kitchen.

> EWAN
> (to JOHN BRIGSON)
> Stop your blether and get back to your work.

> JOHN BRIGSON
> (hurt)
> Yes, sir.

EWAN walks through the kitchen towards the stairs.

> CHRIS
> What's wrong?

> EWAN
> Nothing!

He goes upstairs.

> CUT TO:

348. INT. KITCHEN - DAY.

CHRIS drying then dressing YOUNG EWAN. HOLD on them. EWAN is making a great deal of noise upstairs. She finishes and as she does so she hears EWAN's footsteps on the stairs then coming into the kitchen. She looks up.

CUT TO:

349. INT. KITCHEN - DAY.

CHRIS's POV EWAN dressed in his Sunday best.

CUT TO:

350. INT. KITCHEN - DAY.

CHRIS puzzled and worried.

> CHRIS
> Where are you going?

> EWAN
> (walking past her and out)
> To Aberdeen, if you'd like to know.

She watches him go.

DISSOLVE TO:

351. INT. BEDROOM - EARLY EVENING.

She puts the sleeping YOUNG EWAN to bed.

DISSOLVE TO:

352. INT. PARLOUR - EARLY EVENING.

She goes through the parlour and looks at the clock ticking in the silence.

DISSOLVE TO:

353. INT. KITCHEN - NIGHT.

She sits down and listens for a long time then she goes to the kitchen door, opens it and looks out. Nothing. She puts her coat on and runs out.

DISSOLVE TO:

354. EXT. ROAD - NIGHT.

She comes running down the turnpike, stops, waits and listens in the darkness.

Silence. Then a car flashes past containing soldiers and is gone. She stands in the darkness.

HOLD. Then she walks back to Blaewearie.
                                              DISSOLVE TO:

355. INT. KITCHEN - NIGHT.

She is sitting in the quiet kitchen lit only by the fire and a lamp. She listens and waits. Silence. JOHN BRIGSON knocks softly on the door and comes in.

                        CHRIS
        I'm sorry, John, for the master this morning. He's been
                    worried about business.

                        JOHN BRIGSON
        Never heed, mistress, he'll be as right as rain when
                        he's back tonight.

                        CHRIS
                    Goodnight John.

                        JOHN BRIGSON
                    Goodnight mistress.

He leaves. She sits there in the semi-darkness.
                                              DISSOLVE TO:

356. INT. KITCHEN - DAY.

OVER THE DISSOLVE.

                        EWAN (VOICE OVER)
I've joined the North Highlanders. I'm off to the war. I'll let you know where they send me. Don't worry. I am yours truly ... Ewan.

JOHN BRIGSON and CHRIS at the table reading the letter.

                        CHRIS
            He's enlisted. He's gone to fight.

                        JOHN BRIGSON
                    (trying to be positive)
        It'll soon be over. I see the Germans are retreating
                    on all fronts, they say.

CHRIS sits there quite stunned.
Silence.
                        JOHN BRIGSON (CONT'D)
            You're not to worry. Ewan will be fine.

TRACK AWAY from them to the kitchen door. Then TRACK FORWARD beyond it.

      CHRIS (VOICE OVER)
   Oh, but that Spring was long ...

              DISSOLVE TO:

TRACK FORWARD to distant fields. CHRIS and JOHN BRIGSON drilling the earth. CONTINUE TRACK FORWARD (from behind them).

     CHRIS (VOICE OVER) (CONT'D)
But the hills flowed up and down day after day and Chris saw the harvest near, so near, a good harvest in spite of all things ...

              DISSOLVE TO:

CONTINUE TO TRACK FORWARD across the fields. The harvest in and haystacks.

     CHRIS (VOICE OVER) (CONT'D)
 Soon maybe the war would end and they'd all be back in Kinraddie as once they had been ... Long Rob and Chae and her dark lad Ewan ...

              DISSOLVE TO:

CONTINUE TO TRACK FORWARD to the house following a TELEGRAPH BOY on his bike. BOY stops, knocks on door and CHRIS opens it. BOY hands her the telegram. She opens it, reads it and her face becomes radiant.

      EWAN (VOICE OVER)
 Home on leave from Lanark tonight before going to France.

        BOY
     Any reply?

       CHRIS
     Any what?
        BOY
     Any reply?

       CHRIS
      No!
                CUT TO:

357. INT. BEDROOM - DAY.

The bed made with the best linen and jars of honeysuckle all around.
              CUT TO:

358. INT. PARLOUR - DAY.

Shining and clean.

                                                           CUT TO:

359. INT. KITCHEN - DAY.

Shining and clean and the table laden with everything for a fine meal. CHRIS waiting in the doorway. JOHN BRIGSON goes by her.

                       JOHN BRIGSON
This is hardly the place for me with your man come home, I'll away to Bervie then for the night.

She goes indoors and closes the door.

                                                           CUT TO:

360. INT. KITCHEN - DAY.

The kitchen door flies open. EWAN standing there in his uniform and drunk. She runs to him.

                             EWAN
                     (looking down)
Hell, Chris, what a bloody place!

She is horrified at the change in him but she smiles and kisses him. He responds by roughly running his hands over her breasts and buttocks and trying to lift her skirt. She pulls away from him and goes to the child.

                     CHRIS (to CHILD)
Ewan, who's this?

The child doesn't answer, just looks at EWAN.

                     CHRIS (CONT'D)
It's Father.

EWAN throws his pack on the floor.

                             EWAN
                      (laughing)
Well, we'll hope so, eh, Chris! Any supper left - unless you're too bloody stand-offish even to have that?

She goes to him and tries to hold him but he pushes her away and sits down.

                     EWAN (CONT'D)
For Christ's sake let a man sit down.

He slumps down, first throwing onto the floor a child's colouring book.

> EWAN (CONT'D)
> Here, give us some tea.

She sits down beside him, pours the tea and serves him. He doesn't notice the meal laid out for him, he just drinks cup after cup of tea - fast and coarse.

CHRIS becoming more and more repelled by him. EWAN looks at her with simmering anger.

> EWAN (CONT'D)
> Well, damn't, don't you have anything to say to me now I've come home?

She sits there, unable to speak and trying desperately not to cry.

> EWAN (CONT'D)
> I'd've done better to spend the night with a tart in the town.

She can no longer prevent herself from crying.

> EWAN (CONT'D)
> God Almighty, what are you snivelling about now? You're always snivelling.

> CHRIS
> (getting up from the table)
> Ewan ...

> EWAN
> Alright! Alright!

She goes to move away from him but he grabs her by the wrist and pulls her onto his lap.

> EWAN (CONT'D)
> Be stand-offish now if you can ...

She struggles to get free as he holds her tight, slobbers over her and forces his kisses on her.

> EWAN (CONT'D)
> What I get regular in Lanark I now want from you ... what do you think I came home for?

She frees herself but falls on the floor.

                    EWAN (CONT'D)
              Now that you know ... Get!

She just stands there. She smothers her tears and EWAN picks up a lamp and goes upstairs. He tramps up the stairs.

                    EWAN (CONT'D)
                      (shouting)
              For God's sake, hurry up!

She picks up the child and goes upstairs.
                                                    CUT TO:

361. INT. CHILD'S BEDROOM - NIGHT.

CHRIS puts YOUNG EWAN to bed.

                    YOUNG EWAN
              I don't like him ... that soldier.

                    CHRIS
              No, Ewan, you must never say that again.

She kisses him.

                    EWAN (VOICE OVER)
                      Chris!
                                                    CUT TO:

362. INT. BEDROOM - NIGHT.

EWAN already undressed and half in bed. CHRIS comes in and goes to blow out the lamp.

                    EWAN
              I'll do that!

He gets out of bed naked and grabs her, pulling her down to the floor and pushing her skirts up.

                    CHRIS
                      (terrified)
              Oh, Ewan, put out the light! Put out the light!

He doesn't do so and he has her against her will.

                                                    CUT TO:

363. INT. KITCHEN - MORNING.

CHRIS making breakfast. YOUNG EWAN playing.

EWAN comes in from upstairs just in his kilt. He goes to the sink and starts washing.

YOUNG EWAN stops playing and looks at him.

> EWAN
> (turning around)
> God, what a damned glower! Eyes like your mother and a nature the same.

> CHRIS
> Will you wear a suit, Ewan?

> EWAN
> What, me, dress like a bloody conchie! I'll need some money. I'm off to Drumlithie.

She gives it to him without a murmur but he detects her reluctance.

> EWAN (CONT'D)
> I'm entitled to what's my own.

Silence.

> EWAN (CONT'D)
> I'm no longer the young fool I was content to slave here without so much as a dram ... nothing but a wife you hardly dare touch in case you put her in the family way.

CUT TO:

364. INT. BEDROOM - NIGHT.

Both in bed. Both awake. EWAN drunk. CHRIS lying awake tense and frightened. Gradually EWAN snores into sleep.

HOLD on CHRIS a LONG time.

When she is sure he won't hear her, she gets up and goes downstairs.

CUT TO:

365. INT. KITCHEN - NIGHT.

She lights a lamp and gets the fire going and makes some tea. She sits down.

HOLD on her. Slowly the dawn comes up.

DISSOLVE TO:

366. INT. KITCHEN - MORNING.

CHRIS still sitting there. YOUNG EWAN playing outside.

> EWAN (VOICE OVER)
> When the hell are you bringing some breakfast?

She just smiles and goes to the sink and begins washing up. EWAN comes banging downstairs and into the kitchen.

> EWAN (CONT'D)
> Have you gone clean deaf?

> CHRIS
> (turning round, defiant)
> If you're in need of breakfast ... get it!

EWAN goes to her and grabs her and spins her around. She pushes him away with great strength.

> CHRIS (CONT'D)
> I'll not be treated like a Lanark tart!

EWAN recovers himself and goes to lunge at her, he is very angry. CHRIS picks up a bread knife.

> EWAN
> You bitch!

> CHRIS
> I'm not frightened of you!

EWAN stops and looks at her.

> EWAN
> No ... you can afford to be brave, you're not the one who's got to go to France ...

> CHRIS
> Then why did you enlist?

> EWAN
> Because I was sick of folk laughing and jeering at me for a coward. And you're blethering because your man's no longer "polite"!

A tense silence between them. He sinks into a chair and she throws the knife on the table.

He gets up and leaves and goes upstairs.

> CHRIS
> (quietly)
> Oh Ewan ... I didn't know ...

She turns back to the sink and continues the washing up.

CUT TO:

367. EXT. HOUSE - DAY.

She goes out and begins to feed the hens and then goes to YOUNG EWAN playing.

                                                                                  CUT TO:

368. EXT. HOUSE - DAY.

SHOT of EWAN coming out of the house in his uniform and pack. He walks towards the gate at the end of the close.

                                                                                  CUT TO:

369. EXT. HOUSE - DAY.

CHRIS refuses to look at him and goes on feeding the hens.

                                                                                  CUT TO:

370. EXT. HOUSE - DAY.

SHOT of EWAN going through the gate and banging it behind him. He stops, lights a cigarette, then walks off.

                                                                                  CUT TO:

371. EXT. HOUSE - DAY.

TWO SHOT of CHRIS and YOUNG EWAN. He watches his father go but CHRIS does not. She then walks back into the house. PAN to kitchen window. She comes to the window and now looks after EWAN. She has a curious smile on her face.

                                                                                  CUT TO:

372. EXT - DAY.

LONG SHOT of EWAN walking away in the distance. A cloud passes across the sun and EWAN is gone.

HOLD until he disappears. In the distance a train whistle is heard. Then nothing.

                                                                                  CUT TO:

373. EXT - DAY.

CHRIS slowly coming outside, white as a sheet.

                            CHRIS
              (completely bereft, but softly)
         Oh ... Ewan ... I didn't mean it.

PAN UP to the high bright sky.

HOLD.

SUNSET SONG

> CHRIS (VOICE OVER) (CONT'D)
> Nothing stays the same when your're mad with grief ... Everything was changing and as the land changed so did Chris ... She looked for the days gone by ... She looked to see the faces of her mother and father in the firelight before the lamps were lit ... Faces dear and close to her ... She wanted the words they'd known and used ... Forgotten in the far off youngness of their lives, Scots words to tell to your heart how they wrung it and held it through all the toil of their days, and the unending fight with the land.

THEN PAN DOWN TO:

374. EXT. FIELD - MORNING.

CHRIS and JOHN BRIGSON stooking behind rig. HOLD on them as they work.

THEN PAN AWAY TO:

375. EXT. ANOTHER FIELD - LATE AFTERNOON.

They are stacking the sheaves.

HOLD.

THEN PAN AWAY TO:

376. EXT. ROAD - EARLY EVENING.

The road leading back to the house.

JOHN BRIGSON and CHRIS weary from the work walk back home. CHRIS carries YOUNG EWAN.

HOLD.

THEN PAN AWAY TO:

377. EXT. HOUSE - NIGHT.

They walk towards it and go in.

CUT TO:

378. INT. KITCHEN - NIGHT.

They sit down absolutely exhausted from the work.

> JOHN BRIGSON
> I'll put Ewan to bed.

He takes EWAN upstairs.

CHRIS sits in the chair too tired to move, then gets up and goes to the parlour.

                                                                       CUT TO:

379. INT. PARLOUR - NIGHT.

She sees her reflection in the mirror. She looks thin and worn. She goes up to bed.

                                                                       CUT TO:

380. INT. BEDROOM - NIGHT.

Too tired to undress, she gets into bed.

PAN TO window.

HOLD on window.

Then It is morning. The sun comes flooding in.

                                    PAN AWAY AND DISSOLVE TO:

381. INT. PARLOUR.

The parlour is dark. HOLD.

Then it is morning, the sun comes flooding in.

HOLD.

                           THEN PAN AWAY AND DISSOLVE TO:

382. INT. KITCHEN.

The kitchen is dark. Then it is morning. The sun comes flooding in.

                                   PAN AWAY AND DISSOLVE TO:

383. EXT. CLOSE - MORNING.

CHRIS is sitting outside mending YOUNG EWAN's clothes. She hears the gate click and a cycle. She looks up.

                                                                       CUT TO:

384. EXT. GATE AND CLOSE - DAY.

CHRIS's POV of TELEGRAPH BOY. He comes to her and she stands. He gives her the telegram and rides away. She opens, then reads the telegram. She cannot believe its contents.

                    CHRIS
                 (whispering)
        What do I do? Oh ... what do I do?
        (she looks up and now speaks out loud)
                 What do I do?

JOHN BRIGSON comes running to her.

                 JOHN BRIGSON
             Did you cry me, Chris?

                    CHRIS
             (giving him the telegram)
        What do I do now, John? Do I go to France?

He reads the telegram.

                 JOHN BRIGSON
        God, mistress, this is sore news, but he died like a man
             out there, your Ewan died fine.

                    CHRIS
                  (suddenly)
        It's a lie! They're lying! He isn't dead.
                 My Ewan's not dead!

She runs to the house, JOHN BRIGSON is following her.
She is screaming, "IT'S A LIE!"

                                                    CUT TO:

385. INT. KITCHEN - DAY.

JOHN BRIGSON helplessly watching as she stalks around the kitchen mad with grief.

                    CHRIS
        Country and King? What have they to do with my Ewan?
        Blaewearie's his land ... those English generals in
        London, they're lying, the cowards ... they're just
                 tormenting me. IT'S A LIE!

Then she stops.
Silence.
Then she sits down and begins to rock and moan, rock and moan, rock and moan.

                                                 DISSOLVE TO:

386. EXT. SKY AND LAND – DAY.

A massive sky above the land, tranquil and soft.

                CHRIS (VOICE OVER)
And when she'd finished she went quiet and cold. Morning came up, noons with their suns, rains came, soft and grey and quiet across the land but they brought her neither terror nor hope, now that her man had been murdered for nothing ...

                                      DISSOLVE TO:

387. INT. KITCHEN – DAY.

JOHN BRIGSON at the door.

                JOHN BRIGSON
The Government men are here mistress.

                                        CUT TO:

CLOSE UP CHRIS. She does not respond.

                                          CUT TO:

CLOSE UP of JOHN BRIGSON.

                JOHN BRIGSON (CONT'D)
                To fell the trees.

Still no response.

                                        CUT TO:

388. EXT. BLAWEARIE – DAY.

One tree after another comes crashing down into frame.

                                      DISSOLVE TO:

389. EXT. BLAWEARIE – DAY.

SHOT of the rows of stumps of the felled beeches.

                                      DISSOLVE TO:

390. INT. KITCHEN – DAY.

CHAE STRACHAN knocks at the open door – the kitchen empty. CHRIS comes in and stops when she sees him.

                        CHRIS
        Ewan? Chae ... Chae ... he's not living?

SUNSET SONG

                    CHAE STRACHAN
        Ewan's dead, don't vex yourself hoping else.

She sits down and CHAE joins her.

                    CHAE STRACHAN (CONT'D)
        They can't hurt him anymore. Even this can't hurt him. But I
                know right well you should know it, Chris.

                                                        CUT TO:

391. INT. KITCHEN - DAY.

CLOSE UP CHRIS.

                    CHAE STRACHAN (VOICE OVER)
        Ewan was shot as a coward and a deserter out there in France.

HOLD on CHRIS. Then:
                                                        DISSOLVE TO:

392. EXT - DAY.

The sun. Round and glorious.

                    EWAN (VOICE OVER) OVER DISSOLVE
                        (tearful yet ecstatic)
                    Oh Chris!

HOLD on the sun. Then:
                                                        DISSOLVE TO:

393. INT. CELL/HUT - DAWN.

THREE-QUARTER VIEW of EWAN looking out in the dawn drizzle. He wears a kilt and is in shirt sleeves.

                    CHAE STRACHAN (VOICE OVER)
        But why did you do it Ewan? You might well have known
                    you'd never get free.

                    EWAN
                (turning to CHAE)
        I did it for Chris, Chae. I did it for Blaewearie.

                                                        CUT TO:

394. INT. CELL/HUT - DAWN.

CLOSE UP CHAE. He sits down. Silence. EWAN remains at the window and looking out.

                              EWAN
                There's bare a quarter of an hour now, Chae.

                                                            CUT TO:

CHAE overcome. He cannot speak.
                                                       CUT TO EWAN:

                          EWAN (CONT'D)
                            (anguished)
             She didn't even come to give me a kiss at goodbye ...
                       Chae, we never said goodbye ...

                                                       CUT TO CHAE:

He is at a loss to speak.

                                                       CUT TO EWAN:

                          EWAN (CONT'D)
              Oh man mind me when you're next at Blaewearie.
              Look at my lass for me when you see her again for
                       that kiss I'll never give her.
                                                       CUT TO CHAE:

He is weeping.
                                                       CUT TO EWAN:

He is not.
                          EWAN (CONT'D)
              She'll think I died like the rest. Don't tell, you're
                      not to tell my dear Chris.

                                                       CUT TO CHAE:

He is unable to control himself and he moves to EWAN.

                          EWAN (CONT'D)
             D'you remember the night of the storm with the horses
             Chae? That was the night I knew Chris liked me well ...
             And her singing when we wed ... What was it that Chris
                                sang then?

CHAE shakes his head.

SOUNDTRACK: "The Flowers of the Forest" sung by Ronnie Brown is heard.

                                                            CUT TO:

2-SHOT. They embrace. Then shake hands.

CHAE leaves. EWAN sits down.

                                                            CUT TO:

395. EXT. CELL/HUT - DAWN.

SOUNDTRACK: "The Flowers of the Forest" continues.

A fine drizzle, showering down over the shattered remains of a farm. EWAN led out - just in kilt and shirt sleeves.

PAN WITH HIM and GUARD (R-L).

A chair has been placed with its back to us, EWAN sits down facing us. A black 'X' on his shirt just above his heart.

CUT TO:

396. EXT. CELL/HUT - DAWN.

SHOT of firing squad. They are brought to attention.

SOUNDTRACK: "The Flowers of the Forest" continues.

TRACK along firing squad (R-L). TRACK STOPS when squad is framed. They take aim. They fire.

CUT ON THE GUNSHOT TO:

397. EXT. CELL/HUT - DAWN.

SOUNDTRACK: "The Flowers of the Forest" continues. The bullets hit EWAN in a hail and he falls backwards, a little life flickering in him still. His eyes look up.

CUT TO:

EWAN'S POV of OFFICER pointing his revolver at EWAN to give him the coup de grace. He fires.

CUT TO EWAN:

His body jerks, his eyes flicker and life goes out within. He is still. Dying at last.

SOUNDTRACK: "The Flowers of the Forest" continues.

DISSOLVE TO:

398. INT. KITCHEN - IT IS NOW TWILIGHT.

CHAE and CHRIS still sitting there.

SOUNDTRACK: "The Flowers of the Forest" continues.

CHAE
Better always to know what's truth in a thing, for lies come creeping home to roost, Chris. You're young yet, you've hardly begun to live and I swore to myself I'd tell you all so that you'd never be vexed with me.

                              CHRIS
                            (quietly)
         I'll not be vexed with you for telling me this. It was
                         best! It was best.

They both go to the open door of the kitchen and stand there.

                           CHAE STRACHAN
                     The beech trees have gone.

                              CHRIS
                   Yes. The Government men felled them.

                           CHAE STRACHAN
                         (suddenly angry)
              They're ruining the land! The bastards!

Silence.

                              CHRIS
                         How is the war?

                           CHAE STRACHAN
              It's not so bad if it weren't for the lice.

Pause.

                       CHAE STRACHAN (CONT'D)
                     (bending down to kiss her)
                         That's from Ewan.

Her arms go around his neck and she draws him to her and kisses him deeply.

                       CHAE STRACHAN (CONT'D)
                       Chris ... We mustn't ...

But the kissing gets more and more passionate between them. They seem to melt into each others arms.

Then MORPH into next SHOT.

CHRIS is on FRAME LEFT, CHAE FRAME RIGHT but this becomes:

399. INT. BEDROOM - TWILIGHT.

CHRIS holding EWAN's clothes sits on bed with them. She takes his clothes in her arms and embraces them and softly, repeatedly kisses them.

SOUNDTRACK: "The Flowers of the Forest" continues, then ends.

CHRIS
Oh, Ewan, sleep quiet and sound now, lad, I understand! You did it for me and I'm proud - for me and Blaewearie ... My dear ... my dear ... sleep quiet and brave for I've understood.

DISSOLVE TO:

400. EXT. HILL LEADING TO STANDING STONES - DAY.

Snipes calling, clouds passing in front of the sun.
CHRIS walks slowly up the hill towards the stones.
TRACK BACK in front of her. She hears something and stops.

CUT TO:

401. EXT. STANDING STONES - DAY.

Her POV Nothing but the stones and the whispering silence - then - someone is heard whistling.

CUT TO:

402. EXT. HILL - DAY.

CHRIS hears the whistling and moves up the hill.

CHRIS
Ewan?

CUT TO:

403. EXT. STONES - DAY.

HER POV EWAN's ghost preceding her up the hill, stops whistling and turns around and looks at her.

EWAN
I've come home lass ...

CUT TO:

404. EXT. HILL - DAY.

CHRIS radiant.

CHRIS
Oh Ewan - Ewan!

CUT TO:

405. EXT. STONES - DAY.

SHOT of EWAN's wraith as it melts into the stone.

                        EWAN
                    I've come home.

He melts and is gone.

PAN AROUND (R-L).

                                                   DISSOLVE TO:

406. EXT. HILL - GLOAMING.

The whole of Kinraddie streaming up the hill (including CHRIS and YOUNG EWAN) for a memorial service.

                    CHRIS (VOICE OVER)
        We came for all those who died - Long Rob, Chae Strachan
                   and Ewan - all of them.

PAN with them (L-R) to FRAME the Standing Stones and the MINISTER.

Silence.

NB: This should be INTERCUT with SHOTS of the VILLAGERS. (The funeral in "Shane" to be the template.)

Then:

                        MINISTER
    "For I will give you the morning star." In the sunset of
    an age and an epoch we may write that for epitaph of the
    men who were of it. They went quiet and brave from the
    lands they loved, though seldom of that love might they
    speak, it was not in them to tell in words of the earth
    that moved and lived and abided, their life and enduring
    love. And who knows at the last what memories of it were
        with them, the springs and the winters of this land
        and all the sounds and scents of it that had once been
        theirs, deep, and a passion of their blood and spirit,
        those who died in France? With them we may say there
                died a thing older than themselves.

    It was old Scotland that perished with them. A new
    generation comes up that will know them not, except as a
    memory in a song. Nothing, it has been said, is true but
        change, nothing abides, and here in Kinraddie we must
        give heed that a new spirit shall come to the land. For
        greed of place and possession and great estate those men
        had little heed, the kindness of friends and the warmth
        of toil and the peace of rest - they asked no more from
        God or man, and no less would they endure. So, lest we
    shame them, let us believe that the new oppressions and
            foolish greeds are no more than mists that pass.

SUNSET SONG

> They died for a world that is past, these men, but they did not die for this that we seem to inherit. Beyond it and us there shines a greater hope and a newer world, undreamt when these men died. But need we doubt which side the battle they would range themselves did they live today, need we doubt the answer they cry to us even now, from the places of the sunset?

It is now getting dark.

A PIPER begins to play "The Flowers of the Forest" and to step slowly around the outer edge of the Stone Circle.

INTERCUT with SHOTS of the CROWD - some weeping, some grey-faced.

> CHRIS (VOICE OVER)
> He could fair play, that piper, he tore at your heart with the tune echoing across the loch .. it rose and rose and wept ...

The CROWD begin slowly to stream down the hill as the PIPER continues.

SHOT of the MINISTER against the sky.

SHOT of CHRIS and YOUNG EWAN silhouetted against the sky.

SHOT of the lone PIPER - no longer marching around the Stones - but standing still, silhouetted against the sky and the dying light.

The PIPER finishes.

> CHRIS (VOICE OVER) (CONT'D)
> They'd the last of the light with them up there ...

PAN UP to the dark sky.

> CHRIS (VOICE OVER) (CONT'D)
> And maybe they did not need it or heed it - you can do without day if you've a lamp quiet-lighted and kind in your heart.

SLOW FADE

THE END

THE CONTRIBUTORS

Terence Davies (1945–2022) was born in Liverpool into a large working-class Catholic family. Inspired by his love for cinema, he began writing short stories from the age of 16 and took up acting while working for over a decade as an accounts clerk. His trilogy – *Children* (1976), *Madonna and Child* (1980) and *Death and Transfiguration* (1983) – established his distinctive voice as a filmmaker. Profoundly influenced by T. S. Eliot's *Four Quartets*, he developed a lyrical, meditative style shaped by the nature of memory, time and longing. He went on to make nine feature films, including *Distant Voices, Still Lives* (1988), winner of the International Critics' Prize at Cannes, *The Long Day Closes* (1992), *The House of Mirth* (2000), *Of Time and the City* (2008) and *Benediction* (2021). His novel, *Hallelujah Now*, was first published in 1984.

James Dowling is the co-representative of the Terence Davies Estate and was a close friend of Terence during the last years of his life. He began working with Davies on his later film projects (including the script for *Firefly*) and editing collections of his poetry. James has continued to honour Davies's legacy through film, making two short films based on Terence's poetry: *Passing Time* (2023), commissioned by Film Fest Gent, and *Home! Home!* (2024), commissioned by the Centre Pompidou, Paris, as part of a major retrospective.

Lillian Crawford is a writer and curator. She is currently researching a PhD on Screen Two at Royal Holloway, University of London in collaboration with the BBC. Her first book, *The Mind of the Doctor: Across the Neurodiverse Universe of Doctor Who*, is published by Herne Books in 2026.

Mark Cousins is a film director, producer, and writer best known for his 15-hour documentary *The Story of Film: A Odyssey* (2011). Mark has worked on numerous cine-essays. These include *A Story of Children and Film* and *I Am Belfast*, in which the city is personified by a 10,000 year old woman. Mark is also a presenter and critic, known for his work on *Scene by Scene* and *Elsewhere*.